FANTASY FOOTBALL HANDBOOK
1998/99

FANTASY FOOTBALL HANDBOOK 1998/99

Bruce Smith

CollinsWillow
An Imprint of HarperCollins*Publishers*

First published in 1998
by CollinsWillow
an imprint of HarperCollins*Publishers*
London

© Bruce Smith 1998

1 3 5 7 9 8 6 4 2

All rights reserved. No part of this publication may be reproduced, stored in a retrieval system, or transmitted, in any form or by any means, electronic, mechanical, photocopying, recording or otherwise, without the prior written permission of the publishers

The Author asserts the moral right to be
identified as the author of this work

A CIP catalogue record for this book is
available from the British Library

ISBN 0 00 218856 2

Photographs supplied courtesy of Empics

Layouts by Mick Sanders

Printed in Great Britain by
The Bath Press, Bath

Contents

Introduction	7
Game Guide	9
Choosing and Using	10
Selecting and Managing the Team	15
Top Performers	21
Final Tables and Scorers 1997-98	24
Club Guide	29
Player Directory	91
Appearance Files	321

Introduction

The *Fantasy Football Handbook* is designed to help you get the most out of your particular game of fantasy football management. It contains all the facts and figures you need to create your own fantasy team. It centres on the twenty teams who will take their place in the 1998-99 FA Premier League and the 400 plus players who will make up the squads of these teams. The facts and figures regarding the team players are possibly the most comprehensive available in any publication and come from my own Premiership database.

How you play the game is your decision and the aim here is not to tell you who to pick but more to outline the individual strengths and weaknesses of teams, managers and their players. Taking this in combination with the various information listed and your understanding of the way your fantasy league operates, you should stand a more than reasonable chance of success.

But fantasy management, just like the real thing, requires time, effort, skill and a good deal of luck – as mentioned above a thorough understanding of the way your league works is vitally important and with this you can start to formulate tactics and the best way to use players to their full.

Because of the wide range of games available, this handbook does not aim to go into detail about any one version.

However it does start by outlining the various types of game there are and provides you with some useful strategies that you might want to employ to take full advantage.

Following this you will find selections of teams from a couple of the bigger newspaper versions of the game and you may want to think about using these as your foundation stones. Beware though, players change, as does their form, and it is not just the initial team you pick that is important but also the way you handle the likes of transfers and injuries during the course of the season. It is up to you, and only you, to stay on top of your games. Absolutely no slacking allowed!

Beyond this you will find the Club Guide and this aims to provide you with background information on what the team achieved last year and who were the stars and, perhaps more importantly, who their stars will be in the 1998-99 season. This is followed by a detailed look at each club v club home record in the Premiership since its inception and a listing of transfers throughout the 1997-98 season, right up to 12 July 1998.

The Player Directory provides profiles of around 430 players who will make up the bulk of the squads of the 20 Premiership teams during the season. This is supplemented with three years' worth of facts and figures that will provide you with their underlying performance profile – you want the best for your team but you also want those who perform the most consistently. These Form Factors will help you choose. Note that all these figures, like all those given in this Handbook, relate specifically to FA Carling Premiership matches unless otherwise stated.

Finally there is a player by player summary of how each of the squad players competed last season, with a detailed analysis of appearances numbers.

In short, you'll find everything you need to choose and maintain your fantasy team and players. Now go and find your own luck and with skill, who knows? You could be on the road to a championship season. Here's hoping!

The Author

Bruce Smith is an award winning journalist and author. He has written over 150 books on a variety of subjects. His most popular annual publications include the *FA Carling Premiership Pocket Annual* and *Grand Prix Formula 1 Pocket Annual*. A former BBC Radio commentator he most recently appeared on Channel 4's 'The Big Breakfast' as their World Cup Monitor Man.

Acknowledgments

The author would like to thank David Tavener for his help, in particular the assistance with the player profiles. Thanks also to Mark Webb.

Contact

If you have any suggestions regarding details you would like to see in future editions of this book then please direct them to me at the following address:

Bruce Smith
PO Box 382
St Albans
Herts
AL2 3JD

Alternatively you can email me at:

Bruce-Smith@msn.com

Printable suggestions only please!

Game Guide

Choosing and Using

National newspapers provide possibly the simplest and most effective way to play fantasy football. Indeed, if the bug really takes you, most newspapers have fantasy games going all year round that allow you to try cricket and Formula 1, for instance, at times when the football season does actually stop. Even then special tournament leagues are often available. The recent World Cup in France spurned a number of fantasy leagues.

These fantasy leagues normally start a few weeks into the season and, although it is generally a good idea to start at this point, you can enter the fun at any time of the year.

The other common way of playing is by taking the play-by-mail approach and take part in one of the many leagues that can be found by looking through the ads and small ads in the back of soccer magazines. The frequency at which these run varies and, although most run in tandem with the football season, they can often run out of season.

There is also a third method which is becoming ever more popular and that is the On-Line Fantasy League. These are leagues run along similar lines to the above which are being set up on the Internet and allow you to interact more directly. Larger newspaper organisations are doing this as a common method to supplement their paper editions.

What is best? It's a matter of personal preference of course and largely depends on how much time you can spare and how seriously you are willing to take it. The newspaper versions are normally less complex in nature and also more accessible because they tend to be based solely on actual events and players. The performance of your team is based on how your players performed, or didn't perform, in their matches each weekend. This means that it is possible for you to calculate the points your players scored if you wish or simply wait for them to be published in the paper during the following week.

In these versions of games it is often just a matter of selecting a team, registering it and making sure you manage any transfers that are permissible to best effect.

Play-by-Mail editions can offer a greater depth of play and often allow you to take account of other options. Players may not be generally available and have to be selected from an overall pool of players that the league's Gamesmaster (he's the organiser) originates and can only be with one team at a time and are therefore bought and sold by making bids. Some games go even further and allow you to develop a whole infrastructure around your team and include stadiums and boardroom decisions, to name but two!

Play-by-Mail, rather obviously, also

relies on you having to send in weekly sheets (called Turnsheets) and then wait for the result to come back. If you miss the deadline you could find yourself slipping. Many of these leagues also allow you to contact other managers in your league by publishing a list of contact numbers in a weekly circular.

On-Line versions allow you to make changes right up to the posted deadlines and results are also posted back to you more quickly. Their rules follow similar lines to the ones in any associated publications but quite often differ in several fundamental ways. For instance you may be able to register a squad of players rather than just a single team of players. If you have Internet access then use your browser's search engine to locate the appropriate sites. Simply search for 'Fantasy Football' and see what it returns. Beware that there are a lot of fantasy football sites in North America, but their football relates to that played on a gridiron.

If you have only tried one version, it is worth experimenting with the other just to see if it is more suitable to what you want and expect out of playing a game of fantasy football. Details for these are readily available in newspapers and magazines and it is simply a matter of contacting the telephone number or address shown and awaiting a reply.

All versions of the game cost money to play and this may not just be the cost of a stamp or two, so take this into account when you are selecting the game of your choice.

Whichever version of fantasy football you decide to opt for, it cannot be overstressed how important it is for you to be familiar with its rules. Sometimes this can take a while and, despite plenty of study work and scouring the competition rule book, it often only fully falls into place when you have played your brand of game for a while.

No matter what version of the game you are opting for – get yourself organised. You will start collecting bits of paper and making notes everywhere and the best place for these and any other paperwork is in a suitable folder or filing system. It is no fun looking for bits of paper and scribbled notes when you have a deadline to meet – I have proved this on many occasions.

If you are using a folder or a good filing system, keep room at the start of it to record all the vital information you will need to have at your fingertips. This includes phone number, address and often a PIN number.

Let's now look at team selection and strategy in some detail. Much of what follows is written with the newspaper version of fantasy football games in mind. However, salient points concerning the Play-by-Mail games are included at the appropriate points.

Planning

Once you have decided what type of game you are opting for, you should get things underway.

The key to good planning is this: Start early, register late.

By starting to plan as early as possible you are giving yourself time to succeed. Get the new rules as soon as they come out and make yourself fully conversant with them. Jot down notes and key items that you might otherwise forget or miss and start to think about how best you can use the limitations the rules impose to your best advantage.

The Leagues will give you a deadline by which time your team must be registered. They will impress upon you the need to do this as early as possible. Why? To ensure you get the best players available. Well, yes, that is certainly the case where there is only a limited set of players to select from and you want to ensure you have the best in your teams. But in the bigger games run by the daily nationals in which all players are available to you, it is just a matter of administration. They want you to get your entry in to ensure they keep the rush at the end to a minimum. This is understandable but if you are playing through a newspaper, do as I say and get your entry in at the last moment as this could, and probably will, suit you. The reason behind this tactic will become clearer as we progress.

Team Names

It may come to you in a flash or you may spend all your time fretting about what to call your team. Many Play-by-Mail games allow you to choose a real team name like Arsenal, Barcelona or Stevenage – but to do this you have to be first in because the more popular teams, such as the three examples given, go quickly. If your name is already taken then the next available name is given to you.

In general, newspapers allow you to select your own team names and this is where you can be wonderfully creative or dreadfully dull. 'Money Blaggers United' is a bit more entertaining than 'Monitor Men'. Some of the names that caught my eye during the 1997-98 season were:

Hodsonshotshotstwo
Des Lynham Town
Thick As A Parrot

If you do well enough to get into the top listings you may well find your name, and your team's, appearing in the regular listings printed in respective newspapers – you can't do a lot about the former (especially if your name is Smith) so be really creative about the second. Watch out for the obvious though, make sure you don't exceed the number of characters permissible in the name and don't be offensive.

The Players

There are normally a number of restrictions that will apply when you decide to select your team. To prevent you simply naming 11 players from the Manchester United starting line-up, there are normally two simple rules to follow:

1. There is a limited amount of money for you to spend on players.
2. There is a limit to the number of players from one team you can pick.

Each of the players who will be listed as starters in your league are assigned a transfer value. This value is what you have to spend to secure them for your team, and there is always an upper limit or ceiling on what you are allowed to spend. The amount available can depend on what the prices assigned for each player are, these figures can vary a good deal from league to league. The upper limit of some games for the 1997-98 season was as much as £45 million and this may well increase to perhaps £50 million for the 1998-99 season.

The players per club restriction prevents you snapping up all of your players from one or two clubs, even if the budget allowed you to do so. The number of players limit can again vary between the leagues, but two seems to be fairly normal.

In essence these two simple, but fundamental rules make the game one that makes you think and really does start to test your knowledge of football. The key about the second basic rule is that the club a player is allocated to is the one he was with at the time the player lists were printed and distributed. This means that he may well have actually transferred to another club during the course of time between the list being printed and the season getting underway. This is something you can use to your advantage and is why I mentioned earlier that you should leave your entry to the last possible moment. For example when your player list was published, Teddy Sheringham might still have been playing for Tottenham but then started the season with Manchester United. For all playing purposes, Sheringham would still be regarded as a Tottenham player, so in this respect you could effectively have three Manchester United players in your own fantasy team, even if the limit was two!

There is also often another restriction that is imposed, in that you must make your selection from position categories. In this case players are categorised by their position – the categories are normally:

Goalkeepers
Fullbacks
Centre Backs
Midfielders
Strikers

Your 11 team players have to come from these areas and there can be restrictions such that your 11 players may be selected as:

Goalkeepers   1
Fullbacks   2
Centre Backs 2
Midfielders   4
Strikers   2

This is in playing terms a 4-4-2 formation but in fantasy football would be referred to as a 1-2-2-4-2 formation.

All this will provide you with some debate. Firstly you'll scream and marvel at some of the valuations put on players and this is where your bargain hunting ability comes into play. On the other hand, though, you'll find that some players get assigned funny classifications which can work to your benefit. For example, if a player that you and I would regard as an out-and-out striker is listed as a midfield player. Identifying these irregularities, for want of a better word, allows you to run with what is effectively a 4-3-3 formation. They can also mean you score a lot more points. A free-scoring midfield player may get more points than a similar player classed as a striker who is supposed to score. Examples where confusion could occur are players such as Marc Overmars – a winger, but classified as a midfield player by many newspapers.

Other positions to watch are fullbacks classified as midfielders, especially when their own teams like to use wing-backs.

Beware though because it can operate in reverse where a midfielder is classified as a striker and therefore doesn't seem to pick up as many points for your team as he should.

Some leagues, especially those of an on-line nature, allow you to register a whole squad of players. In these cases you will have more money available to spend – say £55 million, but will still face the other limitations already outlined.

Registering

Once you have done your ground work, made your selections and named your team, you will need to register it. Again the documentation that will have been supplied with the starter pack you

FANTASY FOOTBALL HANDBOOK 1998/99

originally requested will contain the information on how to do this. The two traditional methods are by filling out a registration form or by calling a hotline phone number.

Whatever method you go for, make sure you have all the facts and figures to hand. Players are allocated identification numbers that will need to be recorded, as well as their values. Double check your values and the total because if you go over the limit your application will be rejected and you could miss the start of the season.

Under Way

Once the season is under way, the rules of the game will determine what you can, and can't, do. Transfers will have an important role to play and these are discussed in a little more detail later on. You may also decide to keep track of your own players and how they are scoring for your team. This will certainly help you identify who might need to leave the club!

If you are in a Play-By-Mail league then your scores and associated facts and figures will be posted back to you. If you are in an On-Line version you can log on to your particular web site and find out how well you are doing. Newspaper versions of the game will generally print the full list of players available in their game once a week and alongside the players they will normally list how many points they did or didn't score the previous week and their running aggregate total. Using this you can keep a list of how well you are doing, simply by checking the numbers. Another option often available is the premium-priced hotline where you can use your game PIN to access your own standing and details.

Some versions, such as the Interactive Team Football run by The Times in conjunction with Sky Sports allows you to update and see your performance on your TV screen, via the Astra satellite in combination with a touch-tone telephone. Other newspapers allow you to order a print out of player scorers by phoning a premium rate number and ordering what is called a 'matrix'.

Scoring

How you score points again relies on the manner in which your league is run. The most basic, simplest and often therefore the most popular might go something like this:

For every goal scored by any player
    3 points
For any assist by any of your players
    2 points
For every clean sheet kept by your goalkeeper or defender
    2 points
For every goal conceded by your goalkeeper or defender
    1 point

These criteria are applied to each member of your team to give them their weekly totals – which can be positive or negative. This is added to the previous week's values to provide a total aggregate score. The higher your aggregate score, the nearer the top of the league you will be.

Selecting and Managing the Team

Team selection is a very personal thing. Who you consider to be a good player will not be rated by another. No doubt your selection will also be influenced by your own bias towards or against real sides. But remember you don't just want good players, you want players who are:

- going to score you points
- not going to lose you points

You will ultimately develop your own method of picking a team and this will probably depend on how much time you can spend studying the form of individual players. The most obvious way to start is to go for all the big name players and use this as a reference point that you can work back from as you will almost certainly be over budget. The real expertise comes from being able to pick out 'winners' – that's players breaking on to the scene who score points and are good value for money.

A strategy that is employed by many other players is to spend a big chunk of their money on attackers and then do as best they can with the money that is left over. This is fine in theory but my view is that while you want a top scorer in your side you also want all your other players to contribute to the team performance and not effectively lose you points by low scores or even negative scores. It can prove false economics and this should be borne out in some of the examples that follow on below.

The player and team outlines in this book should allow you to come up with some real gems but a good way to start is to look at past performances.

Getting Value for Money

One method to see just how well your players, potential or otherwise, have performed is to do a little homework when the year's final results are published. Some players can earn excellent points one week, only to lose them again the next. The true value of a player is not just his total number of points at the end of the season, but how much of your budget he cost you to obtain those points. In these cases I calculate what I call the player's PPM – that stands for Points Per Million. I divide the number of points the player scored by the amount he cost. This can provide some interesting results.

Consider Chris Sutton – the Premiership's joint top scorer last season. In one newspaper his end of season total was 50. However, Sutton is always going to be one of the most expensive players you can buy – £6 million in this particular game. This gave him a PPM of 8.3. In the same league, Dion Dublin accumulated 61 points and cost £5.6 million – giving a rating of 10.89. Much better value.

Picking good buys can be very lucrative. Anyone who selected Michael Owen at the start of last year could have got him for £5.0 million in some games, yet he returned 74 points giving a PPM rating of 14.80! He'll be worth a tad more in the coming seasons though and so his PPM rating will inevitably drop.

The tables below show how some of the best players in each category performed. That said, there are bargains to be had and if you have a computer spreadsheet available, you can set up a worksheet so that you can monitor players' performances to date and see which are earning the points for minimal costs. These should be the targets of any transfers you undertake.

Categorically the Best

Goalkeepers

Name	£	Pts	PPM
Neil Sullivan	2.6	23	8.85
Peter Schmeichel	3.7	31	8.37
David Seaman	3.4	24	7.06
David James	3.1	21	6.77
Kasey Keller	2.4	22	9.17

Fullbacks

Name	£	Pts	PPM
Paul Telfer	2.5	33	13.20
Nigel Winterburn	3.7	46	12.43
Pontus Kaamark	2.4	28	11.67
Phil Neville	3.7	37	10.00
Gary Neville	3.9	41	10.52
Dan Petrescu	3.8	34	8.95
Gary Kelly	3.5	28	8.00

Central Defenders

Name	£	Pts	PPM
Matt Elliott	2.7	43	15.93
Tony Adams	3.9	51	13.10
Frank Leboeuf	3.5	44	12.57
Gary Rowett	2.4	28	11.67
David Wetherall	3.2	27	8.44

Midfielders

Name	£	Pts	PPM
Alan Thompson	3.1	41	13.23
David Beckham	4.1	51	12.44
Steve McManaman	4.0	48	12.00
Julian Joachim	3.0	34	11.33
Eyal Berkovic	3.3	37	11.21
Rod Wallace	3.0	32	10.67
Ryan Giggs	4.0	42	10.50
Matt Le Tissier	4.8	51	10.63
Paulo Di Canio	4.6	49	10.65

Strikers

Name	£	Pts	PPM
Paulo Wanchope	4.0	53	13.25
Michael Owen	5.7	74	12.98
Dion Dublin	5.6	61	10.89
Francesco Baiano	4.8	50	10.42
JF Hasselbaink	5.5	55	10.00
John Hartson	5.6	54	9.64
Dennis Bergkamp	6.4	57	8.90
Chris Sutton	6.1	50	8.19

Best Not

The above method allows you to start making selections based on how well the players were actually performing in your own league, but how does that relate to what is actually perceived of their performance? There is one way to examine this which can have a practical benefit.

The Professional Footballer's Association (PFA) vote for their best player every year – not only that they also vote for their team of the year and I have listed their 1997-98 choice below and have included the value they were assigned and the points they returned, had I chosen them in my particular league (which I didn't!).

PFA Team Performance

Player	Team	£	Pts
Nigel Martyn	Leeds U.	3.2	19
Gary Neville	Manchester U.	3.7	37
Colin Hendry	Blackburn R.	3.2	13
Gary Pallister	Manchester U.	3.8	22
Graeme Le Saux	Chelsea	3.7	17
David Beckham	Manchester U.	4.1	51
David Batty	Newcastle U.	2.9	5
Nicky Butt	Manchester U.	3.0	13
Ryan Giggs	Manchester U.	4.2	40
Michael Owen	Liverpool	5.7	74
Dennis Bergkamp	Arsenal	6.4	57

As you can see the choice of the professionals shouldn't necessarily be the choice of you or me! At £43.9 million it would be within the budget of many leagues but the selection of four Manchester United players would almost certainly not be allowed.

However, the team provides a good starting point to work from and, looking retrospectively, to determine what changes can be made to maximise points. Looking straight through the team we can see that Colin Hendry, David Batty, Nicky Butt and even Nigel Martin provided poor returns.

From my basic list of top PPM performers above I would immediately substitute Neil Sullivan for Nigel Martyn, Matt Elliott for Colin Hendry, Alan Thompson for David Batty and Paulo Di Canio for Nicky Butt. That would give me a lot of extra points and for less fantasy cash!

Private Selection

The above method is fine if you have direct access to all players in your league. This is normally the case when you are playing in a newspaper or magazine league. However it is often not the case when you are playing one of the Play-by-Mail leagues. In many of these games you will be required to join an auction for players when the league is about to get underway.

How the auction is held will depend on your league. It may involve placing bids, it may be on a first come first serve basis – but whichever it is, you can prepare yourself in much the same way, although you will need to have back-up players available in your base selection list just in case one or more of your bids fails.

If you join a league that is already underway then you will probably be supplied with a set of players by the league. This is your starting point and it will be up to you to watch your league's transfer market so that you can mould your own team in the fullness of time. Hey, just like the real thing!

Transfers

Transfer policies vary from league to league. Some allow you to do them all the time. In many Play-by-Mail leagues you simply bid and bid and hope that they are accepted by the managers who currently own the rights to the players. The policy of newspaper and magazine games varies as well. Some allow you to make them only a few times per season and then there may be a limit on the number of players you can transfer, while others allow you to make transfers on a weekly basis, again with an upper limit on the number you can make. In all cases you can only make transfers that will keep you within your budget. Thus if there are two players

Fantasy Football Handbook 1998/99

totalling £6 million that you want for your team, you must first transfer out two players to that value or more.

If you are only allowed limited transfers then you need to plan and pick wisely – don't make a change for change's sake!

If you are only allowed a limited number of transfers over a season then there are two reasons why you might consider making a change to your starting line-up. Firstly you have an injured player to replace and secondly you have a player who is not doing the business.

In the case of injured players think carefully. An injured player is not earning you points but equally he isn't costing you points! If you have a midfield player who has scored a total of 30 points for you up to Christmas and then breaks a leg is it really worth getting rid of him? If you refer back to the lists presented earlier you'll see that there aren't too many midfield players who score 30 points at the end of the season let alone half way through it! This is one reason why it is worth keeping track of points scored by players other than those on your team – so that you have the best possible choices available to you when you want to replace an injured or a poor performing player.

Remember that in both of these cases you'll only earn the points that the player scores after you assigned him to your team. Games that allow just the occasional updates often add new players to their lists at the same point to take account of any new arrivals, so keep abreast of the transfer market and how well these players have been performing.

In Leagues that allow weekly transfers you can make them for all the above reasons but you can also use them for tactical reasons.

For example, suppose you have Tony Adams, David Seaman and Michael Owen in your team. The week arrives when Arsenal play Liverpool. There are winner and loser conflicts amongst your own team here. If Michael Owen scores then both Seaman and Adams are going to lose points. If Owen (and Liverpool) are shut out then Seaman and Adams score points but Owen doesn't.

The sensible option here might be to transfer Michael Owen out and look for a replacement for a week. If you have been keeping track of players then you will have the ready-made replacement.

Obviously in these matters it pays to keep track of the fixture list a week or two ahead but you can also look beyond and into the fixture list if you are clever enough. And we are.

In the Club Guide you will find a list of each club's Premiership home records against the other 19 teams that make up the Premier League for 1998-99. Tradition plays a big part in results and if you scour through the fixtures as they come you will find out how teams have traditionally fared against each other. Take Liverpool v Chelsea. Liverpool have a 100% home record against Chelsea over the last six years of the Premiership. Manchester United have a 100% record over Southampton at Old Trafford. Therefore if you have Chelsea players going away to Liverpool players, you may want to consider making some short-term transfers. The same goes for any Southampton players you have, when United are about to take them on at home.

The listing below provides you with what I call some home bankers – these are matches in the past five years that have always favoured the home team!

Home Bankers

Match/Event	P	W	D	L	F	A	Pts	%
Aston Villa v Derby	2	2	0	0	4	1	6	100.00
Blackburn Rovers v Newcastle United	5	5	0	0	6	1	15	100.00
Chelsea v Derby County	2	2	0	0	7	1	6	100.00
Chelsea v Leicester City	3	3	0	0	7	1	9	100.00
Chelsea v Middlesbrough	3	3	0	0	10	0	9	100.00
Derby County v Coventry City	2	2	0	0	5	2	6	100.00
Derby County v Middlesbrough	1	1	0	0	2	1	3	100.00
Derby County v Tottenham Hotspur	2	2	0	0	6	3	6	100.00
Derby County v West Ham United	2	2	0	0	3	0	6	100.00
Liverpool v Chelsea	6	6	0	0	18	6	18	100.00
Liverpool v Derby County	2	2	0	0	6	1	6	100.00
Liverpool v Middlesbrough	3	3	0	0	10	2	9	100.00
Manchester United v Crystal Palace	3	3	0	0	6	0	9	100.00
Manchester United v Southampton	6	6	0	0	13	4	18	100.00
Manchester United v West Ham United	5	5	0	0	10	2	15	100.00
Middlesbrough v Blackburn Rovers	3	3	0	0	7	3	9	100.00
Middlesbrough v Derby County	1	1	0	0	6	0	3	100.00
Middlesbrough v West Ham United	2	2	0	0	8	3	6	100.00
Newcastle United v Aston Villa	5	5	0	0	14	5	15	100.00
Newcastle United v Everton	5	5	0	0	9	1	15	100.00
Newcastle United v Middlesbrough	2	2	0	0	4	1	6	100.00
Newcastle United v Nottingham Forest	3	3	0	0	10	2	9	100.00
Sheffield Wednesday v Leicester City	3	3	0	0	4	1	9	100.00
Southampton v Middlesbrough	3	3	0	0	8	2	9	100.00
West Ham United v Leicester City	3	3	0	0	6	3	9	100.00
Arsenal v Sheffield Wednesday	6	5	1	0	12	4	16	88.89
Arsenal v Southampton	6	5	1	0	16	7	16	88.89
Blackburn Rovers v Chelsea	6	5	1	0	11	2	16	88.89
Blackburn Rovers v Sheffield Wed.	6	5	1	0	19	5	16	88.89
Blackburn Rovers v Southampton	6	5	1	0	10	4	16	88.89
Manchester United v Coventry City	6	5	1	0	14	1	16	88.89
Manchester United v Sheffield Wed.	6	5	1	0	18	4	16	88.89
Manchester United v Tottenham Hotspur	6	5	1	0	11	2	16	88.89
Leeds United v West Ham United	5	4	1	0	9	3	13	86.67
Newcastle United v Chelsea	5	4	1	0	12	4	13	86.67
Newcastle United v Coventry City	5	4	1	0	15	0	13	86.67
Southampton v Newcastle United	5	4	1	0	10	5	13	86.67
West Ham United v Southampton	5	4	1	0	11	6	13	86.67
Aston Villa v Liverpool	6	5	0	1	11	6	15	83.33
Blackburn Rovers v Nottingham Forest	4	3	1	0	15	2	10	83.33
Liverpool v Aston Villa	6	5	0	1	15	5	15	83.33
Liverpool v Leeds United	6	5	0	1	16	2	15	83.33
Liverpool v Nottingham Forest	4	3	1	0	9	4	10	83.33

FANTASY Football Handbook 1998/99

Match/Event	P	W	D	L	F	A	Pts	%
Liverpool v Sheffield Wednesday	6	5	0	1	10	3	15	83.33
Manchester United v Wimbledon	6	5	0	1	13	4	15	83.33
Nottingham Forest v Tottenham Hotspur	4	3	1	0	8	5	10	83.33
Wimbledon v Nottingham Forest	4	3	1	0	5	2	10	83.33
Blackburn Rovers v West Ham United	5	4	0	1	13	7	12	80.00
Everton v West Ham United	5	4	0	1	8	3	12	80.00
Liverpool v Newcastle United	5	4	0	1	11	8	12	80.00
Newcastle United v Sheffield Wed.	5	4	0	1	11	6	12	80.00
Newcastle United v Wimbledon	5	4	0	1	15	5	12	80.00

Keeping Track

Part of the fun behind playing fantasy football is to check out how your team are going and to plan ahead – the reasons for which have already been outlined above. Play-by-Mail games will normally send you a sheet each week showing you just how your players and your team are doing.

Newspaper versions of the game will publish the weekly and aggregate performances of players to date and, if you're good enough, your name and the teams in their top performers list.

If you don't play the transfer market at all, preferring to let your team 'ride', then you can simply total up the aggregates for your players as and when you want to get your points totals at any one time.

However, if you are planning on a game where you will be hyper-active in the transfer market then you will need to keep on top of the administrative management of the team so that you can keep track of your players and the points that they are accumulating for you.

There are several ways to do this. If you have access to a computer you might be able to set everything up on a spreadsheet. This is simple if you don't plan too many transfers, but you will need to think carefully about the design of the spreadsheet if you plan to make regular dealings. Remember, you will need to keep track of the points, positive or negative, that players accumulated for you prior to their departure. This book isn't a spreadsheet primer, but one way to do this is to create a worksheet for each of the players you use with a cell for each week of the season. Into each cell add points at the appropriate time and total these to be carried forward into a main summary worksheet.

This same method can be used for the pen and paper approach and you may find a ruled hardback book convenient for this.

Top Performers

The following lists should give you an even better indication as to the sort of players you should be selecting. Remember that it is not necessarily the best individual players that win the most points, but those that work with their team. The best goalkeeper in the world is not going to score as many points behind a leaky defence as he will by playing behind a watertight one!

The points totals given are my own figures based on how the players performed across some of the top newspaper based fantasy leagues. Only players who score 10 points or more across the course of the season are included.

Goalkeepers

Name	Club	Points
SCHMEICHEL	Manchester U.	31
KELLER	Leicester C.	25
SEAMAN	Arsenal	24
SULLIVAN	Wimbledon	23
JAMES	Liverpool	21
MARTYN	Leeds U.	21
DE GOEY	Chelsea	18
MANNINGER	Arsenal	18
HEDMAN	Coventry C.	16
FLOWERS	Blackburn R.	13
OGRIZOVIC	Coventry C.	11
POOM	Derby Co.	11
FORREST	West Ham U.	10

Fullbacks

Name	Club	Points
WINTERBURN	Arsenal	46
G NEVILLE	Manchester U.	36
P NEVILLE	Manchester U.	36
PETRESCU	Chelsea	33
TELFER	Coventry C.	33
KAAMARK	Leicester C.	31
DIXON	Arsenal	30
KELLY	Leeds U.	30
McATEER	Liverpool	30
BURROWS	Coventry C.	27
NILSSON	Coventry C.	27
CUNNINGHAM	Wimbledon	23
IRWIN	Manchester U.	22
ERANIO	Derby Co.	21
DODD	Southampton	20
ROBERTSON	Leeds U.	20
ATHERTON	Sheffield W.	17

Fantasy Football Handbook 1998/99

Name	Club	Points
BJORNEBYE	Liverpool	17
KIMBLE	Wimbledon	17
LE SAUX	Chelsea	17
THATCHER	Wimbledon	16
WRIGHT	Aston Villa	16
WATSON	Newcastle U.	15
HALL	Coventry C.	14
POWELL	Derby Co.	13
BABAYARO	Chelsea	12
GRAYSON	Aston Villa	12
BARTON	Newcastle U.	11
PISTONE	Newcastle U.	11
KENNA	Blackburn R.	10

Central Defenders

Name	Club	Points
ADAMS	Arsenal	51
ELLIOTT	Leicester C.	46
LEBOEUF	Chelsea	41
JOHNSEN	Manchester U.	29
WETHERALL	Leeds U.	29
BLACKWELL	Wimbledon	25
ROWETT	Derby Co.	25
KEOWN	Arsenal	24
PERRY	Wimbledon	24
BREEN	Coventry C.	22
WALSH	Leicester C.	22
BOULD	Arsenal	20
HALLE	Leeds U.	19
PALLISTER	Manchester U.	19
PRIOR	Leicester C.	18
BERG	Blackburn R.	17
EHIOGU	Aston Villa	17
GRIMANDI	Arsenal	17
KVARME	Liverpool	17
MATTEO	Liverpool	17
SHAW	Coventry C.	17
CLARKE	Chelsea	16
DUBERRY	Chelsea	16
HARKNESS	Liverpool	16
VEGA	Tottenham H.	16
RADEBE	Leeds U.	15
SOUTHGATE	Aston Villa	15
UNSWORTH	Everton	15
MOLENAAR	Leeds U.	14
STAUNTON	Aston Villa	14
STIMAC	Derby Co.	14
ALBERT	Newcastle U.	12
SINCLAIR	Chelsea	12
HENCHOZ	Blackburn R.	11

Midfielders

Name	Club	Points
DI CANIO	Sheffield W.	49
BECKHAM	Manchester U.	48
LE TISSIER	Sothampton	48
McMANAMAN	Liverpool	48
THOMPSON	Bolton W.	41
GIGGS	Manchester U.	39
OVERMARS	Arsenal	39
GINOLA	Tottenham H.	36
JOACHIM	Aston Villa	34
BERKOVIC	West Ham U.	33
SCHOLES	Manchester U.	32
WALLACE	Leeds U.	32
REDFEARN	Barnsley	30
GUPPY	Leicester C.	28
CARBONE	Sheffield W.	27
IZZET	Leicester C.	26
INCE	Liverpool	23
LEONHARDSEN	Liverpool	23
SPEED	Everton/Newcastle	23
GILLESPIE	Newcastle U.	22
PETIT	Arsenal	22
TAYLOR	Aston Villa	22
DI MATTEO	Chelsea	21
SHERWOOD	Blackburn R.	21
BARNES	Liverpool	20
HUGHES	West Ham U.	20
WHELAN	Coventry C.	20
BOWYER	Leeds U.	19
DRAPER	Aston Villa	19
BULLOCK	Barnsley	18
FRANDSEN	Bolton W.	18
HAALAND	Leeds U.	18
PEMBRIDGE	Sheffield W.	18
WHITTINGHAM	Sheffield W.	18
KETSBAIA	Newcastle U.	17
PARLOUR	Arsenal	17
FOX	Tottenham H.	16

Name	Club	Points
KEWELL	Leeds U.	16
LEE	Newcastle U.	16
NIELSEN	Tottenham H.	15
PALMER	Leeds U.	15
REDKNAPP	Liverpool	15
LOMBARDO	C.Palace	14
RIBEIRO	Leeds U.	14
EARLE	Wimbledon	13
PARKER	Leicester C.	13
PLATT	Arsenal	13
POYET	Chelsea	13
RODGER	C.Palace	13
LAMPARD	West Ham U.	12
LOMAS	West Ham U.	12
RIPLEY	Blackburn R.	12
VIEIRA	Arsenal	12
BERGER	Liverpool	11
NICHOLLS	Chelsea	11
SOLTVEDT	Coventry C.	11
WILCOX	Blackburn R.	11
BERTI	Tottenham H.	10
BUTT	Manchester U.	10
FLITCROFT	Blackburn R.	10
HARTE	Leeds U.	10
LAZARIDIS	West Ham U.	10
LENNON	Leicester C.	10
SAVAGE	Leicester C.	10
SELLARS	Bolton W.	10

Strikers

Name	Club	Points
OWEN	Liverpool	67
DUBLIN	Coventry C.	58
BERGKAMP	Arsenal	57
HASSELBAINK	Leeds U.	55
COLE	Manchester U.	54
HARTSON	West Ham U.	54
WANCHOPE	Derby Co.	50
BAIANO	Derby Co.	48
SUTTON	Blackburn R.	47
HUCKERBY	Coventry C.	44
GALLACHER	Blackburn R.	41
FERGUSON	Everton	40
BLAKE	Bolton W.	39
OSTENSTADT	Southampton	39
FLO	Chelsea	38
ZOLA	Chelsea	38
FOWLER	Liverpool	37
HIRST	Sheffield W.	37
STURRIDGE	Derby Co.	37
SHERINGHAM	Manchester U.	35
WARD	Derby Co.	34
HESKEY	Leicester C.	32
HUGHES	Chelsea	32
KLINSMANN	Tottenham H.	32
MILOSEVIC	Aston Villa	31
YORKE	Aston Villa	31
ANELKA	Arsenal	30
DAVIES	Southampton	29
VIALLI	Chelsea	28
SHIPPERLEY	C.Palace	27
SOLSKJAER	Manchester U.	26
BOOTH	Sheffield W.	25
COLLYMORE	Aston Villa	25
WRIGHT	Arsenal	25
BARMBY	Everton	20
MADAR	Everton	19
MARSHALL	Leicester C.	18
BURTON	Derby Co.	17
ARMSTRONG	Tottenham H.	15
RIEDLE	Liverpool	15
FERDINAND	Tottenham H.	12
DAHLIN	Blackburn R.	11
EUELL	Wimbledon	11
FJORTOFT	Barnsley	11
HOLDSWORTH	Wimbledon	11
HRISTOV	Barnsley	11
WREH	Arsenal	11
SHEARER	Newcastle U.	10

Final Tables and Scorers 1997-98

FA Carling Premiership

	P	W	D	L	F	A	W	D	L	F	A	Pts
		HOME					*AWAY*					
Arsenal	38	15	2	2	43	10	8	7	4	25	23	78
Manchester United	38	13	4	2	42	9	10	4	5	31	17	77
Liverpool	38	13	2	4	42	16	5	9	5	26	26	65
Chelsea	38	13	2	4	37	14	7	1	11	34	29	63
Leeds United	38	9	5	5	31	21	8	3	8	26	25	59
Blackburn Rovers	38	11	4	4	40	26	5	6	8	17	26	58
Aston Villa	38	9	3	7	26	24	8	3	8	23	24	57
West Ham United	38	13	4	2	40	18	3	4	12	16	39	56
Derby County	38	12	3	4	33	18	4	4	11	19	31	55
Leicester City	38	6	10	3	21	15	7	4	8	30	26	53
Coventry City	38	8	9	2	26	17	4	7	8	20	27	52
Southampton	38	10	1	8	28	23	4	5	10	22	32	48
Newcastle United	38	8	5	6	22	20	3	6	10	13	24	44
Tottenham Hotspur	38	7	8	4	23	22	4	3	12	21	34	44
Wimbledon	38	5	6	8	18	25	5	8	6	16	21	44
Sheffield Wednesday	38	9	5	5	30	26	3	3	13	22	41	44
Everton	38	7	5	7	25	27	2	8	9	16	29	40
Bolton Wanderers	38	7	8	4	25	22	2	5	12	16	39	40 R
Barnsley	38	7	4	8	25	35	3	1	15	12	47	35 R
Crystal Palace	38	2	5	12	15	39	6	4	9	22	32	33 R

FA Carling Premiership Top Scorers

Player	Club	Goals	All-time Total
Dion DUBLIN	Coventry City	18	61
Michael OWEN	Liverpool	18	19
Chris SUTTON	Blackburn Rovers	18	77
Dennis BERGKAMP	Arsenal	16	39
Kevin GALLACHER	Blackburn Rovers	16	47
Jimmy HASSELBAINK	Leeds United	16	16
Andy COLE	Manchester United	15	88
John HARTSON	West Ham United	15	34
Darren HUCKERBY	Coventry City	14	19
Paulo WANCHOPE	Derby County	13	14
Francesco BAIANO	Derby County	12	12
Nathan BLAKE	Bolton Wanderers	12	13
Paolo DI CANIO	Sheffield Wednesday	12	12
Marc OVERMARS	Arsenal	12	12
Dwight YORKE	Aston Villa	12	60

FA Carling Premiership Club Top Scorers

Club	Scorers
Arsenal	16 – Bergkamp; 12 – Overmars; 10 – Wright
Aston Villa	12 – Yorke; 8 – Joachim; 7 – Milosevic
Barnsley	10 – Redfearn; 8 – Ward; 6 – Fjortoft
Blackburn Rovers	18 – Sutton; 16 Gallacher; 5 – Sherwood
Bolton Wanderers	12 – Blake; 9 – Thompson
Chelsea	11 – Flo, Vialli; 9 – M. Hughes; 8 – Zola
Coventry City	18 – Dublin; 14 – Huckerby; 6 – Whelan
Crystal Palace	7 – Shipperley; 5 – Bent, Lombardo
Derby County	13 – Wanchope; 12 – Baiano, 9 – Sturridge
Everton	11 – Ferguson; 7 – Speed; 6 – Madar
Leeds United	16 – Hasselbaink; 10 – Radebe
Leicester City	10 – Heskey; 7 – Elliott
Liverpool	18 – Owen; 11 – McManaman; 9 – Fowler
Manchester United	16 – Cole; 9 – Sheringham; 8 – Giggs, Scholes
Newcastle United	6 – Barnes; 4 – Lee, Gillespie
Sheffield Wednesday	12 – Di Canio; 9 – Carbone
Southampton	11 – Le Tissier, Ostenstad; 9 – Davies, Hirst
Tottenham Hotspur	9 – Klinsmann; 5 – Ferdinand, Armstrong
West Ham United	15 – Hartson; 7 – Berkovic, Sinclair
Wimbledon	4 – Cort, Ekoku, Euell, M. Hughes, Leaburn

Nationwide League Division 1

	P	W	D	L	F	A	Pts	
Nottingham Forest	46	28	10	8	82	42	94	P
Middlesbrough	46	27	10	9	77	41	91	P
Sunderland	46	26	12	8	86	50	90	
Charlton Athletic	46	26	10	10	80	49	88	P
Ipswich Town	46	23	14	9	77	43	83	
Sheffield United	46	19	17	10	69	54	74	
Birmingham City	46	19	17	10	60	35	74	
Stockport County	46	19	8	19	71	69	65	
Wolverhampton W.	46	18	11	17	57	53	65	
WBA	46	16	13	17	50	56	61	
Crewe Alexandra	46	18	5	23	58	65	59	
Oxford United	46	16	10	20	60	64	58	
Bradford City	46	14	15	17	46	59	57	
Tranmere Rovers	46	14	14	18	54	57	56	
Norwich City	46	14	13	19	52	69	55	
Huddersfield Town	46	14	11	21	50	72	53	
Bury	46	11	19	16	42	58	52	
Swindon Town	46	14	10	22	42	73	52	
Port Vale	46	13	10	23	56	66	49	
Portsmouth	46	13	10	23	51	63	49	
QPR	46	10	19	17	51	63	49	
Manchester City	46	12	12	22	56	57	48	R
Stoke City	46	11	13	22	44	74	46	R
Reading	46	11	9	26	39	78	42	R

Nationwide League Division 2

	P	W	D	L	F	A	Pts	
Watford	46	24	16	6	67	41	88	P
Bristol City	46	25	10	11	69	39	85	P
Grimsby Town	46	19	15	12	55	37	72	P
Northampton Town	46	18	17	11	52	37	71	
Bristol Rovers	46	20	10	16	70	64	70	
Fulham	46	20	10	16	60	43	70	
Wrexham	46	18	16	12	55	51	70	
Gillingham	46	19	13	14	52	47	70	
Bournemouth	46	18	12	16	57	52	66	
Chesterfield	46	16	17	13	46	44	65	
Wigan	46	17	11	18	64	66	62	
Blackpool	46	17	11	18	59	67	62	
Oldham Athletic	46	15	16	15	62	54	61	

Fantasy Football Handbook 1998/99

	P	W	D	L	F	A	Pts	
Wycombe Wanderers	46	14	18	14	51	53	60	
Preston NE	46	15	14	17	56	56	59	
York City	46	14	17	15	52	58	59	
Luton Town	46	14	15	17	60	64	57	
Millwall	46	14	13	19	43	54	55	
Walsall	46	14	12	20	43	52	54	
Burnley	46	13	13	20	55	65	52	
Brentford	46	11	17	18	50	71	50	R
Plymouth Argyle	46	12	13	21	55	70	49	R
Carlisle United	46	12	8	26	57	73	44	R
Southend United	46	11	10	25	47	79	43	R

Nationwide League Division 3

	P	W	D	L	F	A	Pts	
Notts County	46	29	12	5	82	43	99	P
Macclesfield Town	46	23	13	10	63	44	82	P
Lincoln City	46	20	15	11	60	51	75	P
Colchester United	46	21	11	14	72	60	74	P
Torquay United	46	21	11	14	68	59	74	
Scarborough	46	19	15	12	67	58	72	
Barnet	46	19	13	14	61	51	70	
Scunthorpe United	46	19	12	15	56	52	69	
Rotherham	46	16	19	11	67	61	67	
Peterborough United	46	18	13	15	63	51	67	
Leyton Orient *	46	19	12	15	62	47	66	
Mansfield Town	46	16	17	13	64	55	65	
Shrewsbury	46	16	13	17	61	62	61	
Chester City	46	17	10	19	60	61	61	
Exeter City	46	15	15	16	68	63	60	
Cambridge United	46	14	18	14	63	57	60	
Hartlepool United	46	12	23	11	61	53	59	
Rochdale	46	17	7	22	56	55	58	
Darlington	46	14	12	20	56	72	54	
Swansea	46	13	11	22	49	62	50	
Cardiff City	46	9	23	14	48	52	50	
Hull City	46	11	8	27	56	83	41	
Brighton & HA	46	6	17	23	38	66	35	
Doncaster Rovers	46	4	8	34	30	113	20	R

* Leyton Orient deducted three points for fielding ineligible players.

FANTASY FOOTBALL HANDBOOK 1998/99

Club Guide

Arsenal

The potential Arsenal showed in flashes during the 1996-97 season was fulfilled in 1997-98 when they became only the second club to complete the double for a second time. Arsène Wenger became the first non-British manager to claim the greatest prize in English football. But it had hardly looked on the cards the day that a woeful performance enabled visiting Blackburn Rovers to hint at their potential championship prospects by producing a stunning 3-1 win in North London. Just days before Christmas many Gooners supporters must have left the stands wishing they had joined the shopping brigade.

Ironically it would be at Ewood Park several months later that the Gunners would deliver an emphatic win and an even more enlightening display to leave the Sky TV audience in no doubt as to their real credentials as champions elect.

The win in Lancashire came in the midst of a ten match winning run that started on the 11 March at Wimbledon and culminated at a rocking Highbury on 3 May with the 4-0 drubbing of Everton. Commentator Martyn Tyler caught the Arsenal mood perfectly when he exclaimed "That sums it all up" at the moment skipper Tony Adams – Mr Arsenal – thundered the ball home after running onto Steve Bould's gloriously weighted through ball. It smacked of Steve Williams and Tony Woodcock at their best. But this move came from the heart of the boring, boring Arsenal defence.

Club Data File

Responsibility

Top Scorers: Dennis Bergkamp (16), Marc Overmars (12), Ian Wright (10)

Sent Off: Martin Keown, Manu Petit, Patrick Vieira

Usage

Total: 504 players used

Substitutes: 86 used, 104 not used

Players 1997-98

Most Used Subs: David Platt (20), Luis Boa Morte (11)

Most SNU: Alex Manninger (24), John Lukic (14), Steven Hughes (10)

Most Subbed: Ray Parlour (15), Marc Overmars (13), Nicolas Anelka (13)

Five-Year Form

	Div.	P	W	D	L	F	A	Pts	Pos
93-94	PL	42	18	17	7	53	28	71	4
94-95	PL	42	13	12	17	52	49	51	12
95-96	PL	38	17	12	9	49	32	63	5
96-97	PL	38	19	11	8	62	32	68	3
97-98	PL	38	23	9	6	68	33	78	1

The season had started with Arsenal in championship form. The arrival of Marc Overmars was the catalyst that ultimately converted Arsenal's championship charge as 1998 broke onto the scene. At £7m the flying Dutchman has proved a snip and added his own weight in goals. His link-play with the non-flying Dutchman was in equal presence during the World Cup.

Ronaldo may have the power, Zidane the drive, but there is no more gifted player in world football than Dennis Bergkamp. With sixteen goals in 28 games he was the Gunners' leading scorer and if fantasy points were awarded for the quality of his goals then he would probably be priced beyond any budget you may have for your team. The only player ever to get a 1-2-3 placing in the Match of the Day's Goal of the Month competition, the double winning footballer of the year (PFA and FWA) could well produce another double this year.

For those awards he may have another challenger within the red ranks. Patrick Vieira was one of seven Arsenal players to gain votes in the FWA Player of the Year award. His power, control and pace from his own box to the opponents' box is something to behold. Like Bergkamp though, he was prone to see another sort of red last term and this nearly cost their team dear. Indeed, had the Frenchman not got his marching orders at Stamford Bridge in the Coca-Cola Cup semi-final then who is to say that Arsenal may not have been celebrating a first ever Treble?

Vieira's partnership with World Cup colleague Manu Petit bloomed in the second half of the season. Amazingly hard working, the pair worked in tandem covering, backing up and supporting both defence and attack. And never any sign of fatigue even when most were predicting it.

Only one Arsenal player appeared more

Arsène Wenger

Cucumbers are decidedly hot compared to the Arsenal manager. His association with the Highbury outfit began nearly ten years ago when he started to provide some scouting expertise for them. How past managers must have wished they had listened to his suggestions then! Now he may well become the greatest Highbury gaffer of all-time. Even the legend of Herbert Chapman looks under threat.

He has left most Arsenal supporters in a quandary – having to deal with the fact that neutrals and even Tottenham supporters like and praise their team. He has made Arsenal fashionable.

When the games were coming thick and fast as the prizes drew near there was only the merest hint of perspiration. His manner has clearly been an influence on his team and he knows that the challenges, and even the expectations, will be greater this time around.

There will be new arrivals at Highbury and Wenger's international standing ensures that they will also be the best available.

times in the Premiership than the evergreen Nigel Winterburn and that was the re-kindled Ray Parlour. At a time when so many are concerned at the effect imported players will have on our home-grown talent, not least in restricting their appearances, here is a native who has blossomed into a player of international quality. Yet, Glenn Hoddle could not find a place for him, other than the bench in Switzerland.

There were concerns about the depth of the Gunners' squad at the start of 1997-98 but almost all of manager Wenger's 'minor' buys developed into exciting talent. Nicolas Anelka looked a sure-fire winner and looks set to be the long-term successor to the departed Ian Wright, while the likes of Wreh and Boa Morte will push hard for places. Even England's Number One David Seaman may be under pressure given the vital displays of Austrian keeper Alex Manninger in goal.

Despite making just seven Premiership appearances last season, he not only won Player of the Month but also was awarded a Championship medal by the Premier League in recognition of his contribution.

Arsenal players are a must in your fantasy team but just which ones you pick is one of the biggest challenges of your own managerial reign this year!

Arsenal v Opponents Record

Opponents	92-3	93-4	94-5	95-6	96-7	97-8	P	W	D	L	F	A	Pts	%
Aston Villa	0-1	1-2	0-0	2-0	2-2	0-0	6	1	3	2	5	5	6	33.33
Blackburn Rovers	0-1	1-0	0-0	0-0	1-1	1-3	6	1	3	2	3	5	6	33.33
Charlton Athletic	-	-	-	-	-	-	0	0	0	0	0	0	0	0.00
Chelsea	2-1	1-0	3-1	1-1	3-3	2-0	6	4	2	0	12	6	14	77.78
Coventry City	3-0	0-3	2-1	1-1	0-0	2-0	6	3	2	1	8	5	11	61.11
Derby County	-	-	-	-	2-2	1-0	2	1	1	0	3	2	4	66.67
Everton	2-0	2-0	1-1	1-2	3-1	4-0	6	4	1	1	13	4	13	72.22
Leeds United	0-0	2-1	1-3	2-1	3-0	2-1	6	4	1	1	10	6	13	72.22
Leicester City	-	-	1-1	-	2-0	2-1	3	2	1	0	5	2	7	77.78
Liverpool	0-1	1-0	0-1	0-0	1-2	0-1	6	1	1	4	2	5	4	22.22
Manchester United	0-1	2-2	0-0	1-0	1-2	3-2	6	2	2	2	7	7	8	44.44
Middlesbrough	1-1	-	-	1-1	2-0		3	1	2	0	4	2	5	55.56
Newcastle United	-	2-1	2-3	2-0	0-1	3-1	5	3	0	2	9	6	9	60.00
Nottingham Forest	1-1	-	1-0	1-1	2-0		4	2	2	0	5	2	8	66.67
Sheffield Wednesday	2-1	1-0	0-0	4-2	4-1	1-0	6	5	1	0	12	4	16	88.89
Southampton	4-3	1-0	1-1	4-2	3-1	3-0	6	5	1	0	16	7	16	88.89
Tottenham Hotspur	1-3	1-1	1-1	0-0	3-1	0-0	6	1	4	1	6	6	7	38.89
West Ham United	-	0-2	0-1	1-0	2-0	4-0	5	3	0	2	7	3	9	60.00
Wimbledon	0-1	1-1	0-0	1-3	0-1	5-0	6	1	2	3	7	6	5	27.78

Transfers

In

Month	Player	Signed From	Fee
Aug-97	Christopher Wreh	Monaco	Free
Jun-98	David Grodin	Saint Etienne	£500,000

Out

Month	Player	Signed For	Fee
Oct-97	Ian Selley	Fulham	£500,000
Sep-97	Paul Shaw	Millwall	£250,000
Oct-97	Glenn Helder	NAC Breda	Undisclosed
Feb-98	Jehad Muntasser	Bristol C.	Free
Feb-98	Valur Gislason	Stromsgodset	Undisclosed
Mar-98	Vince Bartram	Gillingham	Free
Jul-98	Scott Marshall	Southampton	Free
Jul-98	Ian Wright	West Ham	Undisclosed

Aston Villa

Football is a game of chance and a manager's career is often defined by the roll of the dice that is the football transfer market. A good buy, a bad buy can make or break a team. At the start of the 1997-98 season Brian Little decided to play his cards and twist in the direction of Liverpool and Stan Collymore. At £7m it seemed a huge gamble for a player who had not really ever proved his worth in those terms but it was hoped that a partnership with Dwight Yorke and Savo Milosevic would ignite Villa into the top three places. As ever it was the vastly underrated Yorke who again provided the fire-power and consistency of performance. His 12 goals seemed scant reward for his efforts while his two strikers managed as many combined but often felt the wrath of the Villa Park faithful for a seeming lack of commitment.

Villa took four games to get their first goals, by Yorke and Collymore at Tottenham, but it was in their fifth match, at home to Leeds, that they picked up their first points of the season when Yorke scored the winner.

Curiously it was another, semi-forgotten striker who made his way back into the fold. Julian Joachim may have made 10 of his 26 appearances from the bench but his eight goals were often of the match winning variety.

Ultimately though, the discord grew and in the end Little offered his resignation and was replaced by former favourite John Gregory, then at Wycombe. During his time as Villa boss, Little spent close on £30m on players and recouped around £18m. The new broom worked and a mini-revival saw Villa move back up the table to finish in seventh place, ending the season with a 1-0 win

Club Data File

Responsibility

Top Scorers:	Dwight Yorke (12), Julian Joachim (8)
Sent Off:	Stan Collymore, Ego Ehiogu

Usage

Total:	472 players used
Substitutes:	55 used, 135 not used

Players 1997-98

Most Used Subs:	Julian Joachim (10)
Most SNU:	Michael Oakes (29), Fernando Nelson (110), Gary Charles (11)
Most Subbed:	Savo Milosevic (7)

Five-Year Form

	Div.	P	W	D	L	F	A	Pts	Pos
93-94	PL	42	15	12	15	46	50	57	10
94-95	PL	42	11	15	16	51	56	48	18
95-96	PL	38	18	9	11	52	35	63	4
96-97	PL	38	17	10	11	47	34	61	5
97-98	PL	38	17	6	15	49	48	57	7

over newly crowned champions Arsenal – a win that saw them back in Europe.

Indeed it was the UEFA Cup that provided the highlights to Villa's season and only an away goal by Atletico Madrid prevented them passing into the semi-finals.

Linchpins Alan Wright and Ugo Ehiogu once again proved to be Villa's most consistent performers, missing just one game apiece in the Premier League. The regularly changing defensive personnel around them though was probably one of the main reasons they conceded significantly more goals than they had in the previous two seasons. Curiously, despite only having one goalscorer in double figures, the Villa attack managed two goals more than 1996-97 and only three less than 1995-96 when they finished fifth and fourth respectively. Goals were shared amongst ten players in all. Whether Gregory keeps faith in his under fire strikers remains to be seen but it is the continuing development of Joachim as a potential full-time strike partner of Yorke where Villa's attacking potential might lie.

In defence Gareth Southgate seems to be recapturing the form that forced him into the England reckoning prior to Euro 96, while in midfield Mark Draper will need to put an indifferent season behind him, a performance which was perhaps not aided by the curious departure of Andy Townsend to Middlesbrough early on.

John Gregory

When Brian Little departed from Villa Park on 24 February his replacement seemed to be immediately waiting. Perhaps not surprisingly as he had arrived at Villa Park with Little at the end of 1994 as part of the management team to replace Ron Atkinson. John Gregory fulfilled the role of coach for two years before accepting an offer to join Wycombe in October 1996.

He had a degree of success there, guiding the Adams Park side away from what looked to be impending relegation.

Prior to Wycombe, Gregory was assistant and then manager at Portsmouth before teaming-up with Little as his coach at Leicester.

As a player he started at Northampton before making his name at Villa and then moving onto Brighton, QPR and Derby. As a midfield player he won six caps for England.

Aston Villa v Opponents Record

Opponents	92-3	93-4	94-5	95-6	96-7	97-8	P	W	D	L	F	A	Pts	%
Arsenal	1-0	1-2	0-4	1-1	2-2	1-0	6	2	2	2	6	9	8	44.44
Blackburn Rovers	0-0	0-1	0-1	2-0	1-0	0-4	6	2	1	3	3	6	7	38.89
Charlton Athletic	-	-	-	-	-	-	0	0	0	0	0	0	0	0.00
Chelsea	1-3	1-0	3-0	0-1	0-2	0-2	6	2	0	4	5	8	6	33.33
Coventry City	0-0	0-0	0-0	4-1	2-1	3-0	6	3	3	0	9	2	12	66.67
Derby	-	-	-	-	2-0	2-1	2	2	0	0	4	1	6	100.00
Everton	2-1	0-0	0-0	1-0	3-1	2-1	6	4	2	0	8	3	14	77.78
Leeds United	1-1	1-0	0-0	3-0	2-0	1-0	6	4	2	0	8	1	14	77.78
Leicester City	-	-	4-4	-	1-3	1-1	3	0	2	1	6	8	2	22.22
Liverpool	4-2	2-1	2-0	0-2	1-0	2-1	6	5	0	1	11	6	15	83.33
Manchester United	1-0	1-2	1-2	3-1	0-0	0-2	6	2	1	3	6	7	7	38.89
Middlesbrough	5-1	-	-	0-0	1-0		3	2	1	0	6	1	7	77.78
Newcastle United	-	0-2	0-2	1-1	2-2	0-1	5	0	2	3	3	8	2	13.33
Nottingham Forest	2-1	-	0-2	1-1	2-0		4	2	1	1	5	4	7	58.33
Sheffield Wednesday	2-0	2-2	1-1	3-2	0-1	2-2	6	2	3	1	10	8	9	50.00
Southampton	1-1	0-2	1-1	3-0	1-0	1-1	6	2	3	1	7	5	9	50.00
Tottenham Hotspur	0-0	1-0	1-0	2-1	1-1	4-1	6	4	2	0	9	3	14	77.78
West Ham United	-	3-1	0-2	1-1	0-0	2-0	5	2	2	1	6	4	8	53.33
Wimbledon	1-0	0-1	7-1	2-0	5-0	1-2	6	4	0	2	16	4	12	66.67

Transfers

In

Month	Player	Signed From	Fee
Nov-97	David Curtolo	Vastras	Nominal
Jun-98	Alan Thompson	Bolton Wanderers	£4.5m
Jul-98	Fabio Ferraresi	Cesana	Free

Out

Month	Player	Signed For	Fee
Sep-97	Stuart Brock	Kidderminster H.	Free
Sep-97	Matthew George	Sheffield U.	Free
Dec-97	Scott Murray	Bristol C.	£150,000
Jul-98	Steve Staunton	Liverpool	Free
Jul-98	Fernando Nelson	FC Porto	£1.1m

Blackburn Rovers

Blackburn made what could only be described as a flying start to the 1997-98 season, taking 13 points from their opening five games. The only doubt though during this early surge in form related to the relatively small size of their squad, not helped in the least by the sale of former bedrock players such as Graeme Le Saux and Henning Berg plus other squad players. Nevertheless they were still very much in touch when they produced one of their best displays of the season, winning 3-1 at Highbury just days before Christmas.

New manager Roy Hodgson used his international experience to bring in new talent in the continental form of Stephane Henchoz, Martin Dahlin and Anders Andersson. Despite the arrival of Swedish striker Dahlin, Chris Sutton and Kevin Gallacher remained Rovers' main strike force and were Blackburn's leading scorers for a second successive year with 18 and 16 respectively.

Aston Villa were thrashed 4-0 at Villa Park with Sutton scoring a hat-trick on the opening day of the season and when Sheffield Wednesday were annihilated 7-2 at Ewood Park, Rovers were being taken very seriously. Indeed the only defeat suffered in the first 15 Premiership matches was another goal feast, with Leeds winning 4-3 at Ewood Park.

Sutton's early season form had the media calling for his return to the England set-up but his rejection of a B-team place may have cost him his international career under Hoddle.

What happened to the Rovers' challenge remains largely a mystery. For the most part they had a settled squad

Club Data File

Responsibility

Top Scorers: Chris Sutton (18), Kevin Gallacher (16)

Sent Off: Tim Flowers, Chris Sutton, Patrick Valery, Jason Wilcox (twice)

Usage

Total: 492 players used

Substitutes: 93 used, 97 not used

Players 1997-98

Most Used Subs: Lars Bohinen (10), Martin Dahlin (10)

Most SNU: Alan Fettis (20), Marlon Broomes (14)

Most Subbed: Stuart Ripley (14)

Five-Year Form

	Div.	P	W	D	L	F	A	Pts	Pos
93-94	PL	42	25	9	8	63	36	84	2
94-95	PL	42	27	8	7	80	39	89	1
95-96	PL	38	18	7	13	61	47	61	7
96-97	PL	38	9	15	14	42	43	42	13
97-98	PL	38	16	10	12	57	52	58	6

with 14 players making in excess of 20 appearances each. Injury to Tim Flowers – the leading Premiership player in terms of total Premier League appearances – certainly didn't help. There was also a goal drought. After scoring 18 times in their first six games, Rovers suddenly found goals hard to come by with just five being scored in the next seven games. On the plus side the defence tightened up and just three goals were conceded during the same period. By the end of the year Blackburn trailed United by five points but with only two victories over the next ten weeks the title bid vanished.

Jeff Kenna led the way in appearances, missing just one Premiership game while Flitcroft, Gallacher, Henchoz, Hendry, McKenna, McKinlay, Sherwood and Sutton all played in over 30 games each. Transfer speculation continued to surround skipper Tim Sherwood and may increase with the emerging talent of Damien Duff.

Just as Arsenal had found in 1996-97, chasing Manchester United required a season of near constancy. With a bigger, more experienced squad Rovers may mount a more seriously long-term challenge in 1998-99. The £7.5m signing of Kevin Davies from Southampton – a player with just 25 Premiership appearances behind him – may well help. But where he fits in the pecking order of Rovers' established dynamic front duo remains to be seen.

Roy Hodgson

At more than one point last season most people wouldn't have bet against Roy leading Rovers to at least one piece of silverware. In the end though, the lack of depth in his squad probably cost them in the championship race. He has sought to increase numbers in this area recently and the arrival of young talent Kevin Davies may just be the start.

Hodgson came to the fore via the European game. It is doubtful many fans will have heard of him before he took Switzerland through to the World Cup finals in the USA in 1994.

He did in fact spend two years in charge at Bristol in the early Eighties, sandwiched in between spells in Sweden where he managed Halmstads, Obebro and Malmo.

In 1990 he moved to Switzerland and to a position with Xamax Neuchatel before being offered, and accepting, the Swiss national job in 1995. His success ultimately saw him move to Italy and a degree of achievement with Internazionale.

Now he starts his second year in charge at Ewood Park and it is likely that honours will be forthcoming, if not this year, then in the near future.

Blackburn Rovers v Opponents Record

Opponents	92-3	93-4	94-5	95-6	96-7	97-8	P	W	D	L	F	A	Pts	%
Arsenal	1-0	1-1	3-1	1-1	0-2	1-4	6	2	2	2	7	9	8	44.44
Aston Villa	3-0	1-0	3-1	1-1	0-2	5-0	6	4	1	1	13	4	13	72.22
Charlton Athletic							0	0	0	0	0	0	0	0.00
Chelsea	2-0	2-0	2-1	3-0	1-1	1-0	6	5	1	0	11	2	16	88.89
Coventry City	2-5	2-1	4-0	5-1	4-0	0-0	6	4	1	1	17	7	13	72.22
Derby County	-	-	-	-	1-2	1-0	2	1	0	1	2	2	3	50.00
Everton	2-3	2-0	3-0	0-3	1-1	3-2	6	3	1	2	11	9	10	55.56
Leeds United	3-1	2-1	1-1	1-0	0-1	3-4	6	3	1	2	10	8	10	55.56
Leicester City	-	-	3-0	-	2-4	5-3	3	2	0	1	10	7	6	66.67
Liverpool	4-1	2-0	3-2	2-3	3-0	1-1	6	4	1	1	15	7	13	72.22
Manchester United	0-0	2-0	2-4	1-2	2-3	1-3	6	1	1	4	8	12	4	22.22
Middlesbrough	1-1	-	-	1-0	0-0		3	1	2	0	2	1	5	55.56
Newcastle United	-	1-0	1-0	2-1	1-0	1-0	5	5	0	0	6	1	15	100.00
Nottingham Forest	4-1	-	3-0	7-0	1-1		4	3	1	0	15	2	10	83.33
Sheffield Wednesday	1-0	1-1	3-1	3-0	4-1	7-2	6	5	1	0	19	5	16	88.89
Southampton	0-0	2-0	3-2	2-1	2-1	1-0	6	5	1	0	10	4	16	88.89
Tottenham Hotspur	0-2	1-0	2-0	2-1	0-2	0-3	6	3	0	3	5	8	9	50.00
West Ham United	-	0-2	4-2	4-2	2-1	3-0	5	4	0	1	13	7	12	80.00
Wimbledon	0-0	3-0	2-1	3-2	3-1	0-0	6	4	2	0	11	4	14	77.78

Transfers

In

Month	Player	Signed From	Fee
Sep-97	Alan Fettis	N. Forest	£300,000
Feb-98	Callum Davidson	St Johnstone	£1.75m
May-98	Jimmy Corbett	Gillingham	£525,000
Jun-98	Darren Peacock	Newcastle United	Free
Jun-98	Kevin Davies	Southampton	£7.25m
Jul-98	Sebastian Perez	Bastia	£3.0m

Out

Month	Player	Signed For	Fee
Aug-97	Graeme Le Saux	Chelsea	£5.0m
Aug-97	Graham Fenton	Leicester C.	£1.1m
Aug-97	Henning Berg	Manchester U.	£5.0m
Sep-97	Ian Pearce	West Ham U.	£1.6m rising to £2.3m
Oct-97	George Donnis	Released	Free
Dec-97	Chris Coleman	Fulham	£2.1m
Mar-98	Lars Bohinen	Derby Co.	£1.45m
Jul-98	Stuart Ripley	Southampton	£1.5m
Jul-98	James Beattie	Southampton	£1.0m

Charlton Athletic

Charlton Athletic have brought top division football back to The Valley for the first time in 41 years. There are considerable doubts as to their ability to stay there however.

Leicester City and Derby County have proved it can be done, but contrary to popular belief getting through and surviving your first season isn't enough on its own. Ask Bolton, Middlesbrough and Nottingham Forest. Alan Curbishley requires not just money but a good deal of luck if the Addicks are to survive. His early close-season signings did look sensible though. Chris Powell from Derby County will add experience, as will the former Barnsley skipper Neil Redfearn – talented and under-rated. Certainly he has the battle experience for the lower reaches of the Premier League where Charlton will probably be based.

Charlton's saving grace could be their striking star Clive Mendonca whose value may have increased seven fold since his £700,000 transfer from Grimsby Town. His strike rate of over two goals per game in Nationwide Division 1 last season was a major reason behind his team's promotion push. His ability to finish is in little doubt. The key may lie in the ability of his midfield to get him the ball, hence the importance of the incoming Redfearn who himself managed 10 goals in Barnsley's campaign last season.

Mark Kinsella, with a new five-year contract, will be equally important.

While Mendonca was a consistent scorer last season, no other Charlton player managed to reach double figures. Robinson netted eight while the much-travelled Steve Jones, with Premiership experience with West Ham, contributed seven along with the vastly experienced Mark Bright. Brighty, with over 100 Premiership appearances and nearly 50 goals, will provide the mainstay of

Club Data File

Responsibility

Top Scorers: Clive Mendonca (23)

Usage

Total: 611 players used

Substitutes: 95 used, 43 not used

Players 1997-98

Most Used Subs: Kevin Lisbie (16)

Most SNU: Bradley Allen (9), Tony Barness (9)

Most Subbed: Shaun Newton (9)

Five-Year Form

	Div.	P	W	D	L	F	A	Pts	Pos
93-94	1	46	19	8	19	61	58	65	11
94-95	1	46	16	11	19	58	66	59	15
95-96	1	46	17	20	9	57	45	71	6
96-97	1	46	16	11	19	52	66	59	15
97-98	1	46	26	10	10	80	49	88	4

FANTASY FOOTBALL HANDBOOK 1998/99

experience and can point to the fact that, with seven goals in his 14 appearances, his goal every two games strike rate remains intact.

At the back Curbishley did some amazing business as well. £550,000 took on board Eddie Youds from Bradford in March and his performances in just nine games helped with Charlton's play-off push. But perhaps the biggest coup came in the form of a free transfer from non-league St Leonards – goalkeeper Sasa Ilic, whose form was priceless and whose penalty save provided the play-off victory at Wembley.

At the start of the 1997-98 season Charlton, rated no higher than 16th for promotion by the bookies, made a mediocre start with defeats by Middlesbrough, Wolves and Stockport within the opening eight games, but also showed their credentials in that time with 4-0 and 4-1 wins over Norwich and Bradford. The Norwich match featured Mendonca's first hat-trick. The defeat by Stockport was Charlton's only home reversal of the season – a record only bettered by Macclesfield – and they bounced back with a seven match unbeaten run. That spell of success was ended by a crushing 5-2 defeat at Nottingham Forest. Again Charlton hit back well with five wins in six games and by the turn of the year they had taken up residency in a play-off position. An important showdown with Middlesbrough at the Valley ended in an emphatic 3-0 success for Curbishley's side with Shaun Newton – 42 appearances during the league season – scoring twice. Charlton's hopes of gaining an automatic promotion place were boosted at the start of March when Forest and Middlesbrough both lost heavily while the Londoners beat Huddersfield and West Brom, the latter 5-0. But one point from two games against Ipswich and Sunderland reduced their sights to a top six finish. Even though Charlton embarked on a breathtaking run of eight consecutive wins they still required, and achieved, a draw at Birmingham on the last day to clinch a shot at the play-offs.

Then a Clive Mendonca hat-trick helped achieve a scintillating 4-4 draw with Sunderland and set the way for Sasa Ilic to make his dramatic contribution in the penalty shoot-out. These two players will have major roles to play if the Addicks are to stay where they now find themselves.

Alan Curbishley

Alan Curbishley has gone about his job as manager at The Valley in the same way he played the game: a mixture of skill and graft combined with great vision. In many respects he was the archetypal West Ham player. He arrived at Charlton as a player and stepped into the position of first team coach in 1990. He shared the manager's post with Steve Gritt for a while and saw the club through their traumatic time away from the Valley when home games were played at Upton Park.

When Charlton returned home, Curbishley was given total team control in 1995. It proved a successful appointment by MD Richard Murray. Within a year he had guided the Addicks to a losing play-off game at Wembley and two years later had repeated the play-off feat, but this time with success. He now faces his biggest challenge.

Charlton Athletic v Opponents Record

Opponents	92-3	93-4	94-5	95-6	96-7	97-8	P	W	D	L	F	A	Pts	%
Arsenal	-	-	-	-	-	-	0	0	0	0	0	0	0	0.00
Aston Villa	-	-	-	-	-	-	0	0	0	0	0	0	0	0.00
Blackburn Rovers	-	-	-	-	-	-	0	0	0	0	0	0	0	0.00
Chelsea	-	-	-	-	-	-	0	0	0	0	0	0	0	0.00
Coventry City	-	-	-	-	-	-	0	0	0	0	0	0	0	0.00
Derby County	-	-	-	-	-	-	0	0	0	0	0	0	0	0.00
Everton	-	-	-	-	-	-	0	0	0	0	0	0	0	0.00
Leeds United	-	-	-	-	-	-	0	0	0	0	0	0	0	0.00
Leicester City	-	-	-	-	-	-	0	0	0	0	0	0	0	0.00
Liverpool	-	-	-	-	-	-	0	0	0	0	0	0	0	0.00
Middlesbrough	-	-	-	-	-	-	0	0	0	0	0	0	0	0.00
Manchester United	-	-	-	-	-	-	0	0	0	0	0	0	0	0.00
Newcastle United	-	-	-	-	-	-	0	0	0	0	0	0	0	0.00
Nottingham Forest	-	-	-	-	-	-	0	0	0	0	0	0	0	0.00
Sheffield Wednesday	-	-	-	-	-	-	0	0	0	0	0	0	0	0.00
Southampton	-	-	-	-	-	-	0	0	0	0	0	0	0	0.00
Tottenham Hotspur	-	-	-	-	-	-	0	0	0	0	0	0	0	0.00
West Ham United	-	-	-	-	-	-	0	0	0	0	0	0	0	0.00
Wimbledon	-	-	-	-	-	-	0	0	0	0	0	0	0	0.00

Transfers

In

Month	Player	Signed From	Fee
Sept-97	Mark Bowen	Shimizu S-Pulse	Free
Mar-98	Eddie Youds	Bradford C.	£550,000
Jun-98	Chris Powell	Derby Co.	£825,000
Jun-98	Neil Redfearn	Barnsley	£1.0m

Out

Month	Player	Signed For	Fee
Aug-97	David Kerkslake	Ipswich T.	Free
Sept-97	Paul Linger	L. Orient	Free
Oct-97	David Whyte	Ipswich T.	Monthly
Nov-97	Sasa Ilic	Welling U.	NC
Jan-98	Carl Leaburn	Wimbledon	£300,000

Chelsea

A few years ago AC Milan set their stall out to capture the Italian Championship and Champions' Cup by having two first team squads, one for each competition, or at least a pick 'n' mix for the two competitions. Developments at Chelsea leave me wondering if deep down that was what Ruud Gullit was initially seeking to achieve, a plan which is now being implemented by Gianluca Vialli – the Italian player-manager about to embark on his first full season in the Stamford Bridge hot-seat.

There was no doubting the team's success last year. The Coca-Cola Cup (now Worthington Cup) and Cup-Winners' Cup were both captured. And for a brief period Chelsea, until Arsenal won in May, also held the FA Cup. Three cups at one time – is that a record?

Thirty-two players had roles to play in the Chelsea blue last season. Only Petrescu, Di Matteo and Leboeuf managed to make 30 appearances plus in the Premiership. The championship though remained and remains the holly grail. During the close season the imports came in almost bigger and better than even in Gullit's reign. Desailly and Brian Laudrup were perhaps the biggest of the signings. Championship consistency invariably comes from a settled side so it remains to be seen if Chelsea can contest the Premiership title.

The talking point last season, almost overshadowing the cup triumphs, was Gullit's dismissal, netto or otherwise on 12 February after, apparently, making excessive wage demands.

In many respects Vialli simply finished what Gullit had started and the Dutchman's pre-season signings of

Club Data File

Responsibility

Top Scorers:	Tore Andre Flo (11), Gianluca Vialli (11)
Sent Off:	Bernard Lambourde, Frank Leboeuf, Frank Sinclair

Usage

Total:	500 players used
Substitutes:	82 used, 108 not used

Players 1997-98

Most Used Subs:	Tore Andre Flo (18)
Most SNU:	Kevin Hitchcock (36), Gianluca Vialli (10)
Most Subbed:	Dan Petrescu (13), Gianluca Vialli (11)

Five-Year Form

	Div.	P	W	D	L	F	A	Pts	Pos
93-94	PL	42	13	12	17	49	53	51	14
94-95	PL	42	13	15	14	50	55	54	11
95-96	PL	38	12	14	12	46	44	50	11
96-97	PL	38	16	11	11	58	55	59	6
97-98	PL	38	20	3	15	71	43	63	4

goalkeeper Ed de Goey and striker Tore Andre Flo were amongst the best. He also retrieved Graeme Le Saux from Blackburn for £5m.

Goals were aplenty for Chelsea early on, with 21 being scored in the first seven games. Six came at Barnsley with Vialli netting four. After a run of four straight wins, Chelsea's first real test was at home to Arsenal when the visitors gained the advantage with a 3-2 victory. Within the next fortnight a win over Newcastle was offset by just one point being gathered from away games with Manchester United and Liverpool. Consistency was proving to be beyond Chelsea's capabilities, until November when five of six games were won. Tottenham were slaughtered 6-1 at White Hart Lane with Flo notching a hat-trick. Chelsea were now just three points behind Manchester United and maintained the challenge when dishing out a 4-1 defeat for Sheffield Wednesday. But thereafter Chelsea's form was again inconsistent. Gullit's final league match was a 2-0 defeat at Arsenal and when the next three games were also lost without scoring, the Blues were eyeing the cups for silverware. There were still some high points to be enjoyed, chiefly a 4-1 thrashing of Liverpool, a 6-2 drubbing of Palace and the completion of the double over Spurs. The season was concluded by a home win over Bolton which relegated the visitors.

Gianluca Vialli

He started last season on the bench and seemingly in dispute with Ruud Gullit but ended it as player/coach and with two trophies under his belt. After the surprise sacking of Gullit, Vialli was an equally surprising choice to take the hot-seat at Stamford Bridge. His honesty amongst the players seems to have stood him in good stead and they responded well to his requests, although the influence of assistant Graham Rix should not be underestimated. His standing in the international scene has ensured a new influx of foreign superstars during the close season. The only question to be answered in 1998-99 is can he do it again and call the triumphs his own work, or was he simply finishing off what Gullit started last year?

For fantasy managers Chelsea players look inviting but beware the real manager's selection policies. While players cannot lose you points by not playing, they equally cannot score you points while sitting on the bench – and this is where many Chelsea players will find themselves during the 1998-99 season. If you are looking for a Stamford Bridge selection then on last season's stats, only a few can look forward to having a major role to play.

Chelsea v Opponents Record

Opponents	92-3	93-4	94-5	95-6	96-7	97-8	P	W	D	L	F	A	Pts	%
Arsenal	1-0	0-2	2-1	1-0	0-3	2-3	6	3	0	3	6	9	9	50.00
Aston Villa	0-1	1-1	1-0	1-2	1-1	0-1	6	1	2	3	4	6	5	27.78
Blackburn Rovers	0-0	1-2	1-2	2-3	1-1	0-1	6	0	2	4	5	9	2	11.11
Charlton Athletic	-	-	-	-	-	-	0	0	0	0	0	0	0	0.00
Coventry City	2-1	1-2	2-2	2-2	2-0	3-1	6	3	2	1	12	8	11	61.11
Derby County	-	-	-	-	3-1	4-0	2	2	0	0	7	1	6	100.00
Everton	2-1	4-2	0-1	0-0	2-2	2-0	6	3	2	1	10	6	11	61.11
Leeds United	1-0	1-1	0-3	4-1	0-0	0-0	6	2	3	1	6	5	9	50.00
Leicester City	-	-	4-0	-	2-1	1-0	3	3	0	0	7	1	9	100.00
Liverpool	0-0	1-0	0-0	2-2	1-0	4-1	6	3	3	0	8	3	12	66.67
Manchester United	1-1	1-0	2-3	1-4	1-1	0-1	6	1	2	3	6	10	5	27.78
Middlesbrough	4-0	-	-	5-0	1-0		3	3	0	0	10	0	9	100.00
Newcastle United	-	1-0	1-1	1-0	1-1	1-0	5	3	2	0	5	2	11	73.33
Nottingham Forest	0-0	-	0-2	1-0	1-1		4	1	2	1	2	3	5	41.67
Sheffield Wednesday	0-2	1-1	1-1	0-0	2-2	1-0	6	1	4	1	5	6	7	38.89
Southampton	1-1	2-0	0-2	3-0	1-0	4-2	6	4	1	1	11	5	13	72.22
Tottenham Hotspur	1-1	4-3	1-1	0-0	3-1	2-0	6	3	3	0	11	6	12	66.67
West Ham United	-	2-0	1-2	1-2	3-1	2-1	5	3	0	2	9	6	9	60.00
Wimbledon	4-2	2-0	1-1	1-2	2-4	1-1	6	2	2	2	11	10	8	44.44

Transfers

In

Month	Player	Signed From	Fee
Aug-97	Graeme Le Saux	Blackburn R.	£5.0m
May-98	Pierluigi Casiraghi	Lazio	£5.4m
Jun-98	Marcel Desailly	AC Milan	£4.6m
Jun-98	Albert Ferrer	Barcelona	£2.2m
Jun-98	Brian Laudrup	Rangers	Free

Out

Month	Player	Signed For	Fee
Oct-97	Daniel Potter	Colchester U.	Free
Jan-98	Frode Grodas	Tottenham H.	£250,000
Jun-98	Danny Granville	Leeds United	£1.6m
Jul-98	Mark Hughes	Southampton	£650,000

Coventry City

The times are a changing. Be honest. How many times would you even consider a Coventry City player for your fantasy team? Hardly ever? Not surprising really. As a team, the Sky Blues were always battling it out. But they have always been survivors, proved by the fact that the club successfully battled against relegation on the final day of the season for three consecutive years.

But now Coventry City are a force to be reckoned with. Under Gordon Strachan they attained their joint highest Premiership position and their second highest Premiership points total. More impressively it has been done with hard work, application and some very astute moves in the transfer market. Prior to the start of the 1997-98 season he spent just £2.2m to bring in Simon Haworth, Markus Hedman, Trond Egil Soltvedt, Kyle Lightbourne, Roland Nilsson and Martin Johansen. The £500,000 invested in Lightbourne was recouped later in the season when he left the club. Amongst those also departing were John Filan, Eoin Jess and Peter Ndlovu.

Strachan was also able to hang-on to prize asset Dion Dublin who ended the 1997-98 season as joint top Premiership scorer and showing enough form to win him his first England cap and be in contention for a World Cup place.

Coventry made a sensational start with Dublin scoring a match-winning hat-trick. The win over Chelsea, though, was one of only two successes in 12 games and by the end of October a run of five draws and a defeat in six games left them just three points clear of the bottom three. The Sky Blues had yet to lose at

Club Data File

Responsibility

Top Scorers: Dion Dublin (18), Darren Huckerby (14)

Sent Off: George Boateng, Gary Breen, Dion Dublin, Paul Williams (twice)

Usage

Total: 473 players used

Substitutes: 55 used, 135 not used

Players 1997-98

Most Used Subs: Willie Boland (11)

Most SNU: Marcus Hedman (23), Steve Ogrizovic (13), Gavin Strachan (11)

Most Subbed: Trond Soltvedt (10), Darren Huckerby (9)

Five-Year Form

	Div.	P	W	D	L	F	A	Pts	Pos
93-94	PL	42	14	14	14	43	45	56	11
94-95	PL	42	12	14	16	44	62	50	16
95-96	PL	38	8	14	16	42	60	38	16
96-97	PL	38	9	14	15	38	54	41	17
97-98	PL	38	12	16	10	46	44	52	11

Highfield Road but somewhat embarrassingly they were the only club in the Premiership and the Nationwide League still to score on their travels. Coventry put that record straight on 1 November with a 2-1 win at Selhurst Park over Wimbledon which also ended a goal drought lasting 458 minutes. Unfortunately, Coventry again failed to build on a good result and lost their unbeaten record at Highfield Road when Leicester won 2-0. That defeat was sandwiched between 3-1 and 3-0 defeats at Derby and Aston Villa.

Strachan broke the club transfer record to sign Romanian international Viorel Moldovan in December and the month started well on the pitch for the Sky Blues with Spurs being hammered 4-0; the exciting Darren Huckerby scored two of his season's tally of 14 goals. Two more away games were lost before Coventry helped to prise open the title race with two late goals from the deadly duo of Huckerby and Dublin which clinched a 3-2 win over league leaders Manchester United just after Christmas. The new year kicked off with defeat at Chelsea but Coventry were not to lose another league match until April. Arsenal drew at Highfield Road before Bolton were thrashed 5-1 at the Reebok Stadium while other lower mid-table sides Sheffield Wednesday, Southampton, Barnsley and Palace were also beaten, along with a couple of cup victories to help Coventry equal the club record of seven straight wins.

Although only two of the last ten league games were won, a good number of draws left Coventry reflecting on an outstanding record of one defeat from their final 15 outings.

Huckerby's form attracted attention and, if continued, should give him an international chance. Telfer, Shaw, Breen and Borrows were the other unsung heroes in what has to be viewed as an encouraging season for the Highfield Road faithful. It was also a season that saw manager Gordon blood his son Gavin in the first team to complete another remarkable milestone in Premiership history.

Gordon Strachan

If passion counted towards team points then the Sky Blues would be amongst the Premiership challengers year after year. Now in his second full season in charge, Strachan has waved a magic wand at Highfield Road. The small gap between winning and losing those big matches is something that still has to be breached though – but there are signs that a silverware return might not be that far off.

Having had an illustrious player career, Strachan was eased into the hot-seat at Coventry via a player/coach role with the guiding experience of Ron Atkinson. As Big Ron moved up and ultimately out, Strachan made the inevitable progression.

His passion often gets him into trouble with refs but he remains one of the game's true personalities.

Coventry City v Opponents Record

Opponents	92-3	93-4	94-5	95-6	96-7	97-8	P	W	D	L	F	A	Pts	%
Arsenal	0-2	1-0	0-1	0-0	1-1	2-2	6	1	3	2	4	6	6	33.33
Aston Villa	3-0	0-1	0-1	0-3	1-2	1-2	6	1	0	5	5	9	3	16.67
Blackburn Rovers	0-2	2-1	1-1	5-0	0-0	2-0	6	3	2	1	10	4	11	61.11
Charlton Athletic	-	-	-	-	-	-	0	0	0	0	0	0	0	0.00
Chelsea	1-2	1-1	2-2	1-0	3-1	3-2	6	3	2	1	11	8	11	61.11
Derby County	-	-	-	-	1-2	1-0	2	1	0	1	2	2	3	50.00
Everton	0-1	2-1	0-0	2-1	0-0	0-0	6	2	3	1	4	3	9	50.00
Leeds United	3-3	0-2	2-1	0-0	2-1	0-0	6	2	3	1	7	7	9	50.00
Leicester City	-	-	4-2	-	0-0	0-2	3	1	1	1	4	4	4	44.44
Liverpool	5-1	1-0	1-1	1-0	0-1	1-1	6	3	2	1	9	4	11	61.11
Manchester United	0-1	0-1	2-3	0-4	0-2	3-2	6	1	0	5	5	13	3	16.67
Middlesbrough	2-1	-	-	0-0	3-0		3	2	1	0	5	1	7	77.78
Newcastle United	-	2-1	0-0	0-1	2-1	2-2	5	2	2	1	6	5	8	53.33
Nottingham Forest	0-1	-	0-0	1-1	0-3		4	0	2	2	1	5	2	16.67
Sheffield Wednesday	1-0	1-1	2-0	0-1	0-0	1-0	6	3	2	1	5	2	11	61.11
Southampton	2-0	1-1	1-3	1-1	1-1	1-0	6	2	3	1	7	6	9	50.00
Tottenham Hotspur	1-0	1-0	0-4	2-3	1-2	4-0	6	3	0	3	9	9	9	50.00
West Ham United	-	1-1	2-0	2-2	1-3	1-1	5	1	3	1	7	7	6	40.00
Wimbledon	0-2	1-2	1-1	3-3	1-1	0-0	6	0	4	2	6	9	4	22.22

Transfers

In

Month	Player	Signed From	Fee
Dec-97	George Boateng	Feyenoord	£250,000
Dec-97	Viorel Moldovan	Grasshopper	£3.25m
Mar-98	Phillippe Clement	Racing Genk	£625,000
Jun-98	Jean-Guy Wallemme	Lens	£700,000
Jun-98	Ian Brightwell	Manchester City	Free

Out

Month	Player	Signed For	Fee
Sep-97	Kevin Richardson	Southampton	£150,000
Nov-97	Brian Borrows	Swindon T.	Free
Mar-98	John Salako	Bolton W.	Free
Jul-98	Viorel Moldovan	Fenerbache	£4.0m

Derby County

Having secured a safe mid-table position in their first season of Premiership football, Derby County looked forward to the second campaign with increased expectations as the club moved to its new Pride Park Stadium. Manager Jim Smith kept faith in those who cemented the club's position in the Premiership with Sean Flynn and veteran Paul McGrath being the only departures from the previous campaign's regulars. Smith invested £1m in Portsmouth striker Deon Burton, and just over that figure to acquire the services of Francesco Baiano from Fiorentina and Jonathan Hunt from Birmingham. Later in the season he added Blackburn's Norwegian international midfielder Lars Bohinen to the squad.

Baiano was the most influential of the signings and his 12 goals an added bonus from his 33 starts. The two Powell's lead the way in appearances with 36 apiece but Chris found himself on his way to Charlton after the 1997-98 season had been completed. Mart Poom, the Rams' Estonian international goalkeeper, proved himself a quality buy in his first full Premiership season as did Costa Rican striker Paulo Wanchope who completed his first full season as top scorer. His gangly, loping run was the torment of many a defender. His international team-mate Solis though found his appearances limited due to an agreement on the number of non-European players that can feature in Premiership sides.

The season began disappointingly for Derby with 1-0 defeats at Blackburn and Tottenham, but once installed in their new stadium the Rams went on the rampage. Stefano Eranio, from the penalty spot, clinched Derby's first points at Pride Park, against Barnsley, and Everton were then

Club Data File

Responsibility

Top Scorers:	Paulo Wanchope (13), Francesco Baiano (12)
Sent Off:	Stefano Eranio (twice)

Usage

Total:	507 players used
Substitutes:	89 used, 101 not used

Players 1997-98

Most Used Subs:	Deon Burton (17), Jonathan Hunt (12)
Most SNU:	Russell Hoult (34), Robert Kozluk (11)
Most Subbed:	Francesco Baiano (16)

Five-Year Form

	Div.	P	W	D	L	F	A	Pts	Pos
93-94	1	46	20	11	15	73	68	71	6
94-95	1	46	18	12	16	66	51	66	9
95-96	1	46	21	16	9	71	51	79	2
96-97	PL	38	11	13	14	45	58	46	12
97-98	PL	38	16	7	15	52	49	55	9

seen off 3-1 with Hunt scoring his first, and last, Premiership goal of the season. After a defeat at Aston Villa, Derby ended a wait of more than six decades for a win at Hillsborough with Baiano scoring twice in a 5-2 romp. The Italian had also scored at Villa and went on a marvellous run of scoring in six consecutive Premiership games, including a brace in successive matches against Wednesday, Southampton and Leicester. Baiano's run coincided with a five-match unbeaten run for the Rams, which was their best spell of the season. Liverpool brought the sequence to its conclusion with a 4-0 reversal at Anfield but Derby stayed in excellent touch at Pride Park and only fell at the 13th attempt when Aston Villa completed the double. Indeed, their outstanding home form was in stark contrast to that of their away performances which were inconsistent in the extreme. After losing their first three away games, the next two were won. Fifteen goals were then leaked in four ventures away from Pride Park which was followed by conceding just two goals in four away games.

But once the Pride Park fortress had been breached Derby fell to a couple of spectacular defeats, with Leeds and Leicester winning 5-0 and 4-0 respectively at the new ground. The defeat by Leeds sparked a run of four games – 410 minutes in total – without a goal, which ended with a 4-0 drubbing of Bolton. Another three successive defeats, including being Crystal Palace's first victims at Selhurst Park, ensured that the Rams would not claim a UEFA Cup place.

Jim Smith

With well over 1000 games in charge as manager in professional football, Jim Smith remains not only the most experienced manager in the Premiership, but in British football. To say that has given him a good eye for a player and a bargain player at that would be an understatement. His dealings in the transfer market have been exceptional. Watch out for his pre and early season signings at Pride Park. You may not have heard of the players, or their club or even their homeland, but be assured that he has probably found a bargain.

Smith is also one of those rare managers who calls it as it is and is always first to praise a superior opposition. Now embarking on his fourth year at Derby, his previous clubs include Boston, Colchester, Blackburn, Birmingham, Oxford, Newcastle and Portsmouth.

Derby County v Opponents Record

Opponents	92-3	93-4	94-5	95-6	96-7	97-8	P	W	D	L	F	A	Pts	%
Arsenal	-	-	-	-	1-3	3-0	2	1	0	1	4	3	3	50.00
Aston Villa	-	-	-	-	2-1	0-1	2	1	0	1	2	2	3	50.00
Blackburn Rovers	-	-	-	-	0-0	3-1	2	1	1	0	3	1	4	66.67
Charlton Athletic	-	-	-	-	-	-	0	0	0	0	0	0	0	0.00
Chelsea	-	-	-	-	3-2	0-1	2	1	0	1	3	3	3	50.00
Coventry City	-	-	-	-	2-1	3-1	2	2	0	0	5	2	6	100.00
Crystal Palace	-	-	-	-	-	0-0	1	0	1	0	0	0	1	33.33
Everton	-	-	-	-	0-1	3-1	2	1	0	1	3	2	3	50.00
Leeds United	-	-	-	-	3-3	0-5	2	0	1	1	3	8	1	16.67
Leicester City	-	-	-	-	2-0	0-4	2	1	0	1	2	4	3	50.00
Liverpool	-	-	-	-	0-1	1-0	2	1	0	1	1	1	3	50.00
Manchester United	-	-	-	-	1-1	2-2	2	0	2	0	3	3	2	33.33
Middlesbrough	-	-	-	-	2-1		1	1	0	0	2	1	3	100.00
Newcastle United	-	-	-	-	0-1	1-0	2	1	0	1	1	1	3	50.00
Nottingham Forest	-	-	-	-	0-0		1	0	1	0	0	0	1	33.33
Sheffield Wednesday	-	-	-	-	2-2	3-0	2	1	1	0	5	2	4	66.67
Southampton	-	-	-	-	1-1	4-0	2	1	1	0	5	1	4	66.67
Tottenham Hotspur	-	-	-	-	4-2	2-1	2	2	0	0	6	3	6	100.00
West Ham United	-	-	-	-	1-0	2-0	2	2	0	0	3	0	6	100.00
Wimbledon	-	-	-	-	0-2	1-1	2	0	1	1	1	3	1	16.67

Transfers

In

Month	Player	Signed From	Fee
Aug-97	Deon Burton	Portsmouth	£1.0m
Feb-98	Rory Delap	Carlisle U.	£500,000 rising to £1.0m
Mar-98	Lars Bohinen	Blackburn R.	£1.45m
May-98	Horacio Carbonari	Rosario Central	£2.7m
Jul-98	Stefan Schnoor	Hamburg	Free

Out

Month	Player	Signed For	Fee
Aug-97	Kevin Cooper	Stockport Co.	£150,000
Aug-97	Sean Flynn	WBA	£260,000
Sep-97	Ashley Ward	Barnsley	£1.3m
Sep-97	Andrew Tretton	Gresley R.	Free
Oct-97	Wayne Sutton	Woking	Free
Nov-97	Paul Trollope	Fulham	£600,000
Nov-97	Paul Simpson	Wolverhampton W.	£75,000
Jan-98	Aljosa Asanovic	Napoli	£350,000
Jan-98	Matt Carbone	WBA	£800,000
Feb-98	Nick Wright	Carlisle U.	£35,000
Jun-98	Chris Powell	Charlton Ath	£850,000
Jul-98	Dean Yates	Watford	Free
Jul-98	Robin Van Der Laan	Barnsley	£325,000

Everton

Everton's problems in recent years seem to have stemmed from their inability to attract a big name manager to take over one of the most difficult jobs in Premiership football. The tide might just have turned. The arrival of former Rangers manager Walter Smith at Goodison Park for the start of the 1998-99 season is possibly the most significant signing for the Toffees in the past ten years. No single manager has won more in British football in the past decade – the test now comes to see if he can do it at a more competitive level. But there are few more stressful places to work than Ibrox one would assume – even with a winning team.

Everton maintained their Premiership status by the skin of their teeth. But 1997-98 had started with renewed optimism. After battling against relegation for three of the previous four seasons, Everton looked to turn back time in the summer of 1997 with the appointment of Howard Kendall as manager. Kendall enjoyed great success as Everton boss during the previous decade, but a second spell in the early '90s was less profitable and the first season of his third stint almost ended in complete disaster with the drop only being avoided on the final day of the campaign. History would repeat itself.

Kendall spent almost £7.5m in the close season in attracting to Goodison Park Slaven Bilic, John Oster, Gareth Farrelly and Tony Thomas. Departures included Paul Rideout, Marc Hottiger and David Unsworth. Bilic was seen as a more than useful acquisition but the Croatian defender spent a good part of the season on the sidelines following three dismissals – he made just 24 appearances.

The midfield was strengthened later in the season with the signing of Don

Club Data File

Responsibility

Top Scorers:	Duncan Ferguson (11)
Sent Off:	Slaven Bilic (three times), Duncan Ferguson, Andy Hinchcliffe

Usage

Total:	503 players used
Substitutes:	85 used, 105 not used

Players 1997-98

Most Used Subs:	John Oster (15)
Most SNU:	Paul Gerrard (28),
Most Subbed:	Mickael Madar (11)

Five-Year Form

	Div.	P	W	D	L	F	A	Pts	Pos
93-94	PL	42	12	8	22	42	63	44	17
94-95	PL	42	11	17	14	44	51	50	15
95-96	PL	38	17	10	11	64	44	61	6
96-97	PL	38	10	12	16	44	57	42	15
97-98	PL	38	9	13	16	41	56	40	17

Hutchison from West Ham while £8.5m was collected from the sale of Gary Speed and Andy Hinchcliffe. Both were curious departures given Everton's predicament throughout the season.

Everton kicked off the season with three successive home games but despite Duncan Ferguson scoring in the opening game against Crystal Palace, the Toffeemen went down to a 2-1 defeat. Goals by the soon departing Speed and Graham Stuart saw off West Ham, but when Manchester United won at Goodison the writing was on the wall for another season of struggle. Everton were unbeaten for the next three home games but it was only a temporary reprieve before slipping into serious relegation problems. Away from home Everton had a disastrous time with only two successes all season, the first of which didn't arrive until just before Christmas when Speed's last-minute penalty at Leicester ended an inglorious run of one year and four days without a victory on opposition turf.

A sequence of five consecutive defeats, begun at Goodison Park by Southampton on 2 November and ended 27 days later by Tottenham in Neville Southall's 750th match between the sticks, saw Everton plummet from 16th to bottom. With just one defeat from the next nine games – including wins over fellow strugglers Bolton and Palace – Everton rose to 15th, some five points clear of the bottom three.

But it was a false dawn and Kendall's side could muster just two wins from the last 15 outings. One win from the final three games would probably guarantee safety but their survival went to the wire after defeats by Sheffield Wednesday and Arsenal when they were totally outclassed by the new champions. With an early strike against Coventry, Farrelly repaid his £900,000 transfer fee in one swoop but when the visitors grabbed a late equaliser Everton still had to rely on Bolton losing at Chelsea for their own safety to be secured.

It will be interesting to see how top scorer Duncan Ferguson takes to the arrival of his former Rangers manager and whether the new man can get the spark back into Nick Barmby's play. The talent is undoubtedly at Goodison Park and it awaits the right catalyst.

Walter Smith

Everton have waited a long time for a big name manager who will be able to walk in new and sweep away the cobwebs that have threatened to strangle the club. Walter Smith is arguably the most successful manager in British football over the past decade. His achievements at Rangers included a run of nine successive championship titles. The Glasgow club's holy grail of a European title went unfulfilled though and this may cast just a small doubt as to his potential to wake up the slumbering Goodison giant. His ability to deal with top international stars will be of considerable benefit. His long-term assistant Archie Knox travels south with him so the trophy winning team remains intact. But, the clock is ticking.

Everton v Opponents Record

Opponents	92-3	93-4	94-5	95-6	96-7	97-8	P	W	D	L	F	A	Pts	%
Arsenal	0-0	1-1	1-1	0-2	0-2	2-2	6	0	4	2	4	8	4	22.22
Aston Villa	1-0	0-1	2-2	1-0	0-1	1-4	6	2	1	3	5	8	7	38.89
Blackburn Rovers	2-1	0-3	1-2	1-0	0-2	1-0	6	3	0	3	5	8	9	50.00
Charlton Athletic	-	-	-	-	-	-	0	0	0	0	0	0	0	0.00
Chelsea	0-1	4-2	3-3	1-1	1-2	3-1	6	2	2	2	12	10	8	44.44
Coventry City	1-1	0-0	0-2	2-2	1-1	1-1	6	0	5	1	5	7	5	27.78
Derby County	-	-	-	-	1-0	1-2	2	1	0	1	2	2	3	50.00
Leeds United	2-0	1-1	3-0	2-0	0-0	2-0	6	4	2	0	10	1	14	77.78
Leicester City	-	-	1-1	-	1-1	1-1	3	0	3	0	3	3	3	33.33
Liverpool	2-1	2-0	2-0	1-1	1-1	2-0	6	4	2	0	10	3	14	77.78
Manchester United	0-2	0-1	1-0	2-3	0-2	0-2	6	1	0	5	3	10	3	16.67
Middlesbrough	2-2	-	-	4-0	1-2		3	1	1	1	7	4	4	44.44
Newcastle United	-	0-2	2-0	1-3	2-0	0-0	5	2	1	2	5	5	7	46.67
Nottingham Forest	3-0	-	1-2	3-0	2-0		4	3	0	1	9	2	9	75.00
Sheffield Wednesday	1-1	0-2	1-4	2-2	2-0	1-3	6	1	2	3	7	12	5	27.78
Southampton	2-1	1-0	0-0	2-0	7-1	0-2	6	4	1	1	12	4	13	72.22
Tottenham Hotspur	1-2	0-1	0-0	1-1	1-0	0-2	6	1	2	3	3	6	5	27.78
West Ham United	-	0-1	1-0	3-0	2-1	2-1	5	4	0	1	8	3	12	80.00
Wimbledon	0-0	3-2	0-0	2-4	1-3	0-0	6	1	3	2	6	9	6	33.33

Transfers

In

Month	Player	Signed From	Fee
Aug-97	Danny Williamson	West Ham U.	Swap + £1.0m
Nov-97	Carl Tiler	Sheffield U.	Swap
Nov-97	Mitch Ward	Sheffield U.	Swap
Nov-97	Thomas Myhre	Viking Stavanger	£800,000
Dec-97	Mickael Madar	Dep La Coruna	Free
Jan-98	John O'Kane	Manchester U.	£250,000 rising to £450,000
Feb-98	Don Hutchison	Sheffield U.	£1.0m
Jul-98	Marco Materazzi	Perugia	£2.8m

Out

Month	Player	Signed For	Fee
Aug-97	David Unsworth	West Ham U.	Swap
Nov-97	Graham Stuart	Sheffield U.	£500,000
Jan-98	Andy Hinchcliffe	Sheffield W.	£3.0m
Feb-98	John Hills	Blackpool	£75,000
Feb-98	Gary Speed	Newcastle U.	£5.5m
Feb-98	Jon O'Connor	Sheffield U.	Swap
Feb-98	Earl Barrett	Sheffield W.	Free
Feb-98	Mark Quayle	Southport	Non-contract
Mar-98	Neville Southall	Stoke C.	Free

Leeds United

The signs are there. Leeds United are on the move and maybe the Graham magic is about to rekindle itself at Elland Road. Certainly the season-by-season building block improvements are there to be seen.

Having shored up a leaking defence, there was a definite need to improve an attack which scored just 28 times in the Premiership during 1996-97. Graham parted company with striker Brian Deane for £1.5m and brought in Dutchman Jimmy Floyd Hasselbaink for £2m. The investment was quickly justified with Hasselbaink going on to be Leeds' top scorer with 22 league and cup goals, 14 more than the previous season's top scorer. This performance earned the Dutchman a place in Holland's World Cup squad.

In total Graham released five players during the summer and made several significant signings, including David Hopkin for £3.25m, Alf-Inge Haaland for £1.6m and Bruno Ribeiro and David Robertson for a combined fee of £1m. Early in the new season Graham helped balance the books when collecting £2m from the sale of Tony Yeboah and Carlton Palmer. One transfer which didn't work out was that of Tomas Brolin, whose 19 games for the club cost somewhere in the region of £6m. Another out of favour player was Rod Wallace who, nevertheless, chipped in with 13 goals, of which just two were at Elland Road and several of which proved to be match winners.

On the pitch, Leeds achieved their highest points total and scored their most goals from a 38-match programme, as the

Club Data File

Responsibility

Top Scorers: Jimmy Floyd Hasselbaink (16)

Sent Off: Alf Inge Haaland, Gunnar Halle, Gary Kelly, Harry Kewell, Lucas Radebe

Usage

Total: 473 players used

Substitutes: 55 used, 135 not used

Players 1997-98

Most Used Subs: Derek Lilley (12)

Most SNU: Mark Beeney (35), Derek Lilley (13)

Most Subbed: David Hopkin (8), JF Hasselbaink (7)

Five-Year Form

	Div.	P	W	D	L	F	A	Pts	Pos
93-94	PL	42	18	16	8	65	39	70	5
94-95	PL	42	20	13	9	59	38	73	5
95-96	PL	38	12	7	19	40	57	43	13
96-97	PL	38	11	13	14	28	38	46	11
97-98	PL	38	17	8	13	57	46	59	5

club reclaimed fifth position after two seasons in the lower half of the table, although the number of clean sheets dropped from 20 to 11.

Although Leeds secured a place in the UEFA Cup, their start to the season was indifferent. An opening day draw with Arsenal was followed by victory at Sheffield Wednesday but Leeds failed to score in the next three games, all of which were lost including a 2-0 defeat by Hopkin's old club Crystal Palace. United's season stepped up a gear in mid September with a pulsating 4-3 win at Ewood Park over the previously all-conquering Blackburn; Wallace scored twice, having done likewise at Hillsborough. But Leicester handed Leeds a third successive defeat at Elland Road before United started to climb the table with victory at Southampton and a 1-0 home success over Manchester United in front of their best home gate of the season.

The win over Southampton ignited an impressive run of just one defeat in 12 games which took Leeds to fourth, although Manchester United were still a healthy nine points away. Along the way Newcastle were rolled over 4-1 and Derby, having led 3-0 after just 33 minutes, were defeated 4-3 with Lee Bowyer grabbing a last-minute winner. Leeds won the return 5-0, having beaten Blackburn 4-0 four days earlier. Both of those results came in the wake of a disappointing FA Cup exit at the hands of Wolves. A remarkable point was taken off Chelsea in spite of having Kelly and Haaland sent off inside 20 minutes. A trip to West Ham brought that flurry of success to a close but it was overshadowed by events later in the night as the aircraft in which the team travelled was forced to abort its take-off. Fortunately, there were no serious casualties.

Leeds benefited from a tight squad in which 14 players contributed 20 appearances or more. David Wetherall was again an impressive performer as was Australian Harry Kewell, a player who could well become one of the stars of the Premiership.

George Graham

Last season Graham addressed many of the problems he was presented with during his first season in charge at Elland Road. Not least up front where the arrival of Hasselbaink and the maturing of Kewell have helped address Leeds' attacking balance. Perhaps more importantly he also kept clear of the headlines that had troubled him at Arsenal and ultimately lead to his, albeit temporary, ban from the game.

The signs are there and it would seem only a matter of time until he achieves his first silverware success for the Yorkshire club. Graham has been successful as both player and manager but the skilful application of the first has been in stark contrast to the sterile nature of the second.

His greatest triumph as a player was being a member of the Arsenal Double side of 1971 and as a manager he was in charge of the same team who won 2–0 at Anfield to snatch the title from Liverpool in what ranks as one of the most dramatic games of football ever played. The Gunners repeated the feat two seasons later despite having points deducted and went on to complete the first ever domestic cup double in 1993.

FANTASY FOOTBALL HANDBOOK 1998/99

Leeds United v Opponents Record

Opponents	92-3	93-4	94-5	95-6	96-7	97-8	P	W	D	L	F	A	Pts	%
Arsenal	3-0	2-1	1-0	0-3	0-0	1-1	6	3	2	1	7	5	11	61.11
Aston Villa	1-1	2-0	1-0	2-0	0-0	1-1	6	3	3	0	7	2	12	66.67
Blackburn Rovers	5-2	3-3	1-1	0-0	0-0	4-0	6	2	4	0	13	6	10	55.56
Charlton Athletic	-	-	-	-	-	-	0	0	0	0	0	0	0	0.00
Chelsea	1-1	4-1	2-3	1-0	2-0	3-1	6	4	1	1	13	6	13	72.22
Coventry City	2-2	1-0	3-0	3-1	1-3	3-3	6	3	2	1	13	9	11	61.11
Derby County	-	-	-	-	0-0	4-3	2	1	1	0	4	3	4	66.67
Everton	2-0	3-0	1-0	2-2	1-0	0-0	6	4	2	0	9	2	14	77.78
Leicester City	-	-	2-1	-	3-0	0-1	3	2	0	1	5	2	6	66.67
Liverpool	2-2	2-0	0-2	1-0	0-2	0-2	6	2	1	3	5	8	7	38.89
Manchester United	0-0	0-2	2-1	3-1	0-4	1-0	6	3	1	2	6	8	10	55.56
Middlesbrough	3-0	-	-	0-1	1-1		3	1	1	1	4	2	4	44.44
Newcastle United	-	1-1	0-0	0-1	0-1	4-1	5	1	2	2	5	4	5	33.33
Nottingham Forest	1-4	-	1-0	1-3	2-0		4	2	0	2	5	7	6	50.00
Sheffield Wednesday	3-1	2-2	0-1	2-0	0-2	1-2	6	2	1	3	8	8	7	38.89
Southampton	2-1	0-0	0-0	1-0	0-0	0-1	6	2	3	1	3	2	9	50.00
Tottenham Hotspur	5-0	2-0	1-1	1-3	0-0	1-0	6	3	2	1	10	4	11	61.11
West Ham United	-	1-0	2-2	2-0	1-0	3-1	5	4	1	0	9	3	13	86.67
Wimbledon	2-1	4-0	3-1	1-1	1-0	1-1	6	4	2	0	12	4	14	77.78

Transfers

In

Month	Player	Signed From	Fee
May-98	Clyde Wijnhard	Willem II	£1.5m
Jun-98	Danny Granville	Chelsea	£1.6m

Out

Month	Player	Signed For	Fee
Aug-97	Ian Rush	Newcastle U.	Free
Aug-97	Tony Dorigo	Torino	Free
Sep-97	Tony Yeboah	Hamburg	£1.0m
Sep-97	Carlton Palmer	Southampton	£1.0m
Jan-98	Pierre Laurent	Bastia	£500,000
Jan-98	Tomas Brolin	C. Palace	Free
Mar-98	Sean Hessey	Huddersfield T.	Free
Mar-98	Richard Jobson	Manchester C.	Free

Leicester City

It was back to reality for City in 1997-98 following a season in which they won their first silverware for 33 years and claimed a position inside the top ten of the Premiership for the first time. By slipping one place in the table and making early exits in the cups it could be said that Leicester failed to match the achievements of the previous campaign. Certainly they did not threaten to repeat their Coca-Cola Cup success but Leicester established themselves firmly amongst the middle group and, despite finishing a place lower than in 1996-97, the Foxes did actually improve their points total by six to 53.

O'Neill was able to build his side around a core of eight players who featured in at least 33 of the side's Premiership fixtures. This included the excellent Matt Elliott – who also weighed in with seven goals from centre half and forced his way into Scotland's World Cup squad. The other seven were Steve Guppy, Emil Heskey, Muzzy Izzett, Pontus Kaamark, Kasey Keller, Neil Lennon and Robbie Savage. Elliott, Guppy and Lennon played in every minute of their 37 games apiece.

O'Neill made just two signings during the close season: Graham Fenton and Robbie Savage for a combined total of just £1.4m. Before August was out the experienced Tony Cottee moved to Filbert Street for £500,000. Six players were released, the most significant being Simon Grayson to Aston Villa for £1.3m.

With an Ian Marshall goal seeing off Villa on the first day of the season and efforts from Matt Elliott and Fenton clinching an excellent victory at Liverpool, Leicester made their best start since 1956 and it took champions Manchester United (0–0) to deny the

Club Data File

Responsibility

Top Scorers:	Emile Heskey (10)
Sent Off:	Emile Heskey, Robert Ullathorne

Usage

Total:	497 players used
Substitutes:	79 used, 111 not used

Players 1997-98

Most Used Subs:	Gary Fenton (14), Tony Cottee (12)
Most SNU:	Pegguy Arphexad (23), Gary Fenton (14)
Most Subbed:	Ian Marshall (10)

Five-Year Form

	Div.	P	W	D	L	F	A	Pts	Pos
93-94	1	46	19	16	11	72	59	73	4
94-95	PL	42	6	11	25	45	80	29	21
95-96	1	46	19	14	13	66	60	71	5
96-97	PL	38	12	11	15	46	54	47	9
97-98	PL	38	13	14	11	51	41	53	10

Foxes a winning hat-trick which would have equalled their best start for 75 years. Leicester scored three times in the closing minutes of a fiery clash with Arsenal to preserve their unbeaten start with a 3-3 draw before the first reversal was suffered at Sheffield Wednesday. But Leicester bounced back well with three wins and a draw lifting them to third, just a point behind leaders Arsenal.

The bubble burst with a home defeat by Derby and with just one win from six games Leicester gradually slid out of the frame. Leicester's inability to convert draws into wins cost them precious points and ultimately a place in the UEFA Cup. Indeed only Coventry drew more games in total. Goals were difficult to come by at Filbert Street, and only two sides scored less at home than Leicester.

Tony Cottee scored his first goal for City at Old Trafford and earned an unlikely victory over Manchester United. It was followed with home wins over Leeds and Chelsea and a draw at Tottenham. Leicester, not for the first time, failed to maintain the momentum and went down to three successive defeats.

The form of Steve Guppy, who O'Neill nurtured while in charge of the then non-league Wycombe Wanderers, was good enough to earn him an England squad call-up not least for his ability to whip in crosses when they are least expected. Emile Heskey finished top scorer for the second consecutive season but still has to make the transition from Under-21 level to the full England squad. Hopefully he can do this under O'Neill, who agreed to stay at Filbert Street after concerns over backroom control had lead him to indicate he might move on. Under him Leicester have not finished outside the top ten in the Premier League.

Martin O'Neill

It was late June when Martin O'Neill finally committed himself to Filbert Street for at least another year. Concerned about control of team affairs, with pending changes within the plc owned club, had prompted the likeable Irishman to make his stand. It worked and O'Neill can look ahead to a season in which to further build on success. The 1997-98 season though was a bit of an anticlimax after the trophy win in 1996-97. But realistically, the Foxes are not going to win trophies that regularly. What O'Neill will be seeking though is another stab at Europe after their curious exit from the competition in the first round last season.

A dynamic player with Nottingham Forest, O'Neill won the games' top honours. He learnt his managerial trade at the footballing bastions of Grantham and Shepshed before enjoying outstanding success at Wycombe, taking them to two FA Trophy triumphs at Wembley, a Conference title and promotion to the Football League.

Eventually he answered the call of Norwich City and, although he didn't see the season out with them, he did with Leicester and took them through to triumph in the Coca-Cola Cup.

Leicester City v Opponents Record

Opponents	92-3	93-4	94-5	95-6	96-7	97-8	P	W	D	L	F	A	Pts	%
Arsenal	-	-	2-1	-	0-2	3-3	3	1	1	1	5	6	4	44.44
Aston Villa	-	-	1-1	-	1-0	1-0	3	2	1	0	3	1	7	77.78
Blackburn Rovers	-	-	0-0	-	1-1	1-1	3	0	3	0	2	2	3	33.33
Charlton Athletic	-	-	-	-	-	-	0	0	0	0	0	0	0	0.00
Chelsea	-	-	1-1	-	1-3	2-0	3	1	1	1	4	4	4	44.44
Coventry City	-	-	2-2	-	0-2	1-1	3	0	2	1	3	5	2	22.22
Derby County	-	-	-	-	4-2	1-2	2	1	0	1	5	4	3	50.00
Everton	-	-	2-2	-	1-2	0-1	3	0	1	2	3	5	1	11.11
Leeds	-	-	1-3	-	1-0	1-0	3	2	0	1	3	3	6	66.67
Liverpool	-	-	1-2	-	0-3	0-0	3	0	1	2	1	5	1	11.11
Manchester United	-	-	0-4	-	2-2	0-0	3	0	2	1	2	6	2	22.22
Middlesbrough	-	-	-	-	1-3		1	0	0	1	1	3	0	0.00
Newcastle United	-	-	1-3	-	2-0	0-0	3	1	1	1	3	3	4	44.44
Nottingham Forest	-	-	2-4	-	2-2		2	0	1	1	4	6	1	16.67
Sheffield Wednesday	-	-	0-1	-	1-0	1-1	3	1	1	1	2	2	4	44.44
Southampton	-	-	4-3	-	2-1	3-3	3	2	1	0	9	7	7	77.78
Tottenham Hotspur	-	-	3-1	-	1-1	3-0	3	2	1	0	7	2	7	77.78
West Ham United	-	-	1-2	-	0-1	2-1	3	1	0	2	3	4	3	33.33
Wimbledon	-	-	3-4	-	1-0	0-1	3	1	0	2	4	5	3	33.33

Transfers

Out

Month	Player	Signed For	Fee
Sep-97	Mike Whitlow	Bolton W.	£700,000
Mar-98	Steve Claridge	Wolverhampton W.	£350,000

Liverpool

The legacy of the past remains with Liverpool and will do so until the Anfield side capture their first Premiership title. They have arguably the greatest talent in English football. Having scored just once in 1996-97, Michael Owen burst onto the Mersey scene and then into the World Cup shop window. Not that he will be going anywhere in the short term. His 18 goals in 1997-98 placed him joint top of the Premiership scoring list, while his strikes for England, not least his sensational goal against Argentina, will make him coveted by managers everywhere – real or fantasy.

Under fire manager Roy Evans used Owen well and helped his development with some impressive signings before 1997-98 got under way. England star Paul Ince returned to this country from Italy for £4.2m. Oyvind Leonhardsen joined for £3.5m. Karl-Heinz Riedle moved to Anfield for £1.6m and an eventual £3m will be invested in the exciting talent of Crewe's 20 year old midfielder Danny Murphy. Murphy could well develop an Owenesk sparkle in the seasons ahead. With the transfer of Anfield misfit Stan Collymore to Aston Villa, £7m was quickly recouped while John Barnes left on a free.

Owen lost his main strike partner when injury ruled Robbie Fowler out of the second half of the season. Riedle, despite his European experience, contributed just six goals in a disappointing first season. But foreign stars can take time to settle – if allowed to do so.

Liverpool began slowly with two away draws and a home defeat by Leicester. Already the then 17-year-old Owen had scored twice to demonstrate the talent which, towards the end of the season, was

Club Data File

Responsibility

Top Scorers: Michael Owen (18), Steve McManaman (11)

Sent Off: Robbie Fowler, Michael Owen

Usage

Total: 477 players used

Substitutes: 59 used, 131 not used

Players 1997-98

Most Used Subs: Patrick Berger (16), Danny Murphy (10)

Most SNU: Jorgen Nielson (12), David James (11)

Most Subbed: Oyvind Leonhardsen (7)

Five-Year Form

	Div.	P	W	D	L	F	A	Pts	Pos
93-94	PL	42	17	9	16	59	55	60	8
94-95	PL	42	21	11	10	65	37	74	4
95-96	PL	38	20	11	7	70	34	71	3
96-97	PL	38	19	11	8	62	37	68	4
97-98	PL	38	18	11	9	68	42	65	3

to make him the youngest player this century to play and score for his country. Steve McManaman put behind him rumours of a £12m move to Barcelona to open the scoring at Leeds on 26 August and Liverpool's first win of the season was made safe with Riedle's first goal. Ince scored his first goal in the next match, a 2-1 win over Sheffield Wednesday, as Liverpool embarked on a run of scoring 17 times in five consecutive home wins.

Away from home Liverpool were experiencing problems until winning at Arsenal at the end of November but this performance was followed by a comprehensive 3-1 home defeat by Manchester United. Again they bounced back strongly with five successive wins. But the leaders were still nine points away and hopes of maintaining a title challenge faltered when just one of the next seven games were won. Third place was ultimately secured by emphatic 5-0 and 4-0 wins over West Ham and a depleted Arsenal, but the final game was lost 1-0 at Derby.

A look down the appearance lists shows that Liverpool very rarely fielded the same side twice. Only McManaman and Owen played in over 30 games each, while 13 other players produced 20 or more starts. Fowler's injury limited his goals total to nine – the first time in five seasons he had failed to make double figures. McManaman contributed 11 from his roving midfield role while Ince added eight and Leonhardsen six.

Roy Evans

During four years as manager of Liverpool, Roy Evans has taken the club to two Wembley cup finals and not finished lower than fourth in the Premiership. Maybe given Liverpool's glorious record over the past three decades, it is a record of underachieving and not for the first time the 1997/98 season heard calls for his head. It is a record which most clubs would happily settle for and Evans continues at the helm for another year. You sense though that it is a year in which silverware must return to Anfield.

His side was hit by a number of injuries to key players last season but he was able to call on the talents of Michael Owen. If Evans can help forge a partnership between him and Fowler then the bandwagon will get rolling. But it is on defence that Evans will need to work hardest, not least in determining which of his number ones will be number one.

Evans had only limited action as a first team professional footballer, making just nine appearances for Liverpool as a left-back.

Liverpool v Opponents Record

Opponents	92-3	93-4	94-5	95-6	96-7	97-8	P	W	D	L	F	A	Pts	%
Arsenal	0-2	0-0	3-0	3-1	2-0	4-0	6	4	1	1	12	3	13	72.22
Aston Villa	1-2	2-1	3-2	3-0	3-0	3-0	6	5	0	1	15	5	15	83.33
Blackburn Rovers	2-1	0-1	2-1	3-0	0-0	0-0	6	3	2	1	7	3	11	61.11
Charlton Athletic	-	-	-	-	-	-	0	0	0	0	0	0	0	0.00
Chelsea	2-1	2-1	3-1	2-0	5-1	4-2	6	6	0	0	18	6	18	100.00
Coventry City	4-0	1-0	2-3	0-0	1-2	1-0	6	3	1	2	9	5	10	55.56
Derby County	-	-	-	-	2-1	4-0	2	2	0	0	6	1	6	100.00
Everton	1-0	2-1	0-0	1-2	1-1	1-1	6	2	3	1	6	5	9	50.00
Leeds United	2-0	2-0	0-1	5-0	4-0	3-1	6	5	0	1	16	2	15	83.33
Leicester City	-	-	2-0	-	1-1	1-2	3	1	1	1	4	3	4	44.44
Manchester United	1-2	3-3	2-0	2-0	1-3	1-3	6	2	1	3	10	11	7	38.89
Middlesbrough	4-1	-	-	1-0	5-1		3	3	0	0	10	2	9	100.00
Newcastle United	-	0-2	2-0	4-3	4-3	1-0	5	4	0	1	11	8	12	80.00
Nottingham Forest	0-0	-	1-0	4-2	4-2		4	3	1	0	9	4	10	83.33
Sheffield Wednesday	1-0	2-0	4-1	1-0	0-1	2-1	6	5	0	1	10	3	15	83.33
Southampton	1-1	4-2	3-1	1-1	2-1	2-3	6	3	2	1	13	9	11	61.11
Tottenham Hotspur	6-2	1-2	1-1	0-0	2-1	4-0	6	3	2	1	14	6	11	61.11
West Ham United	-	2-0	0-0	2-0	0-0	5-0	5	3	2	0	9	0	11	73.33
Wimbledon	2-3	1-1	3-0	2-2	1-1	2-0	6	2	3	1	11	7	9	50.00

Transfers

In

Month	Player	Signed From	Fee
Oct-97	Brad Friedel	Columbus Crew	£1.0m
Dec-97	Haukua Gudnason	Keflavik	£150,000
Jun-98	Sean Dundee	Karlsruhe	£2.0m
Jul-98	Steve Staunton	Aston Villa	Free
Jul-98	Vegard Heggem	Rosenborg	£3.5m

Out

Month	Player	Signed For	Fee
Aug-97	John Barnes	Newcastle U.	Free
Nov-97	Paul Dalglish	Newcastle U.	Free
Dec-97	Jason Jones	Swansea	Free
Mar-98	Mark Kennedy	Wimbledon	£1.75m

Manchester United

Up until Christmas Manchester United appeared well on course for an unprecedented third league and cup double and, following excellent form in the Champions' Cup group matches, there was a real belief that a European triumph could be on the cards. Prior to Christmas, United lost just one Premiership match and won five of their six Champions' League fixtures as Alex Ferguson contemplated a clean sweep of the major honours.

But then form took an unexpected dip. It is debatable if an eye on Europe or a comfortable championship lead was the cause of the team's slide. Following defeat at Coventry on 28 December, Ferguson's side went on to suffer more defeats than in any of the previous five years of the Premiership. The Reds also failed to win any more games in Europe. It was the beginning of the end as far as 1997-98 was concerned.

Things had started brightly though with Ferguson strengthening even further a squad that was now devoid of the retired Eric Cantona. Henning Berg and Teddy Sheringham arrived for £5m and £3.5m respectively and United looked ominously good early on.

Five of the first six league games were won and the Premiership had to wait 464 minutes for Peter Schmeichel to concede his first Premiership goal of their season. Chelsea were the first visiting side to take a point from Old Trafford while Leeds handed United their first defeat after eight unbeaten matches. But even that impressive start paled by comparison to a run of eight wins in nine games which included several thrashings: Barnsley 7-0, Sheffield Wednesday 6-1, Wimbledon 5-2 and Blackburn 4-0. Maybe most impressively of all, Liverpool were swept away 3-1 at Anfield. By Boxing Day

Club Data File

Responsibility

Top Scorers: Andy Cole (16), Teddy Sheringham (9)

Sent Off: Gary Pallister, Ole Gunaar Solskjaer

Usage

Total: 494 players used

Substitutes: 76 used, 114 not used

Players 1997-98

Most Used Sub: Brian McClair (11)

Most SNU: Brian McClair (17)

Most Subbed: Paul Scholes (10)

Five-Year Form

	Div.	P	W	D	L	F	A	Pts	Pos
93-94	PL	42	27	11	4	80	38	92	1
94-95	PL	42	26	10	6	77	28	88	2
95-96	PL	38	25	7	6	73	35	82	1
96-97	PL	38	21	12	5	76	44	75	1
97-98	PL	38	23	8	7	73	26	77	2

Fantasy Football Handbook 1998/99

United had scored 47 times in 20 games and led the table by six points. United were now hot favourites, with Andy Cole in hot form, notching 11 goals in ten Premiership matches.

United went into the new year on the back of a 2-0 win over Spurs and despite taking only one point from games with Southampton, Leicester and Bolton, by the end of February United held a seemingly impregnable 11-point lead. Defeat at Sheffield Wednesday slowed the charge and on 14 March Arsenal grabbed a vital victory at Old Trafford which cut United's lead to six points, and the Gunners had three games in hand. Wins over Wimbledon and Blackburn kept United on top but draws at home to Liverpool and Newcastle could not repel Arsenal's ten-match winning run as the Reds' title hat-trick aspirations evaporated.

A defeat by Monaco in the European quarter-finals had done little to lift spirits and Teddy Sheringham, more than any others, looked totally out of sorts as the season progressed. Sheringham would have been looking for more than the nine goals he did manage in the league – a feat matched by midfield maestro David Beckham. Cole finished on 16 while new England arrivals Butt and Scholes also got near double figures. United also managed to force four own goals – the most of any Premiership side. David Beckham missed just one game, while only eight other players broke the 30 appearance barrier.

Alex Ferguson

Just perhaps Alex Ferguson has met his match in the 'wind-up' stakes. The mind games that the most successful manager in English football in recent times has played on his challengers in recent years went un-noticed by the rival to his managerial crown – Arsène Wenger.

Just how he and his brilliant number two, Brian Kidd, get their United juggernaut back on the trophy road will be one of the more interesting developments as the 1998-99 season unfolds. The World Cup will have hindered their plans but it is hard to believe that there will not be major new arrivals at Old Trafford in the aftermath of the Finals.

Ferguson took over in November 1986 and his partnership with Brian Kidd has reaped dividends ever since, bringing the club its first championship in over 25 years and now having secured three of the five Premiership titles available, not to mention two Doubles.

Manchester United v Opponents Record

Opponents	92-3	93-4	94-5	95-6	96-7	97-8	P	W	D	L	F	A	Pts	%
Arsenal	0-0	1-0	3-0	1-0	1-0	0-1	6	4	1	1	6	1	13	72.22
Aston Villa	1-1	3-1	1-0	0-0	0-0	1-0	6	3	3	0	6	2	12	66.67
Blackburn Rovers	3-1	1-1	1-0	1-0	2-2	4-0	6	4	2	0	12	4	14	77.78
Charlton Athletic	-	-	-	-	-	-	0	0	0	0	0	0	0	0.00
Chelsea	3-0	0-1	0-0	1-1	1-2	2-2	6	1	3	2	7	6	6	33.33
Coventry City	5-0	0-0	2-0	1-0	3-1	3-0	6	5	1	0	14	1	16	88.89
Crystal Palace	1-0	-	3-0	-		2-0	3	3	0	0	6	0	9	100.00
Derby County	-	-	-	-	2-3	2-0	2	1	0	1	4	3	3	50.00
Everton	0-3	1-0	2-0	2-0	2-2	2-0	6	4	1	1	9	5	13	72.22
Leeds United	2-0	0-0	0-0	1-0	1-0	3-0	6	4	2	0	7	0	14	77.78
Leicester City	-	-	1-1	-	3-1	0-1	3	1	1	1	4	3	4	44.44
Liverpool	2-2	1-0	2-0	2-2	1-0	1-1	6	3	3	0	9	5	12	66.67
Middlesbrough	3-0	-		2-0	3-3		3	2	1	0	8	3	7	77.78
Newcastle United	-	1-1	2-0	2-0	0-0	1-1	5	2	3	0	6	2	9	60.00
Nottingham Forest	2-0	-	1-2	5-0	4-1		4	3	0	1	12	3	9	75.00
Sheffield Wednesday	2-1	5-0	1-0	2-2	2-0	6-1	6	5	1	0	18	4	16	88.89
Southampton	2-1	2-0	2-1	4-1	2-1	1-0	6	6	0	0	13	4	18	100.00
Tottenham Hotspur	4-1	2-1	0-0	1-0	2-0	2-0	6	5	1	0	11	2	16	88.89
West Ham United	-	3-0	1-0	2-1	2-0	2-1	5	5	0	0	10	2	15	100.00
Wimbledon	0-1	3-1	3-0	3-1	2-1	2-0	6	5	0	1	13	4	15	83.33

Transfers

In

Month	Player	Signed From	Fee
Aug-97	Henning Berg	Blackburn R.	£5.0m
Mar-98	Jonathan Greening	York C.	£1.0m
May-98	Jaap Stam	PSV Eindhoven	£10.75m

Out

Month	Player	Signed For	Fee
Dec-97	Karel Poborsky	Benfica	£3.0m
Jan-98	John O'Kane	Everton	£250,000 rising to £450,000
Jan-98	Neil Mustoe	Wigan A.	Unknown
May-98	Ben Thornley	Huddersfield T.	tbc
Jun-98	Grant Brebner	Reading	£300,000
Jun-98	Kevin Pilkington	Port Vale	Free
Jul-98	Gary Pallister	Middlesbrough	£2.5m

Middlesbrough

Did Middlesbrough's relegation from the Premier League at the end of the 1996-97 season prove that money can't buy you success? If the three points they lost for not turning up for a fixture at Everton had been recouped on appeal, then the answer would probably have been 'yes'. They weren't and Middlesbrough were back in the Nationwide League.

Those big money signings did have one positive effect though in that players such as Juninho were re-sold on at a substantial profit to help finance what has been a more realistic building plan for Bryan Robson's side. Central to this was the arrival of reformed Arsenal winger Paul Merson for £5m and the experienced Andy Townsend for just £500,000 and as deadline day approached Robson invested almost £8.5m on five players including Paul Gascoigne from Rangers and Colombian World Cup player Hamilton Ricard. Merson certainly played his part to the full as he finished the season as Boro's leading scorer. He earned the tag 'Magic Man' on Teesside and forced his way into England's World Cup squad and side. Gary Pallister returned home during the Summer to bring valuable experience to the defence.

Many fully expected Boro to bounce right back – they did but they did not have things all their own way. Their season got off to a good start with a 2-1 victory over Charlton but they then lost to both Stoke and Sheffield United within their first four home games. The latter defeat left Boro down in eighth place some eight points adrift of Forest but with two games in hand. Just one of the next 14 games was lost and despite slipping to a 2-0 defeat at Manchester City and a 3-0 reversal at Charlton, Boro ended the year in pole position.

With a run of seven games undefeated and only four goals conceded, Boro had a chance to open up a six-point lead with a

Club Data File

Responsibility

Top Scorers: Mikkel Beck (14), Paul Merson (12)

Usage

Total: 578 players used

Substitutes: 73 used, 65 not used

Players 1997-98

Most Used Sub: Tony Omerod (7)

Most SNU: Kevin Stamp (8)

Most Subbed: Mikkel Beck (8)

Five-Year Form

	Div.	P	W	D	L	F	A	Pts	Pos
93-94	1	46	18	13	15	66	54	67	9
94-95	1	46	23	13	10	67	40	82	1
95-96	PL	38	11	10	17	35	50	43	12
96-97	PL	38	10	12	16	51	60	39	19
97-98	1	46	27	10	9	77	41	91	2

trip to Forest on 1 March but came away beaten 4-0 and followed it up four days later with a 5-0 drubbing at Queens Park Rangers.

The response was perfect with Branca, Neil Maddison and Armstrong each scoring twice in a 6-0 thrashing of Swindon. Indeed, from conceding nine goals in two games Boro let in just five more in their remaining 11 games and scored 22 in the process, including a 4-1 home win over Oxford City on the final day of the season to clinch the second automatic promotion place at the expense of neighbouring Sunderland.

For the second year running Boro enjoyed great success in the Coca-Cola Cup making it to the final, only to suffer Wembley defeat for the third time in a year. There should be a rule against that.

Bryan Robson used no less than 37 players in Middlesbrough's promotion campaign. Only Paul Merson managed to break the 40 barrier in terms of league appearances. A more settled line-up will be needed if the club from the Riverside are to avoid being the perennial football yo-yo. Only Merson, Townsend and Pallister can count themselves amongst successful Premiership players. The likes of Beck, Vickers, Kinder and even Paul Gascoigne must prove they can be too.

Bryan Robson

If loyalty was repaid with success then you would feel that Middlesbrough have bucket loads of it waiting round the corner. Boro chairman Steve Gibson pledged that Bryan Robson would be staying with the club as their relegation from the Premiership loomed ever nearer at the end of a season when they had invested heavily in a new stadium and even more heavily in players. Votes of confidence are two a penny in football; but at least on Teesside they have meaning. Robson did remain and the confidence has been repaid with him, and his number two Viv Anderson, guiding Boro back to the Premiership.

This time round Robson seems to have a more stable ship. The addition of Merson and Townsend were great signings and both will acquit themselves in the Premiership. His capture of Gary Pallister could make the difference – provided the player can remain free from injury. However, you still wonder about his overall judgement. Paul Gascoigne? Hamilton Ricard? Time will tell.

As a player Robson reached the heights as captain of England and Manchester United. Captain Marvel was his nickname in his playing days. It will be rekindled if Boro maintain their Premiership spot a year hence.

Middlesbrough v Opponents Record

Opponents	92-3	93-4	94-5	95-6	96-7	97-8	P	W	D	L	F	A	Pts	%
Arsenal	1-0	-	-	2-3	0-2	-	3	1	0	2	3	5	3	33.33
Aston Villa	2-3	-	-	0-2	3-2	-	3	1	0	2	5	7	3	33.33
Blackburn Rovers	3-2	-	-	2-0	2-1	-	3	3	0	0	7	3	9	100.00
Charlton Athletic	-	-	-	-	-	-	0	0	0	0	0	0	0	0.00
Chelsea	0-0	-	-	2-0	1-0	-	3	2	1	0	3	0	7	77.78
Coventry City	0-2	-	-	2-1	4-0	-	3	2	0	1	6	3	6	66.67
Derby County	-	-	-	-	6-1	-	1	1	0	0	6	1	3	100.00
Everton	1-2	-	-	0-2	4-2	-	3	1	0	2	5	6	3	33.33
Leeds United	4-1	-	-	1-1	0-0	-	3	1	2	0	5	2	5	55.56
Leicester City	-	-	-	-	0-2	-	1	0	0	1	0	2	0	0.00
Liverpool	1-2	-	-	2-1	3-3	-	3	1	1	1	6	6	4	44.44
Manchester United	1-1	-	-	0-3	2-2	-	3	0	2	1	3	6	2	22.22
Newcastle United	-	-	-	1-2	1-1	-	2	0	1	1	2	3	1	16.67
Nottingham Forest	1-2	-	-	1-1	0-1	-	3	0	1	2	2	4	1	11.11
Sheffield Wednesday	1-1	-	-	3-1	4-2	-	3	2	1	0	8	4	7	77.78
Southampton	2-1	-	-	0-0	0-1	-	3	1	1	1	2	2	4	44.44
Tottenham Hotspur	3-0	-	-	0-1	0-3	-	3	1	0	2	3	4	3	33.33
West Ham United	-	-	-	4-2	4-1	-	2	2	0	0	8	3	6	100.00
Wimbledon	2-0	-	-	1-2	0-0	-	3	1	1	1	3	2	4	44.44

Transfers

In

Month	Player	Signed From	Fee
Sept-97	John O'Loughlin	B'carana Hearts	Non-contract
Oct-97	Neil Maddison	Southampton	£250,000
Feb-98	Hamilton Ricard	Dep. Cali	£2m
Feb-98	Marco Branca	Internazionale	£1m
Feb-98	Alun Armstrong	Stockport Co.	£1.5m
Mar-98	Marlon Beresford	Burnley	£500,000
Mar-98	Paul Gascoigne	Rangers	£3.45m
Jul-98	Gary Pallister	Manchester U.	£2.5m

Out

Month	Player	Signed For	Fee
Sept-97	Alan White	Luton T.	£40,000
Sept-97	Fabrizio Ravanelli	Marseille	£5.3m
Oct-97	Gary Walsh	Bradford C.	£300,000
Dec-97	Chris Freestone	Northampton T.	£75,000
Jan-98	Emerson	Tenerife	£4.2m

Newcastle United

For the first time in five years Alan Shearer failed to reach the 25 Premiership goal mark. A bad pre-season injury ruled the England captain out for most of the season and his two goals in the Premiership did little to revitalise a Newcastle side that sadly lacked his fire power. In truth it was an awful season for the Tynesiders, despite reaching an FA Cup Final they never looked capable of winning.

Yet the season had started full of potential with manager Kenny Dalglish starting his first full year in charge and with the bonus of a UEFA Champions' League programme. Dalglish looked to strengthen his squad accordingly with eight new faces. Many though failed to live up to expectations and price tag. Most expensive was Italian defender Allessandro Pistone at £4.3m while the most experienced were former England stars Stuart Pearce and John Barnes. Other signings included goalkeeper Shay Given, versatile Dane Jon-Dahl Tomasson and colourful Georgian Temuri Ketsbaia. After the turn of the year Dalglish spent around £13m to make several signings including Andreas Andersson and Gary Speed. Dalglish released veteran Peter Beardsley and, more controversially, the enigmatic Asprilla in January for over £6m.

With Shearer injured, Dalglish tried to halt the agreed departure of Les Ferdinand to Tottenham. He failed but Ferdinand himself was to suffer with re-occurring injury problems.

Two goals by Asprilla, against Sheffield Wednesday, got Newcastle's season off to a flying start which was continued with another three wins in the next four games. Despite having 12 points from five games, Newcastle were six points shy of the leaders who had already played an extra

Club Data File

Responsibility

Top Scorer: John Barnes (6)

Sent Off: David Batty (three times)

Usage

Total: 480 players used

Substitutes: 62 used, 128 not used

Players 1997-98

Most Used Sub: Temuri Ketsbaia (15)

Most SNU: Shaka Hislop (18), Shay Given (11), Aaron Hughes (11)

Most Subbed: John Barnes (8), Keith Gillespie (8)

Five-Year Form

	Div.	P	W	D	L	F	A	Pts	Pos
93-94	PL	42	23	8	11	82	41	77	3
94-95	PL	42	20	12	10	67	47	72	6
95-96	PL	38	24	6	8	66	37	78	2
96-97	PL	38	19	11	8	73	40	68	2
97-98	PL	38	11	11	16	35	44	44	13

three matches. Defeat at Chelsea appeared no more than a minor irritation as a last-minute Warren Barton goal beat Tottenham but the Magpies then embarked on a 14-match run which produced just two victories. Goals were proving hard to come by and, but for two goals in five minutes by Keith Gillespie against Barnsley, Newcastle would have gone six consecutive matches without scoring. Two wins in three games looked to have dispelled relegation chatter only for the side to plummet towards the depths again with one lone success from a dozen outings. Back in the fold, Shearer grabbed a vital late winner against Barnsley while safety was finally confirmed in the penultimate league match of the season which saw both Nikolaos Dabizas and Speed score their first Premiership goals in a 3-1 win over Chelsea.

In the Champions' League a stunning hat-trick of headed goals by Asprilla gave Newcastle an unforgettable 3-2 win over Barcelona, but it was the only true highlight performance of the season as the chance for progress into the knock-out stages faded even before it appeared.

United's biggest headlines came against non-league Stevenage in the 4th Round of the FA Cup where the war of words between the two clubs did little to enlighten their meeting on the pitch. Shearer's goals helped them through to the final.

In the ensuing close season, Dalglish again looked to foreign fields to add to his team list. Whether he can find an international gelling agent to provide much needed coherence remains to be seen. A simple statistic showing that John Barnes – a free transfer from Liverpool – was United's top scorer with six goals tells one story. Another is that only two players managed to break the 30 appearance barrier. Ketsbaia was one and

Kenny Dalglish

The Newcastle manager found that Kevin Keegan was a hard act to follow. Not only in the football manager's sense but also in the personality stakes. United fans openly criticised the only manager to win the title with two different clubs in the past decade and talked of a return to the cavalier style that also failed to bring success.

While the Premiership was a struggle, Dalglish did take his team to an FA Cup final. But again St James's Park still waits for its first major silverware in a long time. On the other hand Dalglish has the pedigree to get it right.

As a player and as a manager he has had few peers and trying to cram all of his successes into a couple of paragraphs scarcely does him justice. Suffice to say that he remains Scotland's most capped player (102) and won four Scottish championships and four cups with Celtic. Moving to England, he won five Football League titles, one FA Cup, four League Cups and two Champions' Cups. As a manager he steered Liverpool to a Double and Blackburn to a Premiership title. But is time on his side on Tyneside?

David Batty the other. The Yorkshireman's drive in midfield has never been in doubt, and nor had his temperament until now. His first ever red card was quickly compounded by a further to help reduce his season.

One positive note for Dalglish would have been the form of Dabizas, a late season signing who looks as though he could be a major influence in the months ahead and help clear what might otherwise be an ever thickening fog on the Tyne.

Newcastle United v Opponents Record

Opponents	92-3	93-4	94-5	95-6	96-7	97-8	P	W	D	L	F	A	Pts	%
Arsenal	-	2-0	1-0	2-0	1-2	0-1	5	3	0	2	6	3	9	60.00
Aston Villa	-	5-1	3-1	1-0	4-3	1-0	5	5	0	0	14	5	15	100.00
Blackburn Rovers	-	1-1	1-1	1-0	2-1	1-1	5	2	3	0	6	4	9	60.00
Charlton Athletic	-						0	0	0	0	0	0	0	0.00
Chelsea	-	0-0	4-2	2-0	3-1	3-1	5	4	1	0	12	4	13	86.67
Coventry City	-	4-0	4-0	3-0	4-0	0-0	5	4	1	0	15	0	13	86.67
Derby County	-	-	-	-	3-1	0-0	2	1	1	0	3	1	4	66.67
Everton	-	1-0	2-0	1-0	4-1	1-0	5	5	0	0	9	1	15	100.00
Leeds United	-	1-1	1-2	2-1	3-0	1-1	5	2	2	1	8	5	8	53.33
Leicester City	-	-	3-1	-	4-3	3-3	3	2	1	0	10	7	7	77.78
Liverpool	-	3-0	1-1	2-1	1-1	1-2	5	2	1	2	8	5	8	53.33
Manchester United	-	1-1	1-1	0-1	5-0	0-1	5	1	2	2	7	4	5	33.33
Middlesbrough	-	-	-	1-0	3-1		2	2	0	0	4	1	6	100.00
Nottingham Forest	-	-	2-1	3-1	5-0		3	3	0	0	10	2	9	100.00
Sheffield Wednesday	-	4-2	2-1	2-0	1-2	2-1	5	4	0	1	11	6	12	80.00
Southampton	-	1-2	5-1	1-0	0-1	2-1	5	3	0	2	9	5	9	60.00
Tottenham Hotspur	-	0-1	3-3	1-1	7-1	1-0	5	2	2	1	12	6	8	53.33
West Ham United	-	2-0	2-0	3-0	1-1	0-1	5	3	1	1	8	2	10	66.67
Wimbledon	-	4-0	2-1	6-1	2-0	1-3	5	4	0	1	15	5	12	80.00

Transfers

In

Month	Player	Signed From	Fee
Aug-97	Ian Rush	Leeds U.	Free
Aug-97	John Barnes	Liverpool	Free
Nov-97	Ralf Keidel	FC Schweinfurt	Undisclosed
Nov-97	Paul Dalglish	Liverpool	Free
Nov-97	Carlos Gonzales	Sydney Olympic	Undisclosed
Jan-98	Andreas Andersson	AC Milan	£3.6m
Jan-98	Andrew Griffin	Stoke C.	£1.5m rising to £2.25m
Jan-98	David Terrier	West Ham U.	Free
Feb-98	Gary Speed	Everton	£5.5m
Mar-98	James Coppinger	Darlington	£250,000
Mar-98	Nikolaos Dabizas	Olympiakos	£2m
Jun-98	Stephane Guivarch	Auxerre	£3.5m
Jul-98	Carl Serrant	Oldham A.	£500,000

Out

Month	Player	Signed For	Fee
Aug-97	Peter Beardsley	Bolton W.	£450,000
Jan-98	Faustino Asprilla	Parma	£6.1m
Feb-98	John Beresford	Southampton	£1.5m
Mar-98	Paul Brayson	Reading	£100,000
Mar-98	Jimmy Crawford	Reading	£50,000
Jun-98	Darren Peacock	Blackburn R.	Free
Jun-98	Jon Dahl Tomasson	Feyenoord	£2.5m
Jul-98	Shaka Hislop	West Ham U.	Free

Nottingham Forest

If there is one club which adds substance to the theory that there is a growing gulf between the Premiership and the Nationwide League then it has to be Nottingham Forest. By virtue of winning the Division One Championship for a second time in five years, Forest are the first club to have twice fallen from the Premiership and then won the Football League title at the first time of asking.

It's a trend that manager Dave Bassett will be looking to halt this time around and he may well have the fire power to achieve it now. It could well come in the form of Pierre Van Hooijdonk who was brought in too late from Celtic to save them from their last drop. The Dutchman formed a formidable partnership with Kevin Campbell who answered his critics superbly as the duo scored in excess of 50 league goals between them, with Van Hooijdonk alone scoring 29 times – many in the form of free kick rockets.

Hooijdonk was the start of a rebuilding programme that Bassett engineered after taking over from player manager Stuart Pearce. Bassett collected over £3m from the departure of Alf-Inge Haaland and Bryan Roy. He brought in Andy Johnson and Alan Rogers from Norwich and Tranmere for over £4m and overseas players Marco Pascalo and Jon Olav Hjelde for £1.35m. Bassett also acquired Geoff Thomas and Thierry Bonalair on free transfers.

Forest set a cracking pace from the off with four consecutive wins, including 4-1 and 4-0 thumpings of Norwich and QPR, the latter including Van Hooijdonk's first hat-trick for the club. They were surprisingly brought down to earth when former Forest boss Frank Clark took his Manchester City side to the City Ground and won 3-1. A draw at Swindon, who made a good start, and defeat at Sheffield United sent Forest down to fifth but

Club Data File

Responsibility
Top Scorer: Pierre van Hooijdonk (29)

Usage
Total: 561 players used
Substitutes: 69 used, 69 not used

Players 1997-98
Most Used Sub: Craig Armstrong (13)
Most SNU: Craig Armstrong (17)
Most Subbed: Scot Gemmill (7), Alan Rogers (7)

Five-Year Form

	Div	P	W	D	L	F	A	Pts	Pos
93-94	1	46	23	14	9	74	49	83	2
94-95	PL	42	22	11	9	72	43	77	3
95-96	PL	38	15	13	10	50	54	58	9
96-97	PL	38	6	16	16	31	59	34	20
97-98	1	46	28	10	8	82	42	94	1

victory over Portsmouth returned Bassett's side to the top of the table after eight games. With one defeat from 14 games – two in the first 21 games – Forest were well on the path to promotion and proved their credentials against other top sides. Draws were collected at Sunderland and Middlesbrough while Charlton were thrashed 5-2 with Van Hooijdonk being the destroyer with another hat-trick.

The return match with Middlesbrough was crucial to Forest's title aspirations. Two successive draws had allowed Boro to open up a three-point lead but with Van Hooijdonk scoring twice Forest pulled off an amazing 4-0 victory. Forest failed to capitalise fully on that success and were immediately pegged back by Sunderland who dished out a 3-0 defeat at the City Ground. Unabashed Forest duly put the record straight with a Campbell hat-trick setting up a 4-1 win at Crewe. Forest were now three points clear and, with seven wins in eight games, carried themselves into an unassailable position. Results elsewhere during the final week handed Forest the title and they celebrated with Van Hooijdonk's 34th goal of the season in a 1-1 draw at West Brom.

Goals will come for Forest during 1998-99. Van Hooijdonk's ability from free-kicks at the highest level was underlined with a terrific strike for Holland during their World Cup Finals campaign. It is doubtful that he will match his 29 goals from last year, and therefore much will depend on Kevin Campbell's ability to fulfil his potential at the top level – something that he struggled to do previously with Arsenal.

Dave Bassett

Dave 'Harry' Bassett has started to develop a niche for himself in football. He is a man for a job. In much the same way Texan fire fighters would call in Red Adare to extinguish an oil-well fire, club chairmen who want to get their club on an even keel, with a solid base and moving forward call in Dave Bassett. The magic has worked again at the City Ground. In his first full season in charge he has added wisely to his squad and guided them to the Division One championship at the first time of asking. The key however is can he keep them in the Premiership? This will be his second spell managing in the top flight, having been in control of Sheffield United, who were ultimately relegated at the end of the 1993-94 season. Bassett had taken the Blades into the top flight then. This Forest side look stronger but at the time of writing there had been a general lack of activity in the incoming side of the transfer market. Van Hooijdonk's ability to score at the top may be the key to Bassett's future.

Nottingham Forest v Opponents Record

Opponents	92-3	93-4	94-5	95-6	96-7	97-8	P	W	D	L	F	A	Pts	%
Arsenal	0-1	-	2-2	0-1	2-1	-	4	1	1	2	4	5	4	33.33
Aston Villa	0-1	-	1-2	1-1	0-0	-	4	0	2	2	2	4	2	16.67
Blackburn Rovers	1-3	-	0-2	1-5	2-2	-	4	0	1	3	4	12	1	8.33
Charlton Athletic	-	-	-	-	-	-	0	0	0	0	0	0	0	0.00
Chelsea	3-0	-	0-1	0-0	2-0	-	4	2	1	1	5	1	7	58.33
Coventry City	1-1	-	2-0	0-0	0-1	-	4	1	2	1	3	2	5	41.67
Derby County	-	-	-	-	1-1	-	1	0	1	0	1	1	1	33.33
Everton	0-1	-	2-1	3-2	0-1	-	4	2	0	2	5	5	6	50.00
Leeds United	1-1	-	3-0	2-1	1-1	-	4	2	2	0	7	3	8	66.67
Leicester City	-	-	1-0	-	0-0	-	2	1	1	0	1	0	4	66.67
Liverpool	1-0	-	1-1	1-0	1-1	-	4	2	2	0	4	2	8	66.67
Manchester United	0-2	-	1-1	1-1	0-4	-	4	0	2	2	2	8	2	16.67
Middlesbrough	1-0	-	-	1-0	1-1	-	3	2	1	0	3	1	7	77.78
Newcastle United	-	-	0-0	1-1	0-0	-	3	0	3	0	1	1	3	33.33
Sheffield Wednesday	1-2	-	4-1	1-0	0-3	-	4	2	0	2	6	6	6	50.00
Southampton	1-2	-	3-0	1-0	1-3	-	4	2	0	2	6	5	6	50.00
Tottenham Hotspur	2-1	-	2-2	2-1	2-1	-	4	3	1	0	8	5	10	83.33
West Ham United	-	-	1-1	1-1	0-2	-	3	0	2	1	2	4	2	22.22
Wimbledon	1-1	-	3-1	4-1	1-1	-	4	2	2	0	9	4	8	66.67

Transfers

In

Month	Player	Signed From	Fee
Sept-97	Carlos Merino	Urdaneta Italy	Free
Nov-97	Dave Beasant	Southampton	Free
Feb-98	Glyn Hodges	Hull C.	Free

Out

Month	Player	Signed For	Fee
Sept-97	Alan Fettis	Blackburn R.	£300,000
Oct-97	Gareth Bough	Corby T.	Free
Nov-97	David Phillips	Huddersfield T.	Free
Nov-97	Andrea Silenzi	Released	Free
Nov-97	Vance Warner	Rotherham	Undisclosed
Dec-97	Paul Smith	Lincoln C.	£20,000
Dec-97	Andy Porteous	Manchester C.	Free
Dec-97	Kris Winters	Manchester C.	Non-contract
Dec-97	Dean Saunders	Sheffield U.	Free
Jan-98	Stephen Howe	Swindon T.	£30,000
Feb-98	Daniel George	Doncaster R.	Free

Sheffield Wednesday

What went wrong at Hillsborough remains another one of those footballing questions that will go unanswered. One year on from making their best ever start to a Premiership season, Sheffield Wednesday found themselves on the rocks early in 1997-98 with just one victory in nine Premiership matches. Along the way Wednesday were slaughtered 7-2 at Blackburn and crushed 5-2 at home by Derby. Not that the dire results unsettled Italian Benito Carbone who had seven goals after just ten games.

In reality their poor start was a continuation of the form they had shown in the previous season's final run in. Wednesday won just two of the final nine games of the previous campaign. The close season had done nothing to hinder it.

Manager David Pleat, however, had more faith in his players and by the start of the season had added only Paulo Di Canio from Celtic for £3m and Patrick Blondeau from Monaco for £1.8m to his existing squad. Waving farewell to Hillsborough were Regi Blinker, Orlando Trustfull and three other squad members. In September Jim Magilton joined from Southampton for £1.6m and a month later David Hirst went in the opposite direction for £2m.

After that poor start Pleat was walking a thin line. When four points from two games was followed by defeat at one of his previous clubs, Tottenham, a home reversal by Crystal Palace and another mauling – this time 6-1 at Manchester United, Wednesday decided that Pleat's time was up. Pleat's number two Peter Shreeves took charge of the side for the visit of Bolton and wondered what all the fuss was about as Andy Booth, making his first appearance of the season after injury,

Club Data File

Responsibility

Top Scorer:	Paulo Di Canio (12)
Sent Off:	Earl Barrett, Andy Booth, Dejan Stefanovic

Usage

Total:	505 players used
Substitutes:	87 used, 103 not used

Players 1997-98

Most Used Subs:	Guy Whittingham (11), Wayne Collins (11)
Most SNU:	Matt Clarke (32), Richie Humphreys (1)
Most Subbed:	Mark Pembridge (15)

Five-Year Form

	Div.	P	W	D	L	F	A	Pts	Pos
93-94	PL	42	16	16	10	76	54	64	7
94-95	PL	42	13	12	17	49	57	51	13
95-96	PL	38	10	10	18	48	61	40	15
96-97	PL	38	14	15	9	50	51	57	7
97-98	PL	38	12	8	18	52	67	44	16

Fantasy Football Handbook 1998/99

scored a hat-trick in Wednesday's 5-0 stroll, all the goals coming before half time.

By the time of their next Premiership match a fortnight later Wednesday had appointed Ron Atkinson as manager for his second stint at Hillsborough. Big Ron's first test was a triumph, with Booth scoring again as Arsenal went down to only their second defeat of the season. Mid table Southampton and struggling Barnsley also became victims of the Owls' recovery which saw the talented Di Canio score three times in that four match winning run. A trip to West Ham in December terminated the run and the fact that Atkinson still had plenty of work to do was emphasised by a 4-1 home defeat against Chelsea. Wednesday's form for the rest of the season was erratic to say the least, with never more than two consecutive games being won or lost. Indeed it still needed a 3-1 win at Everton, with Mark Pembridge scoring twice and top scorer Di Canio getting the other, towards the end of the campaign to maintain Wednesday's ever present record in the Premiership. The season closed with successive defeats by Aston Villa and Crystal Palace.

Throughout this Des Walker was probably Wednesday's most consistent player. He was one of the few Premiership players who managed to play in all 38 games, and in Walker's case he started and finished them all. Pressman, Pembridge and imports Carbone and Di Canio were also near ever-presents. Di Canio was also the main source of goals although his total of 12 was nearly matched by his yellow cards.

Danny Wilson

It seemed inevitable that Danny Wilson would ultimately end up in the number one seat at Hillsborough. A crowd favourite as a player, there can be few managers who have managed a side to Premiership relegation with such verve.

The credit through was in taking a club like Barnsley into the Premier League in such style. Had they shown the defensive togetherness in the first part of the season that was apparent in the second half then Wilson may still have been at Oakwell now. Certainly few teams made so many friends, with many supporters regarding the Tykes as their second side.

Wilson moved to Oakwell from Sheffield Wednesday for £200,000 in the summer of 1993 and played close on a hundred games in the Tykes' midfield. He started his playing career at Wigan, joined Bury on a free transfer and went to Hillsborough via Chesterfield, Forest, Scunthorpe, Brighton and Luton.

Now he is faced with a tougher job in Sheffield where the expectations are much higher.

Sheffield Wednesday v Opponents Record

Opponents	92-3	93-4	94-5	95-6	96-7	97-8	P	W	D	L	F	A	Pts	%
Arsenal	1-0	0-1	3-1	1-0	0-0	2-0	6	4	1	1	7	2	13	72.22
Aston Villa	1-2	0-0	1-2	2-0	2-1	1-3	6	2	1	3	7	8	7	38.89
Blackburn Rovers	0-0	1-2	0-1	2-1	1-1	0-0	6	1	3	2	4	5	6	33.33
Charlton Athletic							0	0	0	0	0	0	0	0.00
Chelsea	3-3	3-1	1-1	0-0	0-2	1-4	6	1	3	2	8	11	6	33.33
Coventry City	1-2	0-0	5-1	4-3	0-0	0-0	6	2	3	1	10	6	9	50.00
Derby	-	-	-	-	0-0	2-5	2	0	1	1	2	5	1	16.67
Everton	3-1	5-1	0-0	2-5	2-1	3-1	6	4	1	1	15	9	13	72.22
Leeds United	1-1	3-3	1-1	6-2	2-2	1-3	6	1	4	1	14	12	7	38.89
Leicester City	-	-	1-0	-	2-1	1-0	3	3	0	0	4	1	9	100.00
Liverpool	1-1	3-1	1-2	1-1	1-1	3-3	6	1	4	1	10	9	7	38.89
Manchester United	3-3	2-3	1-0	0-0	1-1	2-0	6	2	3	1	9	7	9	50.00
Middlesbrough	2-3	-	-	0-1	3-1		3	1	0	2	5	5	3	33.33
Newcastle United	-	0-1	0-0	0-2	1-1	2-1	5	1	2	2	3	5	5	33.33
Nottingham Forest	2-0	-	1-7	1-3	2-0		4	2	0	2	6	10	6	50.00
Southampton	5-2	2-0	1-1	2-2	1-1	1-0	6	3	3	0	12	6	12	66.67
Tottenham Hotspur	2-0	1-0	3-4	1-3	2-1	1-0	6	4	0	2	10	8	12	66.67
West Ham United	-	5-0	1-0	0-1	0-0	1-1	5	2	2	1	7	2	8	53.33
Wimbledon	1-1	2-2	0-1	2-1	3-1	1-1	6	2	3	1	9	7	9	50.00

Transfers

In

Month	Player	Signed From	Fee
Aug-97	Paolo Di Canio	Celtic	£3.0m
Sep-97	Bruce Grobbelaar	Oxford U.	Nominal
Sep-97	Jim Magilton	Southampton	£1.6m
Oct-97	Peter Rudi	Molde	£800,000
Dec-97	N. Alexandersson	Gothenburg	£750,000
Jan-98	Andy Hinchcliffe	Everton	£3.0m
Jan-98	Christian Mayrleb	FC Tirol	£200,000
Feb-98	Earl Barrett	Everton	Free
Feb-98	Goce Sedloski	Hajduk Split	£750,000 rising to £1.25m
Mar-98	Emerson Thome	Benfica	Free
Mar-98	Stuart Jones	Weston-S-Mare	£20,000 rising to £100,000

Out

Month	Player	Signed For	Fee
Aug-97	Regi Blinker	Celtic	£1.5m
Aug-97	Orlando Trustfull	Vitesse Arnhem	£800,000
Oct-97	Jonathan Scargil	Chesterfield	Non-contract
Oct-97	David Hirst	Southampton	£2.0m
Nov-97	Steve Lenagh	Chesterfield	Monthly
Jan-98	Patrick Blondeau	Bordeaux	£1.2m
Jan-98	Wayne Collins	Fulham	£400,000 rising to £550,000
Feb-98	Adem Poric	Rotherham	Monthly
Mar-98	O'Neill Donaldson	Stoke C.	Free

Southampton

Southampton are on the verge of becoming a fashionable club. Last season life at the Dell wasn't about a battle against relegation. While a European placing wasn't in view, it may not be totally out of the question in the coming seasons. Such was the impact of new manager Dave Jones. Jones – an outstanding success at Stockport County – brought two of his prodigies to the south coast: goalkeeper Paul Jones – who appeared in every Premiership game – and defender Lee Jones. Manager Jones also benefited from the arrival of Chesterfield striker Kevin Davies just prior to his appointment. He witnessed Davies' value increase ten-fold in the 1997-98 season and sold him to Blackburn Rovers for £7.5m. Davies scored 12 times in 25 appearances in his one season at the Dell where he had been hindered by injury. Jones further increased his squad during the season and opted for more Premiership experience when spending £4.5m on bringing in Carlton Palmer, David Hirst and John Beresford. The books were balanced with Jones releasing several players before the season was out.

Being amongst the favourites to struggle, Southampton gave the bookies plenty to smile about when kicking off the season with three defeats, although two of them were against Manchester United and Arsenal. Neil Maddison celebrated his tenth season with the Saints by scoring their first goal of the season but by then they were on the path to the Arsenal defeat. Davies' first goal clinched victory over Crystal Palace but by the time Derby won 4-0 at Pride Park, Southampton had played nine games and collected just four points. Not surprisingly they were at the

Club Data File

Responsibility

Top Scorers: Matt Le Tissier (11), Egil Ostenstad (11)

Sent Off: Francis Benali (twice), Ken Monkou, Carlton Palmer

Usage

Total: 505 players used

Substitutes: 87 used, 103 not used

Players 1997-98

Most Used Sub: Andy Williams (17)

Most SNU: Kevin Moss (20), Taylor (14)

Most Subbed: Matt Le Tissier (15)

Five-Year Form

	Div.	P	W	D	L	F	A	Pts	Pos
93-94	PL	42	12	7	23	49	66	43	18
94-95	PL	42	12	18	12	61	63	54	10
95-96	PL	38	9	11	18	34	52	38	17
96-97	PL	38	10	11	17	50	56	41	16
97-98	PL	38	14	6	18	50	55	48	12

foot of the table. The return of Matt Le Tissier after breaking his arm during pre-season was instrumental in the Saints edging above Barnsley a week later with a 3-0 win over West Ham. A defeat at Blackburn was followed by Hirst scoring twice on his home debut during a 3-2 win over Tottenham. Further wins over Everton and Barnsley lifted the Saints to 13th.

A run of three more defeats sent Southampton slipping back into trouble before three wins and three draws carried them to the safe sanctuary of mid-table. Two of those wins were high points in Southampton's season with Davies getting the winner at home to both Chelsea and Manchester United. In the other success, against Leicester, Francis Benali finally scored his first goal for the club after 11 years on their books. Arsenal cut short the celebrations with a 3-0 win to put the brakes on the climb but immediately the Saints hit back with two late Hirst goals pulling off a magnificent 3-2 win at Liverpool. A home defeat by Coventry ensued but another three successes raised the possibility of qualifying for Europe before the season ended on the back of two wins in nine games. During the final ten games Le Tissier confirmed his return to form with seven goals.

Le Tissier and the underrated Egil Ostenstad finished the season as joint top scorers for the Saints with 11 each, with Davies and Hirst close behind with nine each. But that particular spread of goals, 40 between four, has to be seen as encouraging, although Jones will be on the lookout for a Davies-made replacement.

The form of Carlton Palmer was also a revelation as the former England man had one of his best seasons in recent years and was a major driving force behind Southampton's push up the table.

Dave Jones

The appointment of Dave Jones as manager of Southampton was a bold move by the Saints and flies in the face of present day appointments in the Premiership which tend to veer towards either overseas coaches or top line foreign players being given their head for the first time. Jones had done an outstanding job in two years as manager of Stockport where he took them to within sight of Wembley in the League Cup and brought his ability to the attention of the nation.

Despite a poor start at the Dell, which included a spell on the bottom of the Premiership, Jones kept his nerve and guided Saints to mid-table respectability.

Jones took over at County in March 1995 and in his first full season in charge they finished ninth in Division Two. He followed that up with a second place and promotion to add to that League Cup run.

Prior to County, Jones' only managerial experience was at non-league Morecambe where he was also a player after a career that started at Everton and went to Preston NE via Coventry and Hong Kong.

Southampton v Opponents Record

Opponents	92-3	93-4	94-5	95-6	96-7	97-8	P	W	D	L	F	A	Pts	%
Arsenal	2-0	0-4	1-0	0-0	0-2	1-3	6	2	1	3	4	9	7	38.89
Aston Villa	2-0	4-1	2-1	0-1	0-1	1-2	6	3	0	3	9	6	9	50.00
Blackburn Rovers	1-1	3-1	1-1	1-0	2-0	3-0	6	4	2	0	11	3	14	77.78
Charlton Athletic	-	-	-	-	-	-	0	0	0	0	0	0	0	0.00
Chelsea	1-0	3-1	0-1	2-3	0-0	1-0	6	3	1	2	7	5	10	55.56
Coventry City	2-2	1-0	0-0	1-0	2-2	1-2	6	2	3	1	7	6	9	50.00
Derby County	-	-	-	-	3-1	0-2	2	1	0	1	3	3	3	50.00
Everton	0-0	0-2	2-0	2-2	2-2	2-1	6	2	3	1	8	7	9	50.00
Leeds United	1-1	0-2	1-3	1-1	0-2	0-2	6	0	2	4	3	11	2	11.11
Leicester City	-	-	2-2	-	2-2	2-1	3	1	2	0	6	5	5	55.56
Liverpool	2-1	4-2	0-2	1-3	0-1	1-1	6	2	1	3	8	10	7	38.89
Manchester United	0-1	1-3	2-2	3-1	6-3	1-0	6	3	1	2	13	10	10	55.56
Middlesbrough	2-1	-	-	2-1	4-0		3	3	0	0	8	2	9	100.00
Newcastle United	-	2-1	3-1	1-0	2-2	2-1	5	4	1	0	10	5	13	86.67
Nottingham Forest	1-2	-	1-1	3-4	2-2		4	0	2	2	7	9	2	16.67
Sheffield Wednesday	1-2	1-1	0-0	0-1	2-3	2-3	6	0	2	4	6	10	2	11.11
Tottenham Hotspur	0-0	1-0	4-3	0-0	0-1	3-2	6	3	2	1	8	6	11	61.11
West Ham United	-	0-2	1-1	0-0	2-0	3-0	5	2	2	1	6	3	8	53.33
Wimbledon	2-2	1-0	2-3	0-0	0-0	0-1	6	1	3	2	5	6	6	33.33

Transfers

In

Month	Player	Signed From	Fee
Aug-97	Stig Johansen	Bodo-Glimt	£600,000
Sep-97	Kevin Richardson	Coventry C.	£150,000
Sep-97	Carlton Palmer	Leeds U.	£1.0m
Oct-97	David Hirst	Sheffield W.	£2.0m
Nov-97	Bjorn Johansen	Tromso	£200,000
Feb-98	John Beresford	Newcastle U.	£1.5m
Jul-98	David Howells	Tottenham H.	Free
Jul-98	Stuart Ripley	Blackburn R.	£1.5m
Jul-98	James Beattie	Blackburn R.	£1.0m
Jul-98	Mark Hughes	Chelsea	£650,000
Jul-98	Scott Marshall	Arsenal	Free

Out

Month	Player	Signed For	Fee
Sep-97	Jim Magilton	Sheffield W.	£1.6m
Oct-97	Christer Warren	Bournemouth	£50,000
Oct-97	Neil Maddison	Middlesbrough	£250,000
Oct-97	Mike Evans	WBA	£750,000
Nov-97	Maik Taylor	Fulham	£700,000
Nov-97	Alan Neilson	Fulham	£250,000
Nov-97	Dave Beasant	N. Forest	Free
Jan-98	Simon Charlton	Birmingham C.	£250,000

Out

Month	Player	Signed For	Fee
Feb-98	Russell Watkinson	Bristol C.	Monthly
Feb-98	Andrew Catley	Exeter C.	Non-contract
Feb-98	Matthew Robinson	Portsmouth	£50,000
Mar-98	Russell Watkinson	Millwall	Free
Mar-98	Robbie Slater	Wolverhampton W.	£75,000
Jun-98	Kevin Davies	Blackburn Rovers	£7.25m
Jul-98	Duncan Spedding	Northampton T.	£60,000
Jul-98	Kevin Richardson	Barnsley	Nominal

Tottenham

Many may have questioned his stomach for a fight when he arrived at White Hart Lane for the start of the 1997-98 season but by the end of it most agreed that he was one of the reasons Tottenham remained in the Premiership. Frenchman David Ginola was a revelation and his hard-working, skill-packed performances for Spurs earned him respect – even from Arsenal fans where his tussles with Lee Dixon have not always been best received.

Was the writing for a struggling season already on the wall when it kicked off? Tottenham supporters were stunned to learn of the departure of Teddy Sheringham to Manchester United for just £3.5m; that Spurs paid almost double for his replacement, Les Ferdinand, caused further consternation. Ferdinand began the season promisingly with three goals in four games but when he joined long-term injury victim Chris Armstrong on the sick list, Spurs struggled for goals.

Opening the season against Manchester United was probably not quite what Spurs wanted and they duly went down 2-0 at White Hart Lane, despite Sheringham missing a penalty. Another defeat at West Ham followed before successive home wins over Derby and Villa eased the early tension. But that was as good as it got and the pressure on Francis grew quickly. With just one success from their next 11 Premiership games, Spurs were heading down the table at pace and the end came for Francis when he resigned on 19 November following three successive defeats, the last being a 4-0 thrashing at Liverpool.

New manager Christian Gross was given as rough a baptism as any with Tottenham, against Crystal Palace, going down to the second of three successive home defeats. Gross looked to be getting

Club Data File

Responsibility

Top Scorer: Jurgen Klinsmann (9)

Sent Off: Justin Edinburgh, Ramon Vega

Usage

Total: 507 players used

Substitutes: 89 used, 100 not used

Players 1997-98

Most Used Sub: Jose Dominguez (10)

Most SNU: Espen Baardsen (26), Gary Mabbutt (11)

Most Subbed: Ruel Fox (9)

Five-Year Form

	Div.	P	W	D	L	F	A	Pts	Pos
93-94	PL	42	11	12	19	54	59	45	15
94-95	PL	42	16	14	12	66	58	62	7
95-96	PL	38	16	13	9	50	38	61	8
96-97	PL	38	13	7	18	44	51	46	10
97-98	PL	38	11	11	16	44	56	44	14

the ship back on an even keel with victory at fellow strugglers Everton only for Chelsea, after being stretched at times in the first half, to hand the club its heaviest home defeat since 1935 with a 6-1 thrashing. Again Spurs performed reasonably well in their next game but still suffered a 4-0 drubbing at Coventry. Gross looked abroad for salvation and found it in the form of fans' favourite Jurgen Klinsmann, who was having a none too happy time in Italy.

But only one more win was achieved before the end of the year, with Barnsley being despatched 3-0 at White Hart Lane, and that was just one of two successes in 11 Premiership games as Spurs slipped into the relegation zone. Gross, according to the press, was living on borrowed time almost from day one and the glowing reviews heaped on neighbours Arsenal did little to appease the Spurs faithful. Klinsmann struggled early on but the news did get better as Armstrong, Ferdinand and even Darren Anderton returned from injury. With Ginola finding his touch, Spurs went on a run of one defeat in five games before another four-match winless run in April plunged them back into trouble. D-Day for Tottenham came at Barnsley on 18 April. Defeat would almost certainly have precipitated relegation but, despite having Ramon Vega dismissed, Gross's side gained a draw through a Colin Calderwood goal and suddenly the pressure seemed to ease. One week later a fine performance secured a vital 2-0 win over Newcastle before safety was secured on the back of four Klinsmann goals during a 6-2 slaughter of Wimbledon at Selhurst Park.

The World Cup form of Darren 'sick note' Anderton was more than encouraging and his combination with Ginola could be a pointer to what may lie ahead. The arrival of Algerian skipper Moussa Saib late in the season may bode well given the way the midfielder immediately looked at home in the Premiership. Goals though will be the main requirement and the return to fitness of Ferdinand and Armstrong should ensure they finish with more than the six strikes Ginola achieved to earn him the White Hart Lane top marksman award.

Christian Gross

Christian Gross arrived at White Hart Lane as a virtual unknown. With Spurs under achieving and struggling at the wrong end of the Premiership, his brief was simple: survival. In that respect he was a success but it remains to be seen if he can build on that and take Tottenham back up the table and amongst the honours.

A successful club manager in Switzerland with Grasshopper Club, Gross seemed to lack the charisma that characterised the previous incumbents at the Lane. Rumours surrounding clashes with some of the senior players at the club were ever present, not least with Les Ferdinand and ultimately with the returning Klinsmann. He did however seem to bring the best out in David Ginola.

With a full pre-season in charge, a change in fortunes will be expected with immediate effect. That may determine whether Gross remains in charge for his first full season.

Tottenham Hotspur v Opponents Record

Opponents	92-3	93-4	94-5	95-6	96-7	97-8	P	W	D	L	F	A	Pts	%
Arsenal	1-0	0-1	1-0	2-1	0-0	1-1	6	3	2	1	5	3	11	61.11
Aston Villa	0-0	1-1	3-4	0-1	1-0	3-2	6	2	2	2	8	8	8	44.44
Blackburn Rovers	1-2	0-2	3-1	2-3	2-1	0-0	6	2	1	3	8	9	7	38.89
Charlton Athletic	-	-	-	-	-	-	0	0	0	0	0	0	0	0.00
Chelsea	1-2	1-1	0-0	1-1	1-2	1-6	6	0	3	3	5	12	3	16.67
Coventry City	0-2	1-2	1-3	3-1	1-2	1-1	6	1	1	4	7	11	4	22.22
Derby	-	-	-	-	1-1	1-0	2	1	1	0	2	1	4	66.67
Everton	2-1	3-2	2-1	0-0	0-0	1-1	6	3	3	0	8	5	12	66.67
Leeds United	4-0	1-1	1-1	2-1	1-0	0-1	6	3	2	1	9	4	11	61.11
Leicester City	-	-	1-0	-	1-2	1-1	3	1	1	1	3	3	4	44.44
Liverpool	2-0	3-3	0-0	1-3	0-2	3-3	6	1	3	2	9	11	6	33.33
Manchester United	1-1	0-1	0-1	4-1	1-2	0-2	6	1	1	4	6	8	4	22.22
Middlesbrough	2-2	-	-	1-1	1-0		3	1	2	0	4	3	5	55.56
Newcastle United	-	1-2	4-2	1-1	1-2	2-0	5	2	1	2	9	7	7	46.67
Nottingham Forest	2-1	-	1-4	0-1	0-1		4	1	0	3	3	7	3	25.00
Sheffield Wednesday	0-2	1-3	3-1	1-0	1-1	3-2	6	3	1	2	9	9	10	55.56
Southampton	4-2	3-0	1-2	1-0	3-1	1-1	6	4	1	1	13	6	13	72.22
West Ham United	-	1-4	3-1	0-1	1-0	1-0	5	3	0	2	6	6	9	60.00
Wimbledon	1-1	1-1	1-2	3-1	1-0	0-0	6	2	3	1	7	5	9	50.00

Transfers

In

Month	Player	Signed From	Fee
Aug-97	Jose Dominguez	Sporting Lisbon	£1.5m
Dec-97	Jurgen Klinsmann	Sampdoria	£175,000
Jan-98	Frode Grodas	Chelsea	£250,000
Jan-98	Nicola Berti	Internazionale	Free
Feb-98	Moussa Saib	Valencia	£2.3m
Jul-98	Paolo Tramezzani	Piacenza	£1.35m

Out

Month	Player	Signed For	Fee
Aug-97	Ronny Rosenthal	Watford	Free
Sep-97	Leon Townley	Brentford	£50,000
Oct-97	Jason Dozzell	Ipswich T.	Non-contract
Jan-98	Kevin Mather	Southend U.	Free
Mar-98	Stuart Nethercott	Millwall	Free
Mar-98	Paul Mahorn	Port Vale	Non-contract
Jun-98	Jamie Clapham	Ipswich T.	£300,000
Jul-98	David Howells	Southampton	Free
Jul-98	Dean Austin	C. Palace	Free

West Ham United

West Ham United's most successful season of the five years the club has spent in the Premiership was based upon something which the Hammers have not been graced with for many years – a formidable home record. Only Arsenal won more home games but at the end of the season it was poor away form which cost the Hammers the chance of playing in Europe after a 17-year absence.

Manager Harry Redknapp brought in Eyal Berkovic (one of the buys of the season), Andy Impey and Craig Forrest at a cost of almost £3.5m and added David Unsworth three days into the season for a further £1m. In October Ian Pearce was snapped up for £1.6m and after the turn of the year more attacking flair was brought to the side with the £2.3m signing of Trevor Sinclair. With the sale of Slaven Bilic, all Redknapp's summer outgoings were covered in one transfer.

Redknapp had been criticised for seemingly paying over the odds during the previous season for John Hartson, but the Welsh international scored in wins over Barnsley and Tottenham as West Ham won their opening two games for the first time in 11 years. Hartson ended the season as second only to Andy Cole in the league and cup goalscoring stakes. But for disciplinary problems, and suspensions he could well have reached the 30 mark. Injury deprived him of his strike partner Paul Kitson for much of the season – the former Newcastle man making just 13 appearances but still managing to contribute four goals.

Hopes of building on their promising start were undone to some degree by their away record which saw them lose on nine of the next ten trips away from Upton

Club Data File

Responsibility

Top Scorer:	John Hartson (15)
Sent Off:	Samassi Abou, John Hartson (twice), Steve Lomas, David Unsworth

Usage

Total:	469 players used
Substitutes:	51 used, 139 not used

Players 1997-98

Most Used Sub:	Steve Potts (9)
Most SNU:	Craig Forrest (21), Steve Potts (12), Ian Bishop (12)
Most Subbed:	Eyal Berkovic (12)

Five-Year Form

	Div.	P	W	D	L	F	A	Pts	Pos
93-94	PL	42	13	13	16	47	58	52	13
94-95	PL	42	13	11	18	44	48	50	14
95-96	PL	38	14	9	15	43	52	51	10
96-97	PL	38	10	12	16	39	48	42	14
97-98	PL	38	16	8	14	56	57	56	8

Park. But at home West Ham were almost unstoppable, with defeat by Newcastle being the only blemish in the first ten home games. Most impressive victories were over Liverpool 2-1, Crystal Palace 4-1 and Barnsley 6-0 during which French youngster Samassi Abou scored his first two goals for the club. A run of eight consecutive away defeats was halted two days after Christmas when the double was completed over Wimbledon and after a defeat at Tottenham the Hammers won their third and last away match with revenge over Newcastle.

With injuries to goalkeepers, Redknapp brought in Bernard Lama on loan from Paris St-Germain and his form between the sticks helped propel the Hammers towards a European spot. UEFA Cup qualification was a genuine possibility even up until the last day of the season but a run of one win in seven games during April and May dented their prospects. A 4-2 home defeat by Southampton made qualification unlikely but the season had an amazing finale with Hammers' supporters seeing 24 goals in just four games.

Discipline was a major problem for the Upton Park side – their five red cards (including two for Hartson) being shown to key players at vital points in the season.

With players returning from injury and others starting their first full season at West Ham, the Hammers could well provide a few upsets along the way in the season ahead. To sustain a real challenge and ensure the UEFA Cup spot they will be looking for, they will need to take care of their form away from East London.

Harry Redknapp

Having delved into the realm of European stars for 1996-97, the West Ham manager reverted to more locally grown talent for 1997-98 and it proved to be one of the most successful seasons of recent times. Central to this was his capture – ridiculed by many at the time – of John Hartson, followed by the signing of Berkovic.

Redknapp is West Ham, having played there in a distinguished career, often as an old-fashioned winger. He played in more than 170 games but never won any major honours – a semi final League Cup defeat by Stoke City in 1971 being the nearest he came.

He began on the managerial front as an assistant to Bobby Moore at Oxford City before he moved on to Bournemouth and guided them to an Associate Members Cup win and a third division championship title in 1987. Having suffered a serious car injury, he returned to nurture his son Jamie and his move to Liverpool. His chance at Upton Park came as assistant to Billy Bonds in 1991, whom he eventually replaced as manager.

Now in his fourth year in charge, a European placing at the very least should be the minimum the Hammers achieve under him this season.

West Ham United v Opponents Record

Opponents	92-3	93-4	94-5	95-6	96-7	97-8	P	W	D	L	F	A	Pts	%
Arsenal	-	0-0	0-2	0-1	1-2	0-0	5	0	2	3	1	5	2	13.33
Aston Villa	-	0-0	1-0	1-4	0-2	2-1	5	2	1	2	4	7	7	46.67
Blackburn Rovers	-	1-2	2-0	1-1	2-1	2-1	5	3	1	1	8	5	10	66.67
Charlton Athletic	-						0	0	0	0	0	0	0	0.00
Chelsea	-	1-0	1-2	1-3	3-2	2-1	5	3	0	2	8	8	9	60.00
Coventry City	-	3-2	0-1	3-2	1-1	1-0	5	3	1	1	8	6	10	66.67
Derby County	-	-	-	-	1-1	0-0	2	0	2	0	1	1	2	33.33
Everton	-	0-1	2-2	2-1	2-2	2-2	5	1	3	1	8	8	6	40.00
Leeds United	-	0-1	0-0	1-2	0-2	3-0	5	1	1	3	4	5	4	26.67
Leicester City	-	-	1-0	-	1-0	4-3	3	3	0	0	6	3	9	100.00
Liverpool	-	1-2	3-0	0-0	1-2	2-1	5	2	1	2	7	5	7	46.67
Manchester United	-	2-2	1-1	0-1	2-2	1-1	5	0	4	1	6	7	4	26.67
Middlesbrough	-	-	-	2-0	0-0		2	1	1	0	2	0	4	66.67
Newcastle United	-	2-4	1-3	2-0	0-0	0-1	5	1	1	3	5	8	4	26.67
Nottingham Forest	-	-	3-1	1-0	0-1		3	2	0	1	4	2	6	66.67
Sheffield Wednesday	-	2-0	0-2	1-1	5-1	1-0	5	3	1	1	9	4	10	66.67
Southampton	-	3-3	2-0	2-1	2-1	2-1	5	4	1	0	11	6	13	86.67
Tottenham Hotspur	-	1-3	1-2	1-1	4-3	2-1	5	2	1	2	9	10	7	46.67
Wimbledon	-	0-2	3-0	1-1	0-2	3-1	5	2	1	2	7	6	7	46.67

Transfers

In

Month	Player	Signed From	Fee
Aug-97	David Unsworth	Everton	Swap
Sep-97	Ian Pearce	Blackburn R.	£1.6m rising to £2.3m
Sep-97	Andy Impey	QPR	£1.3m
Oct-97	Samassi Abou	Cannes	£300,000
Jan-98	Trevor Sinclair	QPR	£2.3m
Feb-98	Stephen Bywater	Rochdale	£300,000 rising to £2.3m
Mar-98	Mohamed Berthe	Gaz Ajaccio	Free
Jul-98	Shaka Hislop	Newcastle U.	Free
Jul-98	Ian Wright	Arsenal	Undisclosed

Out

Month	Player	Signed For	Fee
Aug-97	Danny Williamson	Everton	Swap + £1.0m
Sep-97	Marc Rieper	Celtic	£1.4m
Sep-97	Michael Hughes	Wimbledon	£800,000 rising to £1.6m
Jan-98	David Terrier	Newcastle U.	Free
Jan-98	Iain Dowie	QPR	Swap
Jan-98	Keith Rowland	QPR	Swap
Mar-98	Steven Blaney	Brentford	Free
Mar-98	Ian Bishop	Manchester C.	Free

Fantasy Football Handbook 1998/99

Wimbledon

Wimbledon started and finished the 1997-98 season poorly but in between did just enough to take their remarkable run in the top flight of English football into a 13th year. Yet again manager Joe Kinnear will not have been in the running for the Manager of the Year Award, but the achievements of a club still searching for its own permanent home are a tribute to the former Eire international. Time and again the Dons have been written off but it does look as though Kinnear will need to modify his squad during the close season after ending the campaign with one win in ten games and only scoring in three of those matches.

The Dons made just one summer signing with Ceri Hughes joining from Luton at an eventual cost of £1.15m while £3.5m was collected from Oyvind Leonhardsen's move to Liverpool. Close on that figure was also made from Dean Holdsworth's move to Bolton and in March the notorious Vinnie Jones moved across the capital to QPR for £500,000. Early in the season Kinnear brought in Michael Hughes for £800,000 and as the transfer deadline moved closer he also signed Andy Roberts, Mark Kennedy and Carl Leaburn for a little over £3m.

Wimbledon began the season with three successive home matches. Marcus Gayle and Jason Euell scored in draws with Liverpool and Sheffield Wednesday before Chelsea won 2-0 at Selhurst Park.

Defeat at West Ham handed the Dons an early visit to the foot of the table but a fine 3-1 win at Newcastle and, two matches later, a 4-1 home win over Barnsley, gave them breathing space. A draw at Tottenham suggested that Wimbledon were on the way up only for Blackburn to win the next match at Selhurst Park. Indeed the Dons had to wait until February until they won two consecutive matches with a 3-0 win over

Club Data File

Responsibility

Top Scorers:	Four goals – multiple
Sent Off:	Ben Thatcher (twice)

Usage

Total:	487 players used
Substitutes:	69 used, 121 not used

Players 1997-98

Most Used Sub:	Andy Clarke (13)
Most SNU:	Paul Heald (38), Andy Clarke (13)
Most Subbed:	Marcus Gayle (13)

Five-Year Form

	Div.	P	W	D	L	F	A	Pts	Pos
93-94	PL	42	18	11	13	56	53	65	6
94-95	PL	42	15	11	16	48	65	56	9
95-96	PL	38	10	11	17	55	70	41	14
96-97	PL	38	15	11	12	49	46	56	8
97-98	PL	38	10	14	14	34	46	44	15

Crystal Palace and a 2-1 success against Aston Villa. Leaburn scored three times in those two games, having joined the club a month earlier from Charlton Athletic where he earned a reputation for being a striker who couldn't score goals. On the flipside, Wimbledon's longest losing run was also just two games while their total of 14 draws was the second highest in the Premiership.

The Dons' run over the last ten games is particularly alarming as they failed to score in seven of the games, drew five of those matches 0–0 and were hammered 5-0 and 6-2 by Arsenal and Spurs. Peter Fear scored two excellent goals against Tottenham, which were his first Premiership goals for the club since December 1994.

Scoring goals was ultimately the problem for Wimbledon who achieved their lowest goals for tally – just 34 – since they were promoted into the professional ranks. Nevertheless they remained as tight as ever at the back with Neil Sullivan being ever present and conceding just 44 goals – only bettered three times in the same period. The Dons' tally of just 10 wins was their lowest ever for a season.

Joe Kinnear

How much longer Joe Kinnear can produce the drive and commitment that have kept the Dons in the top flight in recent year on a small budget remains to be seen. One suspects that the lure of a 'big' club with 'big' resources will ultimately prove too much to resist. Last year did not provide the sparkle that had been present in his teams play in previous seasons.

Kinnear was appointed the Dons' manager at the start of 1992 having previously held the position of coach and assistant manager at the club. His managerial career started at Doncaster Rovers where he began as an assistant to Dave Mackay, ultimately taking over as manager for a three month period at the end of the 1988-89 season.

Kinnear played most of his professional football at Tottenham, making the full-back position his own and playing over 300 games in a period from 1963 to 1975. A Republic of Ireland international he won medals in the FA Cup, the League Cup (twice) and UEFA Cup with Spurs, before injury ended his career during a spell at Brighton.

Wimbledon v Opponents Record

Opponents	92-3	93-4	94-5	95-6	96-7	97-8	P	W	D	L	F	A	Pts	%
Arsenal	3-2	0-3	1-3	0-3	2-2	0-1	6	1	1	4	6	14	4	22.22
Aston Villa	2-3	2-2	4-3	3-3	0-2	2-1	6	2	2	2	13	14	8	44.44
Blackburn Rovers	1-1	4-1	0-3	1-1	1-0	0-1	6	2	2	2	7	7	8	44.44
Charlton Athletic	-	-	-	-	-	-	0	0	0	0	0	0	0	0.00
Chelsea	0-0	1-1	1-1	1-1	0-1	0-2	6	0	4	2	3	6	4	22.22
Coventry City	1-2	1-2	2-0	0-2	2-2	1-2	6	1	1	4	7	10	4	22.22
Derby County	-	-	-	-	1-1	0-0	2	0	2	0	1	1	2	33.33
Everton	1-3	1-1	2-1	2-3	4-0	0-0	6	2	2	2	10	8	8	44.44
Leeds United	1-0	1-0	0-0	2-4	2-0	1-0	6	4	1	1	7	4	13	72.22
Leicester City	-	-	2-1	-	1-3	2-1	3	2	0	1	5	5	6	66.67
Liverpool	2-0	1-1	0-0	1-0	2-1	1-1	6	3	3	0	7	3	12	66.67
Manchester United	1-2	1-0	0-1	2-4	0-3	2-5	6	1	0	5	6	15	3	16.67
Middlesbrough	2-0	-	-	0-0	1-1		3	1	2	0	3	1	5	55.56
Newcastle United	-	4-2	3-2	3-3	1-1	0-0	5	2	3	0	11	8	9	60.00
Nottingham Forest	1-0	-	2-2	1-0	1-0	-	4	3	1	0	5	2	10	83.33
Sheffield Wednesday	1-1	2-1	0-1	2-2	4-2	1-1	6	2	3	1	10	8	9	50.00
Southampton	1-2	1-0	0-2	1-2	3-1	1-0	6	3	0	3	7	7	9	50.00
Tottenham Hotspur	1-1	2-1	1-2	0-1	1-0	2-6	6	2	1	3	7	11	7	38.89
West Ham United	-	1-2	1-0	0-1	1-1	1-2	5	1	1	3	4	6	4	26.67

Transfers

In

Month	Player	Signed From	Fee
Sep-97	Michael Hughes	West Ham U.	£800,000 rising to £1.6m
Oct-97	Staale Solbakken	Lillestrom	£250,000
Jan-98	Carl Leaburn	Charlton A.	£300,000
Mar-98	Andy Roberts	C. Palace	£1.2m rising to £1.6m
Mar-98	Mark Kennedy	Liverpool	£1.75m

Out

Month	Player	Signed For	Fee
Oct-97	Dean Holdsworth	Bolton W.	£3.5m
Jun-98	Alan Reeves	Swindon Town	Free

Player Directory

Guide to Player Directory

The Player Directory contains details of over 400 potential Premiership footballers and provides vital three-season form information which will help you make your fantasy selections. Each entry follows the same format, although there are some differences for goalkeeper entries and these are outlined below. Use the Player Directory information along with that provided in the Team Directory and the various tables throughout this book to ensure you get the best value from your purchasing budget. Remember that you are seeking consistent performers and sometimes the big-name players can obscure the performances of the majority of the players who provide the backbone of their team.

Star Ratings

Each entry starts with the player's name and the club he was registered with at the time of writing. This is followed by his position and a star rating. Ratings are out of five: a player who has ❶❷❸❹❺ is considered a top buy, while a rating of a ❶ suggests that he probably isn't worth considering for your team! However don't immediately dismiss any player. A rating can also mean that he is simply unlikely to be in the side's starting line-up. Read the text because, should an injury thrust the player into the limelight, you could find yourself with a real bargain on your hands!

This information is followed by the player's full name and date/place of birth. The body of the entry is the pen pic – a profile of the player which summarises his strengths and weaknesses, together with some general information regarding his performances last season.

Form Factors

Form Factors provide the hard stats behind the player in the Premiership for the previous three-season period. Note that only Premiership details are listed here, thus if a player has been out of the top flight, or has missed a year, the seasons listed might not be concurrent and may not finish with the 1997-98 season. This is especially true of course with the three promoted teams. However, more detailed figures relating to all players including the promoted teams can be found in the section headed Appearance Fact File. This includes details you are unlikely to find elsewhere, including how many times a player was subbed last year, for example.

Back to the Player Directory: The format and information differ according to the position in which the player plays. For example, a goalkeeper entry concentrates on goals conceded and clean sheets as opposed to an entry for a forward, which concentrates on goals scored and the percentage of the goals he gets for his team.

Nevertheless the arrangement is

straightforward and provides some basic information about the number of games the player appeared in, both as a starter and as a sub, along with details on the number of yellow and red cards they accumulated. Remember that red cards mean missed matches and yellow cards can mean suspensions as well. As a rule of thumb, five yellow cards will earn the recipient a suspension.

The key to these stats is as follows:
Tot   Total appearances for the season
St   Starting appearances
Sb   Sub appearances
Y   Yellow cards received
R   Red cards received

These figures are provided for all players and are followed by a look inside the numbers and an attempt to analyse the player's contribution to his team for each season. These are done on a strict season-by-season basis even if the player has played for two Premiership clubs in a season. In this case the numbers for the season are combined and the percentages calculated from the combined figures where appropriate.

There are therefore two possible sets of information. For all outfield players (not goalkeepers) the following information is provided:

GP   Game Percentage – this is the percentage of the Premiership games the player played in for that season. Thus a player with a 50.00 rating here would have played in half of the team's Premier League games.

GG   Game Goals – this is the number of games a player takes to score a goal. A rating of 5.25 would means the player scores a goal every 5.25 games. A figure of 0.00 indicates no goals.

GF   Goals For – the goals the player's team scored in the season.

GS   Goals Scored – the goals the player scored that season.

TGR   Team Goal Ratio – the percentage of the team's goals that the player scored.

Goalkeeper summaries concentrate on the number of goals they have or haven't conceded as the case may be. The key here is:

GA   Goals Against – the goals the 'keeper's team conceded in the relevant season.

GkA   Goals 'Keeper Against – the number of goals that the goalkeeper conceded for the season.

GAp   Goals/Appearance Ratio – the average number of goals the 'keeper concedes in a game.

CS   Clean Sheets – the number of occasions the 'keeper didn't concede a goal in a game.

SO   Shut Outs – the most number of full games in succession a goalkeeper went without conceding a goal.

R   Repeated – How often the shut-out was repeated.

An Example

An example Form Factors entry can be seen below. From this we can see that the player played for Arsenal in the Premiership during the past three seasons. Most of the time the player started games but the yellow and red card count shows that a large number of games could have been lost through suspensions in this period.

Form Factors

Season	Team	Tot	St	Sb	Y	R
95-96	Arsenal	27	27	0	4	1
96-97	Arsenal	21	21	0	4	1
97-98	Arsenal	28	27	1	5	2
Total		76	75	1	13	4

	GP	GG	GF	GS	TGR
95-96	64.29	9.00	52	3	5.77
96-97	55.26	21.00	49	1	2.04
97-98	73.68	9.33	62	3	4.84
Averages	64.41	13.11	54.33	2.33	4.22

The total averages on the final line show that the 76 games played during the three seasons amounted to a little over 64% of the club's Premiership games with the player scoring a goal on average every 13th game or so – this accounting for 4.22% of the team's goals during the three-year period.

Below is the second half of the Form Factors entry as it might appear for a goalkeeper. From the first line – season 1995-96 – we can see that his team conceded 56 goals, 43 of which the 'keeper was in goal for. This worked out to an average of 1.43 goals per game. Obviously this figure (GAp) is a key one as it tells you a lot about the 'keeper and his defence. The lower this figure the better for your fantasy team!

Beyond that we can see that there were six clean sheets in those games and the longest shut out was two games and this wasn't repeated.

	GA	GkA	GAp	CS	SO	R
95-96	56	43	1.43	6	2	0
96-97	35	34	0.89	13	2	0
97-98	34	17	0.85	9	2	0
Total	125	94	1.07	28	6	

The final line is simply a totalling of the figure above with an overall average given for the GAp total.

ABOU, Samassi

West Ham U.   ①② S
Fullname: Samassi Abou
DOB: 04-04-73 Gabnoa, Ivory Coast

Despite being substituted in six of his 12 Premiership starts for West Ham last season, Abou was quickly accepted by the Hammers' faithful and by the end of the season had scored five goals in 19 league games; he also scored once in seven cup ties. Skilful striker who looks as though he could be a real handful over the coming months and revels in the 'a-boooo' chants which echo around Upton Park whenever he is possession. A French Under-21 international.

Form Factors

Season	Team	Tot	St	Sb	Y	R
97-98	West Ham U.	19	12	7	1	1
Total		19	12	7	1	1

	GP	GG	GF	GS	TGR
97-98	50.00	3.80	56	5	8.93
Averages	50.00	3.80	56.00	5.00	8.93

ADAMS, Tony

Arsenal   ①②③④⑤ CB
Fullname: Anthony Alexander Adams
DOB: 10-10-66 Romford, Essex

Possibly the most respected defender in the Premiership and, despite the hounding he gets from opposition supporters, Adams is the central defender that every fan would love to have in their side. Was at the heart of the Arsenal defence for their championship successes of '89 and '91 and overcame personal problems and injury to lead them to a glorious league and cup double last season. The title celebrations went into

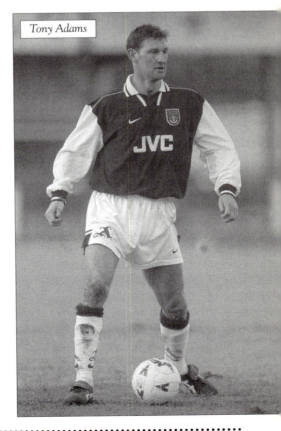

Tony Adams

Fantasy Football Handbook 1998/99

full swing once Adams scored with a powerful drive during a win over Everton which clinched the championship. It was one of three Premiership goals he scored last season taking his career total in the league with Arsenal to 30 in 421 games.

Crowned a magnificent year with what is likely to be his final World Cup campaign in France 98.

Since joining Arsenal as a schoolboy he has won Football League and Premier championships, the FA Cup, Coca Cola Cup and the Cup Winners' Cup. What he may now lack in speed he more than compensates for with a masterful reading of the game and will continue to be a major influence at Highbury during the 1998-99 season.

Form Factors

Season	Team	Tot	St	Sb	Y	R
95-96	Arsenal	21	21	0	4	1
96-97	Arsenal	28	27	1	5	2
97-98	Arsenal	26	26	0	6	0
Total		75	74	1	15	3

	GP	GG	GF	GS	TGR
95-96	55.26	21.00	49	1	2.04
96-97	73.68	9.33	62	3	4.84
97-98	68.42	8.67	68	3	4.41
Averages	65.79	13.00	59.67	2.33	3.76

AGOGO, Junior

Sheffield W. ❶ S

Fullname: Junior Agogo
DOB: 1-08-79 Ghana

Made his Sheffield Wednesday debut when coming on as a substitute during the Owls' first Premiership match of last season but unfortunately for him it proved to be his only taste of first team football that season.

Tall and powerfully built, the teenage striker will doubtless be looking to make further inroads at Hillsborough this season but it may be a bit early to include him in your fantasy team.

ALBERT, Philippe

Newcastle U. ❶❷ CB

Fullname: Philippe Albert
DOB: 10-08-67 Bouillon, Belgium

Elegant Belgian defender who has played five times for his country, and with his willingness to move forward with the ball he was one of the stars of Kevin Keegan's Newcastle but has found his chances more limited under Kenny Dalglish. Failed to score during 1997-98 for only the second time in 11 years as a professional but that probably reflects more on Newcastle's approach to the game rather than any failings on Albert's part. Played 23 times in the Premiership last season but regularly fell foul of match officials as he collected eight yellow cards.

Joined Newcastle in 1994 from Anderlecht for £2.65m having previously played on the continent for Mechelen and Charleroi.

Form Factors

Season	Team	Tot	St	Sb	Y	R
95-96	Newcastle U.	23	19	4	5	0
96-97	Newcastle U.	27	27	0	6	0
97-98	Newcastle U.	23	21	2	8	0
Total		73	67	6	19	0

	GP	GG	GF	GS	TGR
95-96	60.53	5.75	66	4	6.06
96-97	71.05	13.50	73	2	2.74
97-98	60.53	0.00	35	0	0.00
Averages	64.04	6.42	58.00	2.00	2.93

ALEXANDERSSON, Niclas

Sheffield W. ❶ M

Fullname: Niclas Alexandersson
DOB: 29-12-71 Vessigebro, Sweden

Swedish international Alexandersson created a good impact at Hillsborough when making his debut on Boxing Day last season during a 0-0 draw with Blackburn Rovers. Looks to be an excellent purchase at just £750,000 and has plenty of top level experience having played for two seasons in the Champions League with IFK Gothenburg. Unfortunately it seems unlikely that he will be able to aid Sheffield Wednesday's cause until the turn of the year after cruelly suffering a cruciate ligament injury after just seven games and one goal for the Owls.

Form Factors

Season	Team	Tot	St	Sb	Y	R
97-98	Sheffield W.	6	5	1	0	0
Total		6	5	1	0	0

	GP	GG	GF	GS	TGR
97-98	15.79	0.00	52	0	0.00
Averages	15.79	0.00	52.00	0.00	0.00

ALLEN, Bradley

Charlton A. ❶ S

Fullname: Bradley James Allen
DOB: 13-09-71 Romford

Since making a move from Queens Park Rangers to Charlton Athletic on transfer deadline day in 1996 Allen has endured little but setbacks with a succession of injuries. When he did regain his fitness during last season his place in the side had already been taken and he faced a frustrating wait on the sidelines.

Prior to his latest blow Allen possessed a very decent goals per game ratio but throughout his career the number of games played, 121 league games in 10 years, has always been low. In that time he has scored 36 goals.

ALLEN, Graham

Everton ❶❷ FB

Fullname: Graham Allen
DOB: 08-04-77 Franworth

Defender who made his Everton debut on Boxing Day 1996 and continued to make progress during 1997-98 despite only starting in two Premiership matches. Made three further appearances when coming on as a substitute and has become very much a part of the first team squad with seven other occasions when he was an unused substitute. A one time Everton trainee who has won caps with England at youth level.

Form Factors

Season	Team	Tot	St	Sb	Y	R
96-97	Everton	1	0	1	0	0
97-98	Everton	5	2	3	1	0
Total		6	2	4	1	0

	GP	GG	GF	GS	TGR
96-97	2.63	0.00	44	0	0.00
97-98	13.16	0.00	41	0	0.00
Averages	7.89	0.00	42.50	0.00	0.00

ALLEN, Rory

Tottenham H. ❶❷ S

Fullname: Rory William Allen
DOB: 17-10-77 Beckenham

Made a big impression during his early games in the Tottenham first team but then failed to hold down a regular place in the side. Played just four times for Spurs last season but had a successful spell on loan to Luton Town where his six goals in eight games helped the Hatters escape relegation.

During this past summer he played for England Under-21s in the Toulon tournament in France. Spurs have a great deal of faith in his ability and he could yet force his way through to the first team.

Form Factors

Season	Team	Tot	St	Sb	Y	R
96-97	Tottenham H.	12	9	3	4	0
97-98	Tottenham H.	13	13	0	0	0
Total		25	22	3	4	0

	GP	GG	GF	GS	TGR
96-97	31.58	6.00	44	2	4.55
97-98	34.21	0.00	44	0	0.00
Averages	32.89	3.00	44.00	1.00	2.27

ANDERSSON, Anders

Blackburn R. ❶❷❸ M

Fullname: Anders Andersson
DOB: 15-03-74 Tomellia, Sweden

No stranger to manager Roy Hodgson who brought him through the ranks at Malmo prior to returning to England. Andersson joined Blackburn Rovers in July 1997 with a good pedigree as a Swedish international but had to be content with a squad place in his first season at Ewood Park. A midfielder, he is likely to come more to the fore this season.

Form Factors

Season	Team	Tot	St	Sb	Y	R
97-98	Blackburn R.	4	1	3	0	0
Total		4	1	3	0	0

	GP	GG	GF	GS	TGR
97-98	10.53	0.00	57	0	0.00
Averages	10.53	0.00	57.00	0.00	0.00

ANDERSSON, Andreas

Newcastle U. ❶❷❸❹ S

Fullname: Andreas Andersson
DOB: 10-04-74 Stockholm, Sweden

Kenny Dalglish finally got his man in January 1998 when he signed Andersson from AC Milan for £3.6m, having previously attempted to sign the Swedish international during his time as manager of Blackburn. A powerful figure when surging forward with the ball, he moved to Newcastle after failing to establish himself at Milan. Played for several clubs in his homeland with a move to Gothenburg setting a record for a transfer between two Swedish clubs.

Form Factors

Season	Team	Tot	St	Sb	Y	R
97-98	Newcastle U.	12	10	2	0	0
Total		12	10	2	0	0

	GP	GG	GF	GS	TGR
97-98	31.58	6.00	35	2	5.71
Averages	31.58	6.00	35.00	2.00	5.71

ANDERTON, Darren

Tottenham H. ❶❷❸❹ M

Fullname: Darren Robert Anderton
DOB: 03-03-72 Southampton

Darren Anderton

Possibly one of the most gifted and exciting players currently playing in the Premiership but has seldom been able to demonstrate his quality over the past three seasons due to injury. England coach Glenn Hoddle, like his predecessor, was prepared to overlook his absence from the Tottenham team to gamble on his fitness for France 98. Anderton justified Hoddle's faith with some superb right-sided performances and the first goal in a crucial 2-0 win over Colombia.

A fully fit Anderton will be a huge bonus for Spurs as they look to climb out of Arsenal's shadow with Chris Armstrong and Les Ferdinand likely to benefit most from his return.

Anderton's injuries restricted him to just seven starts for Tottenham last season – he only played a full 90 minutes in two of those games – and his last goal was against Liverpool in May 1997 but if he can steer clear of injury then he should chip in with a good number of goals of his own and be a good point accumulator in fantasy football.

Form Factors

Season	Team	Tot	St	Sb	Y	R
95-96	Tottenham H.	8	6	2	0	0
96-97	Tottenham H.	16	14	2	4	0
97-98	Tottenham H.	15	7	8	0	0
Total		39	27	12	4	0

Season	GP	GG	GF	GS	TGR
95-96	21.05	4.00	50	2	4.00
96-97	42.11	5.33	44	3	6.82
97-98	39.47	0.00	44	0	0.00
Averages	34.21	3.11	46.00	1.67	3.61

ANELKA, Nicolas

Arsenal ❶❷❸ S

Fullname: Nicolas Anelka
DOB: 27-03-79 Versailles

Manager Arsène Wenger has taken great pains to shield the shy Anelka from the limelight and this approach has paid rich dividends in the teenage Frenchman's first season in the Premiership. He made 26 appearances in the Premiership last season but of these just three lasted for the full 90 minutes. Despite the regularity with which he was withdrawn he scored a very creditable six league goals and two in the FA Cup including the Gunners' second in the final against Newcastle.

Is likely to come even more to the fore this season as Wenger is almost certain to let him off the leash for longer periods with his dynamic pace, control and pinpoint passing being central to Arsenal's chances of glory in the Champions League.

Form Factors

Season	Team	Tot	St	Sb	Y	R
96-97	Arsenal	4	0	4	0	0
97-98	Arsenal	26	16	10	3	0
Total		30	16	14	3	0

	GP	GG	GF	GS	TGR
96-97	10.53	0.00	62	0	0.00
97-98	68.42	4.33	68	6	8.82
Averages	39.47	2.17	65.00	3.00	4.41

ARDLEY, Neal

Wimbledon ❶❷ M

Fullname: Neal Christopher Ardley
DOB: 01-09-72 Epsom

Has become an established member of Joe Kinnear's Wimbledon side over the past two years missing just eight Premiership matches during that time and is in line to play his 150th game in the Premiership early in 1998-99. A former England Under-21 international who, like many of his team-mates down the years, has worked his way through the ranks at Wimbledon after joining as a trainee. Although a ball-playing midfielder with a high workrate, Ardley will not get you many goals with his best return of four goals coming during the 1992-93 season.

Nicolas Anelka

100   Fantasy Football Handbook 1998/99

Neal Ardley

Form Factors

Season	Team	Tot	St	Sb	Y	R
95-96	Wimbledon	6	4	2	1	0
96-97	Wimbledon	34	33	1	1	0
97-98	Wimbledon	34	31	3	1	0
Total		74	68	6	3	0

	GP	GG	GF	GS	TGR
95-96	15.79	0.00	55	0	0.00
96-97	89.47	17.00	49	2	4.08
97-98	89.47	17.00	34	2	5.88
Averages	64.91	11.33	46.00	1.33	3.32

ARMSTRONG, Alun

Middlesbrough ❶ S

Fullname: Alun Armstrong
DOB: 22-02-75 Gateshead

A former Newcastle United trainee who returned to the north-east just before the transfer deadline to become an important part in Middlesbrough's push for a place in the Premiership. A back injury restricted him to just seven starts but he still smashed in seven goals to give Robson's side the impetus it needed to see off Sunderland's brave challenge.

Given Boro's other big money signing at around the same time, the acquisition of Armstrong, who scored 36 times in three full seasons with Stockport County, is definitely one for the future and he could well be one to look out for if you need a striker on the cheaper side to complete your attack.

Fantasy Football Handbook 1998/99

ARMSTRONG, Chris

Tottenham H. ❶❷❸ S

Fullname: Christopher Peter Armstrong
DOB: 19-06-71 Newcastle

Undoubtedly a top quality striker who will score goals but, along with a good number of his Tottenham team-mates, has been sidelined by injury for much of the past two seasons. Missed Spurs' first nine games of the 1997-98 season and then sat out the middle three months of the campaign with a foot injury. Managed to squeeze in 22 appearances, seven as sub, and score four times in the Premiership and once in the Coca Cola Cup. If his injury hit days are behind him then he should flourish with the return of Darren Anderton.

Started his career with spells at Wrexham and Millwall and signed for Spurs from Crystal Palace for a club record £4.5m in July 1995. A successful season could yet see Armstrong back in the frame for an England call up.

Form Factors

Season	Team	Tot	St	Sb	Y	R
95-96	Tottenham H.	36	36	0	5	0
96-97	Tottenham H.	12	12	0	2	0
97-98	Tottenham H.	19	13	6	2	0
Total		67	61	6	9	0

	GP	GG	GF	GS	TGR
95-96	94.74	2.40	50	15	30.00
96-97	31.58	2.40	44	5	11.36
97-98	50.00	3.80	44	5	11.36
Averages	58.77	2.87	46.00	8.33	17.58

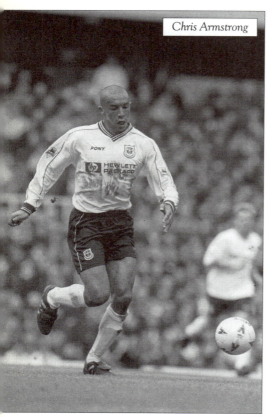

Chris Armstrong

ARMSTRONG, Craig

Nottingham F. ❶❷ M

Fullname: Steven Craig Armstrong
DOB: 23-05-75 South Shields

Spent five fruitless seasons at Nottingham Forest before finally making the breakthrough last season with 17 Football League appearances although only four of those games were from the start. A midfielder, he also scored his first goal for the club last season as Forest bowed out of the Coca Cola Cup at Walsall. Gained his first experience of senior football while on loan to Burnley in December 1994 and then made 14 loan appearances with Bristol Rovers the following season.

ARPHEXAD, Pegguy

Leicester C. ❶❷ GK
Fullname: Pegguy Arphexad
DOB:

French Under-21 goalkeeper who joined Leicester from Racing Club Lens after the 1996-97 season and had five run-outs in the Premiership last season. Conceded six goals in his five games at an average of 1.2 per game which was just above Leicester's Premiership average for the season of almost 1.1. His hopes of an extended run were partly dashed by injury which sidelined him for three months. Will have a tough task on his hands over the coming months to dislodge Kasey Keller.

Form Factors

Season	Team	Tot	St	Sb	Y	R
97-98	Leicester C.	5	5	0	0	0
Total		5	5	0	0	0

	GA	GkA	GAp	CS	SO	R
97-98	41	4	0.80	1	1	0
Averages	41	4	0.80	1	1	0

ATHERTON, Peter

Sheffield W. ❶❷❸ FB
Fullname: Peter Atherton
DOB: 06-04-70 Orrell

Sheffield Wednesday captain who, in a generally disappointing season for the Owls, performed consistently well by winning 75% of his tackles. But he had his campaign hindered by a long-term injury.

Joined Wednesday back in 1994 from Coventry City and in his first three seasons at Hillsborough missed just four Premiership matches, which put him third in the list of all time Premiership appearances. Injury restricted him to 26 league games in 1997-98, taking his total Premiership appearances to 219. Was switched to midfield last season and scored three times which is his best return in a career which has also taken in five years at Wigan Athletic and three seasons with Coventry. A former England Under-21 international who collected the Player of the Year award in his first season at Sheffield Wednesday.

Form Factors

Season	Team	Tot	St	Sb	Y	R
95-96	Sheffield W.	35	35	0	6	0
96-97	Sheffield W.	37	37	0	7	0
97-98	Sheffield W.	27	27	0	7	0
Total		99	99	0	20	0

	GP	GG	GF	GS	TGR
95-96	92.11	0.00	48	0	0.00
96-97	97.37	18.50	50	2	4.00
97-98	71.05	9.00	52	3	5.77
Averages	86.84	9.17	50.00	1.67	3.26

BAARDSEN, Espen
Tottenham H. ❶❷ GK

Fullname: Espen Baardsen
DOB: San Rafael, Ca.

A full and Under-21 international goalkeeper with Norway who was actually born in California and represented the USA at Under-18 level. Made his debut in the Premiership for Tottenham Hotspur during the 1996-97 season and thanks to an injury sustained by Ian Walker enjoyed a run of 11 consecutive games for Spurs last season, nine in the league. Conceded 14 goals during his 11 games and kept three clean sheets and will go into the 1998-99 season once again as understudy to Walker but seems to have successfully seen off the challenge of midseason signing fellow Norwegian keeper Frode Grodas from Chelsea.

Form Factors

Season	Team	Tot	St	Sb	Y	R
96-97	Tottenham H.	2	1	1	0	0
97-98	Tottenham H.	9	9	0	0	0
Total		11	10	1	0	0

	GA	GkA	GAp	CS	SO	R
96-97	51	2	1.00	0	0	
97-98	56	10	1.11	3	1	0
Averages	53.50	6.00	1.06	1.50	0.5	0

BABAYARO, Celestine
Chelsea ❶❷❸ FB

Fullname: Celestine Babayaro
DOB: 29-08-78 Nigeria

Nigerian international who has been plagued by injury since signing for Chelsea from Anderlecht for £2.25m in the summer of 1997. His first injury setback came when celebrating a goal in a friendly and he was sidelined again in December with a toe injury. Played just 13 times for Chelsea last season but figured in Nigeria's France 98 side and earlier in his career won Olympic gold with his national side.

A left wing-back signed by Ruud Gullit at Chelsea he should, injury not withstanding, play a major part in Vialli's plans this season and at just 20 years old will be around for many years to come.

Form Factors

Season	Team	Tot	St	Sb	Y	R
97-98	Chelsea	8	8	0	0	0
Total		8	8	0	0	0

	GP	GG	GF	GS	TGR
97-98	21.05	0.00	71	0	0.00
Averages	21.05	0.00	71.00	0.00	0.00

BABB, Phil

Liverpool ❶❷ CB
Fullname: Phillip Andrew Babb
DOB: 30-11-70 London

Eire international defender who has struggled to hold down a first team place at Anfield over the past two seasons but he remains a versatile player who shines best in the middle of the defence. Comfortable on the ball, he slots in nicely with Liverpool's passing style but despite his dominance in the air at the back his quota of goals has dried up in recent years with the back of the net being found just once in the past four seasons.

A star of Eire's 1994 World Cup bid he began his career with Millwall – he was born in Lambeth – before scoring 14 times in two seasons with Bradford City. Spent just over two years with Coventry City before joining Liverpool in a £3.6m deal in September 1995, a move which made him the most expensive defender in Britain.

Form Factors

Season	Team	Tot	St	Sb	Y	R
95-96	Liverpool	28	28	0	2	0
96-97	Liverpool	22	21	1	5	0
97-98	Liverpool	19	18	1	0	5
Total		69	67	2	7	5

	GP	GG	GF	GS	TGR
95-96	73.68	0.00	70	0	0.00
96-97	57.89	22.00	62	1	1.61
97-98	50.00	0.00	68	0	0.00
Averages	60.53	7.33	66.67	0.33	0.54

BAIANO, Francesco

Derby County ❶❷❸❹ S
Fullname: Francesco Baiano
DOB: Napoli

Making the transition from Serie A to the Premiership proved little problem for Baiano whose £1.3m transfer from Fiorentina to Derby County in the summer of 1997 culminated a year later with the former Italian international picking up the Rams' Player of the Year award. With a dozen goals the 30 year old was Derby's second highest scorer in the Premiership but it was not only his goals which caught the eye but also his unselfish ability to bring others into play

Francesco Baiano

FANTASY Football Handbook 1998/99   **105**

and create scoring chances for his team-mates.

Baiano featured in 33 of Derby's 38 league games and somewhat strangely for a player who enjoyed so much personal success he was the most substituted player in the Premiership with manager Jim Smith calling him out of the action early on no less than 16 occasions.

Form Factors

Season	Team	Tot	St	Sb	Y	R
97-98	Derby Co.	33	30	3	2	0
Total		33	30	3	2	0

	GP	GG	GF	GS	TGR
97-98	86.84	2.75	52	12	23.08
Averages	86.84	2.75	52.00	12.00	23.08

BALL, Michael

Everton ❶❷❸ M

Fullname: Michael Ball
DOB: 02-10-77 Liverpool

Local born midfielder who really came to prominence last season. Made his first team debut for Everton towards the end of the 1996-97 season and after not being included in any of Everton's first six matches of 1997-98 scored in his first start against Arsenal in September. But it was only on Boxing Day, against Manchester United, that he became a regular with an unbroken run through to the end of the season.

Ball has played for England Youth and Under-21 and has shown himself to be a versatile player turning out in defence and at left wing-back. Composed on the ball he possesses a long throw and may be one of the best youngsters to shine in the Premiership this season.

Form Factors

Season	Team	Tot	St	Sb	Y	R
96-97	Everton	5	2	3	1	0
97-98	Everton	25	21	4	2	0
Total		30	23	7	3	0

	GP	GG	GF	GS	TGR
96-97	13.16	0.00	44	0	0.00
97-98	65.79	25.00	41	1	2.44
Averages	39.47	12.50	42.50	0.50	1.22

BALMER, Stuart

Charlton A. ❶❷ CD

Fullname: Stuart Murray Balmer
DOB: 20-09-69 Falkirk

After three fruitless years with Celtic, central defender Balmer tried his luck south of the border with a £120,000 move to Charlton Athletic in August 1990. Since then the right-footed Scot, who has also played at right-back, has made a big impression on Addicks fans with his sheer consistency. He is good in possession, looks to use the ball sensibly and, crucially for a central defender, positive in dealing with aerial attacks.

Was kept out of the side for over four months last season after having an operation on a cartilage in his knee. Was not on the scoresheet in his 16 Nationwide League appearances last season which is the first time in six years he has failed to score.

BARMBY, Nicky

Everton ❶❷❸ F

Fullname: Nicholas Jonathan Barmby
DOB: 11-02-74 Hull

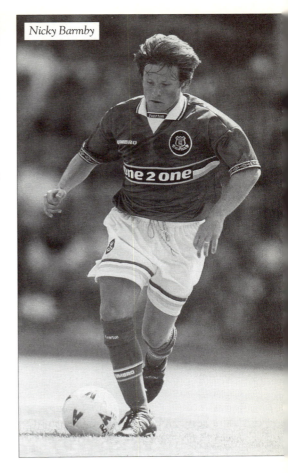
Nicky Barmby

Became one of the hottest properties in British football after breaking into the Tottenham Hotspur first team during the 1992-93 season. Found the back of the net 20 times in 87 league games for Spurs prior to a £5.25m move back north to Middlesbrough. Surprisingly stayed just 15 months on Teesside before switching across to Everton in another expensive, £5.75m, transfer. Barmby's career did not flourish as anticipated at Goodison Park during his early days on Merseyside but during the latter part of the 1997-98 season he showed signs of regaining much of his earlier flamboyance, and at just 24-years-old will almost certainly add to his 10 England appearances and three goals in the years to come.

Made 33 league and cup appearances for Everton last season scoring five times, and as a new regime looks to build a new era at Goodison Park Barmby is certain to be a vital part of those plans.

Form Factors

Season	Team	Tot	St	Sb	Y	R
96-97	Middlesbrough	10	10	0	0	0
96-97	Everton	25	22	3	0	0
97-98	Everton	30	26	4	0	7
Total		65	58	7	0	7

	GP	GG	GF	GS	TGR
96-97	26.32	10.00	51	1	1.96
96-97	65.79	6.25	44	4	9.09
97-98	78.95	15.00	41	2	4.88
Averages	57.02	10.42	45.33	2.33	5.31

Fantasy Football Handbook 1998/99

BARNES, John
Newcastle U. ❶❷ M
Fullname: John Charles Bryan Barnes
DOB: 07-11-63 Jamaica, W Indies

Very much at the veteran stage of his career but what Barnes may now lack in pace he conceals with his indisputable skills on the ball. Started the 1997-98 season as an unused substitute with Liverpool prior to a free transfer to Newcastle United which presented him with the opportunity to team up with long-time colleagues Kenny Dalglish and Ian Rush. Figured in 26 of Newcastle's relegation threatened Premiership matches, scoring six times, and made five appearances in the Magpies' run to the FA Cup final coming on as a substitute during the defeat by Arsenal at Wembley.

Will probably be used more sparingly in the future but can reflect on a highly successful career which includes 79 caps and 11 goals for England, two League championship successes with Liverpool and also FA Cup and Coca Cola Cup winners medals with the Reds.

Form Factors

Season	Team	Tot	St	Sb	Y	R
95-96	Liverpool	36	36	0	0	0
96-97	Liverpool	35	34	1	0	0
97-98	Newcastle U.	26	22	4	0	0
Total		97	92	5	0	0

	GP	GG	GF	GS	TGR
95-96	94.74	12.00	70	3	4.29
96-97	92.11	8.75	62	4	6.45
97-98	68.42	4.33	35	6	17.14
Averages	85.09	8.36	55.67	4.33	9.29

BARNESS, Anthony
Charlton A. ❶❷ D
Fullname: Anthony Barness
DOB: 25-03-73 Lewisham

Defender who seldom gets ruffled under pressure and is currently enjoying the most successful spell of his career. Originally with Charlton Athletic he returned to the Addicks after an unsuccessful three years at Chelsea which included loan periods with Middlesbrough and Southend United.

Missed just one game in 1996-97, scored his first goals for five years in the process, but was out of favour for a large part of last season although he did manage 30 league appearances of which nine were from the bench. Predominently played at left-back for Charlton but can also play on the right.

Form Factors

Season	Team	Tot	St	Sb	Y	R
92-93	Chelsea	2	2	0	0	0
94-95	Chelsea	12	10	2	1	0
95-96	Chelsea	0	0	0	0	0
Total		14	12	2	1	0

	GP	GG	GF	GS	TGR
92-93	5.26	0.00	51	0	0.00
94-95	31.58	0.00	50	0	0.00
95-96	0.00	0.00	46	0	0.00
Averages	12.28	0.00	49.00	0.00	0.00

BARRETT, Earl
Sheffield W ❶❷ FB
Fullname: Earl Delisser Barrett
DOB: 28-04-67 Rochdale

Experienced one time England defender who moved to Sheffield Wednesday on a free transfer in February 1998 from Everton having had a loan spell at Sheffield United. But Barrett did not experience the best of starts with the Owls as Wednesday won just three of their ten games with him in the side while Barrett himself picked up four yellow cards. Also had problems with referees at Everton with three more bookings being picked up in 13 games for the Merseysiders, all this in stark contrast to earlier in his career when he was seldom suspended.

Started his career with Manchester City and on loan to Chester City before teaming up with Joe Royle at Oldham Athletic where he made 183 league appearances. Signed for Aston Villa in a £1.7m deal before joining forces again with Royle at Everton. One of the best tacklers and man-markers in the Premiership in recent years but don't look for him to get you the occasional goal – his last strike was in February 1993.

Form Factors

Season	Team	Tot	St	Sb	Y	R
96-97	Everton	36	36	0	1	0
97-98	Everton	13	12	1	0	3
97-98	Sheffield W.	10	10	0	1	1
Total		59	58	1	2	4

	GP	GG	GF	GS	TGR
96-97	94.74	0.00	44	0	0.00
97-98	34.21	0.00	41	0	0.00
97-98	26.32	0.00	52	0	0.00
Averages	51.75	0.00	45.67	0.00	0.00

BART-WILLIAMS, Chris
Nottingham F. ❶❷❸ M
Fullname: Christopher Gerald Bart-Williams
DOB: 16-06-74 Freetown, Sierra Leone

Moved to Nottingham Forest at the end of the 1994-95 season for £2.5m and was immediately switched from a wide attacking position to more of a holding role in midfield. As a hardworking player it was something Bart-Williams could cope with but Forest only really began to get value for money when he was pushed forward again by new boss Dave Bassett.

Although not a prolific scorer he chipped in with four goals of his own last season, but his greatest contribution is his all-round commitment to the side as he works tirelessly to win possession.

Former England Under-21 international who started his career with Leyton Orient.

Form Factors

Season	Team	Tot	St	Sb	Y	R
94-95	Sheffield W.	38	32	6	6	0
95-96	N. Forest	33	33	0	2	0
96-97	N. Forest	16	16	0	1	0
Total		87	81	6	9	0

	GP	GG	GF	GS	TGR
94-95	100.00	19.00	49	2	4.08
95-96	86.84	0.00	50	0	0.00
96-97	42.11	16.00	31	1	3.23
Averages	76.32	11.67	43.33	1.00	2.44

BARTON, Warren

Newcastle U. ❶❷❸ FB

Fullname: Warren Dean Barton
DOB: 19-03-69 Stoke Newington

Started his career with two since defunct clubs, Leytonstone Ilford and Maidstone United, before embarking on five successful years with Wimbledon where he really made his mark as an attack-minded defender. Joined Newcastle in the summer of 1995 and made 31 Premiership appearances in 1995-96 under Kevin Keegan but has in the past two seasons has played fewer times under Kenny Dalglish although he was in Newcastle's FA Cup final side last May. Won his three England caps as a defender but was used quite often in midfield at St. James's Park last season. Needs just 29 games to complete 300 league appearances.

Form Factors

Season	Team	Tot	St	Sb	Y	R
95-96	Newcastle U.	31	30	1	3	0
96-97	Newcastle U.	18	14	4	1	0
97-98	Newcastle U.	23	17	6	7	0
Total		72	61	11	11	0

	GP	GG	GF	GS	TGR
95-96	81.58	0.00	66	0	0.00
96-97	47.37	18.00	73	1	1.37
97-98	60.53	7.67	35	3	8.57
Averages	63.16	8.56	58.00	1.33	3.31

BASHAM, Steve

Southampton ❶❷ S

Fullname: Steven Basham
DOB: 02-12-77 Southampton

Local-born Southampton forward who was used nine times as a substitute last season following six appearances the previous season as he is gradually eased into the first team. Has started in just one Premiership match thus far, against Manchester United, but has gained further experience whilst on loan to Wrexham. Solid centre-forward who shields the ball well, is good in the air and can shoot quite happily with either foot.

Form Factors

Season	Team	Tot	St	Sb	Y	R
96-97	Southampton	6	1	5	0	0
97-98	Southampton	9	0	9	0	0
Total		15	1	14	0	0

	GP	GG	GF	GS	TGR
96-97	15.79	1.00	50	6	12.00
97-98	23.68	0.00	50	0	0.00
Averages	19.74	0.50	50.00	3.00	6.00

BATTY, David

Newcastle U. ❶❷❸❹ M

Fullname: David Batty
DOB: 02-12-68 Leeds

Has become one of the most respected midfielders in the Premiership but suffered criticism during the World Cup for seemingly taking a negative option after winning possession. Whatever the merits of that criticism, Batty is one of the hardest and most successful tacklers in the game though taking penalties is clearly not one of his best points.

Has enjoyed success throughout his career starting with Leeds United where he was a member of their championship-winning side. Blackburn signed him early in the 1993-94 season for a bargain £2.7m. He won another championship medal during his two and a bit years at Ewood Park before signing for Newcastle in a £4.5m deal. Finished second with Newcastle in 1997 and made his first appearance in an FA Cup final a year later.

With the right players around him Batty will help revive Newcastle's league fortunes, but don't expect him to get many goals for your fantasy team; he has scored just once in each of the past four seasons and only once scored more than one goal in 11 years as a professional. You may also need to keep an eye on his discipline; he was dismissed three times last season and has collected 19 yellow cards over the past two seasons.

Form Factors

Season	Team	Tot	St	Sb	Y	R
95-96	Newcastle U.	11	11	0	2	0
96-97	Newcastle U.	32	32	0	10	1
97-98	Newcastle U.	32	32	0	9	3
Total		75	75	0	21	4

	GP	GG	GF	GS	TGR
95-96	28.95	11.00	66	1	1.52
96-97	84.21	32.00	73	1	1.37
97-98	84.21	32.00	35	1	2.86
Averages	65.79	25.00	58.00	1.00	1.91

BEASANT, Dave

Nottingham Forest ⑫ GK

Fullname: David John Beasant
DOB: 20-03-59 Willesden

Ten years on from his famous FA Cup final penalty save for Wimbledon against Liverpool, Dave Beasant achieved more success as Nottingham Forest regained their place in the Premiership at the first attempt. It was a bold move by the veteran keeper to drop out of the Premiership to join Forest from Southampton but he continued to show his quality in making 39 Nationwide League appearances behind a defence

Dave Beasant

which kept 22 clean sheets in its 46 league games. On the downside Beasant suffered the first dismissal of his career.

How much longer Beasant can continue playing at the top level must be open to question but he has confounded the critics by rebuilding his career which appeared to be on the decline prior to a move from Chelsea to Southampton in 1993. He played two games for England in 1990 whilst at Chelsea and has also had a spell with Newcastle United.

Form Factors

Season	Team	Tot	St	Sb	Y	R
94-95	Southampton	13	12	1	0	0
95-96	Southampton	36	36	0	0	0
96-97	Southampton	14	13	1	0	0
Total		63	61	2	0	0

	GA	GkA	GAp	CS	SO	R
94-95	63	16	1.23	4	2	0
95-96	52	49	1.36	10	2	2
96-97	56	24	1.71	2	1	0
Averages	57.00	29.67	1.43	5.33	1.67	0.67

BEATTIE, James
Southampton ❶❷ S

Fullname: James Scott Beattie
DOB: 27-02-78 Lancaster

A prolific goalscorer in youth football Beattie made his Premiership debut for Blackburn Rovers in October 1996, during a 2-0 home defeat by Arsenal, but was not called upon again for first team action for almost a year when he played in a Coca Cola Cup tie against Preston North End. Ended the season with three further Premiership appearances under his belt, all from the subs bench, and will be looking for an extended run this year to prove his goalscoring abilities at the highest level. Moved to Southampton for £1.0m in the close season so may get more first-team opportunities.

Form Factors

Season	Team	Tot	St	Sb	Y	R
97-98	Blackburn Rovers	3	0	3	0	0
Total		3	0	3	0	0

	GP	GG	GF	GS	TGR
97-98	7.89	0.00	57	0	0.00
Averages	7.89	0.00	57.00	0.00	0.00

BECK, Mikkel
Middlesbrough ❶❷ S

Fullname: Mikkel Beck
DOB: 12-05-73 Arhus, Denmark

Danish international who joined Middlesbrough early in the 1996-97 season but with just five goals in 25 matches he could do little to halt the club's slide towards relegation. A season in the Nationwide League has done his confidence no harm and with 14 league goals in 38 appearances he was Boro's top scorer. He will pose problems for defences but his total of 37 goals in 155 league games for B1909, Fortuna Koln and now Middlesbrough suggests that he could find it hard going back in the Premiership.

Form Factors

Season	Team	Tot	St	Sb	Y	R
96-97	Middlesbrough	25	22	3	0	0
Total		25	22	3	0	0

	GP	GG	GF	GS	TGR
96-97	65.79	5.00	51	5	9.80
Averages	65.79	5.00	51.00	5.00	9.80

BECKHAM, David

Manchester U. ①②③④⑤ M

Fullname: David Robert Beckham
DOB: 02-05-75 Leytonstone

Petulant pain or genius? In France 98 Beckham displayed pure class with his free kick goal against Colombia only to follow it with incredible stupidity against Argentina which may or may not have cost England the World Cup.

His questionable temperament to one side, he has the skill and tenacity to be one of the greats of the modern era and in less than three seasons as a Manchester United regular Beckham has become a regular part of the England set-up.

The 1997-98 season may have been one in which Manchester United failed to live up to expectations but for Beckham personally he returned his best figures to date of nine goals in 37 Premiership matches. As with previous seasons his nine goals included many spectacular efforts. Scoring goals though is just one string in Beckham's bow; there are few better creative players in the game and he has shown himself to be hardworking and more than adequate when tackling. Prefers playing a more central midfield role than earlier in his career and links well with those around him.

David Beckham

Form Factors

Season	Team	Tot	St	Sb	Y	R
95-96	Manchester U.	33	26	7	5	0
96-97	Manchester U.	36	33	3	6	0
97-98	Manchester U.	37	34	3	6	0
Total		106	93	13	17	0

	GP	GG	GF	GS	TGR
95-96	86.84	4.71	73	7	9.59
96-97	94.74	5.14	76	7	9.21
97-98	97.37	4.11	73	9	12.33
Averages	92.98	4.66	74.00	7.67	10.38

BEENEY, Mark
Leeds United ❶ GK
Fullname: Mark Raymond Beeney
DOB: 30-12-67 Tunbridge Wells

Goalkeeper who got to know the bench very well during his time at Elland Road. Started in just one Premiership match for Leeds United during 1997-98 when he stood-in for the suspended Nigel Martyn. Played one other game for United when he was called into action following Martyn's dismissal in the FA Cup against Oxford United.

In five full seasons with Leeds, Beeney has played just 34 times in the league and his total appearances in three of those seasons amount to a dismal two games. Is unlikely to earn your fantasy team many points if both he and Martyn remain at Elland Road. Has previously played in the Football League with Aldershot, Maidstone United and Gillingham, joined Leeds in a £350,000 transfer in April 1993.

Form Factors

Season	Team	Tot	St	Sb	Y	R
95-96	Leeds U.	10	10	0	0	1
96-97	Leeds U.	1	1	0	0	0
97-98	Leeds U.	1	1	0	0	0
Total		12	12	0	0	1

	GA	GlA	GAp	CS	SO	Rp
95-96	57	15	1.50	3	2	0
96-97	38	0	0.00	1	1	0
97-98	46	2	2.00	0	0	0
Averages	47.0	5.67	1.17	1.33	1.0	0

BENALI, Francis
Southampton ❶❷ FB
Fullname: Francis Vincent Benali
DOB: 30-12-68 Southampton

Benali's 10th season in the Southampton first team contained something which none of his previous nine had – a goal! The Southampton-born defender finally broke his duck on 13 December with the Saints' second goal in a 2-1 win over Leicester and he had further cause for celebration come Christmas as the normally suspension-collecting defender had not been booked come Yuletide. By the end of the season though he had two yellow and two red cards against his name – not ideal for winning points for your fantasy team. Even so, it was an improvement on the previous season when his disciplinary problems resulted in him being sidelined for 12 games.

Benali actually started out as a striker with England Youth and the Saints' reserves before being converted into a defender by the time he made his Southampton debut on 1 October 1998. Has since made 253 league appearances for his only club.

Form Factors

Season	Team	Tot	St	Sb	Y	R
95-96	Southampton	30	29	1	6	0
96-97	Southampton	18	14	4	3	1
97-98	Southampton	33	32	1	2	2
Total		81	75	6	11	3

	GP	GG	GF	GS	TGR
95-96	78.95	0.00	34	0	0.00
96-97	47.37	0.00	50	0	0.00
97-98	86.84	33.00	50	1	2.00
Averages	71.05	11.00	44.67	0.33	0.67

BERESFORD, John

Southampton ❶❷❸ M

Fullname: John Beresford
DOB: 04-09-66 Sheffield

Experienced midfielder who has given his Premiership career a new lease of life with a £1.5m move to Southampton in February 1998 after 179 league appearances in five and a half seasons at Newcastle United. One thing the move has not altered though is Beresford's success rate in the penalty area as his goal drought stretches back to 7 April 1983 when he converted a penalty against Barnsley, one of his former clubs.

Beresford joined Barnsley from Manchester City – where he failed to make the first team – before having his first spell on the south coast with Portsmouth. Was transferred from Pompey to Newcastle for just £650,000. By signing for Southampton he may have greatly enhanced his chances of playing for a couple more seasons in the top flight.

Form Factors

Season	Team	Tot	St	Sb	Y	R
96-97	Newcastle U.	19	18	1	4	0
97-98	Newcastle U.	18	17	1	3	0
97-98	Southampton	10	10	0	0	0
Total		47	45	2	7	0

	GP	GG	GF	GS	TGR
96-97	50.00	0.00	73	0	0.00
97-98	47.37	9.00	35	2	5.71
97-98	26.32	0.00	50	0	0.00
Averages	41.23	3.00	52.67	0.67	1.90

BERG, Henning

Manchester U. ❶❷❸❹ FB

Fullname: Henning Berg
DOB: 01-09-69 Eidsvell

Highly accomplished Norwegian international defender who joined Manchester United at the start of last season from Blackburn Rovers for £5m after just over four years at Ewood Park. The move was certainly good business for Blackburn who signed him from Lillestrom for £400,000 in January 1993.

An excellent tackler who is comfortable on the ball and is seldom injured, having missed just five games during four full seasons at Blackburn but only played 27 times in the Premiership with Manchester United last season. Played on the right side of the defence on his arrival in England but has since blossomed in the middle of the back-line.

Strangely has a better strike rate when playing for Norway than he does in domestic football, having scored just four times with United and Rovers.

Form Factors

Season	Team	Tot	St	Sb	Y	R
95-96	Blackburn R.	38	38	0	5	1
96-97	Blackburn R.	36	36	0	3	0
97-98	Manchester U.	27	23	4	2	0
Total		101	97	4	10	1

	GP	GG	GF	GS	TGR
95-96	100.00	0.00	61	0	0.00
96-97	94.74	18.00	42	2	4.76
97-98	71.05	13.50	73	2	2.74
Averages	88.60	10.50	58.67	1.33	2.50

BERGER, Patrik
Liverpool ❶❷ S
Fullname: Patrik Berger
DOB: 10-11-73 Prague

Scored the goal which put the Czech Republic ahead against Germany in the final of Euro 96 and it was his performances in that competition, although troubled by illness, which persuaded Liverpool to sign him from Borussia Dortmund for £3.25m. Unfortunately has never really settled at Anfield and after making 23 Premiership appearances in 1996-97 he was in the starting line-up for just six league games last season though he was used as a sub on no less than 16 other occasions.

Has the skill in either foot to really set the Premiership alight but having been signed as a goalscoring attack-minded midfielder his tally of nine goals in two seasons does not yet justify his large fee.

Form Factors

Season	Team	Tot	St	Sb	Y	R
96-97	Liverpool	23	13	10	0	0
97-98	Liverpool	22	6	16	0	0
Total		45	19	26	0	0

	GP	GG	GF	GS	TGR
96-97	60.53	3.83	62	6	9.68
97-98	57.89	7.33	68	3	4.41
Averages	59.21	5.58	65.00	4.50	7.04

BERGKAMP, Dennis
Arsenal ❶❷❸❹❺ S
Fullname: Dennis Nicolaas Bergkamp
DOB: 18-05-69 Amsterdam

A season in which Bergkamp oozed class ended in disappointment in one way for the Dutch striker as injury ruled him out of his first FA Cup final but, having already won both the PFA and the Writers Player of the Year awards, there was no doubting his contribution to Arsenal's second league and cup double.

Bergkamp was into his stride early in the season and was running along at a goal a game after 10 Premiership matches; his return of 16 league goals by the end of the season is his best in three years at Highbury despite playing less games than in his two previous seasons with the club.

A key member of Holland's France 98 campaign, Bergkamp appears to be at the peak of his powers at the present time and if he can stay injury-free – and overcome his fear of flying – then Arsenal will not only successfully defend their title but could also bring the European Champions Cup back to England.

Form Factors

Season	Team	Tot	St	Sb	Y	R
95-96	Arsenal	33	33	0	5	0
96-97	Arsenal	29	28	1	6	1
97-98	Arsenal	28	28	0	6	0
Total		90	89	1	17	1

	GP	GG	GF	GS	TGR
95-96	86.84	3.00	49	11	22.45
96-97	76.32	2.42	62	12	19.35
97-98	73.68	1.75	68	16	23.53
Averages	78.95	2.39	59.67	13.00	21.78

BERKOVIC, Eyal

West Ham U. ①②③④ M

Fullname: Eyal Berkovic
DOB: 02-04-72 Haifa

Diminutive, speedy Israeli international midfielder who has made a big impact in the Premiership since his arrival from Maccabi Haifa. With his exceptional close ball skills Berkovic quickly catches the eye and would be a useful addition to any fantasy team. Although best known for his creative abilities he does chip in with a reasonable number of goals, averaging six a season since making his debut for Maccabi. Was signed by the then Southampton manager Graeme Souness at the start of the 1996-97 season for £1m and a year later was transferred to West Ham United for £1.75m where his skills compliment the Hammers' renowned passing game.

Eyal Berkovic

Form Factors

Season	Team	Tot	St	Sb	Y	R
96-97	Southampton	28	26	2	4	0
97-98	West Ham U.	35	34	1	2	0
Total		63	60	3	6	0

	GP	GG	GF	GS	TGR
96-97	73.68	7.00	50	4	8.00
97-98	92.11	5.00	56	7	12.50
Averages	82.89	6.00	53.00	5.50	10.25

BERTI, Nicola

Tottenham H. ①②③④ M

Fullname: Nicola Berti
DOB:

Joined Tottenham Hotspur in December 1997 from Internazionale when the Londoners were fast sinking towards the Nationwide League. Berti, a very experienced Italian international who didn't cost Tottenham a fee, played in Spurs' final 18 matches of the season and chipped in with a useful three goals. A hardworking midfielder who, over the past four years, has broken both of his knees and one of his feet.

Was expected only to see out the season with Tottenham but so impressed manager Christian Gross that he has accepted an invitation to stay for a further season at White Hart Lane. Played for several of the top clubs in Italy including Parma and Fiorentina and featured in the Italian side which competed in USA 94.

Form Factors

Season	Team	Tot	St	Sb	Y	R
97-98	Tottenham H.	17	17	0	5	0
Total		17	17	0	5	0

	GP	GG	GF	GS	TGR
97-98	44.74	5.67	44	3	6.82
Averages	44.74	5.67	44.00	3.00	6.82

Slaven Bilic

BILIC, Slaven

Everton ❶❷❸❹ CB

Fullname: Slaven Bilic
DOB: 11-09-68 Croatia

Croatian defender who did his reputation no harm with typically solid performances for his country during France 98. It was playing for Croatia in Euro 96 that he really came to the fore as far as British fans were concerned although four months earlier he had already joined West Ham United from German side Karlsruhe for £1.3m. Began his career with five seasons at Hajduk Split.

Moved to Everton in the summer of 1997 having delayed his transfer to help West Ham in their successful battle against relegation.

In many respects he is an old-fashioned no-nonsense defender but in addition to being dominant in the air he is also deceptively good on the ground. He does though have disciplinary problems, having been booked 10 times in his one full season at Upton Park, although he successfully reduced that figure quite substantially last season only to be sent off three times and miss 11 games through suspension.

Form Factors

Season	Team	Tot	St	Sb	Y	R
95-96	West Ham U.	13	13	0	1	0
96-97	West Ham U.	35	35	0	10	0
97-98	Everton	24	22	2	4	3
Total		72	70	2	15	3

	GP	GG	GF	GS	TGR
95-96	34.21	0.00	43	0	0.00
96-97	92.11	17.50	39	2	5.13
97-98	63.16	0.00	41	0	0.00
Averages	63.16	5.83	41.00	0.67	1.71

BJORNEBYE, Stig

Liverpool ❶❷❸ FB

Fullname: Stig Inge Bjornebye
DOB: 11-12-69 Norway

Norwegian international who, after making just two appearances for Liverpool during 1995-96, then went on an unbroken run of 61 Premiership matches which saw him and David James as the Reds' only ever-present players during 1996-97.

A fine tackler who uses the ball well and has shown himself to be good when going forward from a wing-back position to put over a decent cross. As good as he is at defending, scoring goals is not his forte with just two in his Anfield career to date so don't look for Bjornebye to get you bonus points here.

A member of the Norwegian side which progressed, a touch fortuitously, through to the second stage of France 98 he joined Liverpool in December 1992 for just £600,000 having previously played for Strammen, Kongsvinger and Rosenborg.

Form Factors

Season	Team	Tot	St	Sb	Y	R
95-96	Liverpool	2	2	0	0	0
96-97	Liverpool	38	38	0	3	0
97-98	Liverpool	25	24	1	4	0
Total		65	64	1	7	0

	GP	GG	GF	GS	TGR
95-96	5.26	0.00	70	0	0.00
96-97	100.00	19.00	62	2	3.23
97-98	65.79	0.00	68	0	0.00
Averages	57.02	6.33	66.67	0.67	1.08

BLACKWELL, Dean

Wimbledon ❶❷ CB

Fullname: Dean Robert Blackwell
DOB: 05-12-69 Camden

Another player who is testimony to Wimbledon's excellent record in bringing on home-grown youngsters. Blackwell joined the Dons as a trainee and the 1997-98 season was his 10th in the first team. Has fully recovered from the injuries

Dean Blackwell

Fantasy Football Handbook 1998/99

which decimated his career for two seasons and last season only goalkeeper Nicky Sullivan played in more Premiership matches for the Dons as Blackwell took his total league appearances above 150.

A former England Under-21 international who is quick and strong in the air but seldom uses his strength there to his advantage at set pieces, having scored just once since turning professional.

Form Factors

Season	Team	Tot	St	Sb	Y	R
95-96	Wimbledon	8	8	0	0	0
96-97	Wimbledon	27	22	5	4	0
97-98	Wimbledon	35	35	0	4	0
Total		70	65	5	8	0

	GP	GG	GF	GS	TGR
95-96	21.05	0.00	55	0	0.00
96-97	71.05	0.00	49	0	0.00
97-98	92.11	0.00	34	0	0.00
Averages	61.40	0.00	46.00	0.00	0.00

BOA MORTE, Luis

Arsenal ❶❷ S

Fullname: Luis Boa Morte
DOB: 04-08-78 Lisbon, Portugal

Wide Portuguese midfielder who was afforded few chances to demonstrate his capabilities at Highbury last season but when given the chance showed himself to be extremely nimble and skilful. Made just four league starts, came on from the bench 11 times and was named as an unused sub for eight games.

Formerly with Sporting Lisbon, an Under-21 international in his homeland, he can play as an orthodox winger or as a striker. Cost Arsenal £1.2m.

Form Factors

Season	Team	Tot	St	Sb	Y	R
97-98	Arsenal	15	4	11	2	0
Total		15	4	11	2	0

	GP	GG	GF	GS	TGR
97-98	39.47	0.00	68	0	0.00
Averages	39.47	0.00	68.00	0.00	0.00

BOATENG, George

Coventry C. ❶ D/M

Fullname: George Boateng
DOB: 05-09-75 Accra, Ghana

Made his Coventry City in December last year during a 1-0 defeat at Liverpool following a £250,000 move from Feyenoord. Former Dutch Under-21 captain who already looks to be a bargain buy and with his ability to play either in midfield or defence he should prove an asset for many years to come. The only cloud on the horizon is his discipline following his five bookings in 19 league and cup matches for the Sky Blues.

Form Factors

Season	Team	Tot	St	Sb	Y	R
97-98	Coventry City	14	14	0	4	1
Total		14	14	0	4	1

	GP	GG	GF	GS	TGR
97-98	36.84	14.00	46	1	2.17
Averages	36.84	14.00	46.00	1.00	2.17

BOHINEN, Lars

Derby County ❶❷❸ M

Fullname: Lars Bohinen
DOB: 08-09-69 Vadso, Norway

Experienced Norwegian international midfielder who switched from Blackburn Rovers to Derby County in a £1.5m transfer in March 1998 after two years at Ewood Park. Having played 23 times in the Premiership for Blackburn during 1996-97 Bohinen found his chances limited last season with 10 of his 16 appearances being as a substitute. Played nine times for Derby before the season was out.

Useful at free kicks, he is very much a ball playing midfielder which may be somewhat at odds with the style of his national side. Started his career with Valerengen and had spells with Viking and Young Boys of Berne before joining Nottingham Forest in 1993; moved to Blackburn for £700,000 in early 1995.

Lars Bohinen

Form Factors

Season	Team	Tot	St	Sb	Y	R
96-97	Blackburn R.	23	17	6	6	0
97-98	Blackburn R.	16	6	10	0	0
97-98	Derby Co.	9	9	0	1	0
Total		48	32	16	7	0

	GP	GG	GF	GS	TGR
96-97	60.53	11.50	42	2	4.76
97-98	42.11	16.00	57	1	1.75
97-98	23.68	9.00	52	1	1.92
Averages	42.11	12.17	50.33	1.33	2.81

BOLAND, Willie

Coventry City ❶ M

Fullname: William John Boland
DOB: 06-08-75 Republic of Ireland

A former Eire Under-21 player who looked to be heading for the big time in 1993-94 when he made 27 league appearances for Coventry City in the Premiership but in the following two seasons Boland added just four more games to his tally. Gordon Strachan brought him more into the fold last season with the midfielder making eight starts and 11 substitute appearances; he was also an unused sub on 10 occasions.

Boland has now played 59 times in the Premiership but has yet to score.

Fantasy Football Handbook 1998/99 121

Form Factors

Season	Team	Tot	St	Sb	Y	R
95-96	Coventry C.	3	2	1	0	0
96-97	Coventry C.	1	0	1	0	0
97-98	Coventry C.	19	8	11	4	0
Total		23	10	13	4	0

	GP	GG	GF	GS	TGR
95-96	7.89	0.00	42	0	0.00
96-97	2.63	0.00	38	0	0.00
97-98	50.00	0.00	46	0	0.00
Averages	20.18	0.00	42.00	0.00	0.00

BONALAIR, Thierry

Nottingham F. ❶❷❸ D

Fullname: Thierry Bonalair
DOB: France

Excellent acquisition by Nottingham Forest who signed French international defender on a free transfer in time for last season. With Bonalair's toughness in the tackle, acceleration and good use of the ball, Forest were bolstered considerably from the previous season by Bonalair's arrival.

Bonalair brought with him a good pedigree to the City Ground having won the Player of the Year award for the two previous seasons in Switzerland. Amongst his former clubs are Lille, Nantes, Auxerre and Neuchatel Xamax.

BOOTH, Andy

Sheffield W. ❶❷ S

Fullname: Andrew David Booth
DOB: 06-12-73 Huddersfield

Having finished seventh in the Premiership in 1996-97, Sheffield Wednesday slipped badly a year later with one of the reasons being a couple of injuries to striker Andy Booth. Top scorer during his first season at Hillsborough following a £2.7m transfer from county neighbours Huddersfield Town, Booth featured in just three of the Owls' opening 15 games in 1997-98 before bursting back in style with a hat trick in a 5-0 win over Bolton Wanderers, which is, so far, his only Premiership treble.

Injuries clearly disrupted his progress but Booth still found the net seven times

Andy Booth

in 23 league games although he was scoreless in his last seven games and was dismissed during a 3-1 win at Everton in April.

Providing he can stay clear of injury this time round then he may yet add further international honours to his Under-21 caps.

Form Factors

Season	Team	Tot	St	Sb	Y	R
96-97	Sheffield W.	35	32	3	3	0
97-98	Sheffield W.	23	21	2	1	1
Total		58	53	5	4	1

	GP	GG	GF	GS	TGR
96-97	92.11	3.50	50	10	20.00
97-98	60.53	3.29	52	7	13.46
Averages	76.32	3.39	51.00	8.50	16.73

BOSNICH, Mark

Aston Villa ❶❷❸❹ GK

Fullname: Mark John Bosnich
DOB: 13-01-72 Sydney, Australia

Having found his position as the number one goalkeeper at Aston Villa under threat during the 1996-97 season Mark Bosnich re-established himself as the top keeper at Villa Park last season with nine clean sheets in 30 Premiership appearances.

But in spite of Bosnich's, consistency between the sticks Villa, in a season of transition, did concede their highest number of goals for three seasons. The Australian's best form though, was possibly saved for the UEFA Cup where he conceded a miserly one goal in five appearances, this despite being struck by missiles during the away leg with Atletico Madrid. Agile, a good handler and stylish shot-stopper he should have little trouble in confirming his status as one of the top keepers in the Premiership during 1998-99.

Form Factors

Season	Team	Tot	St	Sb	Y	R
95-96	Aston Villa	38	38	0	1	0
96-97	Aston Villa	20	20	0	2	0
97-98	Aston Villa	30	30	0	1	0
Total		88	88	0	4	0

	GA	GkA	GAp	CS	SO	R
95-96	35	34	0.89	13	2	0
96-97	34	17	0.85	9	2	0
97-98	48	35	1.17	9	2	0
Averages	39.0	28.67	0.97	10.33	2.0	0

Mark Bosnich

BOULD, Steve
Arsenal ❶❷❸ CB
Fullname: Stephen Andrew Bould
DOB: 16-11-62 Stoke

Well into the veteran stage of his career but the long serving central defender was still a major player in Arsenal's glorious Double campaign last season with 24 Premiership appearances taking his league career total in 10 years at Highbury to 268. The only blot in an otherwise memorable 12 months for the one-time England player was the regularity with which he was cautioned, eight times following 13 yellow cards over the previous two seasons.

Rarely amongst the goals himself, he has scored just five league goals in his time with Arsenal, but he is dangerous at set-pieces with clever flick-ons at the near post that create chances for those behind him.

Started his career with his home-town club of Stoke City and had a loan spell with Torquay United prior to moving to Highbury.

Form Factors

Season	Team	Tot	St	Sb	Y	R
95-96	Arsenal	19	19	0	7	1
96-97	Arsenal	33	33	0	6	0
97-98	Arsenal	24	21	3	8	0
Total		76	73	3	21	1

	GP	GG	GF	GS	TGR
95-96	50.00	0.00	49	0	0.00
96-97	86.84	0.00	62	0	0.00
97-98	63.16	0.00	68	0	0.00
Averages	66.67	0.00	59.67	0.00	0.00

BOWEN, Mark
Charlton A. ❶❷ FB
Fullname: Mark Rosslyn Bowen
DOB: 07-12-63 Neath

One of very few players to have joined an English club from a Japanese side but that is what Bowen did when he returned to these shores from Shimizu in September last year. Before heading east he had a season with West Ham which followed on from 320 league games in nine years with Norwich City.

Expected to be no more than cover at the Valley he was ever-present between October and March and finished the campaign with another 40 games under his belt with his total league appearances now standing at 391. But at almost 35 the chances of the veteran of 41 games for Wales going far beyond that figure in the Premiership must be slim.

Form Factors

Season	Team	Tot	St	Sb	Y	R
93-94	Norwich C.	41	41	0	0	0
94-95	Norwich C.	36	34	2	5	0
96-97	West Ham U.	17	15	2	2	0
Total		94	90	4	7	0

	GP	GG	GF	GS	TGR
93-94	107.89	8.20	65	5	7.69
94-95	94.74	18.00	37	2	5.41
96-97	44.74	17.00	39	1	2.56
Averages	82.46	14.40	47.00	2.67	5.22

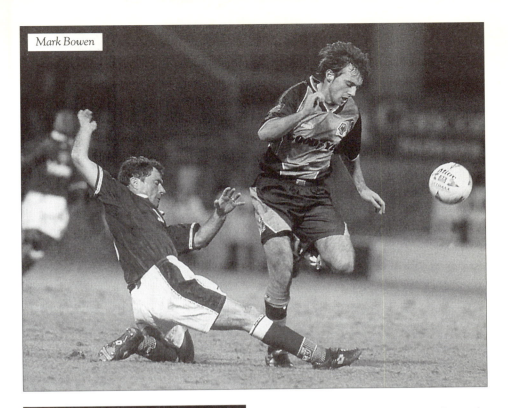

Mark Bowen

BOWYER, Lee

Leeds United ❶❷❸ M

Fullname: Lee David Bowyer
DOB: 03-01-77 London

Bowyer seemed to have the world at his feet when he signed for Leeds United from Charlton Athletic for an initial £2.6m in July 1996 but instead of moving onto the international stage his profile slipped slightly last season as he failed to command a regular place George Graham's side. That said, he was back in favour towards the end of the campaign and a good start to the 1998-99 season could be just the boost he is searching for.

A midfield player possessing bundles of talent that if harnessed correctly will see him fulfil his potential. He is quick, good on the ball although passes occasionally tend to go astray, and has proved that he can score goals.

Form Factors

Season	Team	Tot	St	Sb	Y	R
96-97	Leeds U.	32	32	0	6	0
97-98	Leeds U.	25	21	4	4	0
Total		57	53	4	10	0

	GP	GG	GF	GS	TGR
96-97	84.21	8.00	28	4	14.29
97-98	65.79	8.33	57	3	5.26
Averages	75.00	8.17	42.50	3.50	9.77

Fantasy Football Handbook 1998/99

BRADY, Garry
Newcastle U. ❶❷ M
Fullname: Garry Brady
DOB: 07-09-76 Glasgow

Signed as a professional with Tottenham in September 1993 but had to wait until January this year to make his debut, firstly in the FA Cup and then five days later in the Premiership away to Manchester United. Has played all his career in midfield until having a stint at full-back in the Spurs Reserves last season to accommodate the returning from injury Darren Anderton.

An administrative error by Tottenham allowed Newcastle to snap up the former Scotland Schoolboy and Youth international on a free during the summer.

Form Factors

Season	Team	Tot	St	Sb	Y	R
97-98	Tottenham H.	9	0	9	0	0
Total		9	0	9	0	0

	GP	GG	GF	GS	TGR
97-98	23.68	0.00	44	0	0.00
Averages	23.68	0.00	44.00	0.00	0.00

BRANCA, Marco
Middlesbrough ❶❷❸ S
Fullname: Marco Branca
DOB: 06-01-65

Vastly experienced striker who arrived in time to give Middlesbrough's promotion drive the push it needed last spring. Branca may be getting towards the end of his days at the highest level but it was hard to tell that last season as in 13 games for the Riverside club he weighed in with 10 goals including the one which put Boro on the path to a Coca Cola Cup semi final victory over Liverpool.

With promotion secured Boro may consider his £1m fee a more than worthwhile investment and certainly his background is of the highest order taking in such clubs as Internazionale, Roma, Parma, Fiorentina, Sampdoria and Udinese.

BRANCH, Michael

Everton ❶ S

Fullname: Michael Paul Branch
DOB: 18-10-78 Liverpool

Liverpool born striker who seemed to be making a name for himself on Merseyside when he played in 25 of Everton's Premiership matches during 1996-97 but found himself back on the sidelines last season with just one start in the league – he was substituted during that match – and a further five games from the bench.

A one time England Youth player who certainly has time on his side to re-establish himself and has proved in the past that he can work a good understanding with Duncan Ferguson so may yet come through as a surprise package.

Form Factors

Season	Team	Tot	St	Sb	Y	R
95-96	Everton	3	1	2	0	0
96-97	Everton	25	13	12	2	0
97-98	Everton	6	1	5	0	0
Total		34	15	19	2	0

	GP	GG	GF	GS	TGR
95-96	7.89	0.00	64	0	0.00
96-97	65.79	8.33	44	3	6.82
97-98	15.79	0.00	41	0	0.00
Averages	29.82	2.78	49.67	1.00	2.27

BREACKER, Tim

West Ham U. ❶❷❸ FB

Fullname: Timothy Sean Breacker
DOB: 02-07-65 Bicester

A vital member of the West Ham United defence over the past seven years. Tim Breacker's 1997-98 season came to an abrupt end on 2 March when he picked up an injury against Arsenal which restricted his total of Premiership matches to 19. Injury is not an unknown problem for Breacker with the former England Under-21 full-back managing just 67 Premiership games over the past three seasons due to various ailments.

Right-sided defender who is very suited to playing wing-back but will seldom be found amongst the goalscorers with his most recent successful strike being way back in March 1994.

Form Factors

Season	Team	Tot	St	Sb	Y	R
95-96	West Ham U.	22	19	3	6	0
96-97	West Ham U.	26	22	4	2	0
97-98	West Ham U.	19	18	1	3	0
Total		67	59	8	11	0

	GP	GG	GF	GS	TGR
95-96	57.89	0.00	43	0	0.00
96-97	68.42	0.00	39	0	0.00
97-98	50.00	0.00	56	0	0.00
Averages	58.77	0.00	46.00	0.00	0.00

BREEN, Gary

Coventry City ❶❷❸ CB

Fullname: Gary Patrick Breen
DOB: 12-12-73 Hendon

Having experienced a difficult and disappointing spell shortly after joining Coventry City from Birmingham City in January 1997, Gary Breen fully established himself at the heart of the Sky Blues defence during 1997-98 as Coventry enjoyed their most successful league campaign for many years.

An Eire international he has justified the £2.5m Coventry paid for his services and, unusually for a defender in this era, he only occasionally falls foul of the laws of the game by collecting just two yellow cards in 39 league games although he was also sent off once last season.

Form Factors

Season	Team	Tot	St	Sb	Y	R
96-97	Coventry C.	9	8	1	0	0
97-98	Coventry C.	30	30	0	1	1
Total		39	38	1	1	1

	GP	GG	GF	GS	TGR
96-97	23.68	0.00	38	0	0.00
97-98	78.95	30.00	46	1	2.17
Averages	51.32	15.00	42.00	0.50	1.09

Gary Breen

BRIGHT, Mark

Charlton A. ❶❷❸ S

Fullname: Mark Abraham Bright
DOB: 06-06-62

Mark Bright goes into his 17th year as a professional with a new one-year contract at Charlton Athletic after his seven goals in 17 games last season helped the Addicks secure their return to the Premiership. Initially brought in as cover, he was the ideal man for the job when Charlton sold Leaburn to Wimbledon early in the new year.

Whether he can recapture the form which brought him 56 goals in three years in the Premiership with Sheffield Wednesday remains to be seen. Bright also had an outstanding partnership with Ian Wright at Crystal Palace in the late '80s when he scored 62 goals, again over three years.

He has also played for Leek Town, Port Vale, Leicester City and on loan to Millwall.

Form Factors

Season	Team	Tot	St	Sb	Y	R
94-95	Sheffield W.	37	33	4	3	0
95-96	Sheffield W.	25	15	10	2	0
96-97	Sheffield W.	1	0	1	0	0
Total		63	48	15	5	0

	GP	GG	GF	GS	TGR
94-95	97.37	3.36	49	11	22.45
95-96	65.79	3.57	48	7	14.58
96-97	2.63	0.00	50	0	0.00
Averages	55.26	2.31	49.00	6.00	12.34

BRIGHTWELL, Ian

Coventry C. ①② D/M

Fullname: Ian Robert Brightwell
DOB: 09-04-68 Lutterworth

Although a very capable defender, Ian Brightwell is regarded in the main as a midfield player and following his free transfer from Manchester City adds experience to the Coventry City middle. His departure from Maine Road ends a 12 year stint in the City first team but also offers him the chance to resurrect his Premiership career which came to an abrupt halt when his previous club was relegated in 1996.

Despite his undoubted ability he may have to settle for being a squad member at Highfield Road.

BRISCOE, Lee

Sheffield W. ①② FB

Fullname: Lee Stephen Briscoe
DOB: 30-09-75 Pontefract

Wing-back who unfortunately failed to build on his gradual integration into the Sheffield Wednesday team over the past couple of years during 1997-98 in part to a long-term groin injury. Having to play on whilst carrying the injury did little to accelerate his recovery. Was in the starting line-up for three of the Owls' Premiership matches but was withdrawn in two of those games and his total of seven league games – four as substitute – included two yellow cards. An England Under-21 attack-minded defender who had a spell on loan to Manchester City towards the end of the season.

His most successful season was back in 1995-96 when he featured in 26 of Wednesday's league games.

Form Factors

Season	Team	Tot	St	Sb	Y	R
95-96	Sheffield W.	25	22	3	1	0
96-97	Sheffield W.	6	5	1	0	0
97-98	Sheffield W.	7	3	4	0	0
Total		38	30	8	1	0

	GP	GG	GF	GS	TGR
95-96	65.79	0.00	48	0	0.00
96-97	15.79	0.00	50	0	0.00
97-98	18.42	0.00	52	0	0.00
Averages	33.33	0.00	50.00	0.00	0.00

BROOMES, Marlon
Blackburn R. ❶ CD

Fullname: Marlon Charkes Broomes
DOB: 28-11-77 Birmingham

A former England Schools, Youth and Under-21 international who spent three years with Blackburn Rovers before making his Football League debut whilst on loan to Swindon Town during the 1996-97 season. Used the experience gained there to good effect and made his debut in the Premiership last season with Blackburn but has yet to fully establish himself at Ewood Park. Blackburn are confident that Broomes has the ability to press for a first team place very soon.

Form Factors

Season	Team	Tot	St	Sb	Y	R
97-98	Blackburn R.	4	2	2	1	0
Total		4	2	2	1	0

	GP	GG	GF	GS	TGR
97-98	10.53	0.00	57	0	0.00
Averages	10.53	0.00	57.00	0.00	0.00

BROWN, Steve
Charlton A. ❶❷ D

Fullname: Steven Byron Brown
DOB: 13-05-73 Brighton

A one-club man, a defender who had his second most successful season with Charlton Athletic last season. His 35 Nationwide League appearances was his best total since playing 42 times in 1994-95, incidentally the only other season apart from 1997-98 when he found the back of the net. Would have beaten his previous best total had he not been dislodged from the side in February.

Brown is certainly versatile, being able to play at right back, his strongest side, or centre-half or in midfield. His talents do not end there as he has played in goal for segments of three games and kept a clean sheet in the first two.

BURROWS, David
Coventry City ❶❷ FB

Fullname: David Burrows
DOB: 25-10-68 Dudley

The 1997-98 season was by far the most successful of David Burrows' four years at Highfield Road with the one-time England Under-21 and B international making 32 Premiership appearances for the Sky Blues. During his previous three seasons at Highfield Road Burrows played just 40 league games but if he can avoid injury then his versatility should secure him a big part in manager Gordon Strachan's plans this season.

Has a wealth of top class experience having begun his career at West Bromwich Albion, had almost five years at Liverpool and then spells with West Ham United and Everton prior to joining Coventry.

Form Factors

Season	Team	Tot	St	Sb	Y	R
95-96	Coventry C.	13	13	0	4	0
96-97	Coventry C.	18	17	1	5	0
97-98	Coventry C.	32	32	0	8	0
Total		63	62	1	17	0

	GP	GG	GF	GS	TGR
95-96	34.21	0.00	42	0	0.00
96-97	47.37	0.00	38	0	0.00
97-98	84.21	0.00	46	0	0.00
Averages	55.26	0.00	42.00	0.00	0.00

BURTON, Deon

Derby County ①② S
Fullname: Deon John Burton
DOB: 25-10-76 Ashford

Joined Derby County from one of manager Jim Smith's previous clubs, Portsmouth, for £1m during the close season following the 1996-97 season. Scored a goal every six games during his time at Fratton Park but the '97-98 campaign was very much a season of bedding in at the higher level as 17 of Burton's 29 Premiership appearances were as substitute; only two players came off the bench to be called into action more times.

Prior to leaving Portsmouth he scored twice during five games on loan to Cardiff City and three goals in his first season in the Premiership. A player who you could probably get for your team fairly cheaply – despite his three appearances for Jamaica in France 98 – and may just be the one who makes it big this season.

Form Factors

Season	Team	Tot	St	Sb	Y	R
97-98	Derby Co.	29	12	17	0	0
Total		29	12	17	0	0

	GP	GG	GF	GS	TGR
97-98	76.32	9.67	52	3	5.77
Averages	76.32	9.67	52.00	3.00	5.77

BUTT, Nicky

Manchester U. ①②③④ M
Fullname: Nicholas Butt
DOB: 21-01-75 Manchester

Another in Manchester United's long tradition of producing local talent to make it at the highest level. Still only 23 at the start of the 1998-99 season, Butt has been a regular in Alex Ferguson's side over the past four seasons and will doubtless add to his tally of England caps in the years to come.

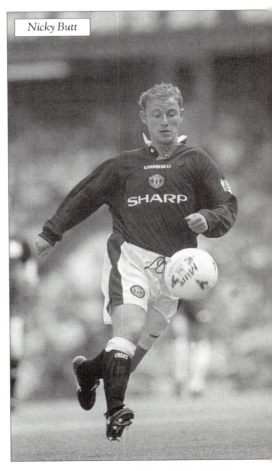

Nicky Butt

Fantasy Football Handbook 1998/99

Excellent in the tackle he has done much to keep United's midfield together following the long term injury which sidelined Roy Keane. Not a renowned goalscorer, he has nonetheless chipped in with 10 during his 115 Premiership games and is dangerous when breaking quickly through the middle of the park. For a player who does not go lightly into tackles he did well to collect just seven yellow cards last season.

Form Factors

Season	Team	Tot	St	Sb	Y	R
95-96	Manchester U.	32	31	1	7	1
96-97	Manchester U.	26	24	2	5	0
97-98	Manchester U.	33	31	2	7	0
Total		91	86	5	19	1

	GP	GG	GF	GS	TGR
95-96	84.21	16.00	73	2	2.74
96-97	68.42	5.20	76	5	6.58
97-98	86.84	16.50	73	2	2.74
Averages	79.82	12.57	74.00	3.00	4.02

BYFIELD, Darren

Aston Villa ● S

Fullname: Darren Byfield
DOB: 29-09-76 Birmingham

After four seasons as a professional at Villa Park, it was fifth time lucky for local born Byfield who made his debut for Aston Villa on December 28 last season during a 1-1 draw away to Leeds United. It was to be his only start but he became a regular in the first team squad with another six Premiership appearances from the bench.

Having made an albeit small breakthrough last season he will be looking to establish himself this season but it would be a brave manager to include him in his fantasy team at this time.

Form Factors

Season	Team	Tot	St	Sb	Y	R
97-98	Aston Villa	7	1	6	1	0
Total		7	1	6	1	0

	GP	GG	GF	GS	TGR
97-98	18.42	0.00	49	0	0.00
Averages	18.42	0.00	49.00	0.00	0.00

CADAMARTERI, Danny

Everton ❶❷❸ S

Fullname: Daniel Leon Cadamarteri
DOB: 12-10-79 Bradford

Having made his first team debut for Everton as a 17-year-old when coming on as substitute for the final match of the 1996-97 season, Cadamarteri really caught the public's imagination last season. With the natural exuberance of a teenager and his dreadlocks he was one of the bright lights to shine in an otherwise dismal season at Goodison Park.

In 26 Premiership appearances – 15 starts and 11 as sub – Cadamarteri scored a creditable four goals which included a goal in the first match he started and the scored goal in a 2-0 win over Liverpool. His goals dried up after that match and he spent practically all of the second half of the season on the bench but he is most definitely one for the future.

Form Factors

Season	Team	Tot	St	Sb	Y	R
96-97	Everton	1	0	1	0	0
97-98	Everton	26	15	11	4	0
Total		27	15	12	4	0

	GP	GG	GF	GS	TGR
96-97	2.63	0.00	44	0	0.00
97-98	68.42	6.50	41	4	9.76
Averages	35.53	3.25	42.50	2.00	4.88

CALDERWOOD, Colin

Tottenham H. ❶❷ CB

Fullname: Colin Calderwood
DOB: 20-01-65 Stranraer

Experienced defender who celebrated his fifth season with Tottenham Hotspur with a place in Scotland's France 98 squad but had to withdraw after two games due to a serious hand injury. Has really flourished at Tottenham since the emergence of Sol Campbell but lost his place in the starting line-up towards the end of last season. Even so he played 26 times in the Premiership last season scoring four times making it his most productive seasons in six years.

At 33 Calderwood could find his opportunities more limited this season but his versatility may well extend his career in the top flight by another year. Joined Spurs from Swindon Town having also played for Mansfield Town.

Form Factors

Season	Team	Tot	St	Sb	Y	R
95-96	Tottenham H.	29	26	3	6	0
96-97	Tottenham H.	34	33	1	6	0
97-98	Tottenham H.	26	21	5	3	0
Total		89	80	9	15	0

	GP	GG	GF	GS	TGR
95-96	76.32	29.00	50	1	2.00
96-97	89.47	0.00	44	0	0.00
97-98	68.42	6.50	44	4	9.09
Averages	78.07	11.83	46.00	1.67	3.70

CAMPBELL, Andy
Middlesbrough ❶ S
Fullname: Andrew Paul Campbell
DOB: 18-04-79 Middlesbrough

During Middlesbrough's previous spell in the top flight Campbell, then just short of his 17th birthday, became the youngest ever player in the Premiership. Upon their return he is still only 19 and has a touch more experience after 15 run-outs for Boro last season in various competitions. A prolific scorer at lower levels he also broke his duck during the 1997-98 season with goals in both the FA Cup and Coca Cola Cup.

CAMPBELL, Kevin
Nottingham F. ❶❷❸ S
Fullname: Kevin Joseph Campbell
DOB: 04-02-70 Lambeth

A free-scoring striker in the Arsenal Youth and Reserve teams but failed to translate that into the first team when given the opportunity at Highbury. Had successful spells on loan to Leyton Orient and Leicester City where he scored a combined total of 14 goals in 27 games. But his form with Arsenal remained patchy with two alternately good seasons being broken up by poor ones. Nottingham Forest paid £3m in 1995 as much for his potential than results but with just nine league goals in 38 games over the next two seasons their investment looked to have failed.

Kevin Campbell

But last season, sharing the attacking responsibilities with flying Dutchman van Hooijdonk, Campbell delivered the goods with 23 goals in 41 Division One appearances. The duo were the most prolific partnership in the English leagues as between them 82 league games produced 52 goals. It now remains to be seen whether Campbell can at last produce that sort of form at the highest level.

Form Factors

Season	Team	Tot	St	Sb	Y	R
94-95	Arsenal	23	19	4	1	0
95-96	N. Forest	21	21	0	2	0
96-97	N. Forest	17	16	1	3	0
Total		61	56	5	6	0

	GP	GG	GF	GS	TGR
94-95	60.53	5.75	52	4	7.69
95-96	55.26	7.00	50	3	6.00
96-97	44.74	2.83	31	6	19.35
Averages	53.51	5.19	44.33	4.33	11.02

CAMPBELL, Sol

Tottenham H.   ❶❷❸❹ CB

Fullname: Sulzeer Jeremiah Campbell
DOB: 18-09-74 Newham, London

Arsenal have Tony Adams, Tottenham have Sol Campbell. But what Campbell does not have with Tottenham is success and if they struggle for a third consecutive year then it is difficult to see how they can hold on to the jewel of their backline. Campbell stands head and shoulders above the rest of the Spurs' defence but in the World Cup he will forever be remembered for that dazzling run against Colombia which so nearly ended in a goal.

Strong in the air, an excellent tackler, good reader of the game and quick to recover lost ground, Campbell is almost

Sol Campbell

Fantasy Football Handbook 1998/99   **135**

the complete defender – a rare commodity at White Hart Lane – and at 24 will be around for a long time to come.

Has made 168 appearances in the Premiership and chipped in with two goals.

Form Factors

Season	Team	Tot	St	Sb	Y	R
95-96	Tottenham H.	31	31	0	2	0
96-97	Tottenham H.	38	38	0	1	0
97-98	Tottenham H.	34	34	0	5	0
Total		103	103	0	8	0

	GP	GG	GF	GS	TGR
95-96	81.58	31.00	50	1	2.00
96-97	100.00	0.00	44	0	0.00
97-98	89.47	0.00	44	0	0.00
Averages	90.35	10.33	46.00	0.33	0.67

CAMPBELL, Stuart
Leicester City ❶❷ M

Fullname: Stuart Pearson Campbell
DOB: 9-12-77 Corby

Former Leicester City trainee who progressed through to the first team to make his debut in a Coca Cola Cup tie during 1996-97 with his league debut coming in December of that season against Middlesbrough. Made 10 league appearances for Leicester that season and figured on the teamsheet for 24 of Leicester's Premiership matches during 1997-98, six of which were in the starting line (he was withdrawn five times), five times he came on during the game and on 13 other occasions he was an unused substitute.

Looks likely to make further progress this season after winning the Foxes' Young Player of the Season award last season.

Form Factors

Season	Team	Tot	St	Sb	Y	R
96-97	Leicester C.	10	4	6	0	0
96-97	Leicester C.	11	6	5	1	0
Total		21	10	11	1	0

	GP	GG	GF	GS	TGR
96-97	26.32	0.00	46	0	0.00
96-97	28.95	0.00	46	0	0.00
Averages	27.63	0.00	46.00	0.00	0.00

CARBONARI, Horacio
Derby County ❶❷❸ D

Fullname: Horacio Carbonari
DOB: Argentina

New to English football for the 1998-99 season is Argentinean defender Carbonari. For a central defender, who is equally good with either foot, he does like to get amongst the goals with 36 in 127 games prior to his move to Derby County in May for £2.7m. A free kick specialist, his powerful shooting ability earned him the nickname 'Bazooka' in his native country.

CARBONE, Benito

Sheffield W. ❶❷❸ M

Fullname: Benito Carbone
DOB: 14-08-71 Bagnara Calabra, Italy

After falling out of favour with his previous club in Italy, Internazionale, Benito Carbone moved to England to become Sheffield Wednesday's then record signing at £3m in October 1996 and quickly won over the Hillsborough faithful. Carbone scored six times in 25 Premiership matches during his first season on these shores and continued that good work last season with another nine league goals from 33 matches.

Carbone, who played for Italy at Under-21 level, will also score you a good number of points through assists from his position just behind Wednesday's main strike force and he has also shown that he will not shirk his defensive responsibilities.

He played a leading role in attracting his compatriot di Canio to Hillsborough.

Form Factors

Season	Team	Tot	St	Sb	Y	R
96-97	Sheffield W.	25	24	1	3	0
97-98	Sheffield W.	33	28	5	8	1
Total		58	52	6	11	1

	GP	GG	GF	GS	TGR
96-97	65.79	4.17	50	6	12.00
97-98	86.84	3.67	52	9	17.31
Averages	76.32	3.92	51.00	7.50	14.65

Benito Carbone

CARR, Stephen

Tottenham H. ❶❷ FB

Fullname: Stephen Carr
DOB: 29-08-76 Dublin

Made his Tottenham Hotspur debut during the 1993-94 season but had to wait a further three years before adding to that game and in 1997-98 he climbed to the top pile by being the only Spurs player to feature in all of their 38 Premiership matches. Somewhat surprisingly for a defender he picked up just three yellow cards last season to go with the one against his name the season before.

Carr is a right-sided full back who supports the attack whenever possible and is capable of sending over good crosses. His patience of a couple of years spent in the reserves has now been fully rewarded with his consistency earning him a call up to the full Eire squad which neatly completes the progression from Schoolboy, Youth and Under-21 levels.

Form Factors

Season	Team	Tot	St	Sb	Y	R
93-94	Tottenham H.	1	1	0	0	0
96-97	Tottenham H.	26	24	2	1	0
97-98	Tottenham H.	38	37	1	2	0
Total		65	62	3	3	0

	GP	GG	GF	GS	TGR
93-94	2.63	0.00	54	0	0.00
96-97	68.42	0.00	44	0	0.00
97-98	100.00	0.00	44	0	0.00
Averages	57.02	0.00	47.33	0.00	0.00

CARRAGHER, Jamie

Liverpool   D M

Fullname: James Lee Carragher
DOB: 28-01-78 Bootle

Having scored in his first start for Liverpool during the 1996-97 season Carragher's star continued in the ascendancy a month later with his first call up to the England Under-21 side and at the end of the season he was a member of the England Under-20 side which competed in the World Youth Tournament in Malaysia.

He didn't disappoint last season when Liverpool manager Roy Evans afforded him much greater exposure in the first team. Although he did not score for Liverpool last season he is certainly one for the future to follow in the long line of home-grown players successfully produced on Merseyside.

Made 20 Premiership appearances for the Reds during '97-98.

Form Factors

Season	Team	Tot	St	Sb	Y	R
96-97	Liverpool	2	1	1	1	0
97-98	Liverpool	20	17	3	2	0
Total		22	18	4	3	0

	GP	GG	GF	GS	TGR
96-97	5.26	2.00	62	1	1.61
97-98	52.63	0.00	68	0	0.00
Averages	28.95	1.00	65.00	0.50	0.81

CARSLEY, Lee
Derby County ❶❷❸ FB
Fullname: Lee Kevin Carsley
DOB: 28-04-74 Birmingham

Spent two years as a professional prior to breaking into the Derby County first team early in the 1994-95 season. Since then he has played 136 league games for the Rams and missed just four Premiership games last season.

An Eire Under-21 international who is recognised as a full back but can also operate from a more attacking position. Suffered a few disciplinary problems last season as he was on the receiving end of 11 yellow cards having been booked just twice during each of the previous two seasons.

Form Factors

Season	Team	Tot	St	Sb	Y	R
96-97	Derby Co.	24	15	9	2	0
97-98	Derby Co.	34	34	0	11	0
Total		58	49	9	13	0

	GP	GG	GF	GS	TGR
96-97	63.16	0.00	45	0	0.00
97-98	89.47	34.00	52	1	1.92
Averages	76.32	17.00	48.50	0.50	0.96

CASIRAGHI, Pierluigi
Chelsea ❶❷❸❹❺ S
Fullname: Pierluigi Casiraghi
DOB: 04-04-69 Monza, Italy

At 29 years old a transfer fee of £5.4m may seem excessive to those outside of Stamford Bridge but Chelsea manager Vialli knows all about his latest Italian import with the duo having played together on many occasions down the years.

A striker of proven ability it was his goal in a qualifying play-off against Russia which took the Italians through to France 98 but he was omitted from the final 22.

CASPER, Chris
Manchester U. ❶ CB
Fullname: Christopher Martin Casper
DOB: 28-04-75 Burnley

Central defender who has played for England Youth and Under-21 but is finding great difficulty in breaking into the Manchester United first team having made just two league appearances during six years as a professional at Old Trafford. Gained some Football League experience with a spell on loan to Bournemouth three seasons ago and had a similar stint with Swindon Town last season. Casper is highly rated at Old Trafford and whether or not he makes it with the Reds he can rightly claim to having played in the Champions League with United.

CASTLEDINE, Stewart

Wimbledon ❶ M

Fullname: Stewart Mark Castledine
DOB: 22-01-73 Wandsworth

For the seventh season out of the past eight Castledine was called into action with the Wimbledon first team but has still to play in more than seven league games in any one season. Indeed his season's best total of seven league games was achieved during a period on loan to Wycombe Wanderers in the 1995-96 season.

Has scored in four separate seasons for the Dons and showed that he knows where goal is during his time at Wycombe with three goals in those seven games.

Form Factors

Season	Team	Tot	St	Sb	Y	R
95-96	Wimbledon	4	2	2	0	0
96-97	Wimbledon	6	4	2	0	0
97-98	Wimbledon	6	3	3	1	0
Total		16	9	7	1	0

	GP	GG	GF	GS	TGR
95-96	10.53	4.00	55	1	1.82
96-97	15.79	6.00	49	1	2.04
97-98	15.79	0.00	34	0	0.00
Averages	14.04	3.33	46.00	0.67	1.29

CHAPPLE, Phil

Charlton A. ❶❷ D

Fullname: Philip Richard Chapple
DOB: 26-11-66 Norwich

Has proved a bargain buy since being snapped up from Cambridge United five years ago for £100,000, since when he has played 142 league games for the Addicks. Has stood in as captain on numerous occasions and to compensate for a lack of speed he is extremely strong in the air and reads the game well. Scored a very useful four goals last season and has bagged at least a brace every season since making his debut with Cambridge in April 1988.

Started his career with his home-town club Norwich City but left Carrow Road without breaking into the first team to join Cambridge United where he spent over five years.

CHARLES, Gary

Aston Villa ❶❷ FB

Fullname: Gary Andrew Charles
DOB: 13-04-70 Newham

Former England defender who missed the whole of the 1996-97 season through injury but battled back well to reclaim his place in the Aston Villa side last season only to spend the second half of the season sitting on the substitutes' bench. Charles made just two appearances in the starting line up after Christmas and it was in one of these, at Everton, that he scored his first goal in almost two years.

Having started his career at full-back he is a natural for the role of wing-back with his tendency to push forward.

Charles started his career with Nottingham Forest and had a spell on loan to Leicester City before joining Derby County and then Villa.

Form Factors

Season	Team	Tot	St	Sb	Y	R
94-95	Aston Villa	16	14	2	0	0
95-96	Aston Villa	34	34	0	1	0
97-98	Aston Villa	18	14	4	1	0
Total		68	62	6	2	0

	GP	GG	GF	GS	TGR
94-95	42.11	0.00	51	0	0.00
95-96	89.47	34.00	52	1	1.92
97-98	47.37	18.00	49	1	2.04
Averages	59.65	17.33	50.67	0.67	1.32

CHETTLE, Steve

Nottingham F. ❶❷❸ D

Fullname: Stephen Chettle
DOB: 27-09-68 Nottingham

Tremendously loyal Nottingham-born defender who celebrated Nottingham Forest's return to the Premiership by scoring his first league goal in four seasons. Has been a model of consistency throughout his career as witnessed by his appearances under different managers. His 41 Nationwide League games last season took his total of league matches played to 368 but that is still almost 250 short of the club record.

Excellent at reading the game, a good header of the ball and solid in the tackle Chettle is one of the most reliable defenders returning to the top flight. Made his Forest debut in 1987 and has not played fewer than 22 league games in any one season since.

Form Factors

Season	Team	Tot	St	Sb	Y	R
94-95	N. Forest	41	41	0	4	1
95-96	N. Forest	37	37	0	4	1
96-97	N. Forest	32	31	1	3	0
Total		110	109	1	11	2

	GP	GG	GF	GS	TGR
94-95	107.89	0.00	72	0	0.00
95-96	97.37	0.00	50	0	0.00
96-97	84.21	0.00	31	0	0.00
Averages	96.49	0.00	51.00	0.00	0.00

CLARKE, Andy

Wimbledon ● S

Fullname: Andrew Weston Clarke
DOB: 22-07-67 Islington

The 1997-98 season was very much in keeping with Clarke's fortunes in recent times as the winger was once again subject to lengthy bouts of watching games from the substitutes' bench. Of his first 100 games for Wimbledon half were as substitute and last season saw him start in just one Premiership match and come on as sub in 13 others; he was also named as an unused sub in another baker's dozen games. Probably not a wise move to include him in your fantasy team unless you are looking for someone to occupy a seat on the subs bench.

Form Factors

Season	Team	Tot	St	Sb	Y	R
95-96	Wimbledon	18	9	9	0	0
96-97	Wimbledon	11	4	7	1	0
97-98	Wimbledon	14	1	13	0	0
Total		43	14	29	1	0

	GP	GG	GF	GS	TGR
95-96	47.37	9.00	55	2	3.64
96-97	28.95	11.00	49	1	2.04
97-98	36.84	0.00	34	0	0.00
Averages	37.72	6.67	46.00	1.00	1.89

Andy Clarke

CLARKE, Matt

Sheffield W. ❶ GK

Fullname: Matthew John Clarke
DOB: 03-11-73 Sheffield

Goalkeeper who has spent a very frustrating two years at Hillsborough following a £300,000 transfer from Yorkshire rivals Rotherham United. Was unjustly dismissed on his Owls' debut in May 1997 and found his chances restricted to just two games during last season. And with seven goals conceded in those two games he quickly lost his place in the side as regular Wednesday keeper Kevin Pressman regained fitness. Hard to see Clarke being offered anything better than understudy again to Pressman during the 1998-99 campaign.

Form Factors

Season	Team	Tot	St	Sb	Y	R
96-97	Sheffield W.	1	0	1	0	1
97-98	Sheffield W.	3	2	1	0	0
Total		4	2	2	0	1

	GA	GkA	GAp	CS	SO	R
96-97	51	0	0.00	0	0	0
97-98	67	7	2.33	1	1	0
Averages	59.0	3.5	1.17	0.5	0.5	0

CLARKE, Steve

Chelsea ❶❷ CB

Fullname: Stephen Clarke
DOB: 29-08-63 Saltcoats

Veteran of over 400 games for Chelsea, well clear of any other member of the current playing staff at Stamford Bridge, and even at the age of 35 looks set for another season of top class football with the Blues. And as Chelsea marched towards glory in both the Cup Winners' Cup and the Coca Cola Cup, Clarke had cause for his own personal celebration by scoring his first goal in seven seasons.

Has been an outstanding servant of Chelsea since joining the club from St. Mirren during the 1986-87 season for £400,000 having only once played less than 20 league games in a season in that time.

Fine passer, excellent at reading the game, controlled in possession and shows no sign of falling below his own high standards with the passing of time. His appointment to player/assistant coach in the close season may indicate that his playing days are limited.

Form Factors

Season	Team	Tot	St	Sb	Y	R
95-96	Chelsea	22	21	1	2	0
96-97	Chelsea	31	31	0	7	0
97-98	Chelsea	26	22	4	2	0
Total		79	74	5	11	0

	GP	GG	GF	GS	TGR
95-96	57.89	0.00	46	0	0.00
96-97	81.58	0.00	58	0	0.00
97-98	68.42	26.00	71	1	1.41
Averages	69.30	8.67	58.33	0.33	0.47

CLEGG, Michael

Manchester U. ❶ FB
Fullname: Michael Jamie Clegg
DOB: 03-07-77 Tameside

Made four appearances in the Premiership with Manchester United during 1996-97 but last season was another of little progress for Clegg who started in just one league game and came on as substitute in two others. He was also a used substitute on the night United bowed out of the Champions Cup with a home draw against Monaco. Hard to see Clegg breaking through in a big way this time round.

Form Factors

Season	Team	Tot	St	Sb	Y	R
96-97	Manchester U.	4	3	1	0	0
97-98	Manchester U.	3	1	2	0	0
Total		7	4	3	0	0

	GP	GG	GF	GS	TGR
96-97	10.53	0.00	76	0	0.00
97-98	7.89	0.00	73	0	0.00
Averages	9.21	0.00	74.50	0.00	0.00

CLEMENCE, Stephen

Tottenham H. ❶❷❸ M
Fullname: Stephen Clemence
DOB: 31-03-78 Liverpool

Clemence, then a teenager, made his Tottenham first team debut on the opening day of last season to complete a rise from the FA School of Excellence and through the ranks at White Hart Lane. Although reduced to a place on the bench by the end of the campaign it had been a good season for the Liverpool-born midfielder who can expect to make bigger in-roads into the Premiership this season. Highly rated at Tottenham, the former England Youth player made 21 appearances and scored his first goal during an FA Cup win over Fulham.

Form Factors

Season	Team	Tot	St	Sb	Y	R
97-98	Tottenham H.	17	12	5	1	0
Total		17	12	5	1	0

	GP	GG	GF	GS	TGR
97-98	44.74	0.00	44	0	0.00
Averages	44.74	0.00	44.00	0.00	0.00

CLEMENT, Phillippe

Coventry C. ❶❷ M
Fullname: Phillippe Clement
DOB: Belgium

Unknown in this country, Clement is set to make his debut at the start of this season having joined Coventry City on a four year deal on transfer deadline day last season. A 23 year old Belgian international midfielder who cost the Sky Blues £650,000. His previous clubs include Racing Genk, St. Anneke Sport and Beerschot!

exceptional, in 230 league games he has scored 124 goals and anything but a continuation of that form this season would be a major surprise. An England recall looks inevitable at some stage.

Form Factors

Season	Team	Tot	St	Sb	Y	R
95-96	Manchester U.	34	32	2	4	0
96-97	Manchester U.	20	10	10	1	0
97-98	Manchester U.	33	31	2	6	0
Total		87	73	14	11	0

	GP	GG	GF	GS	TGR
95-96	89.47	3.09	73	11	15.07
96-97	52.63	3.33	76	6	7.89
97-98	86.84	2.06	73	16	21.92
Averages	76.32	2.83	74.00	11.00	14.96

COLE, Andy

Manchester U. ❶❷❸❹ S
Fullname: Andrew Alexander Cole
DOB: 15-10-71 Nottingham

With the second most successful season of his career Andy Cole proved a great number of doubters wrong during 1997-98 but it was not quite enough to get him on the plane to France 98 with England. Cole found the target in league and cup ties 25 times with the bulk of those goals – 15 – coming during a sensational 13 match run from October to January. Hat-tricks were scored during a 7-0 thrashing of Barnsley and a touch more gloriously during a 3-1 victory in Holland over Feyenoord.

Although the goals came more slowly towards the end of the season Cole could again be the leading scorer in the top flight this season especially with David Beckham and Paul Scholes coming to their creative best.

Cole's record since making his debut for Arsenal during the 1990-91 season is

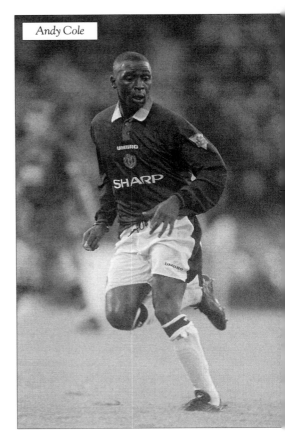
Andy Cole

Fantasy Football Handbook 1998/99   **145**

COLLYMORE, Stan

Aston Villa ①② S

Fullname: Stanley Victor Collymore
DOB: 22-01-71 Stone

A £7m transfer to Aston Villa, the club he supported as a boy, appeared to be the perfect platform upon which Stan Collymore could rebuild his career following an indifferent two years with Liverpool. Unfortunately for Villa fans the script was not adhered to and Collymore, not aided by personal problems, contributed a poor six goals in 25 Premiership outings.

Such a return fell well below even his less than spectacular record at Anfield and does not withstand any sort of comparison with his record during three highly productive campaigns with Southend United and Nottingham Forest. Collymore has everything a striker needs to succeed with speed, strength, good heading ability and an eye for stunning, unexpected goals, all within his range, the only doubt concerns his attitude. Get that right and Collymore could once again be one of the most admired strikers in the Premiership.

Form Factors

Season	Team	Tot	St	Sb	Y	R
95-96	Liverpool	30	29	1	2	0
96-97	Liverpool	30	25	5	3	0
97-98	Aston Villa	25	23	2	4	1
Total		85	77	8	9	1

	GP	GG	GF	GS	TGR
95-96	78.95	2.14	70	14	20.00
96-97	78.95	2.50	62	12	19.35
97-98	65.79	4.17	49	6	12.24
Averages	74.56	2.94	60.33	10.67	17.20

COOPER, Colin

Nottingham F. ①②③ D

Fullname: Colin Terence Cooper
DOB: 28-02-67 Sedgefield

Holder of two England caps, both won during his time at Nottingham Forest, Cooper is a tough-tackling defender who gets forward well at set-pieces and last season, for the second time in three seasons, contributed a very useful five goals. Actually possesses a good record in front of goal for a defender having found the target in 11 of the past 12 seasons.

Cooper has shown his adaptability recently when he played in a midfield position after losing his central defensive slot following a gashed calf injury. Joined Forest for £1.7m in 1993 from Millwall having started out in professional football with Middlesbrough where he spent seven seasons.

Form Factors

Season	Team	Tot	St	Sb	Y	R
94-95	N. Forest	35	35	0	7	0
95-96	N. Forest	37	37	0	7	0
96-97	N. Forest	36	36	0	6	0
Total		108	108	0	20	0

	GP	GG	GF	GS	TGR
94-95	92.11	35.00	72	1	1.39
95-96	97.37	7.40	50	5	10.00
96-97	94.74	18.00	31	2	6.45
Averages	94.74	20.13	51.00	2.67	5.95

CORT, Carl

Wimbledon ①②S

Fullname: Carl Edward Richard Cort
DOB: 01-11-77

Another of Joe Kinnear's kids to have come through the ranks at Wimbledon and at 6'2" tall is very much in the mould of Dons strikers down the years. Made his Football League debut while on loan to Lincoln City during 1996-97 and upon his return to Selhurst Park made his debut as a sub in the Premiership. Was in the starting line-up for the first time in September last year and took his chance well by scoring in a 3-1 win at Newcastle. In his first eight league and cup games of last season he had five goals in the bag but sadly only added one more during the rest of the season and was used mostly as a substitute after the turn of the year.

Quick on the ground and dangerous in the air Cort should make an even bigger impression this season.

Form Factors

Season	Team	Tot	St	Sb	Y	R
96-97	Wimbledon	1	0	1	0	0
97-98	Wimbledon	22	16	6	0	0
Total		23	16	7	0	0

	GP	GG	GF	GS	TGR
96-97	2.63	0.00	49	0	0.00
97-98	57.89	5.50	34	4	11.76
Averages	30.26	2.75	41.50	2.00	5.88

COTTEE, Tony

Leicester C. ①S

Fullname: Anthony Richard Cottee
DOB: 11-07-65 West Ham

After ending his second stint at West Ham United early in the 1996-97 season Cottee's days in the Premiership looked to be over only for the former England striker to return from a spell abroad with Selangor to sign for Leicester City last season. Had a spell on loan to Birmingham City before settling at Filbert Street.

Goals may be harder to come by for the striker who in one spell in the mid-80's missed just three league games in four seasons but he had the satisfaction of scoring his first ever goal at Old Trafford last season and ended the campaign with a brace at Upton Park.

Pace, an eagle-eye for a half-chance and the ability to get around the blind side of defences brought Cottee 187 before adding four more from 19 Premiership matches last season but only seven of those games saw him in the starting line-up. Looks to have a fight on his hands to regain a permanent place in the side.

Form Factors

Season	Team	Tot	St	Sb	Y	R
95-96	West Ham U.	33	30	3	1	0
96-97	West Ham U.	3	2	1	1	0
97-98	Leicester C.	19	7	12	0	0
Total		55	39	16	2	0

	GP	GG	GF	GS	TGR
95-96	86.84	3.30	43	10	23.26
96-97	7.89	0.00	39	0	0.00
97-98	50.00	4.75	51	4	7.84
Averages	48.25	2.68	44.33	4.67	10.37

CROFT, Gary
Blackburn Rovers ❶❷❸ FB
Fullname: Gary Croft
DOB: 17-02-74 Burton on Trent

Took time to settle and establish himself with Blackburn Rovers but has flourished under the management of Roy Hodgson. Has represented England at Under-21 but had just five run-outs during his first full season with Rovers before coming to the fore last season with 23 games in the Premiership and was named a further five times as an unused substitute.

Predominently a defensive player, his good use of the ball makes him suitable to play a more advanced role when required. Scored one goal in the Premiership, that being the winner at home to Chelsea last November. Joined Rovers from Grimsby Town for £1.7m in March 1996.

Form Factors

Season	Team	Tot	St	Sb	Y	R
96-97	Blackburn R.	5	4	1	0	0
97-98	Blackburn R.	23	19	4	0	0
Total		28	23	5	0	0

	GP	GG	GF	GS	TGR
96-97	13.16	0.00	42	0	0.00
97-98	60.53	23.00	57	1	1.75
Averages	36.84	11.50	49.50	0.50	0.88

CRUYFF, Jordi
Manchester U. ❶❷ S
Fullname: Johan Jordi Cruyff
DOB: 09-02-74

As befitting a footballer bearing the legendary name of Cruyff, Jordi is a very skilful player who can play to equal effect on either flank and can also fill in down the middle. Joined Manchester United from Barcelona for £1m following Euro 96 but took time to integrate into a United side already packed with internationals and made just 16 Premiership appearances that season. The 1997-98 campaign was even more disappointing for the Dutch international as injury cut short his bright start after five games and he failed to reclaim his place.

After two undistinguished years at Old Trafford the new season is clearly make or break for the son of one of the sport's greatest ever players.

Form Factors

Season	Team	Tot	St	Sb	Y	R
96-97	Manchester U.	16	11	5	2	0
97-98	Manchester U.	5	3	2	1	0
Total		21	14	7	3	0

	GP	GG	GF	GS	TGR
96-97	42.11	5.33	76	3	3.95
97-98	13.16	0.00	73	0	0.00
Averages	27.63	2.67	74.50	1.50	1.97

CUNNINGHAM, Kenny

Wimbledon ❶❷❸ FB
Fullname: Kenneth Edward Cunningham
DOB: 28-06-71 Dublin

Joined Wimbledon from Millwall in November 1994 for £1.3m after five years at the Den and has been an almost permanent fixture in the Dons side ever since. Over the past three seasons the very reliable Cunningham has missed just 13 league games but mysteriously for a defender who loves to go forward has mustered just one goal and that came in April 1994 during his Millwall days.

A steady defender and Eire international who has played 129 Premiership matches for Wimbledon following his 136 league games for Millwall. A useful addition to your team as he is seldom suspended.

Form Factors

Season	Team	Tot	St	Sb	Y	R
95-96	Wimbledon	33	32	1	5	0
96-97	Wimbledon	36	36	0	5	0
97-98	Wimbledon	32	32	0	2	0
Total		101	100	1	12	0

	GP	GG	GF	GS	TGR
95-96	86.84	0.00	55	0	0.00
96-97	94.74	0.00	49	0	0.00
97-98	84.21	0.00	34	0	0.00
Averages	88.60	0.00	46.00	0.00	0.00

CURTIS, John

Manchester U. ❶❷ D
Fullname: John Curtis
DOB: 03-09-78 Nuneaton

Former Manchester United Youth team defender who ventured into the first team for the first time last season and is seen by many as one who will make the grade, probably as a sweeper. Just months after leading England Under-20s through the group matches of the World Youth Championships in Malaysia, he made his United debut in the Coca Cola Cup defeat at Ipswich and made the first of his eight Premiership appearances during the 7-0 destruction of Barnsley at Old Trafford.

Form Factors

Season	Team	Tot	St	Sb	Y	R
97-98	Manchester U.	8	3	5	0	0
Total		8	3	5	0	0

	GP	GG	GF	GS	TGR
97-98	21.05	0.00	73	0	0.00
Averages	21.05	0.00	73.00	0.00	0.00

DABIZAS, Nikolaos

Newcastle U. ①②③④ CD

Fullname: Nikolaos Dabizas
DOB: 03-08-73

Rated by Newcastle supporters as the most successful of Kenny Dalglish's foreign imports, Dabizas became the first player from his country, Greece, to play at Wembley in the FA Cup final and went close to marking the occasion with a goal as he headed against the woodwork.

Joined the Magpies from Olympiakos for £1.5m just two months before the final. Good at reading the game, he times his tackles well, is a good header and can also play the holding role in midfield. Won two championships during his time in Greece.

Form Factors

Season	Team	Tot	St	Sb	Y	R
97-98	Newcastle U.	11	10	1	2	0
Total		11	10	1	2	0

	GP	GG	GF	GS	TGR
97-98	28.95	11.00	35	1	2.86
Averages	28.95	11.00	35.00	1.00	2.86

Nikolaos Dabizas

DAHLIN, Martin

Blackburn R. ①②③ S

Fullname: Martin Dahlin
DOB: 16-04-68 Lund, Sweden

One of the first major signings of Rovers' manager Roy Hodgson, Dahlin joined Blackburn from AS Roma for £2m in July 1997 but it is questionable whether the club got full value for their money. He appeared in 21 Premiership matches in his first season at Ewood Park although ten of those games were as substitute, and he scored four times.

A Swedish international, he first made his mark with Malmo before joining Borussia Monchengladbach in 1992. Had a very successful USA 94, scoring four times. If fully fit then this could be the season he really shines in England.

Form Factors

Season	Team	Tot	St	Sb	Y	R
97-98	Blackburn R.	21	11	10	2	0
Total		21	11	10	2	0

	GP	GG	GF	GS	TGR
97-98	55.26	5.25	57	4	7.02
Averages	55.26	5.25	57.00	4.00	7.02

DAILY, Christian

Derby County ①②③④ M

Fullname: Christian Eduard Dailly
DOB: 23-10-73 Dundee

Began his career with Dundee, where he was born, before moving to the Premiership with Derby County for the start of the 1996-97 season. Scored in only his second game for the Rams, a 1-1 draw at Tottenham, when playing in a deep midfield position but has since been switched to a more defensive position to great effect. Scotland manager Craig Brown was impressed enough by Dailly's consistency and driving determination to play him in all three of the Scots' Group matches in France 98.

Will again be a big influence on Derby's fortunes this season.

Form Factors

Season	Team	Tot	St	Sb	Y	R
96-97	Derby County	36	31	5	6	0
97-98	Derby County	30	30	0	7	0
Total		66	61	5	13	0

	GP	GG	GF	GS	TGR
96-97	94.74	12.00	45	3	6.67
97-98	78.95	30.00	52	1	1.92
Averages	86.84	21.00	48.50	2.00	4.29

Christian Dailly

DARCHEVILLE, Jean-Claude

Nottingham F. ①② S

Fullname: Jean-Claude Darcheville
DOB: France

Dave Bassett has pledged a lot of faith in the potential of young Frenchman Darcheville by investing £700,000 in the Rennes striker even though his record shows just three goals in 24 games last season. Would take a brave manager to include him in a fantasy team.

DAVIDSON, Callum

Blackburn R. ❶❷ D

Fullname: Callum Davidson
DOB: 25-06-76 Stirling

Defender Davidson was brought to Ewood Park in February 1998 very much with one eye on this season, was given just one run out last season following his £1.75m transfer from St. Johnstone and was an unused substitute for three other games.

Form Factors

Season	Team	Tot	St	Sb	Y	R
97-98	Blackburn Rovers	1	1	0	0	0
Total		1	1	0	0	0

	GP	GG	GF	GS	TGR
97-98	2.63	0.00	57	0	0.00
Averages	2.63	0.00	57.00	0.00	0.00

DAVIES, Kevin

Blackburn B. ❶❷❸❹ S

Fullname: Kevin Cyril Davies
DOB: 26-03-77 Sheffield

Has enjoyed a phenomenal rise over the past two years which culminated just after the close of last season with a £7.1m move from Southampton to Blackburn Rovers. Scored 22 goals in the Football League in 129 games for Chesterfield but it was his four goals – including a hat-trick against Bolton – in Chesterfield's march to the semi final of the FA Cup in 1997 which really brought him national recognition.

Occasionally unorthodox, he learns quickly and with his knack of running at defenders should settle quickly, although it would be a surprise if his first season at Ewood Park were to see an explosion of goals.

Moved to Southampton for just £750,000 and the Saints really pleased their bank manager a year later with his mega-bucks transfer to Blackburn.

Form Factors

Season	Team	Tot	St	Sb	Y	R
97-98	Southampton	25	20	5	5	0
Total		25	20	5	5	0

	GP	GG	GF	GS	TGR
97-98	65.79	2.78	50	9	18.00
Averages	65.79	2.78	50.00	9.00	18.00

DE GOEY, Ed

Chelsea ❶❷❸ GK

Fullname: Ed de Goey
DOB: 20-12-66

Goalkeeper who was held back as cover for Holland's van der Sar during the World Cup after a very successful first season with Chelsea. Signed by former Blues' boss Ruud Gullit from Feyenoord for a hefty £2.25m, de Goey appeared in 28 of Chelsea's Premiership matches last season conceding 31 goals at an average of 1.11 per game which was just below the Blues' overall Premiership average of 1.13. Was in goal for Chelsea's Cup Winners' Cup and Coca Cola Cup wins last season and is likely to start the 1998-99 season in preference to Dmitri Kharine.

Missed just eight games in his seven years with Feyenoord having previously played for Sparta Rotterdam.

Form Factors

Season	Team	Tot	St	Sb	Y	R
97-98	Chelsea	28	28	0	0	0
Total		28	28	0	0	0

	GA	GkA	GAp	CS	SO	R
97-98	43	32	1.00	12	2	0
Averages	43	32	1.00	12	2	0

DELAP, Rory

Derby County   ❶❷❸ S

Fullname: Rory John Delap
DOB: 06-07-76 Sutton Coldfield

An Eire Under-21 international who stepped up to the Premiership with Derby County in February 1998 from Carlisle United at a cost of £500,000 for the Rams. Was quickly given his chance to get accustomed to the speed of the Premiership with a run-out in all of Derby's final 13 matches of the season.

Has plenty of attributes to ensure that he makes a successful transition from Division Three including a more than useful long throw. Has a very powerful right foot and is good at holding the ball up with his tight control.

Form Factors

Season	Team	Tot	St	Sb	Y	R
97-98	Derby County	13	10	3	2	0
Total		13	10	3	2	0

	GP	GG	GF	GS	TGR
97-98	34.21	0.00	52	0	0.00
Averages	34.21	0.00	52.00	0.00	0.00

Ed de Goey

DESAILLY, Marcel

Chelsea   ❶❷❸❹❺ D/M

Fullname: Marcel Desailly
DOB: 07-09-68 France

Although new to the Premiership for 1998-99, Desailly is far from unknown as he stood solid in the heart of the French defence for every game of this summer's World Cup. Very experienced, he can also play in midfield.

He has played on the continent for Marseilles and Milan and like his new teammate Casiraghi has joined Chelsea for what appears a high £4.6m fee for a

FANTASY FOOTBALL HANDBOOK 1998/99   **153**

Marcel Desailly

player who will be 30 within the first few weeks of the season. Went some way to justifying that fee with some outstanding performances in France 98 until his dismissal in the Final.

DI CANIO, Paolo

Sheffield W. ❶❷❸❹❺ S

Fullname: Paolo di Canio
DOB: 9-07-68 Rome

Became Sheffield Wednesday's record signing when he moved to Hillsborough in the summer of 1997 from Celtic in a deal which cost the club £3m plus Regi Blinker who headed in the opposite direction. Justified then manager David Pleat's judgement in paying such a large fee by being the Owls' top scorer last season with 12 Premiership goals, ironically also his tally the previous year with Celtic.

Paolo Di Canio

A flamboyant character on the pitch, with boots to match, he certainly possesses a Latin temperament as 10 yellow cards from his 35 Premiership appearances testify, but regardless of his tendency to get himself into trouble he will almost certainly be amongst the goals again this season and from his favoured wide position and will also provide several assists.

Previous clubs include Scaffhausen, Zurich, Aarau and Lazio from where he joined Chelsea. Is certain to again be one of the star performers during the 1998-99 season.

Form Factors

Season	Team	Tot	St	Sb	Y	R
96-97	Chelsea	34	33	1	5	0
97-98	Chelsea	30	28	2	6	0
Total		64	61	3	11	0

	GP	GG	GF	GS	TGR
96-97	89.47	5.67	58	6	10.34
97-98	78.95	7.50	71	4	5.63
Averages	84.21	6.58	64.50	5.00	7.99

Form Factors

Season	Team	Tot	St	Sb	Y	R
97-98	Sheffield W.	35	34	1	10	0
Total		35	34	1	10	0

	GP	GG	GF	GS	TGR
97-98	92.11	2.92	52	12	23.08
Averages	92.11	2.92	52.00	12.00	23.08

DI MATTEO, Roberto

Chelsea ①②③④⑤ M

Fullname: Roberto Di Matteo
DOB: 29-05-70 Sciaffusa, Switzerland

The man who created FA Cup history with the fastest ever goal in the final, within 42 seconds of the start of Chelsea's win over Middlesbrough in 1997, he had another outstanding season in 1997-98 on his way to repaying another large slice of the club record £4.9m Chelsea invested in him. Midfield general who is excellent on the ball and has shown himself to be no soft touch when looking to win possession. He can also score goals, although his four in 30 Premiership matches was down on his seven for the previous season.

Born in Switzerland he is an Italian international through his parents and played a large part in Italy's run to the quarter finals of the World Cup in France.

Roberto Di Matteo

DICKS, Julian
West Ham Utd ❶❷❸❹ CB

Fullname: Julian Andrew Dicks
DOB: 08-08-68 Bristol

A legend at West Ham, Dicks will be looking to rebuild his Hammers career this season after a pre-season knee injury kept him out for the whole of the 1997-98 campaign and stranded on an excellent 60 goals in 303 league and cup games for the club.

Only Stuart Pearce has come close to matching Dicks' determination to win tackles in recent years but it is a determination not without cost as Dicks has served more than a reasonable number of suspensions. That said, a fit Julian Dicks would figure in many a fantasy team.

Is currently in his second spell at Upton Park having also spent 13 months with Liverpool when he scored three times in 24 league games. Has won England honours at Under-21 and B levels.

Form Factors

Season	Team	Tot	St	Sb	Y	R
94-95	West Ham U.	29	29	0	9	0
95-96	West Ham U.	34	34	0	5	1
96-97	West Ham U.	31	31	0	6	0
Total		94	94	0	20	1

	GP	GG	GF	GS	TGR
94-95	76.32	5.80	44	5	11.36
95-96	89.47	3.40	43	10	23.26
96-97	81.58	5.17	39	6	15.38
Averages	82.46	4.79	42.00	7.00	16.67

DIXON, Lee
Arsenal ❶❷❸ FB

Fullname: Lee Michael Dixon
DOB: 17-03-64 Manchester

Dixon's 28 league appearances last season was his lowest in ten years at Highbury but the former England defender, although 34, is showing no signs of being ready to stand down from Arsenal's magnificent defence of the past nine years and signed a new two-year contract in February.

His main assets include his excellence at timing tackles and being a threat whenever he moves down the flank to send over usually superb crosses.

Spent five years with the likes of Burnley, Chester City, Bury and Stoke City before joining Arsenal where he has won the championship three times, the FA Cup twice and the Cup Winners' Cup and the League Cup once each. Is likely to face a challenge for his place this season as Arsene Wenger looks to bring the European Cup to Highbury but there are still few better right-backs than Dixon.

Form Factors

Season	Team	Tot	St	Sb	Y	R
95-96	Arsenal	38	38	0	2	0
96-97	Arsenal	32	31	1	8	0
97-98	Arsenal	28	26	2	3	0
Total		98	95	3	13	0

	GP	GG	GF	GS	TGR
95-96	100.00	19.00	49	2	4.08
96-97	84.21	16.00	62	2	3.23
97-98	73.68	0.00	68	0	0.00
Averages	85.96	11.67	59.67	1.33	2.44

DODD, Jason

Southampton ❶❷ FB
Fullname: Jason Robert Dodd
DOB: 02-11-70 Bath

After an injury-hit time during 1996-97, Dodd missed the opening two games of last season, again through injury, but they were to be the only times when he was not in Southampton's Premiership line-up. A marvellously consistent performer who is also very adaptable having filled several positions at the Dell including central defence, wing-back and midfield during his nine years in the Southampton first team. Tends to play a defensive role when used in midfield which has restricted Dodd to just seven goals in his 231 league games for the club.

Joined the Saints from Bath City for £50,000 in March 1989.

Form Factors

Season	Team	Tot	St	Sb	Y	R
95-96	Southampton	36	36	0	4	0
96-97	Southampton	23	23	0	2	1
97-98	Southampton	36	36	0	2	0
Total		95	95	0	8	1

	GP	GG	GF	GS	TGR
95-96	94.74	18.00	34	2	5.88
96-97	60.53	23.00	50	1	2.00
97-98	94.74	36.00	50	1	2.00
Averages	83.33	25.67	44.67	1.33	3.29

DRAPER, Mark

Aston Villa ❶❷❸ M
Fullname: Mark Andrew Draper
DOB: 11-11-70 Long Eaton

Reliable midfielder who got into the England squad for a World Cup qualifier against Moldova but was not called up for his first cap. Draper is skilful on the ball, works tirelessly to act as a link between defence and attack, is a particularly good

Mark Draper

FANTASY FOOTBALL HANDBOOK 1998/99

passer and packs a powerful shot although his 10 goals in 135 Premiership matches is not exceptional. An all-round solid midfield player whose great strength is his consistency.

Signed for Aston Villa for £3.25m from Leicester City in July 1995 having joined the Foxes a year earlier for £1.25m after six years with Notts County. A one time England Under-21 international.

Form Factors

Season	Team	Tot	St	Sb	Y	R
95-96	Aston Villa	36	36	0	1	0
96-97	Aston Villa	29	28	1	4	1
97-98	Aston Villa	31	31	0	4	0
Total		96	95	1	9	1

	GP	GG	GF	GS	TGR
95-96	94.74	18.00	52	2	3.85
96-97	76.32	0.00	47	0	0.00
97-98	81.58	10.33	49	3	6.12
Averages	84.21	9.44	49.33	1.67	3.32

DRYDEN, Richard

Southampton ❶❷ CB

Fullname: Richard Andrew Dryden
DOB: 14-06-69 Stroud

Central defender who was given a chance to prove himself at the highest level rather late in his career but has grasped the chance superbly with some stirring performances to the left of the heart of the Southampton defence over the past couple of seasons.

Accomplished ball player and fine tackler, he spent ten years playing for both of the Bristol clubs, Exeter City, Notts County, Birmingham City, Manchester City (loan) and Plymouth Argyle (loan) before signing for Southampton for just £150,000 in August 1996.

Form Factors

Season	Team	Tot	St	Sb	Y	R
96-97	Southampton	29	28	1	5	0
97-98	Southampton	13	11	2	2	0
Total		42	39	3	7	0

	GP	GG	GF	GS	TGR
96-97	76.32	29.00	50	1	2.00
97-98	34.21	0.00	50	0	0.00
Averages	55.26	14.50	50.00	0.50	1.00

DUBERRY, Michael

Chelsea ❶❷ CB
Fullname: Michael Wayne Duberry
DOB: 14-10-75 London

Was one of the most highly touted youngsters to break into the Premiership during the 1995-96 season – following a spell on loan to Bournemouth – only for injuries, including a snapped achilles tendon, to hinder his progress a year later. Returned to form last season although Chelsea's rotating team selection and an ankle injury sustained in September restricted his Premiership appearances to 23 games. A good header of the ball, he is also the quickest player at the club and wins the most unlikely of tackles.

Has played for England at Under-21 and has the potential to make it into the senior side.

Form Factors

Season	Team	Tot	St	Sb	Y	R
95-96	Chelsea	22	22	0	3	0
96-97	Chelsea	15	13	2	4	0
97-98	Chelsea	23	23	0	2	0
Total		60	58	2	9	0

	GP	GG	GF	GS	TGR
95-96	57.89	0.00	46	0	0.00
96-97	39.47	15.00	58	1	1.72
97-98	60.53	0.00	71	0	0.00
Averages	52.63	5.00	58.33	0.33	0.57

DUBLIN, Dion

Coventry City ❶❷❸❹ S
Fullname: Dion Dublin
DOB: 22-04-69 Leicester

Following an unsuccessful injury-ridden spell with Manchester United, Dublin has done a magnificent job in rebuilding his career with Coventry City and came within a whisker of making Glenn Hoddle's final 22 for the World Cup.

Dublin's success in 1997-98, with a career best 18 Premiership goals, made him the Sky Blues' top scorer, which was in marked contrast to a year earlier when he served a seven match suspension for two consecutive dismissals, was dropped and then spent time playing at centre-half. Now he is one of the most feared strikers in the land despite his unorthodox, almost disjointed mannerisms. His league record at Highfield Road is excellent with 58 goals in 135 games.

He was red carded again last season but should Dublin be able to keep the goals coming then he could well feature in England's Euro 2000 qualifying games.

Form Factors

Season	Team	Tot	St	Sb	Y	R
95-96	Coventry C.	34	34	0	3	0
96-97	Coventry C.	34	33	1	5	0
97-98	Coventry C.	36	36	0	4	1
Total		104	103	1	12	1

	GP	GG	GF	GS	TGR
95-96	89.47	2.43	42	14	33.33
96-97	89.47	2.43	38	14	36.84
97-98	94.74	2.00	46	18	39.13
Averages	91.23	2.29	42.00	15.33	36.44

DUFF, Damien

Blackburn R. ❶❷❸ S

Fullname: Damien Anthony Duff
DOB: 02-03-79 Ballyboden, Eire

Former Eire Youth player who made his first team debut for Blackburn Rovers in the final game of 1996-97 and used that as the launch-pad for a successful campaign the following season. One of the brightest prospects to break through last season Duff has great pace and a trusty left foot. Had to be patient early in the season but went on to play 26 times in the Premiership during 97-98, nine times as substitute, and scored four goals including a brace in a 3-0 win over West Ham. Just 20-years-old he could soon be adding senior honours to his Under-21 caps.

Form Factors

Season	Team	Tot	St	Sb	Y	R
96-97	Blackburn R.	1	1	0	0	0
97-98	Blackburn R.	26	17	9	0	0
Total		27	18	9	0	0

	GP	GG	GF	GS	TGR
96-97	2.63	0.00	42	0	0.00
97-98	68.42	6.50	57	4	7.02
Averages	35.53	3.25	49.50	2.00	3.51

EARLE, Robbie

Wimbledon ❶❷❸ M

Fullname: Robert Gerald Earle
DOB: 27-01-65 Newcastle-under-Lyme

Former Stoke City youngster who had ten years with Port Vale before moving down to south London to sign for Wimbledon in the summer of 1991. Missed just two league games in his first three seasons with the Dons but has played less frequently over the past four seasons. Not especially tall he still gets a good number of his goals with headers and is keen to use a shoot on sight policy when the ball is on the deck.

Has scored 128 times in the league during his long career and will go down in the history books as the player who scored Jamaica's first ever goal in the World Cup finals following his excellent header against Croatia. At 33 he possibly has a couple of seasons left of playing at a high level.

Form Factors

Season	Team	Tot	St	Sb	Y	R
95-96	Wimbledon	37	37	0	2	1
96-97	Wimbledon	32	32	0	3	0
97-98	Wimbledon	22	20	2	0	0
Total		91	89	2	5	1

	GP	GG	GF	GS	TGR
95-96	97.37	3.36	55	11	20.00
96-97	84.21	4.57	49	7	14.29
97-98	57.89	7.33	34	3	8.82
Averages	79.82	5.09	46.00	7.00	14.37

EDINBURGH, Justin

Tottenham H. ❶ FB

Fullname: Justin Charles Edinburgh
DOB: 18-12-69 Brentwood

Given that they only received £150,000 for their left-back in 1990 when Justin Edinburgh joined Tottenham, Southend United can probably feel a bit miffed now that he has made 237 appearances for the north London club. The 1997-98 season though, was not one of his best and his total of 16 league games was his lowest since his first season at White Hart Lane.

A reliable rather than eye-catching defender who will probably, at best, be a squad member for Spurs this season.

Form Factors

Season	Team	Tot	St	Sb	Y	R
95-96	Tottenham H.	22	15	7	5	0
96-97	Tottenham H.	24	21	3	11	0
97-98	Tottenham H.	17	14	3	4	1
Total		63	50	13	20	1

	GP	GG	GF	GS	TGR
95-96	57.89	0.00	50	0	0.00
96-97	63.16	0.00	44	0	0.00
97-98	44.74	0.00	44	0	0.00
Averages	55.26	0.00	46.00	0.00	0.00

EHIOGU, Ugo

Aston Villa ❶❷❸ CB

Fullname: Ugochuku Ehiogu
DOB: 03-11-72 Hackney

Must be just about the best buy any Premiership club has ever made following his move to Aston Villa from West Bromwich Albion for an insignificant £40,000 in July 1991. Made just two league appearances for Albion but since having a few seasons to get accustomed to life at Villa Park has been virtually ever-present. Missed just one match in the Premiership last season taking his total of games missed over the past four seasons to a paltry six.

A tall, muscular central defender who is very quick on the ground and dominant in the air. Usually contributes around three goals a season. Holder of one England cap which was won as a substitute against China in 1996.

Form Factors

Season	Team	Tot	St	Sb	Y	R
95-96	Aston Villa	36	36	0	7	0
96-97	Aston Villa	38	38	0	4	0
97-98	Aston Villa	37	37	0	7	1
Total		111	111	0	18	1

	GP	GG	GF	GS	TGR
95-96	94.74	36.00	52	1	1.92
96-97	100.00	12.67	47	3	6.38
97-98	97.37	18.50	49	2	4.08
Averages	97.37	22.39	49.33	2.00	4.13

EKOKU, Efan
Wimbledon ❶❷❸ S

Fullname: Efangwu Goziem Ekoku
DOB: 08-06-67 Manchester

Well-built centre forward who had his hopes of playing in the World Cup with Nigeria shattered by an injury which kept him out of the Wimbledon side for six months of last season. Managed four goals in his 16 Premiership matches last season which was down on his average of one goal approximately every three games. His record suggests he will get a reasonable number of goals for your fantasy team but probably will not get you amongst the honours.

Made his Football League debut with Bournemouth in 1990, having been signed from Sutton United, and joined Wimbledon from Norwich City for £900,000 in October 1994.

Form Factors

Season	Team	Tot	St	Sb	Y	R
95-96	Wimbledon	31	28	3	5	0
96-97	Wimbledon	30	28	2	4	0
97-98	Wimbledon	16	11	5	0	0
Total		77	67	10	9	0

	GP	GG	GF	GS	TGR
95-96	81.58	4.43	55	7	12.73
96-97	78.95	2.73	49	11	22.45
97-98	42.11	4.00	34	4	11.76
Averages	67.54	3.72	46.00	7.33	15.65

ELLIOTT, Matt
Leicester City ❶❷❸ CB

Fullname: Matthew Stephen Elliott
DOB: 01-11-68 Wandsworth

It does Matt Elliott a great disservice to habitually describe him as a bargain buy but it must be said that in an age of over-inflated fees and egos his success with Leicester City following a £1.6m move from Oxford United in January 1997 is one which is celebrated far outside of Filbert Street. A totally committed right-sided central defender who scored the goal which saved City from relegation in 1997 and last season he missed just one Premiership match; he also picked up a relatively low six yellow cards.

His move into the Premiership came quite late in his career but if he can maintain his form of the past two seasons then he should be able to continue playing at this level for possibly another three years. Previous clubs include Scunthorpe United, Torquay United and Charlton Athletic.

Matt Elliott

162   FANTASY Football Handbook 1998/99

Form Factors

Season	Team	Tot	St	Sb	Y	R
96-97	Leicester C.	16	16	0	3	0
97-98	Leicester C.	37	37	0	6	0
Total		53	53	0	9	0

	GP	GG	GF	GS	TGR
96-97	42.11	4.00	46	4	8.70
97-98	97.37	5.29	51	7	13.73
Averages	69.74	4.64	48.50	5.50	11.21

ELLIOTT, Steve
Derby County ❶❷ M

Fullname: Stephen Elliott
DOB: 29-10-78 Derby

Local-born midfielder who was handed his first team Derby County debut in September last season in the Coca Cola Cup prior to making his first appearance in the Premiership in December. Played a total of six league and cup games and finished with the remarkable record of four wins, two draws, no defeats and just one goal conceded.

Given that positive start, and a Man of the Match award on his league debut, it would be no surprise to hear a great deal more of this youngster during the 1998-99 season.

Form Factors

Season	Team	Tot	St	Sb	Y	R
97-98	Derby Co.	3	3	0	0	0
Total		3	3	0	0	0

	GP	GG	GF	GS	TGR
97-98	7.89	0.00	52	0	0.00
Averages	7.89	0.00	52.00	0.00	0.00

ERANIO, Stefano
Derby County ❶❷❸ M

Fullname: Stefano Eranio
DOB: 29-12-66 Genova

Italian midfielder who experienced all the highs and lows of life in the Premiership during his first season with Derby County. Scored a very commendable five goals in 23 league games from the middle of the park – Derby did not lose in any of the five games he scored in – but also received two red cards, the second in his first game back after injury. Also collected an excessive nine yellow cards and his continued absence from the side through suspension is not ideal for a fantasy team.

Despite his disciplinary problems the success he has enjoyed down the years is outstanding with three Italian league championships and the European Cup coming his way. Also played for Italy in qualifying matches for France 98 but did not make the final 22.

Form Factors

Season	Team	Tot	St	Sb	Y	R
97-98	Derby Co.	23	23	0	9	2
Total		23	23	0	9	2

	GP	GG	GF	GS	TGR
97-98	60.53	4.60	52	5	9.62
Averages	60.53	4.60	52.00	5.00	9.62

EUELL, Jason

Wimbledon ❶❷❸ S

Fullname: Jason Joseph Euell
DOB: 06-02-77 Lambeth, London

Has made steady progress with Wimbledon over the past three seasons with the 1997-98 campaign being his most successful to date. A very enthusiastic midfielder who can attack down either flank he is proving to be a regular goalscorer having netted four times in 19 Premiership matches last season and scored twice in each of the two previous seasons without playing more than nine games. Should continue to force his way into the side over the coming months.

Form Factors

Season	Team	Tot	St	Sb	Y	R
95-96	Wimbledon	9	4	5	1	0
96-97	Wimbledon	7	4	3	0	0
97-98	Wimbledon	19	14	5	1	0
Total		35	22	13	2	0

	GP	GG	GF	GS	TGR
95-96	23.68	4.50	55	2	3.64
96-97	18.42	3.50	49	2	4.08
97-98	50.00	4.75	34	4	11.76
Averages	30.70	4.25	46.00	2.67	6.49

FARRELLY, Gareth

Everton ❶❷ M

Fullname: Gareth Farrelly
DOB: 28-08-75 Dublin

Scored the goal last May against Coventry City which could prove to be one of the most financially important in Everton's long and illustrious history. Midfielder Farrelly, who had not scored in any of his previous 29 games for the Toffeemen, notched the goal which ultimately secured the vital point which preserved Everton's Premiership status. His only previous goals came during a loan spell with Rotherham United in 1994-95.

The 1997-98 season was undoubtedly his most successful to date with his 26 league appearances outnumbering his tally from the previous three years as a professional. This season will be a tester as to whether Farrelly has finally arrived or not; certainly he has the determination and temperament to make it.

Form Factors

Season	Team	Tot	St	Sb	Y	R
95-96	Aston Villa	4	1	3	0	0
96-97	Aston Villa	3	1	2	0	0
97-98	Everton	26	18	8	3	0
Total		33	20	13	3	0

	GP	GG	GF	GS	TGR
95-96	10.53	0.00	52	0	0.00
96-97	7.89	0.00	47	0	0.00
97-98	68.42	26.00	41	1	2.44
Averages	28.95	8.67	46.67	0.33	0.81

FEAR, Peter
Wimbledon ❶ M
Fullname: Peter Stanley Fear
DOB: 10-09-73 Sutton

One of many Wimbledon players to progress through from being a trainee but despite being with the first team squad for the past six seasons has yet to command a permanent place in the side. His eight games last season represents a significant drop on the previous season but he did manage to double his goals tally. Going into the season Fear had scored just twice in the Premiership but equalled that total with two stunning efforts during a 6-2 defeat against Tottenham.

Good on the ball he can tackle well and when asked to do so can perform a man-marking job.

Form Factors

Season	Team	Tot	St	Sb	Y	R
95-96	Wimbledon	4	4	0	1	0
96-97	Wimbledon	18	9	9	3	0
97-98	Wimbledon	8	5	3	2	0
Total		30	18	12	6	0

	GP	GG	GF	GS	TGR
95-96	10.53	0.00	55	0	0.00
96-97	47.37	0.00	49	0	0.00
97-98	21.05	4.00	34	2	5.88
Averages	26.32	1.33	46.00	0.67	1.96

FENTON, Graham
Leicester C. ❶❷ S
Fullname: Graham Anthony Fenton
DOB: 22-05-74 Wallsend

Bustling striker who, having been unable to break into the Blackburn Rovers side during 1996-97, due in part to injury, moved in a £1m deal to Leicester for last season but again failed to command a regular place in the starting line-up during his first season at Filbert Street. Figured in 23 of the Foxes' Premiership matches but 14 of these were substitute appearances; he was also an unused sub for 14 matches. Scored in three games last season, all of which were won, including a 2-1 success at Liverpool. Overall the past two seasons have been a big disappointment for him but he still has time to recapture the form of '95-96 when he scored six times in 14 games.

Previously with Aston Villa he also had a spell on loan to West Bromwich Albion.

Form Factors

Season	Team	Tot	St	Sb	Y	R
95-96	Blackburn R.	14	4	10	2	0
96-97	Blackburn R.	13	5	8	3	0
97-98	Leicester C.	23	9	14	1	0
Total		50	18	32	6	0

	GP	GG	GF	GS	TGR
95-96	36.84	2.33	61	6	9.84
96-97	34.21	13.00	42	1	2.38
97-98	60.53	7.67	51	3	5.88
Averages	43.86	7.67	51.33	3.33	6.03

FERDINAND, Les

Tottenham H. ❶❷❸❹ S

Fullname: Leslie Ferdinand
DOB: 18-12-66 Acton

Tottenham caused a stir in the summer of 1997 with the £3.5m sale of Teddy Sheringham being followed by the £6m acquisition of 30-year-old Les Ferdinand from Newcastle United. A Spurs fan, Ferdinand should be very much at home at White Hart Lane but his first season as a Spur was poor due, in the main, to injury. When fully fit he is supreme in the air, a perfect target man and a non-stop danger with lightning pace. But his return of six goals from 23 league and cup matches last season does not do justice to a powerful striker who has a career record of 159 goals in 318 games at club level.

Despite the disappointing facts of last season, Ferdinand is still only second to Shearer in the list of all-time Premiership goalscorers and providing he and his teammates can stay fit he will produce the goods in '98-99.

Les Ferdinand

Form Factors

Season	Team	Tot	St	Sb	Y	R
95-96	Newcastle U.	37	37	0	4	0
96-97	Newcastle U.	31	30	1	3	0
97-98	Tottenham H.	21	19	2	2	0
Total		89	86	3	9	0

	GP	GG	GF	GS	TGR
95-96	97.37	1.48	66	25	37.88
96-97	81.58	1.94	73	16	21.92
97-98	55.26	4.20	44	5	11.36
Averages	78.07	2.54	61.00	15.33	23.72

FERDINAND, Rio

West Ham U. ❶❷❸❹ CB

Fullname: Rio Gavin Ferdinand
DOB: 07-11-78 London

Quite remarkably, Ferdinand only signed schoolboy forms with West Ham as recently as 1994 and just four years later he was in the England squad for France 98. His international debut was delayed as a disciplinary measure after he committed a drink-driving offence. Has made rapid progress over the past two seasons, which also included a spell on loan at Bournemouth, and is now just about the hottest young defensive property in English football. A tall central defender who can also fill the full-back positions and with his assured touch can play midfield as well. Made more starts in the Premiership than any other West Ham player last season and will be the focal point of the Hammers' defence this season as he comes under closer scrutiny. Is the second cousin of Spurs' striker Les Ferdinand.

Form Factors

Season	Team	Tot	St	Sb	Y	R
95-96	West Ham U.	1	0	1	0	0
96-97	West Ham U.	15	11	4	2	0
97-98	West Ham U.	35	35	0	3	0
Total		51	46	5	5	0

	GP	GG	GF	GS	TGR
95-96	2.63	0.00	43	0	0.00
96-97	39.47	7.50	39	2	5.13
97-98	92.11	0.00	56	0	0.00
Averages	44.74	2.50	46.00	0.67	1.71

FERGUSON, Duncan

Everton ❶❷❸❹ S

Fullname: Duncan Ferguson
DOB: 27-12-71 Stirling

During a season in which Everton came so close to surrendering their Premiership status, Ferguson scored 11 league goals to retain his position of leading scorer for a second year. He scored in eight separate games with a match-winning hat-trick against Bolton Wanderers ultimately being the difference between relegation and salvation; it was also his first treble for Everton since his £4.4m move from Rangers in October 1994.

Ferguson's goal ratio remains less spectacular than one would imagine but his threat in the air is undiminished, his favoured left foot also makes him a threat on the ground. May well have made it to France 98 as a part of the Scotland squad but for a self-imposed exile from international football.

Form Factors

Season	Team	Tot	St	Sb	Y	R
95-96	Everton	18	16	2	4	0
96-97	Everton	33	31	2	5	1
97-98	Everton	29	28	1	6	1
Total		80	75	5	15	2

	GP	GG	GF	GS	TGR
95-96	47.37	3.60	64	5	7.81
96-97	86.84	3.30	44	10	22.73
97-98	76.32	2.64	41	11	26.83
Averages	70.18	3.18	49.67	8.67	19.12

Duncan Ferguson

Fantasy Football Handbook 1998/99

FERRARESI, Fabio

Aston Villa ❶ M

Fullname: Fabio Ferraresi
DOB: Italy

Ferraresi can probably be regarded as a player for the future. Signed on a free transfer under the Bosman ruling, Ferraresi was a vital cog in the midfield of the Cesana side that won promotion to Italy's Serie A at the end of last season.

FERRER, Albert

Chelsea ❶❷❸ D

Fullname: Albert Ferrer
DOB: Spain

Very much unknown in England although armchair viewers will have caught him in action for 45 minutes of Spain's exhilarating 3-2 defeat by Nigeria in one of the two outstanding matches of France 98.

Plays on the right of the defence, he is seen as a fast, tough-tackling player who will bolster the Chelsea defence. Has signed a five year deal at Stamford Bridge, on a reputed £750,000 a year, following a £2.2m move from Barcelona.

FESTA, Gianluca

Middlesbrough ❶❷❸ D

Fullname: Gianluca Festa
DOB: 15-03-69 Cagliari, Sardinia

One of the more successful overseas acquisitions of Boro manager Bryan Robson, Festa joined Middlesbrough just too late to stave off relegation two seasons ago but last season he was supreme as Boro bounced back at the first attempt with the Italian playing in 38 of the clubs 46 Division One matches.

His general defensive awareness is excellent and when added to his other attributes of being a solid tackler, powerful in the air and unflustered when moving forward, Boro have the quality they need to avoid an instant demotion. Joined Boro in a £2.7m move from Internazionale having also played for Cagliari and on loan to Fersuicis and Roma.

Form Factors

Season	Team	Tot	St	Sb	Y	R
96-97	Middlesbrough	13	13	0	5	0
Total		13	13	0	5	0

	GP	GG	GF	GS	TGR
96-97	34.21	13.00	51	1	1.96
Averages	34.21	13.00	51.00	1.00	1.96

FETTIS, Alan

Blackburn R. ①②GK
Fullname: Alan William Fettis
DOB: 01-02-71 Belfast

International goalkeeper with Northern Ireland, for whom he played in World Cup qualifying matches, but has managed just 22 league games since the start of the 1995-96 season. Was with Hull City at that time and had a stint on loan to West Bromwich Albion prior to joining Blackburn from Nottingham Forest for £300,000 early last season. Sat on the bench for 20 Premiership matches last season but was between the sticks for eight league games during which time Rovers conceded 18 goals.

Form Factors

Season	Team	Tot	St	Sb	Y	R
96-97	N. Forest	4	4	0	0	0
97-98	Blackburn R.	8	7	1	0	0
Total		12	11	1	0	0

	GA	GkA	GAp	CS	SO	R
96-97	59	7	1.75	1	1	0
97-98	52	19	2.71	0	0	0
Averages	55.5	13.0	2.23	0.5	0.5	0

FILAN, John

Blackburn R. ①②GK
Fullname: John Richard Filan
DOB: 08-02-70 Sydney, Australia

Australian goalkeeper who has been dogged by various grades of misfortune since making his Football League debut with Cambridge United six years ago. Joined Coventry City in 1995 for £300,000 but in more than two years at Highfield Road was afforded just 16 Premiership games due to the brilliance of veteran Steve Ogrizovic. Was snapped up by Blackburn for £700,000 to cover for the injured Tim Flowers only to be on the receiving end of a serious injury himself after just four games for his new club. Is now fully fit but if he is to make it in the Premiership he may need to break away from the shadow cast by Flowers.

Was called up to the Australian national side by Terry Venables during his time Down Under.

Form Factors

Season	Team	Tot	St	Sb	Y	R
95-96	Coventry C.	13	13	0	0	0
96-97	Coventry C.	1	0	1	0	0
97-98	Blackburn R.	7	7	0	0	0
Total		21	20	1	0	0

	GA	GkA	GAp	CS	SO	R
95-96	60	27	2.08	2	1	0
96-97	54	0	0.00	0	0	0
97-98	52	3	0.43	4	2	0
Averages	55.33	10.0	0.84	3	1	0

FLEMING, Curtis
Middlesbrough ❶❷ FB

Fullname: Curtis Fleming
DOB: 08-10-68 Manchester

Enjoyed a very successful 1997-98 season with Middlesbrough, his seventh with the Riverside club, making 37 Nationwide League appearances and scoring his first goal since April 1996, goes into the new season just seven games away from his 200th league game for the club. Very strong when challenging for possession he uses the ball well when moving forward and will have no problems re-acclimatising himself in the Premiership.

An Eire international he began his career with two spells with Irish side St. Patrick's Athletic either side of an unsuccessful stint at Swindon Town.

Form Factors

Season	Team	Tot	St	Sb	Y	R
92-93	Middlesbrough	24	22	2	0	0
95-96	Middlesbrough	14	14	0	2	0
96-97	Middlesbrough	30	30	0	4	0
Total		68	66	2	6	0

	GP	GG	GF	GS	TGR
92-93	63.16	0.00	54	0	0.00
95-96	36.84	14.00	35	1	2.86
96-97	78.95	0.00	51	0	0.00
Averages	59.65	4.67	46.67	0.33	0.95

FLITCROFT, Garry
Blackburn Rovers ❶❷❸❹ M

Fullname: Garry William Flitcroft
DOB: 06-11-72 Bolton

After an injury strewn start to his career with Blackburn Rovers, Flitcroft fully proved himself last season and justified the £2m fee Rovers paid Manchester City for his services in March 1996. A hardworking midfielder he played a big part in Blackburn's revival with his strength in the tackle being one of his main assets. He has proved himself very capable of getting goals in the past but his last successful effort was on the final day of the 1996-97 season. Has won international honours with England at Under-21.

Form Factors

Season	Team	Tot	St	Sb	Y	R
95-96	Blackburn R.	3	3	0	1	1
96-97	Blackburn R.	28	27	1	1	0
97-98	Blackburn R.	33	28	5	0	6
Total		64	58	6	2	7

	GP	GG	GF	GS	TGR
95-96	7.89	0.00	61	0	0.00
96-97	73.68	9.33	42	3	7.14
97-98	86.84	0.00	57	0	0.00
Averages	56.14	3.11	53.33	1.00	2.38

FLO, Tore Andre

Chelsea ❶❷❸❹❺ S

Fullname: Tore Andre Flo
DOB: 15-06-73 Norway

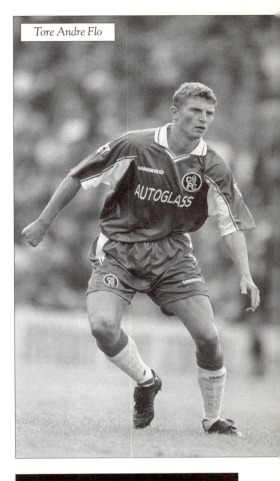

Tore Andre Flo

Tall striker, very good in the air but also a genuine danger of the ground with his lethal turn of speed. Last season was his first with Chelsea and he made his mark by making more Premiership appearances for the Blues than any other player. That said, of his 34 league games 18 were from the bench and of 11 league goals – he was joint top scorer in the league with Vialli – four came when he was summonsed from the bench. The highlight of his season came with a hat-trick during a 6-1 thrashing of Tottenham at White Hart Lane.

His height makes him ideal to play for his country and he had the honour of appearing in all four of Norway's matches in France 98, scoring twice in the process including the equaliser against Brazil.

Previously played for Tromso and SK Brann from where he joined Chelsea for £300,000.

Form Factors

Season	Team	Tot	St	Sb	Y	R
97-98	Chelsea	34	16	18	0	0
Total		34	16	18	0	0

	GP	GG	GF	GS	TGR
97-98	89.47	3.09	71	11	15.49
Averages	89.47	3.09	71.00	11.00	15.49

FLOWERS, Tim

Blackburn R. ❶❷❸❹ GK

Fullname: Timothy David Flowers
DOB: 03-02-67 Kenilworth

Although injury restricted Tim Flowers' Premiership appearances last season to 25, his overall total of 220 games is the highest of any player since the formation of the Premier League. Once fully fit there was little doubt that he would be going to France 98 with England, but also it was no surprise when he was no more than

FANTASY FOOTBALL HANDBOOK 1998/99   171

Tim Flowers

Form Factors

Season	Team	Tot	St	Sb	Y	R
95-96	Blackburn R.	37	37	0	3	1
96-97	Blackburn R.	36	36	0	2	0
97-98	Blackburn R.	25	24	1	1	0
Total		98	97	1	6	1

	GA	GkA	GAp	CS	SO	R
95-96	47	36	0.97	9	2	0
96-97	43	42	1.17	10	3	0
97-98	52	29	1.16	9	3	0
Averages	47.33	35.67	1.10	9.33	2.67	0

understudy to David Seaman. At four years younger than Seaman his chance on the biggest stage may come in the next World Cup providing he maintains his normal high standards.

Conceded 29 Premiership goals in 25 games last season which at 1.16 per game is marginally above his normal average but is considerably better than the 1.53 Blackburn Rovers conceded per game in his absence.

Moved to Blackburn from Southampton in November 1993 for £2m, five months after his England debut, having previously played for Wolverhampton Wanderers.

FORREST, Craig

West Ham U. ①②GK

Fullname: Craig Lorne Forrest
DOB: 20-09-67 Vancouver

Moved to West Ham in the summer of 1997 having spent the previous 13 years with Ipswich Town. Started last season as cover for Miklosko but came into the side for 13 Premiership matches and didn't let anyone down by conceding just one goal a game. He was named as substitute goalkeeper for no less than 21 games.

During his lengthy career, Forrest has had loan spells with Colchester United and Chelsea and is a full international with Canada.

Form Factors

Season	Team	Tot	St	Sb	Y	R
94-95	Ipswich T.	36	36	0	1	0
97-98	West Ham U.	13	13	0	0	0
Total		76	76	0	1	0

	GA	GkA	GAp	CS	SO	R
94-95	93	81	2.25	2	1	1
97-98	57	13	1.00	5	1	2
Averages	60.0	47.0	1.63	3.5	1	1.5

FOWLER, Robbie

Liverpool ❶❷❸ S

Fullname: Robert Bernard Fowler
DOB: 09-04-75 Liverpool

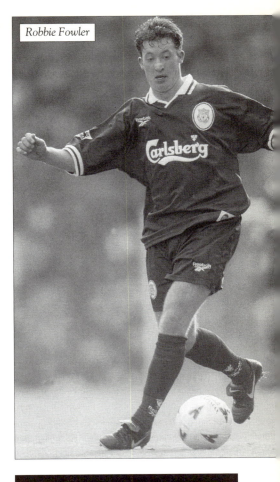
Robbie Fowler

A player who should have been looking to make his name on the world stage suffered damaged medial ligaments and cartilage damage in his left knee against Everton in February which is likely to keep him out until the end of the year. All-in-all it was a troubled season for the England player who could only look on as Michael Owen took on 'god-like' status while Fowler was criticised for alleged excessive wage demands.

The injury came at the end of an unusually lean spell for the Liverpool striker who had scored just once in nine games. Even so, his total for the season was 12, nine in the league, taking his Premiership goals tally to an outstanding 92 in only 160 games but the injury denied him the chance of being top scorer at the club for a fourth consecutive year.

Fowler's accuracy in front of goal is exceptional with his sudden burst of speed getting him into excellent positions. Once back in the side he will again get goals in abundance and the world waits his possible partnership with Owen.

Form Factors

Season	Team	Tot	St	Sb	Y	R
95-96	Liverpool	38	36	2	3	0
96-97	Liverpool	32	32	0	4	1
97-98	Liverpool	20	19	1	1	1
Total		90	87	3	8	2

	GP	GG	GF	GS	TGR
95-96	100.00	1.36	70	28	40.00
96-97	84.21	1.78	62	18	29.03
97-98	52.63	2.22	68	9	13.24
Averages	78.95	1.79	66.67	18.33	27.42

FOX, Ruel

Tottenham H. ❶❷❸ M

Fullname: Ruel Adrian Fox
DOB: 14-01-68 Ipswich

Became Tottenham's second most expensive acquisition when he moved from Newcastle United to White Hart Lane in October 1995 for £4.5m. He played in just under two-thirds of Spurs Premiership matches in his first two seasons with the club but only really seemed to find his best form last season

FANTASY FOOTBALL HANDBOOK 1998/99   **173**

and appeared in 32 league games and five cup ties.

A nippy winger with a good touch, Fox can put over telling crosses and score the occasional goal, current record one every nine games. But despite his return to the first team since Christian Gross' arrival there remains a question mark over his consistency.

Form Factors

Season	Team	Tot	St	Sb	Y	R
95-96	Tottenham H.	26	26	0	1	0
96-97	Tottenham H.	25	19	6	1	0
97-98	Tottenham H.	32	32	0	3	0
Total		83	77	6	5	0

	GP	GG	GF	GS	TGR
95-96	68.42	4.33	50	6	12.00
96-97	65.79	25.00	44	1	2.27
97-98	84.21	10.67	44	3	6.82
Averages	72.81	13.33	46.00	3.33	7.03

FRANCIS, Damien

Wimbledon ❶ M

Fullname: Damien Francis
DOB: 27-02-79 London

After six appearances on the teamsheet as an unused substitute last season, teenager Francis made his Wimbledon debut when coming on as a substitute during a 5-0 drubbing for the Dons at champions-elect Arsenal on 18 April 1998.

A London-born midfielder who made one more appearance before the season was out and is likely to get a few more games under his belt this season but probably an insufficient number to warrant inclusion in your fantasy team.

FRIEDEL, Brad

Liverpool ❶❷ GK

Fullname: Brad Friedel
DOB: 18-05-71 Lakewood, Ohio, USA

American goalkeeper who has experienced an almost meteoric rise over the past 12 months. Was voted as the United States' Major League Soccer Player of the Year for 1997. Joined Liverpool in a £1m deal from Columbus Crew and ousted David James as the number one keeper at Anfield in the spring and then crowned it all with one appearance for his native USA in the World Cup.

Has previous European experience with Brondby and Galatasaray.

Form Factors

Season	Team	Tot	St	Sb	Y	R
97-98	Liverpool	11	11	0	0	0
Total		11	11	0	0	0

	GA	GkA	GAp	CS	SO	R
97-98	42	15	1.36	2	2	0
Averages	42	15	1.36	2	2	0

GALLACHER, Kevin

Blackburn Rovers ❶❷❸❹ M

Fullname: Kevin William Gallacher
DOB: 23-11-66 Clydebank

After just over four, often injury hindered, years with Blackburn Rovers, Scotland striker Gallacher really came into his own last season with his 16 Premiership goals being far and away the best return of his career. Scotland boss Craig Brown was sufficiently impressed to play him in all three of the Scots

Brad Friedel

ultimately unsuccessful Group matches in France 98.

That he was in France at all is testimony to his character having twice come back from a broken leg and a long-term hamstring injury since joining Rovers from Coventry City six seasons ago. Made exactly 100 league appearances for the Sky Blues and 131 for his first club, Dundee United.

Kevin Gallacher

Form Factors

Season	Team	Tot	St	Sb	Y	R
95-96	Blackburn R.	16	14	2	1	0
96-97	Blackburn R.	34	34	0	6	0
97-98	Blackburn R.	33	31	2	0	2
Total		83	79	4	7	2

	GP	GG	GF	GS	TGR
95-96	42.11	8.00	61	2	3.28
96-97	89.47	3.40	42	10	23.81
97-98	86.84	2.06	57	16	28.07
Averages	72.81	4.49	53.33	9.33	18.39

Fantasy Football Handbook 1998/99

GARDE, Remi

Arsenal ❶❷ M

Fullname: Remi Garde
DOB: 03-04-66 L'Arbesle, France

Has been used as cover at Arsenal over the past couple of seasons playing in just 21 of the Gunners' Premiership matches in that time and that situation is unlikely to change during 1998-99. An experienced former French international midfielder who can also play in defence, he made six starts last season and a further four appearances as substitute. Joined Arsenal on a free transfer from Strasbourg just prior to the 1996-97 season.

Form Factors

Season	Team	Tot	St	Sb	Y	R
96-97	Arsenal	11	7	4	2	0
97-98	Arsenal	10	6	4	3	0
Total		21	13	8	5	0

	GP	GG	GF	GS	TGR
96-97	28.95	0.00	62	0	0.00
97-98	26.32	0.00	68	0	0.00
Averages	27.63	0.00	65.00	0.00	0.00

GASCOIGNE, Paul

Middlesbrough ❶❷❸ M

Fullname: Paul J Gascoigne
DOB: 27-05-67 Gateshead

Gascoigne's place in the hall of great players is assured but there will always be thoughts of what might have been when one looks back at the career of probably the most gifted British player since George Best. By joining Middlesbrough just in time for last season's Coca Cola Cup final, in which he was fortunate only to be booked, and successful promotion run-in, he has earned himself one final shot at proving himself in the Premiership.

During his first stint in English football he was spellbinding with no one coming close to matching his creativity in midfield. He could glide past players in the middle of the pitch and in attack with ease and supply a deadly finish at the end. But his problems since those days have been well documented and left him without his sudden bursts of speed and his preferred method of shielding the ball with an outstretched arm has not been well received by match officials.

His talent is unquestionable but his temperament, in the aftermath of his exclusion from the World Cup, is not so

Paul Gascoigne

certain. Following his £3.45m transfer from Rangers in March, Gascoigne made eight league and cup appearances for Boro but failed to score.

GAYLE, Marcus

Wimbledon ❶❷❸ S

Fullname: Marcus Anthony Gayle
DOB: 27-09-70 Hammersmith

Midfielder who glided almost seamlessly from playing for Brentford to the Premiership with Wimbledon in March 1994 and has only rarely been out of the Dons starting line-up since. A formidable figure on the left side of the park, he loves to run at defences and is one of the highest goalscoring midfielders in the Premiership although his tally of two for last season was well down on the norm.

A one time England Youth player, he made 30 appearances last season of which nine were as substitute and was taken off 13 times. Has the remarkable excellent disciplinary record of just four bookings in 133 league games for the Dons.

Form Factors

Season	Team	Tot	St	Sb	Y	R
95-96	Wimbledon	34	21	13	0	0
96-97	Wimbledon	36	34	2	2	0
97-98	Wimbledon	30	21	9	1	0
Total		100	76	24	3	0

	GP	GG	GF	GS	TGR
95-96	89.47	6.80	55	5	9.09
96-97	94.74	4.50	49	8	16.33
97-98	78.95	15.00	34	2	5.88
Averages	87.72	8.77	46.00	5.00	10.43

GEMMILL, Scot

Nottingham F. ❶❷❸ M

Fullname: Scot Gemmill
DOB: 02-01-71 Paisley

Like his father, Scot is a full Scotland international although the two are a different kind of player. A very committed player in the centre of the Nottingham Forest midfield he links well just behind the attack and gets back well to support the defence.

Having struggled a bit during Forest's most recent relegation campaign he regained his regular place in the side last season playing in 43 of their 46 Division One matches on the way to promotion. Made his Forest debut back in the 1990-91 season.

Form Factors

Season	Team	Tot	St	Sb	Y	R
94-95	N. Forest	19	19	0	1	0
95-96	N. Forest	31	26	5	4	0
96-97	N. Forest	24	18	6	6	0
Total		74	63	11	11	0

	GP	GG	GF	GS	TGR
94-95	50.00	19.00	72	1	1.39
95-96	81.58	31.00	50	1	2.00
96-97	63.16	0.00	31	0	0.00
Averages	64.91	16.67	51.00	0.67	1.13

GERRARD, Paul
Everton　　　　　　❶ GK
Fullname:　　　Paul William Gerrard
DOB:　　　　22-01-73 Heywood

Goalkeeper whose performances in 119 league games for Oldham Athletic prompted Everton to fork out £1.5m for his services in August 1996. But despite the high fee Gerrard has been unable to claim a regular place in the first team and his chances of further progress at Goodison Park look remote following the signing of Thomas Myhre.

Was selected for just six league and cup games last season during which time Everton conceded 12 goals.

Form Factors

Season	Team	Tot	St	Sb	Y	R
93-94	Oldham A.	16	15	1	0	0
96-97	Everton	5	4	1	0	0
97-98	Everton	4	4	0	1	0
Total		25	23	2	1	0

	GA	GkA	GAp	CS	SO	R
93-94	68	24	1.50	2	1	0
96-97	58	6	1.20	2	2	0
97-98	56	8	2.00	0	0	0
Averages	60.67	12.67	1.57	1.33	1.0	0

GIGGS, Ryan
Manchester U.　　❶❷❸❹❺ S
Fullname:　　　　Ryan Joseph Giggs
DOB:　　　　　29-11-73 Cardiff

Possibly the most gifted player in the Premiership but not for the first time since breaking into the Manchester United first team at the age of 17 Giggs' season was blighted by injury. Had to sit out a fair part of early spring during which time United crashed out of Europe, the FA Cup and saw Arsenal close in on the championship.

All defenders are aware of his electric pace and the danger he poses from the left wing but there are many other attributes to his game including being a regular goalscorer although he does not always quite notch as many as one would expect. A season of a fully fit Giggs could just be sufficient to bring the title back to Old Trafford but the Welsh international himself will also be pleased when Roy Keane is back in the fold.

Form Factors

Season	Team	Tot	St	Sb	Y	R
95-96	Manchester U.	33	30	3	0	0
96-97	Manchester U.	26	25	1	2	0
97-98	Manchester U.	29	28	1	1	0
Total		88	83	5	3	0

	GP	GG	GF	GS	TGR
95-96	86.84	3.00	73	11	15.07
96-97	68.42	8.67	76	3	3.95
97-98	76.32	3.63	73	8	10.96
Averages	77.19	5.10	74.00	7.33	9.99

GILLESPIE, Keith

Newcastle U. ❶❷❸ S
Fullname: Keith Robert Gillespie
DOB: 18-02-75 Bangor

It is hard to believe that Gillespie, one of the finest and most lethal crossers in the Premiership, is still just 23 years old. Clearly at his best when used almost as an old fashioned winger he is adapting his game to suit that of the modern day wing-back. Equalled his best season for goals last season although that figure is a disappointing four.

Joined Newcastle from Manchester United as part of the deal which saw Andy Cole move in the opposite direction and has since successfully built a reputation of his own and become a regular in the Northern Ireland side. Rarely gets into trouble with referees having never collected a suspension since his move to St. James's Park.

Form Factors

Season	Team	Tot	St	Sb	Y	R
95-96	Newcastle U.	28	26	2	3	0
96-97	Newcastle U.	32	23	9	2	1
97-98	Newcastle U.	29	25	4	2	0
Total		89	74	15	7	1

	GP	GG	GF	GS	TGR
95-96	73.68	7.00	66	4	6.06
96-97	84.21	32.00	73	1	1.37
97-98	76.32	7.25	35	4	11.43
Averages	78.07	15.42	58.00	3.00	6.29

GINOLA, David

Tottenham H. ❶❷❸❹ S
Fullname: David Ginola
DOB: 25-01-67 Gassin, nr St. Tropez, France

The signing of Ginola from Newcastle United in the summer of 1997 for £2m was seen as risky by many pundits but despite Tottenham's general disappointments on the pitch the Frenchman was a success. After falling out at Newcastle, the charismatic striker rediscovered his form at White Hart Lane after a slow start and his total of six goals in 34 games was his best in the league for three years.

His cause was not aided though, by long term injuries to Ferdinand and Armstrong as the main thrust of the attack was not there to take advantage of his usually penetrating crosses. With a fully fit side around him Ginola could be a revelation and should earn you points as a creator and scorer of goals.

Form Factors

Season	Team	Tot	St	Sb	Y	R
95-96	Newcastle U.	34	34	0	5	0
96-97	Newcastle U.	24	20	4	3	0
97-98	Tottenham H.	34	34	0	7	0
Total		92	88	4	15	0

	GP	GG	GF	GS	TGR
95-96	89.47	6.80	66	5	7.58
96-97	63.16	24.00	73	1	1.37
97-98	89.47	5.67	44	6	13.64
Averages	80.70	12.16	61.00	4.00	7.53

GIVEN, Shay

Newcastle U. ①❷ GK

Fullname: Seamus John Givens
DOB: 20-04-76 Lifford, Co Donegal

Top-rated goalkeeper who, during the 1997-98 season, was finally given the extended run he wanted to prove himself but was never going to get as long as he stayed in the shadow of Tim Flowers at Blackburn Rovers. Of the three keepers used by Newcastle last season Given played by far the most games, 24, and acquitted himself well as he kept a clean sheet in a third of them and was beaten 29 times overall.

Given first played under Kenny Dalglish at Blackburn but made just two league appearances for the Ewood Park club although he did gain further experience whilst on loan to Swindon Town and Sunderland where he made a combined total of 22 appearances and boasted an unblemished record in 16 of those games.

Form Factors

Season	Team	Tot	St	Sb	Y	R
96-97	Blackburn R.	2	2	0	0	0
97-98	Newcastle U.	24	24	0	1	0
Total		26	26	0	1	0

	GA	GkA	GAp	CS	SO	R
96-97	43	1	0.50	1	1	0
97-98	44	29	1.21	8	2	0
Averages	43.5	15.0	0.86	4.5	1.5	0

Shay Given

GORDON, Dean

Middlesbrough ①❷❸ FB

Fullname: Dean Dwight Gordon
DOB: 10-02-73 Croydon

Crystal Palace's latest demise from the Premiership was once too often for defender Gordon, who headed north in July to sign for one of the sides replacing his previous club, Middlesbrough. The 25 year old defender looks to be a good addition to the Riverside squad with his tough-tackling and quick use of the ball likely to set up many a counter-attack.

An international with England at Under-21 he has scored an unusually high number of goals and in December 1995 scored a hat-trick against West Bromwich Albion although two of the goals did come from penalties.

Form Factors

Season	Team	Tot	St	Sb	Y	R
92-93	C.Palace	10	6	4	0	0
94-95	C.Palace	41	38	3	4	0
97-98	C.Palace	37	36	1	3	0
Totals		88	80	8	7	0

	GP	GG	GF	GS	TGR
92-93	23.81	0.00	48	0	0.00
94-95	97.62	20.50	34	2	5.88
97-98	97.37	18.50	37	2	5.41
Average	72.93	19.50	39.67	1.33	0.04

GRANT, Tony
Everton ❶ M

Fullname: Anthony James Grant
DOB: 14-11-74 Liverpool

Midfield player who is highly rated at Goodison Park but after a fifth season spent on the verge of the first team one wonders whether his time will ever come. Grant's seven Premiership appearances last season, which included his second goal for the club, was a significant drop from 18 the previous season. The continual change of manager at the club seems to have done little for his long-term ambitions.

Form Factors

Season	Team	Tot	St	Sb	Y	R
95-96	Everton	13	11	2	1	0
96-97	Everton	18	11	7	3	0
97-98	Everton	7	7	0	0	0
Total		38	29	9	4	0

	GP	GG	GF	GS	TGR
95-96	34.21	13.00	64	1	1.56
96-97	47.37	0.00	44	0	0.00
97-98	18.42	7.00	41	1	2.44
Averages	33.33	6.67	49.67	0.67	1.33

GRANVILLE, Danny
Leeds United ❶❷ F

Fullname: Danny Granville
DOB: 19-1-75, Islington

Having started his career at Cambridge United, Granville looked to have broken into the big time when the then Chelsea manager Ruud Gullit signed him for £300,000 in March 1997. His chances were limited during his first full season at Stamford Bridge and with the influx of bigger name players under the Gianluca Vialli regime it was perhaps no surprise that he was allowed to move on, and at a substantial profit, when George Graham signed him for Leeds United for £1.6m.

A skilful left-sided defender or wing-back, he is also an England Under-21 International.

GRAYSON, Simon
Aston Villa ❶❷❸ FB

Fullname: Simon Nicholas Grayson
DOB: 16-12-69 Ripon

Goes into the 1998-99 season, his second at Villa Park, as one of Aston Villa's most reliable players and should continue to feature in a very high percentage of Villa's games as he did last season and during the previous four seasons with Leicester City.

Mostly used as a full-back he can play in midfield, on the right. Scored a couple times in the FA Cup last season but has not found the target in the league since December 1995. It was his goal for Leicester at Wimbledon which took the Foxes through to the Coca Cola Cup final on the away goals rule in 1997. Prior to signing for Villa that summer he was named as Leicester's Player of the Year.

Form Factors

Season	Team	Tot	St	Sb	Y	R
94-95	Leicester C.	34	34	0	7	1
96-97	Leicester C.	36	36	0	4	0
97-98	Aston Villa	33	28	5	2	0
Total		103	98	5	13	1

	GP	GG	GF	GS	TGR
94-95	89.47	0.00	45	0	0.00
96-97	94.74	0.00	46	0	0.00
97-98	86.84	0.00	49	0	0.00
Averages	90.35	0.00	46.67	0.00	0.00

GREENING, Jonathan
Manchester U. ❶❷ M/S

Fullname: Jonathan Greening
DOB: 02-01-79 Scarborough

Yet to make his first team debut for Manchester United but the Reds have high hopes that he will live up to expectations, having invested £1m in him in March 1998. Capable of playing in attack or midfield, Greening's rise to the Premiership has been swift given that last season was his first full campaign in the Football League with Division Two side York City.

GRIFFIN, Andy
Newcastle U. ❶❷ D

Fullname: Andrew Griffin
DOB: 07-03-79 Billinge

Signed for Newcastle United in a £1.5m deal in January 1998 and made four appearances in the Premiership before the season was out. A left back who came through the ranks with Stoke City and only made his debut in the Football League at home to Portsmouth in October 1996. Although he favours the left he plays on either flank. Highly rated, he is expected to take good steps forward this season.

Form Factors

Season	Team	Tot	St	Sb	Y	R
97-98	Newcastle U.	4	4	0	0	0
Total		4	4	0	0	0

	GP	GG	GF	GS	TGR
97-98	10.53	0.00	35	0	0.00
Averages	10.53	0.00	35.00	0.00	0.00

GRIMANDI, Gilles
Arsenal ❶❷❸ D

Fullname: Gilles Grimandi
DOB: 11-11-70 Gap, France

Arsenal boss Arsène Wenger returned to his homeland in the summer of 1997 then came back to England £5m worse off but with Emmanuel Petit and Gilles Grimandi ready to strengthen his side at Highbury. Grimandi featured in the Gunners' first six Premiership matches of the season but thereafter filled in to cover for suspensions and injuries. A composed central defender he is very much in the

French mould with his ability to play out of trouble and reads the game well. Got forward to score one goal in his first season, that being an important three point winning goal at home to Crystal Palace.

Given the advancing years of those he is looking to replace it could be that the 1998-99 season is the one in which he joins fellow countrymen Petit and Vieira as very influential figures at Highbury.

Form Factors

Season	Team	Tot	St	Sb	Y	R
97-98	Arsenal	22	16	6	5	0
Total		22	16	6	5	0

	GP	GG	GF	GS	TGR
97-98	57.89	22.00	68	1	1.47
Averages	57.89	22.00	68.00	1.00	1.47

GRODAS, Frode
Tottenham H. ❶❷❸ GK

Fullname: Frode Grodas
DOB: 24-10-69 Norway

Norwegian international goalkeeper whose days of playing at the highest level looked to be over midway through last season when he left Chelsea to become third choice custodian at Tottenham. He is behind Walker and Baardsen in the pecking order at White Hart Lane but in France 98 he took the number one position with Baardsen reduced to the role of his understudy. Although Grodas took some flack when flapping at crosses in the early games he generally had a sound tournament and may have done enough to convince someone that he could be worth another shot.

Form Factors

Season	Team	Tot	St	Sb	Y	R
96-97	Chelsea	21	20	1	1	1
Total		21	20	1	1	1

	GA	GkA	GAp	CS	SO	R
96-97	55	30	1.43	4	1	0
Averages	55	30	1.43	4	1	-

GRODIN, David
Arsenal ❶ FB

Fullname: David Grodin
DOB: France

In the summer of 1998 Grodin became the sixth Frenchman to join Arsène Wenger at Arsenal following his transfer from St. Etienne. At his best on the left the youngster, who cost Arsenal £500,000, scored in last season's French FA Youth Cup final despite being a defender.

GUIVARCH, Stephane
Newcastle United ❶❷❸ S

Fullname: Stephane Guivarch
DOB: 06-09-70 Concarneau

Top scorer in France last season, Stephane Guivarch won a World Cup winners medal with France in the summer. The national manager had earmarked him as the mainstay of the French attack but he was forced out of a number of games in the finals after picking up an injury in his country's opening game.

He has been likened to Alan Shearer in his style of play and it will be interesting to see how he combines with the England skipper at St James's Park. Certainly his record last season also points the Shearer way. A total of 21 league goals earned him the French Golden Boot and in all competitions he netted 47 times for Auxerre.

Guivarch signed for Auxerre from Guingamp in 1995 but he wasn't able to find the scoring touch so was allowed to move to Rennes. That move sparked the confidence back into him and his 22 goals in 1996-97 earned him another chance at Auxerre which he obviously took.

Kenny Dalglish paid the French side £3.5m for his services before the World Cup Finals, but his performances in France suggest that he still has a lot to prove.

Stephane Guivarch

GUPPY, Steve

Leicester City ❶❷❸ FB

Fullname: Stephen Guppy
DOB: 29-03-69 Winchester

For a while it looked as though Guppy might not make it at the highest level. Had a stab at the Premiership with Newcastle in 1994 but left inside three months without playing a single league game. Regained his confidence in a successful spell with Port Vale from where Leicester signed him for £850,000 in February 1997.

First played under Martin O'Neill's managership in the Conference with Wycombe Wanderers. Played for the England semi-pro side during his non-league days and since teaming up with O'Neill again has won a call up to the England B team. Left sided winger who, on his day, has no peers when it comes to supplying top quality crosses and missed just one match in the Premiership last season.

Form Factors

Season	Team	Tot	St	Sb	Y	R
96-97	Leicester C.	13	12	1	2	0
97-98	Leicester C.	37	37	0	3	0
Total		50	49	1	5	0

	GP	GG	GF	GS	TGR
96-97	34.21	0.00	46	0	0.00
97-98	97.37	18.50	51	2	3.92
Averages	65.79	9.25	48.50	1.00	1.96

HAALAND, Alf-Inge

Leeds United ❶❷❸ M
Fullname: Alf-Inge Haaland
DOB: 23-11-72 Stavanger

Celebrated his first season with Leeds United, 1997-98, by winning United's goal of the season with one of his two strikes in a 4-0 win over Blackburn Rovers. Proved himself to be a popular acquisition following a £1.6m transfer from Nottingham Forest in the summer of 1997 with his quick breaks from midfield to support the attack.

Joined Forest from Bryne in his native Norway back in 1994 and scored seven times in 75 league games for the Reds. Also notched seven goals in just one season with Leeds which somewhat surprisingly did not get him into the Norway squad for France 98.

Form Factors

Season	Team	Tot	St	Sb	Y	R
95-96	N. Forest	17	12	5	4	0
96-97	N. Forest	34	33	1	3	0
97-98	Leeds U.	32	26	6	6	1
Total		83	71	12	13	1

	GP	GG	GF	GS	TGR
95-96	44.74	0.00	50	0	0.00
96-97	89.47	5.67	31	6	19.35
97-98	84.21	4.57	57	7	12.28
Averages	72.81	3.41	46.00	4.33	10.55

HALL, Marcus

Coventry City ❶ FB
Fullname: Marcus Thomas Hall
DOB: 24-03-76 Coventry

After spending the early weeks of last season on the substitutes' bench, Hall forced his way into the Coventry City first team and featured in a run of 19 games out of 20, his second best run in four years as a professional at Highfield Road.

A former England Under-21 international defender who has played in most positions along the backline, and wing-back, although he favours a right-sided position. His 25 games in the Premiership last season included his first goal for the club, the final strike in a 4-0 win over Tottenham. Expect him to up his first team appearances this season.

Form Factors

Season	Team	Tot	St	Sb	Y	R
95-96	Coventry C.	25	24	1	1	0
96-97	Coventry C.	13	10	3	0	0
97-98	Coventry C.	25	20	5	7	0
Total		63	54	9	8	0

	GP	GG	GF	GS	TGR
95-96	65.79	0.00	42	0	0.00
96-97	34.21	0.00	38	0	0.00
97-98	65.79	25.00	46	1	2.17
Averages	55.26	8.33	42.00	0.33	0.72

HALL, Richard

West Ham U. ❶❷❸ CB

Fullname: Richard Anthony Hall
DOB: 14-03-72 Ipswich

Has had his career put on hold since completing a £1.9m move from Southampton to West Ham in the close season of 1996. Injury delayed his debut until the following April. He played the final seven games of that season but has not returned to first team action as injuries continue to blight his time at Upton Park. First gained Football League experience with Scunthorpe United before joining Southampton for £200,000 in February 1991.

Tall, commanding central defender, Hall was on course for a very distinguished career with full international honours with England expected to come his way. Previously capped at Under-21 level.

Form Factors

Season	Team	Tot	St	Sb	Y	R
94-95	Southampton	37	36	1	4	0
95-96	Southampton	30	30	0	6	0
96-97	West Ham U.	7	7	0	1	0
Total		74	73	1	11	0

	GP	GG	GF	GS	TGR
94-95	97.37	9.25	61	4	6.56
95-96	78.95	30.00	34	1	2.94
96-97	18.42	0.00	39	0	0.00
Averages	64.91	13.08	44.67	1.67	3.17

HALLE, Gunnar

Leeds United ❶❷❸ FB

Fullname: Gunnar Halle
DOB: 11-08-65 Oslo, Norway

Gunnar Halle

Very experienced defender who came to this country in 1991 when he signed for Oldham Athletic from Norwegian side Lillestrom. Joined Leeds United for £400,000 in 1996 and made his debut on 14 December in a goalless draw at home to Tottenham. Between then and the end of last season he missed just seven out 60 games and on 15 March scored his first goal for the club during a 5-0 victory at Derby County. His outstanding consistency during last season did not go unnoticed outside of these shores as he was called into the Norway squad for France 98.

Scored 17 times in 188 league games for Oldham.

Form Factors

Season	Team	Tot	St	Sb	Y	R
93-94	Oldham Athletic	23	22	1	0	0
96-97	Leeds U.	20	20	0	2	0
97-98	Leeds U.	33	31	2	5	1
Total		76	73	3	7	1

	GP	GG	GF	GS	TGR
93-94	60.53	23.00	42	1	2.38
96-97	52.63	0.00	28	0	0.00
97-98	86.84	16.50	57	2	3.51
Averages	66.67	13.17	42.33	1.00	1.96

HAMILTON, Des
Newcastle U. ❶❷ M

Fullname: Derrick Vivian Hamilton
DOB: 15-08-76 Bradford

Having played 32 times in Division One for Bradford City during the 1996-97 season, Hamilton had to bide his time for a while at Newcastle after joining the Geordies in a £1.5m transfer in March of that season. Broke into the Newcastle side last season with seven starts in the Premiership and five more run-outs from the bench.

Positive when going in for a tackle he makes dangerous runs from deep positions and displays tremendous stamina. A right-sided player who can operate to equal effect anywhere down that flank. His fee could eventually rise to £2m.

Form Factors

Season	Team	Tot	St	Sb	Y	R
97-98	Newcastle U.	12	7	5	0	0
Total		12	7	5	0	0

	GP	GG	GF	GS	TGR
97-98	31.58	0.00	35	0	0.00
Averages	31.58	0.00	35.00	0.00	0.00

HARKNESS, Steve
Liverpool ❶❷ FB

Fullname: Steven Harkness
DOB: 27-08-71 Carlisle

Tough-tackling left-back who has also featured at centre-half during his nine years at Liverpool. Following on from a season of little action as he recovered from a broken leg, Harkness spent much of the first half of last season on the subs' bench before replacing Bjornebye for the second half of the campaign. Unspectacular but dependable, and a possible threat with free kicks close to the opposition penalty area, he will doubtless face fresh challengers for his place over the coming months.

A run of 18 consecutive league appearances took his total for the season to 25, his best since joining from Carlisle United.

Form Factors

Season	Team	Tot	St	Sb	Y	R
95-96	Liverpool	24	23	1	4	0
96-97	Liverpool	7	5	2	0	0
97-98	Liverpool	25	24	1	6	0
Total		56	52	4	10	0

	GP	GG	GF	GS	TGR
95-96	63.16	24.00	70	1	1.43
96-97	18.42	0.00	62	0	0.00
97-98	65.79	0.00	68	0	0.00
Averages	49.12	8.00	66.67	0.33	0.48

HARTE, Ian

Leeds United ①② S
Fullname: Ian Harte
DOB: 31-08-77 Drogheda

After two seasons of trying to hold down a first team place with Leeds United Ian Harte finally looked to be on the verge of achieving his ambition towards the end of the 1997-98 campaign with an unbroken run of 12 consecutive games in the first team although he was substituted during the final two games. Predominantly a left back Ian Harte is actually two-footed which could aid his case making a good career at Elland Road, especially as the club signed a left back during the summer.

Somewhat bizarrely, as he tried to get into the first team there was a spell when he had appeared more times for his country, Eire, than he had for Leeds United and it does look as though he is more likely to be a squad member this season rather than a point gathering member of a fantasy team.

Form Factors

Season	Team	Tot	St	Sb	Y	R
95-96	Leeds U.	4	2	2	1	0
96-97	Leeds U.	14	10	4	1	0
97-98	Leeds U.	12	12	0	0	0
Total		30	24	6	2	0

	GP	GG	GF	GS	TGR
95-96	10.53	0.00	40	0	0.00
96-97	36.84	7.00	28	2	7.14
97-98	31.58	0.00	57	0	0.00
Averages	26.32	2.33	41.67	0.67	2.38

HARTSON, John

West Ham Utd ①②③④⑤ S
Fullname: John Hartson
DOB: 05-04-75 Swansea

John Hartson took a great deal of pleasure in proving the cynics and the critics wrong last season by making light of his large transfer fee from Arsenal to be the leading scorer in the Premiership and two domestic cup competitions with 24 goals. Hartson was quickly into his stride with goals in the Hammers' opening games against Barnsley and Tottenham but it was in the Coca Cola Cup that he really made hay with six goals in five appearances including a hat-trick against Huddersfield Town.

Powerfully built, with a deceptively good touch he can be lethal from crosses into the danger area and is not afraid to get hurt in the pursuit of goals. Will continue to haunt Premier defences this season and increase his tally of Welsh caps. The one cloud on Hartson's career horizon is a fiery temperament to match his red hair which has already earned him several suspensions.

Was given his chance in professional football with Luton Town from where he joined Arsenal as a teenager for £2.5m and just over two years later went to Upton Park for an initial £3.2m which could rise to £5m.

Form Factors

Season	Team	Tot	St	Sb	Y	R
96-97	Arsenal	19	15	4	9	0
96-97	West Ham U.	11	11	0	3	0
97-98	West Ham U.	32	32	0	4	2
Total		62	58	4	16	2

	GP	GG	GF	GS	TGR
96-97	50.00	6.33	62	3	4.84
96-97	28.95	2.20	39	5	12.82
97-98	84.21	2.13	56	15	26.79
Averages	54.39	3.56	52.33	7.67	14.81

John Hartson

HASSELBAINK, Jimmy Floyd

Leeds United   ❶❷❸❹ S

Fullname: Jimmy Floyd Hasselbaink
DOB: 27-03-72 Surinam

Had a sensational first season with Leeds United following his move to Elland Road in the summer of 1997 from Portuguese side Boavista for £2m. Scored 16 times in the Premiership last season which is only 12 less than Leeds managed in the whole of the previous season. Added a further six goals in cup matches.

After taking time to settle in England and then dismissed in the Coca Cola Cup, Hasselbaink went on to win the Leeds Player of the Year award and his achievements here didn't go unnoticed back home as he was called into Holland's France 98 squad.

A hardworking striker he should continue to rattle in the goals this season.

Jimmy Floyd Hasselbaink

Form Factors

Season	Team	Tot	St	Sb	Y	R
97-98	Leeds U.	33	30	3	5	0
Total		33	30	3	5	0

	GP	GG	GF	GS	TGR
97-98	86.84	2.06	57	16	28.07
Averages	86.84	2.06	57.00	16.00	28.07

HAWORTH, Simon

Coventry C. ❶❷ S

Fullname: Simon Owen Haworth
DOB: 30-03-77 Cardiff

A £500,000 signing made by Coventry City boss Gordon Strachan in the summer of 1997 with one eye very much on the future. Haworth, only 21 going into the 1998-99 season, has already played for Wales at Under-21 and the full side and has the qualities required to make it at the highest level. Tall, powerful in the air and very good on the ground, he played 10 times in the Premiership last season and even though he did not score is certain to be given an extended run this time around.

Spent two seasons with Cardiff City, after working way through from trainee, to score nine league goals in 37 games.

HEALD, Paul

Wimbledon ❶ GK

Fullname: Paul Andrew Heald
DOB: 20-09-68 Wath-on-Dearne

Goalkeeper who has had a stop-start career with last season being very much one of the stop variety as he stayed, unused, on the bench for all 38 of Wimbledon's Premiership matches. Over the past two seasons Heald has had to watch 61 of Wimbledon's league games from the sidelines. His move to Wimbledon at the end of the 1994-95 season came after missing just one match during the previous campaign for Leyton Orient.

Difficult to see him being offered many chances this season given Neil Sullivan's acquisition of international status with Scotland.

Form Factors

Season	Team	Tot	St	Sb	Y	R
95-96	Wimbledon	18	18	0	1	1
96-97	Wimbledon	2	2	0	0	0
97-98	Wimbledon	0	0	0	0	0
Total		20	20	0	1	1

	GA	GkA	GAp	CS	SO	Rp
95-96	70	26	1.44	3	1	0
96-97	48	3	1.50	0	0	0
Averages	59.0	14.5	1.47	1.5	0.5	0

HEDMAN, Magnus
Coventry C. ❶❷❸ GK
Fullname: Magnus Hedman
DOB: 19-03-73 Sweden

Magnus Hedman

The first Swedish goalkeeper to play in the Premiership, Hedman made his debut with Coventry City last season following his transfer from Solna. Seen as the long-term replacement for Ogrizovic, he enjoyed a run of 14 consecutive league and cup appearances and his name was on the teamsheet for no less than 37 Premiership matches, although he was an unused sub for 23 of those games.

Twice a winner in the Swedish Cup he played 14 times in the Premiership last season and let in only 12 goals at 0.86 per game. His very impressive run included six clean sheets and four consecutive shut-outs. Could be one to back.

Form Factors

Season	Team	Tot	St	Sb	Y	R
97-98	Coventry C.	14	14	0	0	0
Total		14	14	0	0	0

	GA	GkA	GAp	CS	SO	Rp
97-98	44	12	0.86	6	2	0
Averages	44	12	0.86	6	2	0

HENCHOZ, Stephane
Blackburn R. ❶❷❸ D
Fullname: Stephane Henchoz
DOB: 07-09-74 Billens, Switzerland

A near ever present at Ewood Park last season, his first in the Premiership, Henchoz was persuaded to move to England by Rovers boss Roy Hodgson under whom he played in club football and the Swiss national side. Settled very quickly to the speed of the British game and missed just two of Blackburn's Premiership games last season.

Form Factors

Season	Team	Tot	St	Sb	Y	R
97-98	Blackburn R.	36	36	0	6	0
Totals		36	36	0	6	0

	GP	GG	GF	GS	TGR
	94.74	0.00	57	0	0.00
Averages	94.74	0.00	57	0	0.00

FANTASY FOOTBALL HANDBOOK 1998/99

HENDRIE, Lee

Aston Villa ❶❷❸ S

Fullname: Lee Andrew Hendrie
DOB: 18-05-77 Birmingham

Local youngster who made good progress in the Aston Villa first team last season having been given a handful of run-outs during the two previous campaigns. Was used in just four games prior to John Gregory's arrival but was ever-present after Gregory took charge. Featured on Villa's Premiership team sheet on no fewer than 26 occasions and made 13 starts with four substitute appearances.

A striker who is not afraid of hard work, he has a very promising future if his three goals last season are anything to go by. An England Under-21 international whose father John played for Birmingham City.

Form Factors

Season	Team	Tot	St	Sb	Y	P
95-96	Aston Villa	3	2	1	1	
96-97	Aston Villa	4	0	4	0	0
97-98	Aston Villa	17	13	4	1	0
Total		24	15	9	2	

	GP	GG	GF	GS	TGR
95-96	7.89	0.00	52	0	0.00
96-97	10.53	0.00	47	0	0.00
97-98	44.74	5.67	49	3	6.12
Averages	21.05	1.89	49.33	1.00	2.04

Colin Hendry

HENDRY, Colin

Blackburn R. ❶❷❸❹❺ CB

Fullname: Edward Colin James Hendry
DOB: 07-12-65 Keith

Distinctive blond central defender who played in Blackburn's promotion winning side of 1992 and the Premiership winning side of three years later. Has also become a vital figure in the Scotland line up with the highlight being appearances in their Euro 96 and France 98 escapades.

Although edging towards the veteran stage of his career Hendry remains as combative and domineering as ever and still pushes forward to boost the attack when the need arises. A good reader of the game who is quick in the tackle and leads by example by never pulling out of a challenge, although despite this he still missed just 16 Premiership matches over the past four seasons.

Started his career with Dundee and in between two lengthy stays at Ewood Park has also played for Manchester City.

Form Factors

Season	Team	Tot	St	Sb	Y	R
95-96	Blackburn R.	33	33	0	9	0
96-97	Blackburn R.	35	35	0	4	0
97-98	Blackburn R.	34	34	0	6	0
Total		102	102	0	19	0

	GP	GG	GF	GS	TGR
95-96	86.84	33.00	61	1	1.64
96-97	92.11	35.00	42	1	2.38
97-98	89.47	34.00	57	1	1.75
Averages	89.47	34.00	53.33	1.00	1.92

HESKEY, Emile

Leicester City ❶❷❸ S

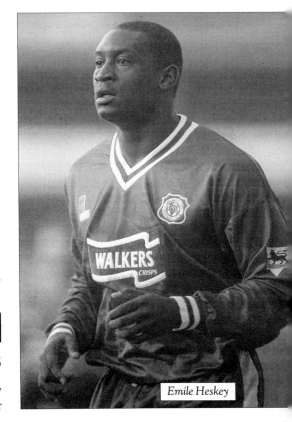

Emile Heskey

Fullname: Emile William Ivanhoe Heskey
DOB: 11-01-78 Leicester

The 1997-98 season saw Heskey score 10 league goals for the second consecutive year and given that he goes into this season still only aged 20 it would be reasonable to expect him to use his experiences of the past couple of seasons to improve upon that total and really push hard for a call up to the England senior squad. Certainly did his chances no harm during the close season when scoring for England Under-21s during the Toulon International Tournament.

Heskey's pace is perhaps his most dangerous weapon but he also has good close skills which enable him to cause havoc with mazy runs. Although he is best known as a striker he has also played many times wide on the right of the midfield which makes it harder to pick him up. Has missed just six Premiership matches over the past two seasons but collected his first red card last season.

Form Factors

Season	Team	Tot	St	Sb	Y	R
94-95	Leicester C.	1	1	0	0	0
96-97	Leicester C.	35	35	0	8	0
97-98	Leicester C.	35	35	0	5	1
Total		71	71	0	13	1

	GP	GG	GF	GS	TGR
94-95	2.63	0.00	45	0	0.00
96-97	92.11	3.50	46	10	21.74
97-98	92.11	3.50	51	10	19.61
Averages	62.28	2.33	47.33	6.67	13.78

HIDEN, Martin

Leeds United ❶❷❸ D
Fullname: Martin Hiden
DOB: 11-03-73 Stainz

Defender who joined Leeds United for £1.5m in February 1998 from Rapid Vienna where he gained Champions League experience. Quickly established himself in the Leeds backline with 12 consecutive appearances towards the end of the season and showed himself to be very adaptable as he played in various positions.

Gained full international honours for the first time shortly after signing for Leeds and was included is Austria's France 98 squad but didn't get a run out during his country's three games. Could prove to be a reasonably priced member of your fantasy team.

Form Factors

Season	Team	Tot	St	Sb	Y	R
97-98	Leeds U.	11	11	0	2	0
Total		11	11	0	2	0

	GP	GG	GF	GS	TGR
97-98	28.95	0.00	57	0	0.00
Averages	28.95	0.00	57.00	0.00	0.00

HINCHCLIFFE, Andy

Sheffield W. ❶❷❸❹ FB
Fullname: Andrew George Hinchcliffe
DOB: 05-02-69 Manchester

Possessor of perhaps the most feared left foot in the Premiership, Hinchcliffe's cultured left peg played a major role in Everton's 1995 FA Cup success and earned him a run in England's France 98 qualifying matches until injury ended his dream of playing in the finals.

Not a renowned goalscorer himself, he notched one in 15 games for Sheffield Wednesday last season, Hinchcliffe has provided the perfect crosses for many others to benefit from and now that he is fully over an injury which cautioned Tottenham against signing him he will doubtless once again fire in his inch-perfect corners over the coming months.

Formerly with Manchester City he spent eight seasons with Everton prior to his £2.75m transfer to Hillsborough in January 1998.

Form Factors

Season	Team	Tot	St	Sb	Y	R
96-97	Everton	18	18	0	2	0
97-98	Everton	17	15	2	3	1
97-98	Sheffield W.	15	15	0	0	0
Total		50	48	2	5	1

	GP	GG	GF	GS	TGR
96-97	47.37	18.00	44	1	2.27
97-98	44.74	0.00	41	0	0.00
97-98	39.47	15.00	52	1	1.92
Averages	43.86	11.00	45.67	0.67	1.40

HIRST, David
Southampton ❶❷❸ S
Fullname: David Eric Hirst
DOB: 07-12-67 Cudworth

Former England striker who moved to Southampton from Sheffield Wednesday in October 1997 for £2m and went on to score nine times in the Premiership in 28 games. His average of a goal every 3.1 games last season was below his average of 2.7 achieved throughout his career with Barnsley and Wednesday.

Hirst is a pacey left-footed player who is good at holding the ball up and leads well from the front. Although not over six feet in height, he is good in the air and providing he can stay injury free should be the Saints' leading scorer this season.

Form Factors

Season	Team	Tot	St	Sb	Y	R
96-97	Sheffield W.	25	20	5	3	1
97-98	Sheffield W.	6	3	3	0	0
97-98	Southampton	28	28	0	0	3
Total		59	51	8	3	4

	GP	GG	GF	GS	TGR
96-97	65.79	4.17	50	6	12.00
97-98	15.79	0.00	52	0	0.00
97-98	73.68	3.11	50	9	18.00
Averages	51.75	2.43	50.67	5.00	10.00

HISLOP, Shaka
West Ham United ❶❷❸ GK
Fullname: Neil Hislop
DOB: 22-02-69 London

Made a close season move from Newcastle United where he'd been for the past three years to join West Ham United. His 13 Premiership games for the Magpies last season, in which he conceded 16 goals, took his career total of league appearances with the Geordies to 53.

Joined Newcastle from Reading for £1.5m during the 1995 close season. Was at Elm Park for three years, the last two of which he was ever present but the best he could manage at Newcastle was 24 games during his first season at St. James's Park. By signing for the Hammers he returns to the city of his birth although he grew up in Trinidad.

Form Factors

Season	Team	Tot	St	Sb	Y	R
95-96	Newcastle U.	24	24	0	0	0
96-97	Newcastle U.	16	16	0	0	0
97-98	Newcastle U.	13	13	0	0	0
Total		53	53	0	0	0

	GA	GkA	GAp	CS	SO	R
95-96	37	19	0.79	8	3	0
96-97	40	21	1.31	3	1	0
97-98	44	14	1.08	2	1	0
Averages	40.33	18.0	1.06	4.33	1.67	0

HITCHCOCK, Kevin

Chelsea ❶ GK

Fullname: Kevin Joseph Hitchcock
DOB: 05-10-62 Canning Town

Hitchcock's days as a goalkeeper in the Premiership appear to be coming to an end if indeed they are not already over. The former Mansfield Town keeper, who joined Chelsea in 1988, had the rare distinction of playing in exactly 12 league games for three consecutive seasons until last season when he sat on the bench for 36 Premiership matches with his only run-outs being a couple of Coca Cola Cup ties.

Form Factors

Season	Team	Tot	St	Sb	Y	R
95-96	Chelsea	12	12	0	0	0
96-97	Chelsea	12	10	2	1	0
97-98	Chelsea	0	0	0	0	0
Total		24	22	2	1	0

	GA	GkA	GAp	CS	SO	R
95-96	44	15	1.25	2	2	0
96-97	55	18	1.50	0	0	0
Averages	49.5	16.5	2.75	1	1	0

HJELDE, Jon Olav

Nottingham F. ❶❷❸ D

Fullname: Jon Olav Hjelde
DOB: Norway

Norwegian defender who settled quickly into English football last season with Nottingham Forest. Was signed for £600,000 at a time when Forest had a lengthy injury list but he did more than fill-in and became a regular in the centre of the defence where his 6'3" frame made him a commanding figure. His height though is not his only asset as he is quick on the ground and uses the ball intelligently. Signed for Forest from Rosenborg with whom he played in the Champions League.

HODGES, Lee

West Ham U. ❶ M

Fullname: Lee Leslie Hodges
DOB: 02-03-78 Plaistow

Made his Premiership debut when coming on as a substitute for West Ham during a 1-0 defeat at Tottenham in January but has yet to appear in the starting line-up for the Hammers. A precise ball-playing midfielder in whom West Ham have a lot of faith and this could be the season when he gets an extended run in the first team. Has had spells on loan to Exeter City and Leyton Orient.

Form Factors

Season	Team	Tot	St	Sb	Y	R
97-98	West Ham U.	2	0	2	0	0
Total		2	0	2	0	0

	GP	GG	GF	GS	TGR
97-98	5.26	0.00	56	0	0.00
Averages	5.26	0.00	56.00	0.00	0.00

HOLMES, Matty

Charlton A. ❶M
Fullname: Matthew Holmes
DOB: 01-08-69 Luton

Since leaving West Ham United in 1995 Holmes has suffered little but misery. He had an unsuccessful two years with Blackburn Rovers during which time he made just nine appearances and moved to Charlton Athletic for £250,000 in August last year. Just five days before the start of the 1997-98 season he was injured in a testimonial match and just 11 games after starting to establish himself in the side he suffered a broken leg and missed the rest of the season.

Prior to hitting this dire run of ill-fortune he was a left-sided midfielder with Bournemouth and then West Ham. Hang on to your lucky rabbit's foot if you put him in your team.

Form Factors

Season	Team	Tot	St	Sb	Y	R
93-94	West Ham U.	34	33	1	1	0
94-95	West Ham U.	24	24	0	4	0
95-96	Blackburn R.	8	7	1	1	0
Total		66	64	2	6	0

	GP	GG	GF	GS	TGR
93-94	89.47	11.33	47	3	6.38
94-95	63.16	24.00	44	1	2.27
95-96	21.05	8.00	61	1	1.64
Averages	57.89	14.44	50.67	1.67	3.43

HOPKIN, David

Leeds United ❶❷❸M
Fullname: David Hopkin
DOB: 21-08-70 Greenock

Had a chance of making his debut in the Premiership with Crysal Palace after his extra time play-off winning goal secured promotion for the Eagles but opted for a £3.25m switch to Leeds United in the summer of 1997. Played in 17 of Leeds' opening 18 games, was substituted in eight of these games but did score his first goal for George Graham's side during this spell. Failed to figure in the starting line up for Leeds' last eight games of the season which pretty much summed up an injury-hit campaign for a player who also lost his place in the Scotland squad. When fully fit and in top form he will be an asset to any midfield as his 21 goals in two seasons with Palace emphasise.

Began his career with three years at Morton and then Chelsea before joining Palace.

Form Factors

Season	Team	Tot	St	Sb	Y	R
93-94	Chelsea	21	12	9	1	0
94-95	Chelsea	15	7	8	0	0
97-98	Leeds U.	25	22	3	5	0
Total		61	41	20	6	0

	GP	GG	GF	GS	TGR
93-94	55.26	0.00	49	0	0.00
94-95	39.47	15.00	50	1	2.00
97-98	65.79	25.00	57	1	1.75
Averages	53.51	13.33	52.00	0.67	1.25

HOULT, Russell

Derby County ❶❷ GK

Fullname: Russell Hoult
DOB: 28-03-71 Leicester

Having played 73 times in two seasons in the Premiership for Derby County former Leicester City goalkeeper Hoult suffered a major setback last season when he was ousted from between the sticks by Mart Poom. Hoult stood in for two league games, conceding one goal in each, and one Coca Cola Cup tie and spent the rest of the season watching from the subs bench. At 6'4" tall he likes to command his penalty area but is also swift at getting down for low shots. Given Poom's consistency last season it would appear that Hoult's chances at Pride Park may be very limited.

Joined Derby for £300,000 in February 1995 having also played on loan to Lincoln City and Bolton Wanderers during his time at Filbert Street.

Form Factors

Season	Team	Tot	St	Sb	Y	R
96-97	Derby Co.	32	31	1	0	0
97-98	Derby Co.	2	2	0	0	0
Total		34	33	1	0	0

	GA	GkA	GAp	CS	SO	Rp
96-97	58	48	1.50	6	1	0
97-98	29	2	1.00	0	0	0
Averages	43.5	25.0	1.25	3.0	0.5	0

HOWELLS, David

Southampton ❶❷ M

Fullname: David Howells
DOB: 15-12-67 Guildford

After 13 years as a member of the Tottenham Hotspur first team Howells was released, perhaps prematurely, at the end of last season and was quickly snapped up on a free transfer by Southampton. Playing just in front of the backline Howells is a non-stop worker in midfield who gets forward well although his goals tally is not overly impressive. Played 20 times in the Premiership for Spurs last season – taking his career tally of league appearances at White Hart Lane to 277 – but will almost certainly play in most of Southampton's games this season and at the age of 30 would be a useful member of your fantasy team.

Form Factors

Season	Team	Tot	St	Sb	Y	R
95-96	Tottenham H.	29	29	0	6	0
96-97	Tottenham H.	32	32	0	7	0
97-98	Tottenham H.	19	13	6	3	0
Total		80	74	6	16	0

	GP	GG	GF	GS	TGR
95-96	76.32	9.67	50	3	6.00
96-97	84.21	16.00	44	2	4.55
97-98	50.00	0.00	44	0	0.00
Averages	70.18	8.56	46.00	1.67	3.52

HOWEY, Steve

Newcastle U. ❶❷ CB

Fullname: Stephen Norman Howey
DOB: 26-10-71 Sunderland

Born in Sunderland but has spent all his career with Newcastle having joined the Magpies as a trainee. An adaptable player who started out as a centre forward and has since moved between defence and midfield. Took three seasons to establish himself in the side and earned four England caps before injury ruled him out of Euro 96. And injuries have also decimated his appearances over the past two seasons although he regained full fitness towards the end of last season and should be in peak condition for the start of 1998-99.

Form Factors

Season	Team	Tot	St	Sb	Y	R
95-96	Newcastle U.	28	28	0	2	0
96-97	Newcastle U.	8	8	0	0	0
97-98	Newcastle U.	14	11	3	0	0
Total		50	47	3	2	0

	GP	GG	GF	GS	TGR
95-96	73.68	28.00	66	1	1.52
96-97	21.05	8.00	73	1	1.37
97-98	36.84	0.00	35	0	0.00
Averages	43.86	12.00	58.00	0.67	0.96

Steve Howey

HUCKERBY, Darren

Coventry City ❶❷❸❹❺ S

Fullname: Darren Carl Huckerby
DOB: 27-04-76 Nottingham

Began his career with Lincoln City and after just 28 games for the Imps was transferred to Newcastle United for £400,000. Unable to break into the side at St James's Park, Huckerby made a £1m move to Coventry and became an instant success. Scored five times in 25 games during the 1996-97 season and improved upon that form last season with 14 goals in 34 Premiership matches. Still only 22 he could really set the world alight this season with his dazzling runs at defences which often appear bemused by his style.

An England Under-21 striker who exudes a refreshingly unorthodox attitude on the pitch although referees were less impressed by it last term as nine yellow cards were waved in his direction.

Form Factors

Season	Team	Tot	St	Sb	Y	R
95-96	Newcastle U.	1	0	1	0	0
96-97	Coventry C.	25	21	4	2	0
97-98	Coventry C.	34	32	2	9	0
Total		60	53	7	11	0

	GP	GG	GF	GS	TGR
95-96	2.63	0.00	66	0	0.00
96-97	65.79	5.00	38	5	13.16
97-98	89.47	2.43	46	14	30.43
Averages	52.63	2.48	50.00	6.33	14.53

Darren Huckerby

HUGHES, Ceri

Wimbledon ❶❷ M

Fullname: Ceri Morgan Hughes
DOB: 26-02-71 Pontypridd

Spent all of his playing career with Luton Town prior to a £750,000 move to Wimbledon ahead of last season. Known for his gritty, bustling attitude in midfield he has fallen foul of match officials in the past but did well to collect just one yellow card in his first season in the Premiership. Looked to have fully established himself in the Dons side when a hamstring injury put him out of action for six weeks.

Spent eight years with Luton where he scored 17 league goals in 175 games and won his first cap for Wales in 1992.

Form Factors

Season	Team	Tot	St	Sb	Y	R
97-98	Wimbledon	17	13	4	1	0
Total		17	13	4	1	0

	GP	GG	GF	GS	TGR
97-98	44.74	17.00	34	1	2.94
Averages	44.74	17.00	34.00	1.00	2.94

HUGHES, David

Southampton ❶M
Fullname: David Robert Hughes
DOB: 30-12-72 St Albans

It could be said that the 1997-98 season was the most successful yet in the Southampton career of David Hughes as he made his most Premiership appearances yet in five years as a member of the Saints first team. Sadly for Hughes though, his total of 13 games included seven as substitute and there must be a question mark as to whether he will eventually hold down a permanent place in the side or not.

A tireless runner in midfield who is partial to going forward and has gained international honours with Wales at Under-21.

Form Factors

Season	Team	Tot	St	Sb	Y	R
95-96	Southampton	11	6	5	1	0
96-97	Southampton	6	1	5	1	0
97-98	Southampton	13	6	7	1	0
Total		30	13	17	3	0

	GP	GG	GF	GS	TGR
95-96	28.95	11.00	34	1	2.94
96-97	15.79	0.00	50	0	0.00
97-98	34.21	0.00	50	0	0.00
Averages	26.32	3.67	44.67	0.33	0.98

HUGHES, Mark

Southampton ❶❷❸S
Fullname: Leslie Mark Hughes
DOB: 01-11-63 Wrexham

When Mark Hughes left Manchester United for Chelsea in 1995, it seemed as though his career was given a tremendous shot in the arm. The 34 year old striker scored 11 goals in all competitions last season taking his total league goals to 129 in 457 games. But scoring is just a part of Hughes' game as his exceptional control and ability to hold the ball up brings teammates into play and creates openings for others to benefit.

Aside from his 65 caps with Wales, during his time with Manchester United he won two Premiership titles, was a winner three times in the FA Cup, and once each in the League Cup and Cup Winners' Cup – the last three were won again at Stamford Bridge.

With his £500,000 move to Southampton in the summer Hughes' incredible career at the top level goes into a 15th year.

Form Factors

Season	Team	Tot	St	Sb	Y	R
95-96	Chelsea	31	31	0	12	1
96-97	Chelsea	35	32	3	6	0
97-98	Chelsea	29	25	4	9	0
Total		95	88	7	27	1

	GP	GG	GF	GS	TGR
95-96	81.58	3.88	46	8	17.39
96-97	92.11	4.38	58	8	13.79
97-98	76.32	3.22	71	9	12.68
Averages	83.33	3.82	58.33	8.33	14.62

HUGHES, Michael

Wimbledon   ①②M

Fullname: Michael Eamonn Hughes
DOB: 02-08-71 Larne

Lively winger who joined Wimbledon in September 1997 for £1.6m after failing to hold down a regular place at the start of the season in Harry Redknapp's West Ham side. Quickly established himself at Selhurst Park and although he can play down either flank he is at his best on the left.

Formerly with Manchester City he spent more than two years in France with Strasbourg before joining West Ham, firstly on loan. A Northern Ireland international, he can be relied upon to score a handful of goals with his four in the Premiership last season being around his average.

Form Factors

Season	Team	Tot	St	Sb	Y	R
96-97	West Ham U.	33	31	2	5	0
97-98	West Ham U.	5	2	3	1	0
97-98	Wimbledon	29	29	0	7	0
Total		67	62	5	13	0

	GP	GG	GF	GS	TGR
96-97	86.84	11.00	39	3	7.69
97-98	13.16	0.00	56	0	0.00
97-98	76.32	7.25	34	4	11.76
Averages	58.77	6.08	43.00	2.33	6.49

HUGHES, Paul

Chelsea   ①②M

Fullname: Paul Hughes
DOB: 19-04-76 Hammersmith

The task of a local player trying to break into the Chelsea first team is not the easiest job in the world over recent seasons and Paul Hughes, who made a dozen appearances in the Premiership during 1996-97, saw his chances limited to just nine games last season of which only five were starts. Given that Chelsea were again one of the major players in the transfer market during the summer his opportunities would look to be further reduced for the coming season.

Even so, he is a hardworking midfielder with no lack of ability who could yet make it at this level.

Form Factors

Season	Team	Tot	St	Sb	Y	R
96-97	Chelsea	12	8	4	1	0
97-98	Chelsea	9	5	4	1	0
Total		21	13	8	2	0

	GP	GG	GF	GS	TGR
96-97	31.58	6.00	58	2	3.45
97-98	23.68	0.00	71	0	0.00
Averages	27.63	3.00	64.50	1.00	1.72

HUGHES, Stephen

Arsenal ❶❷❸ M

Fullname: Stephen John Hughes
DOB: 18-09-76 Wokingham

Former England Under-21 captain who looks to be on the verge of making it big in the Premiership with his one club, Arsenal. A very lively midfielder, he is excellent at running at defenders and uses the ball to great effect. Scored a lot of goals in Youth football and chipped in with a couple in the Premiership last season during his 17 appearances, of which only seven were from the start. Arsenal certainly have no doubts concerning Hughes' ability as they handed him a five year contract in February 1998.

Form Factors

Season	Team	Tot	St	Sb	Y	R
95-96	Arsenal	1	0	1	0	0
96-97	Arsenal	14	9	5	1	0
97-98	Arsenal	17	7	10	0	0
Total		32	16	16	1	0

	GP	GG	GF	GS	TGR
95-96	2.63	0.00	49	0	0.00
96-97	36.84	14.00	62	1	1.61
97-98	44.74	8.50	68	2	2.94
Averages	28.07	7.50	59.67	1.00	1.52

HUMPHREYS, Richie

Sheffield W. ❶ S

Fullname: Richard John Humphreys
DOB: 30-11-77 Sheffield

With three goals – two of them spectacular – in Sheffield Wednesday's first four games of 1996-97, young Richie Humphries appeared to be on the verge something special. And although he was in the side for Wednesday's last two matches of the season a large amount of the campaign had seen him despatched to the bench. Last season saw the continued decline in his fortunes as the lively striker, who can play in midfield and was still only 20 at the end of the season, made just two starts – he was taken off both times – and was used as substitute for a further five games.

The 1998-99 season could well be make-or-break if he is to hold his own in the Premiership.

Form Factors

Season	Team	Tot	St	Sb	Y	R
95-96	Sheffield W.	5	1	4	0	0
96-97	Sheffield W.	29	14	15	2	0
97-98	Sheffield W.	7	2	5	1	0
Total		41	17	24	3	0

	GP	GG	GF	GS	TGR
95-96	13.16	0.00	48	0	0.00
96-97	76.32	9.67	50	3	6.00
97-98	18.42	0.00	52	0	0.00
Averages	35.96	3.22	50.00	1.00	2.00

HUNT, Jonathan
Derby County ❶❷ M
Fullname: Jonathan Richard Hunt
DOB: 02-11-71 Camden, London

A £500,000 signing from Birmingham City in the summer of 1997, he was in the starting line-up for Derby County's first six matches of last season but from then on was only fleetingly seen again in the Rams colours. With his bright start at Pride Park it seemed as though Hunt was successfully rebuilding his career after he lost his place at St. Andrews initially through injury.

Despite his obvious flair on the ball, ability to get goals – he scored 11 times in the league during 1995-96 when he was Birmingham's Player of the Year – and good use of both feet, Hunt looks to have a battle on his hands to reclaim a regular place in the Derby midfield.

Form Factors

Season	Team	Tot	St	Sb	Y	R
97-98	Derby Co.	19	7	12	1	0
Total		19	7	12	1	0

	GP	GG	GF	GS	TGR
97-98	50.00	19.00	52	1	1.92
Averages	50.00	19.00	52.00	1.00	1.92

HUTCHISON, Don
Everton ❶❷ M
Fullname: Donald Hutchison
DOB: 09-05-71 Gateshead

Potentially a very talented midfield player but his sometimes over aggressive tendencies have got him into more than his fair share of disciplinary problems down the years. Is at his best when used in the centre of midfield but can fill other positions if needed.

This is his second stint on Merseyside following over three years at Anfield earlier in the decade. Has also played for Hartlepool United, Sheffield United and West Ham United where he probably enjoyed his most successful spell.

Form Factors

Season	Team	Tot	St	Sb	Y	R
94-95	West Ham U.	23	22	1	6	1
95-96	West Ham U.	5	1	4	0	0
97-98	Everton	11	11	0	2	0
Total		39	34	5	8	1

	GP	GG	GF	GS	TGR
94-95	60.53	2.56	44	9	20.45
95-96	13.16	0.00	43	0	0.00
97-98	28.95	11.00	41	1	2.44
Averages	34.21	4.52	42.67	3.33	7.63

HYDE, Graham
Sheffield W. ❶❷ M
Fullname: Graham Hyde
DOB: 10-11-70 Doncaster

One-club man, born in nearby Doncaster, who began as a trainee with Sheffield Wednesday before making his first team debut in 1991, has since made 170 league

204   Fantasy Football Handbook 1998/99

appearances for the Owls and knocked in 11 goals. A hardworking midfielder he is tenacious in the tackle which led, particularly last season, to disciplinary problems as he collected seven bookings in just 21 Premiership outings. Started in 14 of those 21 games but was substituted 10 times, all that after missing the start of the season through injury.

His best season for goals came four seasons ago when he scored five times in 35 games but he usually chips in with one or two.

Form Factors

Season	Team	Tot	St	Sb	Y	R
94-95	Sheffield W.	35	33	2	7	0
95-96	Sheffield W.	26	14	12	2	0
97-98	Sheffield W.	21	14	7	7	0
Total		82	61	21	16	0

	GP	GG	GF	GS	TGR
94-95	92.11	7.00	49	5	10.20
95-96	68.42	26.00	48	1	2.08
97-98	55.26	21.00	52	1	1.92
Averages	71.93	18.00	49.67	2.33	4.74

ILIC, Sasa

Charlton A. ❶❷❸ GK

Fullname: Sasa Ilic
DOB: Australia

Had an extraordinary rise to fame last season on the back of a penalty shoot-out save at Wembley from Sunderland's Michael Gray which carried Charlton Athletic into the Premiership. Grabbed the goalkeeping jersey at the Valley from fellow Aussie Andy Petterson. Less than a year earlier Ilic was playing in the Dr Martens League with St. Leonards Stamcroft having originally come to this country to study at Sussex University.

Played for Ringwood back in his home country and gained European experience before arriving in England having played for Yugoslavian sides Partisan Belgrade and Radinicki.

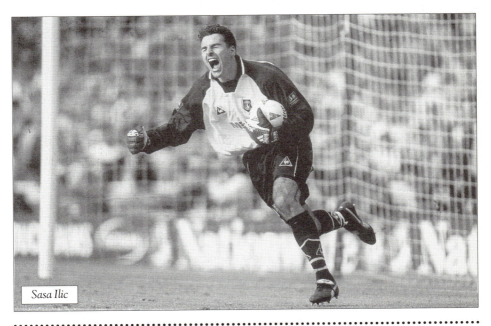

Sasa Ilic

Fantasy Football Handbook 1998/99

IMPEY, Andy
West Ham U. ①②M
Fullname: Andrew Rodney Impey
DOB: 13-09-71 Hammersmith

A £1.2m signing by West Ham from London rivals Queens Park Rangers in the summer of 1997 who was in and out of the Hammers side last season playing in exactly half of their league games. Has found the step up to the Premiership testing after seven years at Loftus Road and he has yet to score his first top flight goal. Voted Player of the Year with Rangers in 1995 he is predominantly a left-sided player whose main asset is his willingness to take players on before sending over crosses for the likes of John Hartson to feed off.

A former England Under-21 international he joined Rangers from nearby Isthmian League side Yeading in August 1990 for £35,000.

Form Factors

Season	Team	Tot	St	Sb	Y	R
94-95	QPR	40	40	0	3	0
95-96	QPR	29	28	1	2	1
97-98	West Ham U.	19	19	0	0	0
Total		88	87	1	5	1

	GP	GG	GF	GS	TGR
94-95	105.26	13.33	61	3	4.92
95-96	76.32	9.67	38	3	7.89
97-98	50.00	0.00	56	0	0.00
Averages	77.19	7.67	51.67	2.00	4.27

INCE, Paul
Liverpool ①②③④M
Fullname: Paul Emerson Carlyle Ince
DOB: 21-10-67 Ilford

Probably the most respected hard-man midfielder in England, he had an excellent France 98 with perhaps his finest match being the showdown with Argentina although he was one of the two unfortunate England players to miss in the penalty shoot-out. A great ball-winner who also likes to use the ball constructively and possesses exceptional stamina with his ability to get between each penalty area simply awesome.

His goalscoring record during his time with West Ham United and Manchester United was pretty ordinary but last season – his first back in the Premiership following a £4.5m transfer from Internazionale – he notched a very healthy eight in 31 league games. Ince, on his form of last season, is irreplaceable.

Form Factors

Season	Team	Tot	St	Sb	Y	R
93-94	Manchester U.	39	39	0	6	0
94-95	Manchester U.	36	36	0	5	0
97-98	Liverpool	31	31	0	8	0
Total		106	106	0	19	0

	GP	GG	GF	GS	TGR
93-94	102.63	4.88	80	8	10.00
94-95	94.74	7.20	77	5	6.49
97-98	81.58	3.88	68	8	11.76
Averages	92.98	5.32	75.00	7.00	9.42

IRWIN, Denis

Manchester U. ❶❷❸❹ FB

Fullname: Joseph Denis Irwin
DOB: 31-10-65 Cork

One of the most consistent defenders ever to play in the Premiership Irwin has proved a steal having been signed from Oldham Athletic in June 1990 for a mere £625,000. Has been involved in all of United's glories of the 1990s with five championship medals, two FA Cup medals and a Cup Winners' Cup medal all going his way. Has also been a long-standing fixture in the Republic of Ireland defence.

His defensive awareness is top class and his forays into attacking positions can be devastating. His fierce free kicks around the opposition penalty area are legendary.

Was sidelined for part of last season when horrendously scythed down in the Champions League away to Feyenoord but if he stays injury free would be an asset to your fantasy team.

Form Factors

Season	Team	Tot	St	Sb	Y	R
95-96	Manchester U.	31	31	0	4	0
96-97	Manchester U.	31	29	2	1	0
97-98	Manchester U.	25	23	2	4	0
Total		87	83	4	9	0

	GP	GG	GF	GS	TGR
95-96	81.58	31.00	73	1	1.37
96-97	81.58	31.00	76	1	1.32
97-98	65.79	12.50	73	2	2.74
Averages	76.32	24.83	74.00	1.33	1.81

IVERSEN, Steffen

Tottenham H. ❶❷❸ S

Fullname: Steffen Iversen
DOB: 10-11-76 Trondheim, Norway

The then Tottenham boss Gerry Francis had to fight hard to sign Norwegian striker Iversen from Rosenborg but the eventual fee of £2.7m looked to be a sound investment as he closed his first season in the Premiership with six goals in 16 games. But being a Tottenham player, he was badly hit by their injury curse last season and added just 13 more appearances to his record, five as a substitute, and did not score at all. His record for Rosenborg was 21 in 65 games. The good news for Tottenham, and possibly fantasy football fans looking for a striker, is that he regained full fitness at the end of the season and scored three times in as many games for Norway's Under-21 side.

Given time, Iversen should mature into a more than useful striker; he certainly has the speed, control, determination near to goal and powerful shot to trouble the tightest of defences.

Form Factors

Season	Team	Tot	St	Sb	Y	R
96-97	Tottenham H.	16	16	0	1	0
97-98	Tottenham H.	13	8	5	1	0
Total		29	24	5	2	0

	GP	GG	GF	GS	TGR
96-97	42.11	2.67	44	6	13.64
97-98	34.21	0.00	44	0	0.00
Averages	38.16	1.33	44.00	3.00	6.82

IZZET, Muzzy
Leicester City ❶❷❸❹ M
Fullname: Mustafa Kemmel Izzet
DOB: 31-10-74 Mile End, London

Since his £800,000 transfer from Chelsea – where he never played in the Premiership – at the end of the 1995-96 season, Izzet has become an integral part of the Leicester City midfield, misssing just five league games in his two seasons at Filbert Street. Has scored seven times over the past two campaigns and notched one during nine games on loan to Leicester which initially prompted manager Martin O'Neill to get the cheque book out.

Was eligible to play for Turkey but has instead opted to gain international honours with Wales.

Form Factors

Season	Team	Tot	St	Sb	Y	R
96-97	Leicester C.	35	34	1	6	0
97-98	Leicester C.	36	36	0	5	0
Total		71	70	1	11	0

	GP	GG	GF	GS	TGR
96-97	92.11	11.67	46	3	6.52
97-98	94.74	9.00	51	4	7.84
Averages	93.42	10.33	48.50	3.50	7.18

JACKSON, Mark
Leeds Utd ❶ CB
Fullname: Mark Graham Jackson
DOB: 30-09-77 Leeds

Having made 17 appearances in the Premiership with Leeds United during the 1996-97 season, Mark Jackson's career suffered a setback last season with the central defender making just one appearance and that from the subs bench. Was an unused substitute on eight other occasions.

Worked his way through from the youth set-up at Elland Road to the first team.

Form Factors

Season	Team	Tot	St	Sb	Y	R
95-96	Leeds U.	1	0	1	0	0
96-97	Leeds U.	17	11	6	1	0
97-98	Leeds U.	1	0	1	4	0
Total		19	11	8	5	0

	GP	GG	GF	GS	TGR
95-96	2.63	0.00	40	0	0.00
96-97	44.74	0.00	28	0	0.00
97-98	2.63	0.00	57	0	0.00
Averages	16.67	0.00	41.67	0.00	0.00

JAMES, David

Liverpool ❶❷❸ GK
Fullname: David Benjamin James
DOB: 01-08-70 Welwyn Garden City

James enjoyed a marvellous unbroken run as Liverpool's first choice goalkeeper for 159 Premiership games but the signing of American Brad Friedel spelt the end of that remarkable run after a 1-1 draw with Everton in February 1998. Throughout his time between the sticks for Liverpool James was beaten less than once a game and even during the 1997-98 season prior to him being dropped he maintained that record with 26 goals conceded in 27 league games.

Despite that record there did appear to be errors creeping into James' games over a long period of time. He has the experience to come good again and will surely be challenging hard this season to win back his place on the side.

An FA Youth Cup winner with Watford in 1989, he joined Liverpool for £1m in 1992 and added the League Cup to his earlier success and in 1997 won what is to date his only England cap.

Form Factors

Season	Team	Tot	St	Sb	Y	R
95-96	Liverpool	38	38	0	1	0
96-97	Liverpool	38	38	0	0	0
97-98	Liverpool	27	27	0	0	0
Total		103	103	0	1	0

	GA	GkA	GAp	CS	SO	R
95-96	34	34	0.89	16	3	0
96-97	37	37	0.97	12	5	0
97-98	42	26	0.96	11	4	0
Averages	37.67	32.33	2.82	13.0	4.0	0

JOACHIM, Julian

Aston Villa ❶❷❸ M
Fullname: Julian Kevin Joachim
DOB: 12-09-74 Peterborough

After struggling to fully establish himself at Villa Park following a £500,000 move from Leicester City, Joachim came to the fore last season with 26 games in the Premiership although 10 of those games were as a substitute. Very highly rated in his younger days he now appears to be rediscovering some of that form and this season could be the one in which he finally makes his mark in the Premiership.

A talented midfielder who knows where the goal is, he got into double figures in each of his first two seasons with Leicester and with eight in the league last season, he was Aston Villa's second highest scorer.

Form Factors

Season	Team	Tot	St	Sb	Y	R
95-96	Aston Villa	11	4	7	0	0
96-97	Aston Villa	15	3	12	0	0
97-98	Aston Villa	26	16	10	0	0
Total		52	23	29	0	0

	GP	GG	GF	GS	TGR
95-96	28.95	11.00	52	1	1.92
96-97	39.47	5.00	47	3	6.38
97-98	68.42	3.25	49	8	16.33
Averages	45.61	6.42	49.33	4.00	8.21

JOHNSEN, Ronnie
Manchester U. ❶❷❸ CB

Fullname: Ronald Jean Johnsen
DOB: 06-10-69

Johnsen's second season with Manchester United, 1997-98, was less successful than his first with the Norwegian international defender in the starting line-up for exactly half of United's Premiership games of which he was substituted seven times. Although good on the ball and fine at tackling he has been caught out of position on occasion which has stopped him from being completely certain of making the starting XI week-in-week-out.

Joined United from Turkish side Besiktas for £1.2m in 1996 as a defender but has also been asked to play in midfield by Alex Ferguson. A regular goalscorer in Norway with Lyn and Lillestrom, he netted his first United goal during last season's 5-1 FA Cup win over Walsall.

Form Factors

Season	Team	Tot	St	Sb	Y	R
96-97	Manchester U.	31	26	5	3	0
97-98	Manchester U.	22	18	4	2	0
Total		53	44	9	5	0

	GP	GG	GF	GS	TGR
96-97	81.58	0.00	76	0	0.00
97-98	57.89	11.00	73	2	2.74
Averages	69.74	5.50	74.50	1.00	1.37

JOHNSON, Andy
Nottingham F. ❶❷ M

Fullname: Andrew James Johnson
DOB: 02-05-74 Bristol

Following his £2.2m transfer from Norwich City in the summer of 1997 to Nottingham Forest, he was seen as one of the building blocks upon which his new club would base their promotion drive. But the midfielder faced a frustrating spell on the subs' bench before securing a place in the starting line-up after the turn of the year. He then began to show the class expected upon his arrival and added three goals of his own to the cause although that was down on the seven and five of his last two seasons at Carrow Road.

JONES, Keith
Charlton A. ❶❷ M

Fullname: Keith Aubrey Jones
DOB: 14-10-65 Dulwich

Midfielder worker who keeps things ticking over in the middle of the park for Charlton Athletic while only rarely catching the eye. Despite a relative diminutive frame Jones is determined when going in for tackles and has a very trusty right foot. Missed just one match last season, having been anything but a permanent member of the side during his first three seasons at the Valley mainly because of injury.

Has played 120 league games for the Addicks with his three goals last season being his first since a solitary strike in the 1994-95 season. One of five

Charlton players well into the thirtysomething bracket which could lead to some rebuilding for manager Alan Curbishley.

JONES, Paul

Southampton ❶❷❸ GK

Fullname: Paul Steven Jones
DOB: 18-04-67 Chirk

One of the stars of Stockport County's magnificent run to the semi final of the Coca Cola Cup in 1996-97, he moved up the ladder when following manager Dave Jones to Southampton in the summer of 1997. Some queried the £1.5m fee for a 30 year old goalkeeper who was untried at the highest level but Jones more than proved himself by playing in all 38 of the Saints' Premiership matches; he conceded 55 goals at 1.45 per game.

On the back of his success with Stockport – they were promoted in the same season of their cup run – Jones won his first international cap with Wales and it would be a big surprise if he were not to gain further caps this season and confirm his position as Southampton's number one.

Keith Jones

Paul Jones

Form Factors

Season	Team	Tot	St	Sb	Y	R
97-98	Southampton	38	38	0	0	0
Total		38	38	0	0	0

	GA	GkA	GAp	CS	SO	R
97-98	55	55	1.45	8	3	2
Averages	55	55	1.45	8	3	2

Fantasy Football Handbook 1998/99

JONES, Rob

Liverpool ❶❷❸ FB

Fullname: Robert Marc Jones
DOB: 05-11-71 Wrexham

Injury decimated Jones's 1996-97 campaign and he was in and out of the side last season until Jason McAteer suffered a serious injury which paved the way for Jones's return. A top quality, pacy defender who wins the ball well and uses it constructively, he would eventually almost certainly have regained his place on merit.

Signed for Liverpool from Crewe Alexandra in October 1991 at a now giveaway price of £300,000. Scored twice in 87 games for Crewe but in 244 league and cup matches for Liverpool he has yet to hit the target. Won eight England caps between 1992-95 and would be an automatic choice at full-back for most clubs.

Form Factors

Season	Team	Tot	St	Sb	Y	R
95-96	Liverpool	33	33	0	2	0
96-97	Liverpool	2	2	0	1	0
97-98	Liverpool	21	20	1	1	0
Total		56	55	1	4	0

	GP	GG	GF	GS	TGR
95-96	86.84	0.00	70	0	0.00
96-97	5.26	0.00	62	0	0.00
97-98	55.26	0.00	68	0	0.00
Averages	49.12	0.00	66.67	0.00	0.00

JONES, Steve

Charlton A. ❶❷ S

Fullname: Stephen Gary Jones
DOB: 17-03-70 Cambridge

Striker with a decent goalscoring record but has experienced problems in fully establishing himself at Charlton Athletic since his £400,000 transfer from West Ham United in February 1997. Picked up a bad injury two games after his arrival at the Valley and when his partnership with new signing Mendonca failed to produce the goods early last season he was dropped and loaned out to Bournemouth around Christmas time. Did well at Dean Court and scored twice on his recall to Charlton but still failed to convince his manager that he was the answer and ended the season back on the sidelines.

Has scored 37 league goals in 124 games but looks unlikely to be adding many more to that tally at the Valley.

Form Factors

Season	Team	Tot	St	Sb	Y	R
93-94	West Ham U.	8	3	5	0	0
94-95	West Ham U.	2	1	1	2	0
96-97	West Ham U.	8	5	3	0	0
Total		18	9	9	2	0

	GP	GG	GF	GS	TGR
93-94	21.05	4.00	47	2	4.26
94-95	5.26	0.00	44	0	0.00
96-97	21.05	0.00	39	0	0.00
Averages	15.79	1.33	43.33	0.67	1.42

JUPP, Duncan

Wimbledon ❶ FB

Fullname: Duncan Alan Jupp
DOB: 25-01-75 Guildford

An Under-21 intenational with Scotland, Jupp goes into his third season with Wimbledon looking to improve upon his total of nine Premiership outings from the past two seasons. Almost a permanent fixture at right-back for Fulham for four years he joined Wimbledon in a £125,000 deal in June 1996 but has yet to convinnce Joe Kinnear that he is up to the demands of the Premiership.

Relatively tall for a full-back he can put over a good cross and is composed on the ball.

Form Factors

Season	Team	Tot	St	Sb	Y	R
96-97	Wimbledon	6	6	0	1	0
97-98	Wimbledon	3	3	0	1	0
Total		9	9	0	2	0

	GP	GG	GF	GS	TGR
96-97	15.79	0.00	49	0	0.00
97-98	7.89	0.00	34	0	0.00
Averages	11.84	0.00	41.50	0.00	0.00

KAAMARK, Pontus

Leicester City ❶❷❸ M

Fullname: Pontus Sven Kaamark
DOB: 05-04-69 Vasteras, Sweden

After two injury hit seasons following an £840,000 move from IFK Gothenburg to Leicester, Kaamark made his first serious impression on the Premiership last season by appearing in 35 of Leicester 38 league games – by his own admission far more games than he is used to in Sweden. Missed the penultimate game of the season, against Barnsley, when he injured himself in the pre-match warm-up. A right-footed defender who can play on the left, is a good man-marker and was a member of the Sweden side which played in the 3rd place play-off of USA 94.

Form Factors

Season	Team	Tot	St	Sb	Y	R
96-97	Leicester C.	10	9	1	0	0
97-98	Leicester C.	35	35	0	2	0
Total		45	44	1	2	0

	GP	GG	GF	GS	TGR
96-97	26.32	0.00	46	0	0.00
97-98	92.11	0.00	51	0	0.00
Averages	59.21	0.00	48.50	0.00	0.00

KEANE, Roy

Manchester U. ①②③④ M

Fullname: Roy Maurice Keane
DOB: 10-08-71 Cork

It was more than by coincidence that with Roy Keane missing from their midfield for all but nine Premiership matches last season, Manchester United did not retain the championship crown most people expected them to collect with ease. United's first defeat of the season, at Leeds on 27 September, came on the day Keane received a cruciate ligament injury which ruled him out for the rest of the season.

Kasey Keller

It was a savage blow for the player himself and it left the club shorn of its captain and principle ball winner in midfield. Added to his tenacity in getting the ball is his phenomenal stamina. Providing he makes a full recovery his return to the side should see United quickly erase from the memory banks last season's trophy-less events.

An Eire international he joined United from Nottingham Forest in July 1993 for a then British record fee of £3.75m. Since coming to England from Cobh Ramblers he has scored a goal approximately every six league games.

Form Factors

Season	Team	Tot	St	Sb	Y	R
95-96	Manchester U.	29	29	0	7	2
96-97	Manchester U.	21	21	0	6	1
97-98	Manchester U.	9	9	0	3	0
Total		59	59	0	16	3

	GP	GG	GF	GS	TGR
95-96	76.32	4.83	73	6	8.22
96-97	55.26	10.50	76	2	2.63
97-98	23.68	4.50	73	2	2.74
Averages	51.75	6.61	74.00	3.33	4.53

KELLER, Kasey

Leicester City ①②③④ GK

Fullname: Kasey Keller
DOB: 27-11-69 Washington USA

After a consistent season between the sticks for Leicester City, Washington-born Keller played in the USA's first two Group matches in France 98. An almost unflappable character who likes to dominate his penalty area, his handling is good and he is a fine shot stopper. Played in America with Portland University before crossing the pond to play for

Millwall where he spent five years. Joined Leicester in a £900,000 deal in 1996 and went onto play in both of the Foxes' Coca Cola Cup final matches with Middlesbrough.

A one-time basketball player who has recently been studying for a degree in sociology. Worth having in your side if still available at a reasonable price.

Form Factors

Season	Team	Tot	St	Sb	Y	R
96-97	Leicester C.	31	31	0	0	0
97-98	Leicester C.	33	33	0	2	0
Total		64	64	0	2	0

	GA	GkA	GAp	CS	SO	R
96-97	54	41	1.32	9	2	0
97-98	41	37	1.11	11	2	1
Averages	47.5	39.0	1.22	10	2	0.5

club Home Farm and played for Eire at USA 94.

Form Factors

Season	Team	Tot	St	Sb	Y	R
95-96	Leeds U.	34	34	0	4	1
96-97	Leeds U.	36	34	2	5	0
97-98	Leeds U.	34	34	0	6	1
Total		104	102	2	15	2

	GP	GG	GF	GS	TGR
95-96	89.47	0.00	40	0	0.00
96-97	94.74	18.00	28	2	7.14
97-98	89.47	0.00	57	0	0.00
Averages	91.23	6.00	41.67	0.67	2.38

KELLY, Gary

Leeds United ❶❷❸❹ FB

Fullname: Gary Kelly
DOB: 09-07-74 Drogheda

Leeds United captain who only turned 24 in the summer of 1998 but has already made 190 league appearances for the Yorkshire club. Made his debut back in the 1991-92 season but had to wait two years before fully establishing himself in the side. Ever present for two consecutive seasons, Kelly has missed just 10 games over the past three seasons and should have few problems in continuing that excellent run this season.

Began his career at full-back before being successfully switched to midfield where he has blossomed into one of the most consistent performers in the Premiership. Signed to Leeds from Irish

Gary Kelly

Fantasy Football Handbook 1998/99 **215**

KENNA, Jeff

Blackburn Rovers ❶❷❸ FB

Fullname: Jeffrey Jude Kenna
DOB: 27-08-70 Dublin

The arrival of Kenna at Blackburn Rovers from Southampton for £1.5m in March 1995 was not one of the most expected transfers but the Dublin-born defender and Eire international has been one of Rovers' most consistent performers and has missed just eight of Blackburn's 123 Premiership games since then.

Good ball player whose great strength is his speed and has proved a valuable acquisition with his comfort at playing in either full-back position. Has played 155 league games for Blackburn, one more than he achieved in seven years as a professional at the Dell.

Form Factors

Season	Team	Tot	St	Sb	Y	R
95-96	Blackburn R.	32	32	0	2	0
96-97	Blackburn R.	37	37	0	2	0
97-98	Blackburn R.	37	37	0	0	0
Total		106	106	0	4	0

	GP	GG	GF	GS	TGR
95-96	84.21	0.00	61	0	0.00
96-97	97.37	0.00	42	0	0.00
97-98	97.37	0.00	57	0	0.00
Averages	92.98	0.00	53.33	0.00	0.00

KENNEDY, Mark

Wimbledon ❶❷ M

Fullname: Mark Kennedy
DOB: 15-05-76 Dublin, Republic of Ireland

Dublin-born striker who joined Liverpool from Millwall for £1.5m in March 1995 but never fully broke into the Reds' first team. Was facing another complete season of frustration at Anfield when Joe Kinnear took him to Wimbledon in a £1.75m transfer during March 1998.

A left-sided forward with great stamina and speed which should enhance the Dons attacking prowess considerably. Now granted an opportunity to enjoy an extended run in the Premiership, he has the potential to be one of the star names of 1998-99 and is already an established international with Eire.

Form Factors

Season	Team	Tot	St	Sb	Y	R
96-97	Liverpool	5	0	5	0	0
97-98	Liverpool	1	0	1	0	0
97-98	Wimbledon	4	4	0	0	0
Total		10	4	6	0	0

	GP	GG	GF	GS	TGR
96-97	13.16	0.00	62	0	0.00
97-98	2.63	0.00	68	0	0.00
97-98	10.53	0.00	34	0	0.00
Averages	8.77	0.00	54.67	0.00	0.00

KEOWN, Martin

Arsenal ❶❷❸❹ CB

Fullname: Martin Raymond Keown
DOB: 24-07-66 Oxford

The improvement in Ray Parlour's game over the past couple of years has been plain to see and in Martin Keown, Arsenal supporters are seeing a player far different to the one sold to Aston Villa for £200,000 in 1986. During what must be considered the latter part of his career, Keown has become a much better player on the ball which makes him more productive when he successfully wins possession, as he invariably does.

He returned to Highbury from Everton in 1993 for £2m and has since justified the increase in his fee with a consistently high standard of performance which sees him excel at man-marking and dominant in the tackle. Has revived his England career in recent seasons and was in the World Cup squad despite missing four months of last season through injury.

Form Factors

Season	Team	Tot	St	Sb	Y	R
95-96	Arsenal	34	34	0	6	0
96-97	Arsenal	33	33	0	7	0
97-98	Arsenal	18	18	0	1	2
Total		85	85	0	14	2

	GP	GG	GF	GS	TGR
95-96	89.47	0.00	49	0	0.00
96-97	86.84	33.00	62	1	1.61
97-98	47.37	0.00	68	0	0.00
Averages	74.56	11.00	59.67	0.33	0.54

KETSBAIA, Temuri

Newcastle U. ❶❷❸ M

Fullname: Temuri Ketsbaia
DOB: 18-03-68 Gale, Georgia

Anyone who witnessed Ketsbaia's celebrations after scoring Newcastle's last minute winner against Bolton in January could justly enquire as to the Georgian's sanity but he came to this country, on a free 'Bosman' transfer from AEK Athens in the summer of 1997, with a good track record. An international midfield player with Georgia he played for various clubs in his home country before moving to Greece where he won a Cup Winners' medal in 1996. Started in 16 Premiership games last season and was called upon 15 times from the bench.

Temuri Ketsbaia

Fantasy Football Handbook 1998/99

Form Factors

Season	Team	Tot	St	Sb	Y	R
97-98	Newcastle U.	31	16	15	3	0
Total		31	16	15	3	0

	GP	GG	GF	GS	TGR
97-98	81.58	10.33	35	3	8.57
Averages	81.58	10.33	35.00	3.00	8.57

KEWELL, Harry

Leeds United ❶❷❸❹ M

Fullname: Harold Kewell
DOB: 22-09-78 Australia

One of the most exciting prospects in the Premiership who burst through in a big way last season after just three league appearances during the two previous seasons. Started the 1997-98 campaign on the bench but forced his way into the starting line up and went onto link well with Hasselbaink. Favoured position is in midfield from where he can run at players with great effect, is also very strong in the air.

Scored five times in the Premiership last season from 29 games and although the surprise element surrounding him will no longer be there he should win you a good number of points over the coming months.

Harry Kewell

Form Factors

Season	Team	Tot	St	Sb	Y	R
95-96	Leeds U.	2	2	0	0	0
96-97	Leeds U.	1	0	1	0	0
97-98	Leeds U.	29	26	3	2	1
Total		32	28	4	2	1

	GP	GG	GF	GS	TGR
95-96	5.26	0.00	40	0	0.00
96-97	2.63	0.00	28	0	0.00
97-98	76.32	5.80	57	5	8.77
Averages	28.07	1.93	41.67	1.67	2.92

KHARINE, Dimitri

Chelsea ❶❷ GK

Fullname: Dimitri Victorvitch Kharine
DOB: 16-08-68 Moscow, Russia

Russian goalkeeper who was in excellent form for his country in the World Cup in 1994 and the European Championships two years later but is no longer first choice between the sticks at Chelsea. Was injured early in the season following Euro 96 and with Chelsea having since signed two other international goalkeepers his chances of reclaiming pole position diminished. When on form Kharine is an acrobatic shot-stopper and looks to start counter-attacks with good quick throw-outs.

Played just 10 times in the Premiership last season, conceding 15 goals, and is unlikely to start the new season ahead of Ed de Goey.

Form Factors

Season	Team	Tot	St	Sb	Y	R
95-96	Chelsea	26	26	0	1	0
96-97	Chelsea	5	5	0	0	0
97-98	Chelsea	10	10	0	0	0
Total		41	41	0	1	0

	GA	GkA	GAp	CS	SO	R
95-96	44	29	1.12	10	2	2
96-97	55	3	0.60	3	3	0
97-98	33	4	0.57	6	6	0
Averages	44.0	12.0	0.76	6.33	3.67	0.67

KIMBLE, Alan
Wimbledon   ❶ FB

Fullname: Alan Frank Kimble
DOB: 06-08-66 Dagenham

After an injury-hit start to his time at Selhurst Park, Kimble has emerged as a vital cog in Joe Kinnear's side, making around 30 league appearances for each of the past four seasons. Not short of speed, he moves forward with confidence from his normal left-back position to occasionally unleash a powerful shot and can be deadly from set-pieces.

Once of Charlton Athletic, he had a spell on loan to Exeter City before spending seven near ever-present seasons with Cambridge United from where he joined Wimbledon for a mere £175,000 in July 1993.

Form Factors

Season	Team	Tot	St	Sb	Y	R
95-96	Wimbledon	31	31	0	2	0
96-97	Wimbledon	31	28	3	2	0
97-98	Wimbledon	25	23	2	7	0
Total		87	82	5	11	0

	GP	GG	GF	GS	TGR
95-96	81.58	0.00	55	0	0.00
96-97	81.58	0.00	49	0	0.00
97-98	65.79	0.00	34	0	0.00
Averages	76.32	0.00	46.00	0.00	0.00

KINDER, Vladimir
Middlesbrough   ❶❷❸ FB

Fullname: Vladimir Kinder
DOB: 09-03-69 Bratislava, Czechoslovakia

A Czechoslovakian and Slovakian international who joined Middlesbrough for £1m in January 1997 having been the Slovakian Player of the Year for the three previous seasons. A robust defender, he was sent off in the FA Cup semi final against Chesterfield. Kinder filled the left-back position 34 times last season as Boro possessed the second meanest defence in Division One of the Nationwide League. He also maintained his record of scoring in all of his eight seasons as a professional with Slovan Bratislava and Middlesbrough.

Form Factors

Season	Team	Tot	St	Sb	Y	R
96-97	Middlesbrough	6	4	2	0	0
Total		6	4	2	0	0

	GP	GG	GF	GS	TGR
96-97	15.79	6.00	51	1	1.96
Averages	15.79	6.00	51.00	1.00	1.96

Mark Kinsella

KINSELLA, Mark

Charlton A. ❶❷❸M

Fullname: Mark Anthony Kinsella
DOB: 12-08-72 Dublin

Player who Charlton believe could make a big impact this season, his first in the Premiership. The Addicks snapped up Kinsella from Colchester United for £200,000 in September 1996 and he was ever present in their promotion-winning campaign last season. Not a prolific scorer from midfield though he does make a useful contribution with one goal just about every seven games and occasionally weighs in with a long-range gem.

Skilful in possession, an exquisite passer and two-footed. All these qualities go together to make Kinsella one of the potential new stars in the Premiership for 1998-99.

Dublin-born he moved to England from renowned Irish side Home Park.

KITSON, Paul

West Ham U. ❶❷❸❹S

Fullname: Paul Kitson
DOB: 09-01-71 Peterlee

The bold move by West Ham manager Harry Redknapp to bring Paul Kitson and John Hartson together as his main strike force may have, in some peoples eyes, been an expensive gamble but it quickly paid rich dividends with the duo going a long way towards helping the Hammers stave off relegation at the end of '96-97. Whilst Kitson was seen as the provider and Hartson the goalscorer it must be said that Kitson has also flourished since moving to Upton Park. Eight goals in 14 games towards the end of 1996-97 should have been a taster of what was to come but tragically he was ruled out for three months of last season with a bad groin injury. Even so, he still scored four times in 13 Premiership games.

A fully fit Kitson, who has also played for Leicester City, Derby County and Newcastle United before his arrival at West Ham, could well provide that extra piece of class the Hammers need to get into Europe.

Form Factors

Season	Team	Tot	St	Sb	Y	R
96-97	Newcastle U.	3	0	3	0	0
96-97	West Ham U.	14	14	0	2	0
97-98	West Ham U.	13	12	1	1	0
Total		30	26	4	3	0

	GP	GG	GF	GS	TGR
96-97	7.89	0.00	73	0	0.00
96-97	36.84	1.75	39	8	20.51
97-98	34.21	3.25	56	4	7.14
Averages	26.32	1.67	56.00	4.00	9.22

KOZLUK, Robert
Derby County ❶❷ M

Fullname: Robert Kozluk
DOB: 05-08-77 Mansfield

Broke into the Derby County first team for the first time last season with nine games in the Premiership, seven from the start, and six more games in the cups. A midfield player who has come through the ranks and is certain to be given more opportunities to show what he can do over the coming months.

Form Factors

Season	Team	Tot	St	Sb	Y	R
97-98	Derby Co.	9	6	3	1	0
Totals		9	6	3	1	0

	GP	GG	GF	GS	TGR
97-98	23.69	0.00	52	0	0.00
Averages	23.69	0.00	52	0	0.00

Paul Kitson

KVARME, Bjorn Tore
Liverpool ❶❷ D

Fullname: Bjorn Tore Kvarme
DOB: 17-07-72 Trondheim, Norway

A one-time striker, Kvarme signed for Liverpool on a free transfer from Rosenborg in January 1997 and slotted in at full-back at Anfield. Did well in his 15 games for Liverpool over the remainder of the season and after missing the first two games of last season went on a run of 25 consecutive appearances. Was dropped following the Reds' shock 3-1 home FA Cup defeat by Coventry City and started in just two other matches before the season was out.

Nevertheless he remains a good dependable defender and at 26 has time to rebuild his Anfield career.

Form Factors

Season	Team	Tot	St	Sb	Y	R
96-97	Liverpool	15	15	0	1	0
97-98	Liverpool	23	22	1	2	0
Total		38	37	1	3	0

	GP	GG	GF	GS	TGR
96-97	39.47	0.00	62	0	0.00
97-98	60.53	0.00	68	0	0.00
Averages	50.00	0.00	65.00	0.00	0.00

LAMPARD, Frank

West Ham U.   ①②❸ M

Fullname: Frank James Lampard
DOB: 21-06-78 Romford

Carrying, as he does, the same christian name as his father, Frank jnr has a lot to live up to at Upton Park but so far has not failed to deliver. After making in-roads to the West Ham first team over the two previous seasons, the 1997-98 campaign was the one in which he began to hold down a regular place in midfield. With his fine touch, precise passing and ability to read the game, he has the potential to keep the Lampard tradition going on the field at Upton Park for many years to come.

His 31 Premiership appearances last season included his first goals, four, for the Hammers.

Form Factors

Season	Team	Tot	St	Sb	Y	R
95-96	West Ham U.	2	0	2	0	0
96-97	West Ham U.	13	3	10	1	0
97-98	West Ham U.	31	27	4	5	0
Total		46	30	16	6	0

	GP	GG	GF	GS	TGR
95-96	5.26	0.00	43	0	0.00
96-97	34.21	0.00	39	0	0.00
97-98	81.58	7.75	56	4	7.14
Averages	40.35	2.58	46.00	1.33	2.38

LAUDRUP, Brian

Chelsea   ①②❸④❺ M/S

Fullname: Brian Laudrup
DOB: 22-02-69 Vienna

Spent the past four years winning three championships in Scotland with Rangers but agreed a move to Chelsea prior to heading for France 98 with Denmark. Playing on the world's largest stage the 29-year-old was in top form scoring twice in Denmark's five games including one against Brazil in an ultimately losing quarter final cause.

His pedigree is irreproachable with his list of previous clubs reading almost like a who's who of European football; Brondby, Bayer Leverkeusen, Bayern Munich, Milan and Fiorentina. The signing of Laudrup can only enhance Chelsea's hopes of winning the Premiership for the first time and being England's top side for the first time in 44 years.

LAURSEN, Jacob
Derby County ❶❷ FB
Fullname: Jacob Laursen
DOB: 06-10-71 Vejle, Denmark

Stylish defender who can effectively fill any of the positions along the backline although he favours playing on the left. Has slotted in very well since joining Derby County in time for the 1996-97 season missing just two Premiership games in Derby's final season at the Baseball Ground.

Danish international who was a member of his nation's France 98 squad but was not used in the competition.

Signed for Derby in a £500,000 move from Silkeborg where he scored eight times in 125 games and has notched one goal in each of his two seasons in England.

Form Factors

Season	Team	Tot	St	Sb	Y	R
96-97	Derby Co.	36	35	1	2	0
97-98	Derby Co.	28	27	1	5	0
Total		64	62	2	7	0

	GP	GG	GF	GS	TGR
96-97	94.74	36.00	45	1	2.22
97-98	73.68	28.00	52	1	1.92
Averages	84.21	32.00	48.50	1.00	2.07

LAZIRIDIS, Stan
West Ham U. ❶❷❸ M
Fullname: Stanley Laziridis
DOB: 16-08-72 Perth, W.Australia

Perth-born Australian international who was in outstanding form last season with his pace down the flank going some way to helping West Ham to their best league placing for several years. 'Stan the Man' missed just five Premiership matches last season, scoring twice, and if he and Paul Kitson can steer clear of injury then the Hammers will continue to be a force at home although the form they display at Upton Park needs to be repeated on opposition soil.

Form Factors

Season	Team	Tot	St	Sb	Y	R
95-96	West Ham U.	4	2	2	0	0
96-97	West Ham U.	22	13	9	2	0
97-98	West Ham U.	28	27	1	2	0
Total		54	42	12	4	0

	GP	GG	GF	GS	TGR
95-96	10.53	0.00	43	0	0.00
96-97	57.89	22.00	39	1	2.56
97-98	73.68	14.00	56	2	3.57
Averages	47.37	12.00	46.00	1.00	2.05

LE SAUX, Graeme
Chelsea ❶❷❸❹ FB
Fullname: Graeme Pierre Le Saux
DOB: 17-10-68 Jersey

Back at Chelsea for a second time, Channel Islander Le Saux enjoyed a successful season with winning appearances in both the Cup Winners' Cup and the Coca Cola Cup being topped by playing for England in France 98. The World Cup though, was not overly kind to the defender who played very much in a wing-back role with his attacking qualities overshadowing his defensive capabilities as unfortunately evidenced by Romania's winning goal.

Excellent at getting up and down the left flank and putting dangerous balls into the box with his speed making him an ideal outlet for a counter-attack. Chelsea originally signed him from his home-town club of St. Paul's on a free transfer but had to hand over £5m to Blackburn Rovers in August 1997 to get him for a second time.

Form Factors

Season	Team	Tot	St	Sb	Y	R
95-96	Blackburn R.	15	14	1	2	0
96-97	Blackburn R.	26	26	0	6	0
97-98	Chelsea	26	26	0	3	0
Total		67	66	1	11	0

	GP	GG	GF	GS	TGR
95-96	39.47	15.00	61	1	1.64
96-97	68.42	26.00	42	1	2.38
97-98	68.42	26.00	71	1	1.41
Averages	58.77	22.33	58.00	1.00	1.81

LE TISSIER, Matthew
Southampton ❶❷❸❹ M
Fullname: Matthew Paul Le Tissier
DOB: 14-10-68 Guernsey

The cries of Le Tissier for England – and France 98 – were strong in the latter part of last winter but in truth Southampton's enigmatic midfield wizard had had a poor first half to the season and his lack of consistency always seemed likely to tell against him. His slow start to the season could possibly be traced to a broken arm suffered in pre-season which delayed his introduction to the side.

On his day, and there have been many down the years at the Dell, Le Tissier has no peers; sublime skills, stunning accuracy with his passing, a thunderous shot, wicked control at set-pieces to leave the best keepers floundering; Le Tissier has the lot, tracking back to defend notwithstanding.

Has been in the Southampton first team for 12 years and was joint top scorer last season with 11 Premiership strikes; his overall total of 91 goals is bettered by only four other players.

Form Factors

Season	Team	Tot	St	Sb	Y	R
95-96	Southampton	34	34	0	11	1
96-97	Southampton	31	25	6	5	0
97-98	Southampton	26	25	1	6	0
Total		91	84	7	22	1

	GP	GG	GF	GS	TGR
95-96	89.47	4.86	34	7	20.5
96-97	81.58	2.38	50	13	26.00
97-98	68.42	2.36	50	11	22.00
Averages	79.82	3.20	44.67	10.33	22.86

LEABURN, Carl
Wimbledon ①② S

Fullname: Carl Winston Leaburn
DOB: 30-03-69 Lewisham

Wimbledon manager Joe Kinnear surprised a few people in January 1998 when he paid Charlton Athletic £300,000 for striker Leaburn. Although useful on the deck and troublesome in the air, his record as a goalscorer left a little to be desired. In 11 years with Charlton he averaged a goal not more regularly than once every six games. Bizarrely he improved upon that record when stepping up to the Premiership with four goals from 16 games. Would do well to hold down a regular place in the Dons' side this season.

Form Factors

Season	Team	Tot	St	Sb	Y	R
97-98	Wimbledon	16	15	1	0	0
Total		16	15	1	0	0

	GP	GG	GF	GS	TGR
97-98	42.11	4.00	34	4	11.76
Averages	42.11	4.00	34.00	4.00	11.76

LEBOEUF, Frank
Chelsea ①②③④⑤ CB

Fullname: Frank Leboeuf
DOB: 22-01-68 Marseille, France

Has enjoyed great success since coming into the Premiership with Chelsea. Joined the Blues from Strasbourg for £2.5m in the summer of 1996 and since then has collected winners medals in the FA Cup and the Cup Winners' Cup. He added the ultimate prize in July when French defender Laurent Blanc got himself sent off in the World Cup semi final which allowed Leboeuf to step in for the final against Brazil.

Reassuring in possession he stays calm in defence and looks to build from the back rather than take the quick option. But Leboeuf is not purely a defensive player as he does like to get forward and scores from open play as well as penalties, as his five goals last season and 40 in five seasons with Strasbourg underlines. Has played 58 times in the Premiership for Chelsea over the past two seasons and that figure would have been greater but for 15 yellow cards.

Form Factors

Season	Team	Tot	St	Sb	Y	R
96-97	Chelsea	26	26	0	7	0
97-98	Chelsea	32	32	0	8	1
Total		58	58	0	15	1

	GP	GG	GF	GS	TGR
96-97	68.42	4.33	58	6	10.34
97-98	84.21	6.40	71	5	7.04
Averages	76.32	5.37	64.50	5.50	8.69

Frank Leboeuf

Fantasy Football Handbook 1998/99

LEE, Robert

Newcastle U.   ❶❷❸❹ M

Fullname: Robert Martin Lee
DOB: 01-02-66 West Ham

Spent ten seasons with Charlton Athletic before stepping into the big time with a £700,000 move to Newcastle in September 1992. Played in the Magpies' promotion and Premiership winning sides of earlier this decade and won his first cap for England in 1995. The Newcastle captain has a ceaseless workrate, seldom gives the ball away cheaply and likes to run at opposition players.

His four goals in 28 league games last season was in keeping with his seasonal average since joining Newcastle. Made a brief appearance for England in the final Group match of France 98.

Form Factors

Season	Team	Tot	St	Sb	Y	R
95-96	Newcastle U.	36	36	0	3	0
96-97	Newcastle U.	33	32	1	7	0
97-98	Newcastle U.	28	26	2	3	0
Total		97	94	3	13	0

	GP	GG	GF	GS	TGR
95-96	94.74	4.50	66	8	12.12
96-97	86.84	6.60	73	5	6.85
97-98	73.68	7.00	35	4	11.43
Averages	85.09	6.03	58.00	5.67	10.13

LENNON, Neil

Leicester City   ❶❷❸ M

Fullname: Neil Francis Lennon
DOB: 25-06-71 Lurgan

One in a line of shrewd purchases by Leicester City manager Martin O'Neill who obtained Lennon from Crewe Alexandra for a bargain £750,000 in February 1996. Missed just one Premiership match last season, through suspension, and hit the headlines through no fault of his own when he was the innocent party in Alan Shearer's infamous 'kick' incident. Ironically was fined by the FA earlier in his career for gestures made towards Newcastle supporters.

A Northern Ireland international who tends to play a containing role in the Leicester midfield. Not noted for his goalscoring prowess, he did get 10 in two seasons towards the end of his days with Crewe.

Form Factors

Season	Team	Tot	St	Sb	Y	R
96-97	Leicester C.	35	35	0	8	0
97-98	Leicester C.	37	37	0	6	0
Total		72	72	0	14	0

	GP	GG	GF	GS	TGR
96-97	92.11	35.00	46	1	2.17
97-98	97.37	18.50	51	2	3.92
Averages	94.74	26.75	48.50	1.50	3.05

LEONHARDSEN, Oyvind

Liverpool   ❶❷❸❹ M

Fullname: Oyvind Leonhardsen
DOB: 17-08-70 Norway

Joe Kinnear conducted his normal excellent business on behalf of Wimbledon in bringing the talented and hardworking Norwegian to the Premiership for just £660,000 in 1994 – three years later he sold his midfield diamond to Liverpool for £3.5m. The former Rosenborg player is tough to shake off the ball and uses it intelligently.

Scored 13 times in 76 league games for the Dons and improved that average in his first season at Anfield with a very useful six goals from 28 games. Played for his country in France 98 and possesses the quality needed to continue his success during the 1998-99 season.

Form Factors

Season	Team	Tot	St	Sb	Y	R
95-96	Wimbledon	29	28	1	6	0
96-97	Wimbledon	27	27	0	0	0
97-98	Liverpool	28	27	1	2	0
Total		84	82	2	8	0

	GP	GG	GF	GS	TGR
95-96	76.32	7.25	55	4	7.27
96-97	71.05	5.40	49	5	10.20
97-98	73.68	4.67	68	6	8.82
Averages	73.68	5.77	57.33	5.00	8.77

LISBIE, Kevin

Charlton A.　　　　　❶ S

Fullname: Kevin Anthony Lisbie
DOB: 17-10-78 Hackney

Youngster who has been on the verge of the first team for a couple of seasons but of his 42 league appearances 37 have been as substitute. Has scored freely at lower levels but, understandably given his few starts, has yet to transfer that to the bigger stage.

A right-sided player, his biggest asset is his speed but he also has good control.

LOMAS, Steve

West Ham U.　　　　❶❷❸ M

Fullname: Stephen Martin Lomas
DOB: 18-01-74 Hanover

Midfielder whose good passing skills make him ideal West Ham material although he is also more than capable of holding his own when going in for a tackle. Joined the Hammers just before the transfer deadline in 1997 for £1.6m and adds pace and a tireless workrate to the side. Spent six years with Manchester City and scored in the 4th Round of the FA Cup against his former club last season. Usually knocks in two or three league goals a season.

German-born midfielder who is an international with Northern Ireland.

Form Factors

Season	Team	Tot	St	Sb	Y	R
95-96	Manchester C.	33	32	1	8	1
96-97	West Ham U.	7	7	0	0	0
97-98	West Ham U.	33	33	0	6	1
Total		73	72	1	14	2

	GP	GG	GF	GS	TGR
95-96	86.84	11.00	33	3	9.09
96-97	18.42	0.00	39	0	0.00
97-98	86.84	16.50	56	2	3.57
Averages	64.04	9.17	42.67	1.67	4.22

LUNDEKVAM, Claus

Southampton ❶❷❸ CB

Fullname: Claus Lundekvam
DOB: 22-02-73 Norway

Norwegian international defender who has slotted into the English game with great ease. Joined Southampton in September 1996 from Brann in Norway and has proved a real asset for the Saints. A ball playing central defender who can play the tradition role of a centre half but is also very comfortable when moving forward to support the midfield, and sometimes the attack such is his comfort on the ball. Has played 60 times in the Premiership since moving to the Dell for a bargain £400,000. Is still awaiting his first goal since turning professional.

Form Factors

Season	Team	Tot	St	Sb	Y	R
96-97	Southampton	29	28	1	6	0
97-98	Southampton	31	31	0	7	0
Total		60	59	1	13	0

	GP	GG	GF	GS	TGR
96-97	76.32	0.00	50	0	0.00
97-98	81.58	0.00	50	0	0.00
Averages	78.95	0.00	50.00	0.00	0.00

LYTTLE, Des

Nottingham F. ❶❷ FB

Fullname: Desmond Lyttle
DOB: 24-09-71 Wolverhampton

Made his debut in the Football League with an ever-present season with Swansea City following his step-up to the big time from non-leaguers Worcester City. His one season at the Vetch Field tempted Nottingham Forest to fork out £375,000 to take him to the City Ground where he has played in a high percentage of the club's games over the past five seasons.

Has been criticised for a sometimes wayward distribution and dubious control but is a tireless worker who uses his pace to maximum benefit. Not the tallest of right-backs but he gets forward well and can put over quality crosses for the likes of Campbell and Van Hooijdonk to convert.

Form Factors

Season	Team	Tot	St	Sb	Y	R
94-95	N. Forest	38	38	0	7	0
95-96	N. Forest	33	32	1	0	0
96-97	N. Forest	32	30	2	5	0
Total		103	100	3	12	0

	GP	GG	GF	GS	TGR
94-95	100.00	0.00	72	0	0.00
95-96	86.84	33.00	50	1	2.00
96-97	84.21	32.00	31	1	3.23
Averages	90.35	21.67	51.00	0.67	1.74

MADAR, Mickael

Everton ❶❷❸ S

Fullname: Mickael Madar
DOB: 08-05-68 Paris

Experienced French international striker who was a free transfer to Everton in December last year from Deportivo la Coruna. Figured in 17 of Everton's Premiership matches but was substituted on 11 occasions. Even so, his quality shone through with six goals including three in as many games which secured four vital points as Everton battled against the drop. A big strong striker with a good touch and could form a very productive partnership with Duncan Ferguson.

Has also played overseas for Sochaux, Cannes and Monaco.

full 90 minutes, he chipped in with four goals which is his highest total for four years.

Not a spectacular player, he has a high workrate and seldom concedes possession cheaply.

Form Factors

Season	Team	Tot	St	Sb	Y	R
95-96	Southampton	15	13	2	1	0
96-97	Southampton	17	14	3	4	0
97-98	Southampton	6	5	1	0	0
Total		38	32	6	5	0

	GP	GG	GF	GS	TGR
95-96	39.47	15.00	34	1	2.94
96-97	44.74	17.00	50	1	2.00
97-98	15.79	6.00	50	1	2.00
Averages	33.33	12.67	44.67	1.00	2.31

Form Factors

Season	Team	Tot	St	Sb	Y	R
97-98	Everton	17	15	2	2	0
Total		17	15	2	2	0

	GP	GG	GF	GS	TGR
97-98	44.74	2.83	41	6	14.63
Averages	44.74	2.83	41.00	6.00	14.63

MADDISON, Neil

Middlesbrough ❶❷ M

Fullname: Neil Stanley Maddison
DOB: 02-10-69 Darlington

After more than nine years with Southampton, midfielder Maddison signed for Middlesbrough last October for an initial fee of just £250,000. Although selected for only 16 Nationwide League matches, of which just seven were for the

Neil Maddison

Fantasy Football Handbook 1998/99 **229**

MAGILTON, Jim
Sheffield W. ❶❷❸ M
Fullname: James Magilton
DOB: 06-05-69 Belfast, N. Ireland

Northern Ireland international whose most successful club days, to date, were probably with Southampton where he spent over three seasons prior to his £1.6m move to Sheffield Wednesday at the end of the 1996-97 season. Ever-present for the Saints in '94-95 he missed just one league game in his final season at the Dell and kicked off his Wednesday career with 13 successive games but did not make the starting line up again during the final five months of Wednesday's Premiership season.

A one time trainee with Liverpool who scored 34 times in 150 league games for Oxford United before signing for Southampton. At 29 Magilton, if selected, could still be a more than useful member of the Wednesday squad.

Form Factors

Season	Team	Tot	St	Sb	Y	R
96-97	Southampton	37	31	6	4	0
97-98	Southampton	5	5	0	1	0
97-98	Sheffield W.	20	13	7	1	0
Total		62	49	13	6	0

	GP	GG	GF	GS	TGR
96-97	97.37	9.25	50	4	8.00
97-98	13.16	0.00	50	0	0.00
97-98	52.63	20.00	52	1	1.92
Averages	54.39	9.75	50.67	1.67	3.31

MANNINGER, Alex
Arsenal ❶❷❸ GK
Fullname: Alex Manninger
DOB: Saltzburg, Austria

The first Austrian goalkeeper to play in the Premiership Manninger possesses a record which, in all probability, will never be bettered. He played in 10 cup ties for Arsenal last season but it was in the Premiership that he set records. Kept waiting until January 31 for his league debut – he stepped in while Seaman was out injured – Manninger then played in six consecutive Premiership matches and did not concede a single goal. He was understandably, though maybe cruelly, left out once Seaman had recovered and had the misfortune to be recalled for one game to play behind a weakened side at Liverpool when the championship was already secured, and on that occasion he was beaten four times.

Certainly one for the future as far as Arsenal are concerned but he has already proved that he is a first class keeper and should be playing first team football.

Form Factors

Season	Team	Tot	St	Sb	Y	R
97-98	Arsenal	7	7	0	0	0
Total		7	7	0	0	0

	GA	GkA	GAp	CS	SO	R
97-98	33	4	0.57	6	6	0
Averages	33	4	0.57	6	6	0

MARSHALL, Ian
Leicester City ❶❷ S

Fullname: Ian Paul Marshall
DOB: 20-03-66 Liverpool

Liverpool-born striker who originally made a name for himself as a rugged central defender and still plays in that position occasionally when requested by the manager. Marshall is the epitome of commitment and has been rewarded with a lengthy career which commenced with his Football League debut with Everton during the 1985-86 FA Cup winning season.

Signed for Oldham Athletic two years later and was with the Latics during their rapid rise into the Premiership. Moved again for the start of the 1992-93 campaign to join Ipswich Town where he stayed until signing for Leicester in an £875,000 deal in August 1996.

His close control, helped by his solid 6'2" frame, makes him difficult to dispossess and his dominance in the air remains undiminished with the passing of time.

Form Factors

Season	Team	Tot	St	Sb	Y	R
94-95	Ipswich T.	18	14	4	0	0
96-97	Leicester C.	28	19	9	1	0
97-98	Leicester C.	24	22	2	2	0
Total		70	55	15	3	0

	GP	GG	GF	GS	TGR
94-95	47.37	6.00	36	3	8.33
96-97	73.68	3.50	46	8	17.39
97-98	63.16	3.43	51	7	13.73
Averages	61.40	4.31	44.33	6.00	13.15

MARTYN, Nigel
Leeds United ❶❷❸❹ GK

Fullname: Nigel Anthony Martyn
DOB: 11-08-66 St Austell

England's first £1m goalkeeper who has had two excellent seasons with Leeds United since joining the Yorkshire club from Crystal Palace in 1996 for another record fee, £2.25m. Has missed just two Premiership matches in his time at Elland Road keeping an outstanding 29 clean sheets, 10 of which were during his first season with the club. With manager George Graham keeping an ever watchful eye on his defence, Martyn has conceded just 82 goals in his 74 Premiership matches at 1.11 per game. The Cornishman's form earned him a place in England's World Cup squad although he did not get a run-out during France 98.

Form Factors

Season	Team	Tot	St	Sb	Y	R
94-95	C. Palace	37	37	0	1	0
96-97	Leeds U.	37	37	0	1	0
97-98	Leeds U.	37	37	0	0	0
Total		111	111	0	2	0

	GA	GkA	GAp	CS	SO	R
94-95	49	41	1.11	14	2	0
96-97	38	38	1.03	20	4	0
97-98	46	44	1.19	11	3	2
Averages	44.3	41.0	1.11	15.0	3.0	0.67

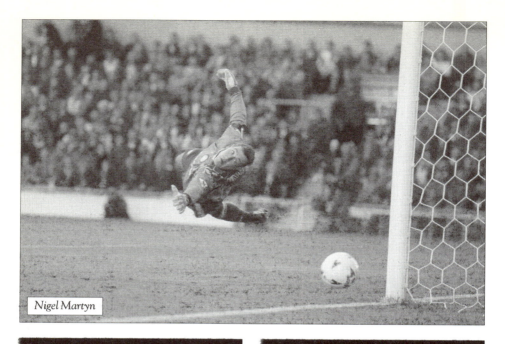
Nigel Martyn

MATERAZZI, Marco

Everton ❶❷ CD

Fullname: Marco Materazzi
DOB: 19-08-73, Lecce, Italy

The giant Italian central defender was Walter Smith's first signing as Everton manager and looks to be lined up as a long term replacement for veteran Dave Watson.

Played with Perugia and came to the fore when the side struggled unsuccessfully against relegation during the 1996-97 season. Despite several Serie A sides seeking his signature Materazzi stayed in Serie B before opting for a move to the Premiership.

MATTEO, Dominic

Liverpool ❶❷❸ D

Fullname: Dominic Matteo
DOB: 28-04-74 Dumfries

Highly skilled England Under-21 defender who has begun to hold down a regular place in the Liverpool backline over the past two seasons. His 25 Premiership appearances was just one down on the previous campaign and given the competition for places at Anfield a similar number of appearances again this season seems likely.

Is at his best on his left side, Matteo can play on the left of the defence or at wing-back with his quick football brain and speed on the ball making him an excellent squad member. Is rarely in trouble with match officials but still awaits his first goal in senior football.

Form Factors

Season	Team	Tot	St	Sb	Y	R
95-96	Liverpool	5	5	0	0	0
96-97	Liverpool	26	22	4	2	0
97-98	Liverpool	25	24	1	1	0
Total		56	51	5	3	0

	GP	GG	GF	GS	TGR
95-96	13.16	0.00	70	0	0.00
96-97	68.42	0.00	62	0	0.00
97-98	65.79	0.00	68	0	0.00
Averages	49.12	0.00	66.67	0.00	0.00

MAY, David
Manchester U. ❶CB

Fullname: David May
DOB: 24-06-70 Oldham

Other than for the 1996-97 season May has struggled to command a first team place at Manchester United since transferring from Blackburn Rovers for £1.4m in July 1994, and events over the past 12 months suggest that life will not get any easier for him. Was selected for just nine Premiership matches last season, of which only seven were starts, and with the arrival of £10.5m central defender Japp Stam it would appear that May's days at Old Trafford are numbered.

His chances of proving of himself at Manchester United were not helped when asked to play at full-back instead of his preferred central position but the high quality of his all round game could resurrect his Premiership career even if it means heading for pastures new.

Form Factors

Season	Team	Tot	St	Sb	Y	R
95-96	Manchester U.	16	11	5	1	0
96-97	Manchester U.	29	28	1	5	0
97-98	Manchester U.	9	7	2	3	0
Total		54	46	8	9	0

	GP	GG	GF	GS	TGR
95-96	42.11	16.00	73	1	1.37
96-97	76.32	9.67	76	3	3.95
97-98	23.68	0.00	73	0	0.00
Averages	47.37	8.56	74.00	1.33	1.77

MAYBURY, Alan
Leeds United ❶FB

Fullname: Alan Maybury
DOB: 08-08-78 Dublin

Right back who made his debut with Leeds United back in February 1996 but had to wait until October 1997 before getting a second chance in the first team. A right-back who has come through the ranks at Elland Road and has won caps with Eire at Under-18 and 21 levels.

Was in the starting line-up for nine Premiership matches last season, used as substitute in three more, but faces a tough task in holding down a regular place this season due to Leeds' strength down the right.

Form Factors

Season	Team	Tot	St	Sb	Y	R
95-96	Leeds U.	1	1	0	0	0
97-98	Leeds U.	12	9	3	0	0
Total		13	10	3	0	0

	GP	GG	GF	GS	TGR
95-96	2.63	0.00	40	0	0.00
97-98	31.58	0.00	57	0	0.00
Averages	17.11	0.00	48.50	0.00	0.00

McALLISTER, Brian
Wimbledon ❶ CB

Fullname: Brian McAllister
DOB: 30-11-70 Glasgow

Goes into the 1998-99 season pretty much as he has done most of his previous ten years with Wimbledon as a fringe player who always fills in ably when required. Did look to be making genuine progress when, following 23 Premiership games during 1996-97, he was frequently on the teamsheet last season only for an achilles tendon injury to put him out of action for almost five months.

Forced his way back into the heart of the Dons' defence before the close of the season and will be hoping for an injury free start to this season to re-stake his claim for a regular place. He is a robust central defender who tackles hard and clears his lines in a no nonsense manner; has also won three caps with Scotland.

Form Factors

Season	Team	Tot	St	Sb	Y	R
95-96	Wimbledon	2	2	0	0	0
96-97	Wimbledon	23	19	4	2	0
97-98	Wimbledon	7	4	3	0	0
Total		32	25	7	2	0

	GP	GG	GF	GS	TGR
95-96	5.26	0.00	55	0	0.00
96-97	60.53	0.00	49	0	0.00
97-98	18.42	0.00	34	0	0.00
Averages	28.07	0.00	46.00	0.00	0.00

McALLISTER, Gary
Coventry City ❶❷❸❹ M

Fullname: Gary McAllister
DOB: 25-12-64 Motherwell

When Gary McAllister made a £3m move from Leeds United to Coventry City in July 1996 it caught everyone by surprise – the Scot had been expected to see out his career at Elland Road. But McAllister settled quickly at Highfield Road and in his first season was ever-present. But tragedy struck in mid December last year when a torn knee cartilage brought his season to a premature end.

A fully fit McAllister would be a massive boost for Coventry as his quality at set-pieces, the precision of his passing, and his regular good quota of goals from midfield would further add to the attacking threat already posed by Dublin and Huckerby. Whether he can attain that level of fitness at going on 34 remains to be seen.

Form Factors

Season	Team	Tot	St	Sb	Y	R
95-96	Leeds U.	36	36	0	1	0
96-97	Coventry C.	38	38	0	1	0
97-98	Coventry C.	14	14	0	1	0
Total		88	88	0	3	0

	GP	GG	GF	GS	TGR
95-96	94.74	7.20	40	5	12.50
96-97	100.00	6.33	38	6	15.79
97-98	36.84	0.00	46	0	0.00
Averages	77.19	4.51	41.33	3.67	9.43

McATEER, Jason
Liverpool ❶❷❸ FB

Fullname: Jason Wynn McAteer
DOB: 18-06-71 Birkenhead

Missed just 10 Pemiership matches in his first two seasons at Anfield following a £4.5m move from Bolton Wanderers but the stylish Eire international suffered a couple of major setbacks last season. Unable to get into the starting line-up to any degree until the end of November, he featured in 14 consecutive games before a broken leg, sustained at home to Blackburn Rovers in late January, shattered his season. Made an excellent recovery in time to score twice in the penultimate match of the season against West Ham.

Was known as a winger during his Bolton days but has adapted supremely to wing-back where he can still get forward to link closely with the attack. Also works as an attacking full-back and like Rob Jones would be virtually ever present at any other club. Played a part in all four of the Republic of Ireland's USA 94 games.

Form Factors

Season	Team	Tot	St	Sb	Y	R
95-96	Liverpool	29	27	2	4	0
96-97	Liverpool	37	36	1	6	0
97-98	Liverpool	21	15	6	3	0
Total		87	78	9	13	0

	GP	GG	GF	GS	TGR
95-96	76.32	0.00	70	0	0.00
96-97	97.37	37.00	62	1	1.61
97-98	55.26	10.50	68	2	2.94
Averages	76.32	15.83	66.67	1.00	1.52

McCANN, Gavin
Everton ❶❷ M

Fullname: Gavin McCann
DOB: 10-01-78 Blackpool

Another in the long line of home-produced youngsters to progress to the first team at Everton. Made his debut as a substitute in September 1997 at Newcastle and was in the starting eleven for the first time during a 1-1 draw at Tottenham the following April. Finished the season with five starts and six substitute appearances under his belt and is expected to make further progress this season.

Form Factors

Season	Team	Tot	St	Sb	Y	R
97-98	Everton	11	5	6	2	0
Total		11	5	6	2	0

	GP	GG	GF	GS	TGR
97-98	28.95	0.00	41	0	0.00
Averages	28.95	0.00	41.00	0.00	0.00

McKINLAY, Billy
Blackburn Rovers ❶❷❸ M

Fullname: William McKinlay
DOB: 22-04-69 Glasgow

Having joined Blackburn Rovers for £1.75m in October 1995, Scottish Under-21 international McKinlay struggled to make an impression under Ray Harford but has since proved himself under caretaker-manager Tony Parks and now Roy Hodgson. A tenacious tackler he plays the holding role just in front of the backline and this deep position has denied him the opportunities required to continue the good goalscoring form shown during his last couple of seasons in Scotland with Dundee United. Featured in 31 of Rovers' league games last season, taking his total of Premiership games to 75.

Form Factors

Season	Team	Tot	St	Sb	Y	R
95-96	Blackburn R.	19	13	6	5	1
96-97	Blackburn R.	25	23	2	12	0
97-98	Blackburn R.	30	26	4	7	0
Total		74	62	12	24	1

	GP	GG	GF	GS	TGR
95-96	50.00	9.50	61	2	3.28
96-97	65.79	25.00	42	1	2.38
97-98	78.95	0.00	57	0	0.00
Averages	64.91	11.50	53.33	1.00	1.89

McMANAMAN, Steve

Liverpool ❶❷❸❹❺ M

Fullname: Steven McManaman
DOB: 11-02-72 Bootle

McManaman has the potential to be the most exciting player in the Premiership when going on one of his numerous surging runs at defences from a deep midfield position. When he is on song it is a great sight with defenders simply bamboozled by his close control, pace and, occasionally as Celtic discovered, lethal shot. But if one has to make a criticism it is that he runs up a blind alley

Steve McManaman

far too often and concedes possession cheaply, which is what stopped him from getting a role in France 98.

Liverpool manager Roy Evans made a shrewd move in giving the England player a free role in front of the midfield and with the shackles off he went on to score a career best 11 league goals last season and with the likes of Owen, and when fit Fowler, in front of him he will also contribute a high number of assists.

Form Factors

Season	Team	Tot	St	Sb	Y	R
95-96	Liverpool	38	38	0	1	0
96-97	Liverpool	37	37	0	5	0
97-98	Liverpool	36	36	0	1	0
Total		111	111	0	7	0

	GP	GG	GF	GS	TGR
95-96	100.00	6.33	70	6	8.57
96-97	97.37	5.29	62	7	11.29
97-98	94.74	3.27	68	11	16.18
Averages	97.37	4.96	66.67	8.00	12.01

McPHAIL, Stephen
Leeds United ❶❷ M

Fullname: Stephen McPhail
DOB: 09-12-79 Dublin

Very highly-rated midfielder who is expected to make in-roads to the Leeds United first team this season having been used sparingly as a substitute on four occasions last term. A former trainee at Elland Road he was the youth Player of the Year when Leeds won the FA Youth Cup in 1997 with his cultured left foot playing a major part in his side's success.

Form Factors

Season	Team	Tot	St	Sb	Y	R
97-98	Leeds U.	4	0	4	0	0
Total		4	0	4	0	0

	GP	GG	GF	GS	TGR
97-98	10.53	0.00	57	0	0.00
Averages	10.53	0.00	57.00	0.00	0.00

MEAN, Scott
West Ham U. ❶ M

Fullname: Scott Mean
DOB: 13-12-73

Midfielder who joined West Ham during the 1996-97 season but had to wait until 30 March 1998 for his debut when coming on as a substitute during a 3-0 win over Leeds United. Was named as substitute, unused, on 11 other occasions.

Form Factors

Season	Team	Tot	St	Sb	Y	R
97-98	West Ham U.	3	0	3	0	0
Total		3	0	3	0	0

	GP	GG	GF	GS	TGR
97-98	7.89	0.00	56	0	0.00
Averages	7.89	0.00	56.00	0.00	0.00

MENDONCA, Clive

Charlton A.   ①②❸ S

Fullname: Clive Paul Mendonca
DOB: 09-09-68 Islington

There cannot be too many players down the years to have scored a hat-trick at Wembley and yet been overshadowed by their own goalkeeper. Such a fate befell Mendonca last May when his triple burst could only secure a 4-4 play-off final draw with Sunderland in one of the greatest matches ever seen at the famous stadium. The accolades went to keeper Ilic for his penalty shoot-out save from Michael Gray which clinched Charlton's place back in the Premiership.

By then Mendonca's work had already been completed; the Addicks record £700,000 signing had scored 23 times in 41 league appearances and then added his three earlier in the afternoon. It was the London-born Sunderland supporter's most successful season and came hot on the heels of his previous best when he scored 17 times in 45 league games for Grimsby Town. Got into double figures in four of his five seasons at Grimsby whom he joined after spells with Sheffield United, Doncaster Rovers on loan and Rotherham United where he first came to prominence as a striker of note.

Clive Mendonca

MERSON, Paul

Middlesbrough   ①❷❸❹ S

Fullname: Paul Charles Merson
DOB: 20-03-68 Harlesden, London

Exciting wide player who won a multitude of honours during 12 years at Arsenal including two league championships. An England regular he was called into the final 22 for France 98 on the back of a memorable first season with Middlesbrough which saw him in amongst the goals again with a dozen, making him their second highest scorer in Nationwide League matches.

Boro paid Arsenal £4.5m to prise him away from Highbury and in return they got a top class winger who can go past players with ease, set up chances for others either with through balls or testing crosses, and has the ability to cut inside and score for himself as his record of 90 league goals implies.

238   FANTASY FOOTBALL HANDBOOK 1998/99

Form Factors

Season	Team	Tot	St	Sb	Y	R
94-95	Arsenal	28	24	4	3	0
95-96	Arsenal	38	38	0	2	0
96-97	Arsenal	32	32	0	1	0
Totals		98	94	4	6	0

	GP	GG	GF	GS	TGR
94-95	73.68	13.00	52	4	7.70
95-96	100.00	9.80	49	5	10.20
96-97	84.21	10.33	62	6	9.67
Averages	85.96	11.04	54.33	5.0	9.19

MIKLOSKO, Ludek

West Ham U.   ❶❷ GK

Fullname: Ludek Miklosko
DOB: 09-12-61 Protesov, Czechoslovakia

Standing at a massive 6'5", Miklosko casts an imposing figure behind the West Ham defence and, having joined the Hammers from Banik Ostrava for £300,000 in

Paul Merson

Ludek Miklosko

Fantasy Football Handbook 1998/99   **239**

February 1990, has proved an outstanding bargain. Given that he will be 37 in December it may be that 'Ludo' may not add too many more games to his impressive 315 league games for West Ham but he, along with Phil Parkes, holds the club record of 21 clean sheets in a season. Before last season, when he made just 13 league appearances – conceding 23 goals – he missed just four league games in five seasons.

Although he didn't get a game, he was in the Czechoslovakia 1990 World Cup squad but did nonetheless accumulate 41 caps with his national side.

Form Factors

Season	Team	Tot	St	Sb	Y	R
95-96	West Ham U.	36	36	0	1	1
96-97	West Ham U.	36	36	0	0	0
97-98	West Ham U.	13	13	0	0	0
Total		85	85	0	1	1

	GA	GkA	GAp	CS	SO	R
95-96	52	47	1.31	11	3	0
96-97	48	46	1.28	9	1	0
97-98	57	23	1.64	0	0	0
Averages	52.3	38.67	1.41	6.67	1.33	0

MILOSEVIC, Savo

Aston Villa ❶❷ S

Fullname: Savo Milosevic
DOB: 02-09-73 Bijeljina, Yugoslavia

Can be an exceptionally gifted striker who can unhinge the tightest of defences but can also display the finishing of a novice. Arrived in England at the start of the 1995-96 season with a wonderful goalscoring record behind him – 64 in 98 games for Partizan Belgrade – but has mustered just 28 in 90 Premiership games for Aston Villa.

Milosevic has an abundance of talent but appeared to be living on borrowed time at Villa Park after spitting at disgruntled supporters following a 5-0 thrashing at Blackburn.

Form Factors

Season	Team	Tot	St	Sb	Y	R
95-96	Aston Villa	37	36	1	6	0
96-97	Aston Villa	30	29	1	6	0
97-98	Aston Villa	23	19	4	5	0
Total		90	84	6	17	0

	GP	GG	GF	GS	TGR
95-96	97.37	3.08	52	12	23.08
96-97	78.95	3.00	47	10	21.28
97-98	60.53	3.29	49	7	14.29
Averages	78.95	3.12	49.33	9.67	19.55

MOLENAAR, Robert

Leeds United ❶❷❸ CB

Fullname: Robert Molenaar
DOB: 27-02-69 Zaandam, Holland

Tall and well built, Dutchman Molenaar has the right credentials to make his mark in the Premiership as a robust central defender. But in keeping with his background in Holland he is also at ease with the ball at his feet. Despite these attributes, he has struggled to hold down a first team place and was in the starting line-up for less than half of Leeds United's league matches last season, his second in England.

Scored three times last season and on each occasion Leeds won the game.

Form Factors

Season	Team	Tot	St	Sb	Y	R
96-97	Leeds U.	12	12	0	5	0
97-98	Leeds U.	22	18	4	4	0
Total		34	30	4	9	0

	GP	GG	GF	GS	TGR
96-97	31.58	12.00	28	1	3.57
97-98	57.89	11.00	57	2	3.51
Averages	44.74	11.50	42.50	1.50	3.54

MONCUR, John

West Ham U. ❶ M

Fullname: John Frederick Moncur
DOB: 22-09-66 Stepney

A well travelled creative midfielder who has improved his ball-winning capabilities as his career has moved on to make his game more complete but the art of goalscoring is something which continues to elude him.

In recent years the effervescent Moncur has been dogged by injury and suspension with his 20 Premiership games last season being about par for the course over the past three years. Is in his fifth season at Upton Park after a nomadic life which saw him loaned out to several clubs by Tottenham to help him gain experience.

Form Factors

Season	Team	Tot	St	Sb	Y	R
95-96	West Ham U.	20	19	1	4	0
96-97	West Ham U.	27	26	1	8	0
97-98	West Ham U.	20	17	3	7	0
Total		67	62	5	19	0

	GP	GG	GF	GS	TGR
95-96	52.63	0.00	43	0	0.00
96-97	71.05	13.50	39	2	5.13
97-98	52.63	20.00	56	1	1.79
Averages	58.77	11.17	46.00	1.00	2.30

MONKOU, Ken

Southampton ❶❷ CB

Fullname: Kenneth John Monkou
DOB: 29-11-64 Necare, Surinam

After a very unhappy time at the Dell during 1996-97 under Graeme Souness, not helped by injury, Monkou was back in a big way last season with 30 appearances in the Premiership following a disappointing 13 games the previous term. Picked up seven yellow cards and one dismissal last season resulting in two suspensions. A Holland Under-21 international defender who is powerful in the air and likes to clear his lines swiftly.

Will be 34 in November and could have a battle on his hands to stay as first choice central defender at the Dell. Joined the Saints in 1992 after more than four years with Chelsea.

Form Factors

Season	Team	Tot	St	Sb	Y	R
95-96	Southampton	32	31	1	7	0
96-97	Southampton	13	8	5	6	0
97-98	Southampton	32	30	2	5	1
Total		77	69	8	18	1

	GP	GG	GF	GS	TGR
95-96	84.21	16.00	34	2	5.88
96-97	34.21	0.00	50	0	0.00
97-98	84.21	32.00	50	1	2.00
Averages	67.54	16.00	44.67	1.00	2.63

Ken Monkou

MOORE, Ian

Nottingham F. ❶❷ S

Fullname: Ian Ronald Moore
DOB: 26-08-76 Birkenhead

Very highly-rated striker who was expected to play a big part in Nottingham Forest's return to the Premiership last season but suffered a pre-season injury and was subsequently put out of action for all but nine league games of which only two were starts. As a 19-year-old striker he played 36 times for Tranmere during the 1995-96 season scoring nine league goals. Struggled the following season having a spell on loan to Bradford before switching to Forest in a £1m deal.

Will be 22 early this season which still leaves him with plenty of time to make the grade at the highest level. He certainly possesses the energy, pace and heading ability to make his mark.

242 FANTASY FOOTBALL HANDBOOK 1998/99

Form Factors

Season	Team	Tot	St	Sb	Y	R
96-97	N. Forest	5	1	4	0	0
Total		5	1	4	0	0

	GP	GG	GF	GS	TGR
96-97	13.16	0.00	31	0	0.00
Averages	13.16	0.00	31.00	0.00	0.00

MORRIS, Jody
Chelsea ❶❷ M

Fullname: Jody Morris
DOB: 22-12-78 Hammersmith

Since breaking into the Chelsea first team just six weeks after his 17th birthday, Morris has been troubled by injury but the signs are that now, hopefully, he is clear of such problems and can become a major player in the Blues' midfield under Vialli's leadership. Morris has tremendous stamina, passes the ball and demonstrated last season that he can get goals with strikes both in the league and Coca Cola Cup.

A one-time captain of England at Under-17 he played in the World Under-20 competition in Malaysia in 1997 but missed out on his first call up to the Under-21 side when injury put him out of action.

Form Factors

Season	Team	Tot	St	Sb	Y	R
95-96	Chelsea	1	0	1	0	0
96-97	Chelsea	12	6	6	1	0
97-98	Chelsea	12	9	3	0	0
Total		25	15	10	1	0

	GP	GG	GF	GS	TGR
95-96	2.63	0.00	46	0	0.00
96-97	31.58	0.00	58	0	0.00
97-98	31.58	12.00	71	1	1.41
Averages	21.93	4.00	58.33	0.33	0.47

MORTIMER, Paul
Charlton A. ❶ M

Fullname: Paul Henry Mortimer
DOB: 08-05-68 Kensington

Very talented, very versatile, very much injury prone and very inconsistent. It is a mix which has stopped Mortimer from having the exciting career which looked to be coming his way in 1991 when he left Charlton for the first time to join Aston Villa for £300,000. His career stalled at Villa Park and he departed for an injury troubled time at Crystal Palace. Returned to Charlton after just 27 games in three years at Palace but found his fortunes little better last season with three interruptions through injury.

It would take a very big 'if' to suggest that the unfortunate Mortimer could win many points for your fantasy team during the coming winter.

MURPHY, Danny
Liverpool ❶❷ M

Fullname: Daniel Benjamin Murphy
DOB: 18-03-77 Chester

Another of Dario Gradi's excellent prodigies to emanate from Crewe Alexandra. One of the most highly rated teenagers in the country in recent years Murphy, now 21, made his Premiership debut with Liverpool last season, following a £1.5m move which could eventually rise to double that figure, and is expected to go onto greater things. Was eased gently into the top flight at Anfield with just two of his 16 league games lasting the full 90 minutes.

Fantasy Football Handbook 1998/99 **243**

Very creative midfielder with an exceptional goalscoring record during his last two seasons at Crewe where he got into double figures on both occasions, but is still awaiting his first goal in the Premiership.

Form Factors

Season	Team	Tot	St	Sb	Y	R
97-98	Liverpool	16	6	10	1	0
Total		16	6	10	1	0

	GP	GG	GF	GS	TGR
97-98	42.11	0.00	68	0	0.00
Averages	42.11	0.00	68.00	0.00	0.00

MUSTOE, Robbie

Middlesbrough ❶❷❸ M

Fullname: Robin Mustoe
DOB: 28-08-68 Oxford

Began his career with his hometown club of Oxford United but after four years at the Manor Ground was transferred to Middlesbrough in a £375,000 deal. He flourished on Teesside with his total commitment in 245 league games for the club winning him many admirers in the north east. A good team player Mustoe has scored 19 times in the league for Boro with a goal coming along approximately every 13 games.

Form Factors

Season	Team	Tot	St	Sb	Y	R
92-93	Middlesbrough	23	21	2	1	0
95-96	Middlesbrough	21	21	0	3	0
96-97	Middlesbrough	31	31	0	9	0
Totals		75	73	2	13	0

	GP	GG	GF	GS	TGR
92-93	54.76	23.0	54	1	1.85
95-96	55.26	21.0	35	1	2.86
96-97	81.58	15.5	51	2	3.92
Averages	63.87	19.83	46.67	1.33	2.88

MYERS, Andy

Chelsea ❶❷ D

Fullname: Andrew John Myers
DOB: 03-11-73 Hounslow

The 1997-98 season was fairly typical in the career of Andy Myers with the very versatile, skilful and fast player being on the fringes of the first team at Stamford Bridge but not able to command a permanent place. His 12 Premiership outings was two games above his average in the seven years since making his debut and the signs are that he will again be a valuable squad member this season without holding down a regular place.

Predominantly a left-sided player, he has been used down that flank as a wing-back and a defender. A former England Under-21 player who has scored twice in his 83 league games for Chelsea.

Form Factors

Season	Team	Tot	St	Sb	Y	R
95-96	Chelsea	20	20	0	2	0
96-97	Chelsea	18	15	3	2	0
97-98	Chelsea	12	11	1	0	0
Total		50	46	4	4	0

	GP	GG	GF	GS	TGR
95-96	52.63	0.00	46	0	0.00
96-97	47.37	18.00	58	1	1.72
97-98	31.58	0.00	71	0	0.00
Averages	43.86	6.00	58.33	0.33	0.57

MYHRE, Thomas

Everton ❶❷❸ GK

Fullname: Thomas Myhre
DOB: 16-10-73 Sarpsborg, Norway

Joined Everton following a one week trial at Goodison Park in November 1997 and was almost immediately installed as the Blues' first choice keeper at the expense of the brilliant long-serving Welshman Neville Southall.

Myhre's initial cost to Everton was £800,000 but that could rise to £1m and given his form during the second half of the season – he kicked off with three successive clean sheets – it will be money well spent. Made 22 league appearances and conceded 29 goals at 1.32 per game.

Was in the Norway squad for France 98 but did not oust Frode Grodas.

Form Factors

Season	Team	Tot	St	Sb	Y	R
97-98	Everton	22	22	0	1	0
Total		22	22	0	1	0

	GA	GkA	GAp	CS	SO	R
97-98	56	29	1.32	7	3	0
Averages	56	29	1.32	7	3	0

Thomas Myhre

NEVILLE, Gary

Manchester U. ❶❷❸❹ FB

Fullname: Gary Alexander Neville
DOB: 18-02-75 Bury

The 1997-98 season saw Gary Neville make more appearances in the Premiership, 34, than in any of his four previous seasons in the Manchester United first team. He may have ended the season medal-less with United but his performances for his country in France 98 were surely his best at international level. He has matured into a top class defender whether playing in the middle of the backline or in his more accustomed right-back position. He is excellent in the tackle, links well with the midfield and can get forward himself to send over telling crosses. Also has the added bonus of being a long throw specialist.

Since progressing from the United youth set-up Gary Neville has won almost every domestic honour going and at 23 he can look forward to adding a multitude of trophies to his collection in the coming years.

Form Factors

Season	Team	Tot	St	Sb	Y	R
95-96	Manchester U.	31	30	1	7	0
96-97	Manchester U.	31	30	1	4	0
97-98	Manchester U.	34	34	0	2	0
Total		96	94	2	13	0
	GP	GG	GF	GS	TGR	
95-96	81.58	0.00	73	0	0.00	
96-97	81.58	1.00	76	31	40.79	
97-98	89.47	0.00	73	0	0.00	
Averages	84.21	0.33	74.00	10.33	13.60	

NEVILLE, Phil

Manchester U.   ❶❷❸ FB

Fullname: Philip John Neville
DOB: 21-01-77 Bury

The younger of the Neville brothers had his most fulfilling year yet with Manchester United last season as he was called into action on 34 occasions and scored his first goals for the club. With his ability to play either at right-back, his best position, or as central defender he would be a useful addition to a fantasy team.

He had to endure a series of setbacks on his way to making it to the highest level but with his strength in the tackle, speed and confidence to move forward he will undoubtedly match his brother's achievements and regain his place in the England set-up. Only 21 and already has Premier League, FA Cup and FA Youth Cup winners medals in his collection.

Form Factors

Season	Team	Tot	St	Sb	Y	R
95-96	Manchester U.	24	21	3	2	0
96-97	Manchester U.	18	15	3	2	0
97-98	Manchester U.	30	24	6	7	0
Total		72	60	12	11	0
	GP	GG	GF	GS	TGR	
95-96	63.16	0.00	73	0	0.00	
96-97	47.37	0.00	76	0	0.00	
97-98	78.95	30.00	73	1	1.37	
Averages	63.16	10.00	74.00	0.33	0.46	

NEWSOME, Jon

Sheffield W.   ❶❷❸ CB

Fullname: Jonathan Newsome
DOB: 06-09-70 Sheffield

Is in his second spell with Sheffield Wednesday having rejoined the club on deadline day in 1996. Injuries restricted him to just ten games during 1996-97 but last season he regained his central defensive position only to miss the final couple of months of the season with another injury.

First played for Wednesday back in September 1989 but transferred to Leeds United in 1991 where he won a championship medal. Moved to Norwich City for £1m in June 1994 before returning to Hillsborough.

Tall, consistent and if he can stay fit would be a useful addition to your team.

Form Factors

Season	Team	Tot	St	Sb	Y	R
95-96	Sheffield W.	8	8	0	1	0
96-97	Sheffield W.	10	10	0	1	0
97-98	Sheffield W.	25	25	0	2	0
Total		43	43	0	4	0

	GP	GG	GF	GS	TGR
95-96	21.05	8.00	48	1	2.08
96-97	26.32	10.00	50	1	2.00
97-98	65.79	12.50	52	2	3.85
Averages	37.72	10.17	50.00	1.33	2.64

Form Factors

Season	Team	Tot	St	Sb	Y	R
95-96	Chelsea	24	21	3	2	0
96-97	Chelsea	15	13	2	2	0
97-98	Chelsea	18	17	1	0	0
Total		57	51	6	4	0

	GP	GG	GF	GS	TGR
95-96	63.16	24.00	46	1	2.17
96-97	39.47	0.00	58	0	0.00
97-98	47.37	0.00	71	0	0.00
Averages	50.00	8.00	58.33	0.33	0.72

NEWTON, Eddie
Chelsea ❶❷ M

Fullname: Edward John Ikem Newton
DOB: 13-12-71 Hammersmith

Popular midfield player who was selected for exactly half of Chelsea's Premiership matches last season which has been just about par for his fortunes over the past three seasons. Often troubled by injury in that time he hit a high in the 1997 FA Cup final with the Blues' second goal in a 2-0 win over Middlesbrough.

Would almost certainly be an automatic choice for most clubs with his ball-winning, distribution and tireless efforts providing the ideal cover in front of an attack-minded defence. His Cup Final goal was a touch unexpected given that he has scored just twice in the league over the past five years.

NEWTON, Shaun
Charlton A. ❶❷❸ S

Fullname: Shaun O'Neill Newton
DOB: 28-08-75 Camberwell

The forgotten man of Wembley. While all the tributes at last season Division One play-off final went to Messrs Ilic, Mendonca and Phillips, there was another goalscorer on that memorable afternoon – Shaun Newton. Has had the sort of career clubs dream of: worked his way through from the youth set-up, missed just a dozen of the past 138 league games and now scored at Wembley - can he make the grade in the Premiership?

Newton has a lot of the attributes to help him succeed in that he is fast, versatile, can get goals but maybe not as many he would like, and is a decent header of the ball. He has been used in a multitude of positions by Charlton, more often than not he is selected as a winger but has been used as a wing-back and a right-back although the results for the latter were none too impressive.

NICHOLLS, Mark

Chelsea ①②S
Fullname: Mark Nicholls
DOB: 30-05-77 Hillingdon

Twenty-one year old striker who scored freely at Youth and Reserve level for Chelsea and last season notched his first at senior level during the 6-1 hammering of Tottenham. Added two more in a 3-1 win over Coventry and all three of his goals came in matches when he was only selected as substitute. Having made eight Premiership appearances in 1996-97, last season was one of great advancement for Nicholls as he was in the side 19 times for league games although 11 of those appearances were as substitute. Could well be worth watching.

Form Factors

Season	Team	Tot	St	Sb	Y	R
96-97	Chelsea	8	3	5	0	0
97-98	Chelsea	19	8	11	2	0
Total		27	11	16	2	0

	GP	GG	GF	GS	TGR
96-97	21.05	0.00	58	0	0.00
97-98	50.00	6.33	71	3	4.23
Averages	35.53	3.17	64.50	1.50	2.11

NICOL, Steve

Sheffield W. ①CB
Fullname: Stephen Nicol
DOB: 11-12-61 Irvine

The curtain finally seems have come down on Steve Nicol's magnificent career at the top level with the vastly experienced and successful Scottish international moving on loan from Sheffield Wednesday to West Bromwich Albion. Made just four starts for Wednesday last season some 16 years after his debut with Liverpool where in 343 league games he was in four title-winning sides and enjoyed one triumph in the European Cup.

Made his breakthrough in the professional game with Ayr United and after leaving Liverpool had a spell with Notts County.

Form Factors

Season	Team	Tot	St	Sb	Y	R
95-96	Sheffield W.	19	18	1	1	0
96-97	Sheffield W.	23	19	4	0	0
97-98	Sheffield W.	7	4	3	1	0
Total		49	41	8	2	0

	GP	GG	GF	GS	TGR
95-96	50.00	0.00	48	0	0.00
96-97	60.53	0.00	50	0	0.00
97-98	18.42	0.00	52	0	0.00
Averages	42.98	0.00	50.00	0.00	0.00

NIELSEN, Allan

Tottenham H. ❶❷❸❹ M
Fullname: Allan Nielsen
DOB: 13-03-71

A £1.6m signing from Brondy who put Tottenham's dismal 1997-98 campaign behind him by playing in all five of Denmark's World Cup matches in France. Nielsen, as he demonstrated in the World Cup, has the potential to fulfil the expectations put upon him as a 17-year-old when Bayern Munich signed him. Although that move didn't work out he has matured into a complete midfield player who can shoot well from around the edge of the penalty area, get up and down the pitch throughout the 90 minutes and links in well just behind the attack.

Has scored a reasonable nine goals in 54 Premiership matches for Spurs and collected Danish League Championship and Cup winners medals prior to moving abroad. Probably set a world record when scoring within one minute of making his international debut.

Form Factors

Season	Team	Tot	St	Sb	Y	R
96-97	Tottenham H.	29	28	1	6	0
97-98	Tottenham H.	25	21	4	2	0
Total		54	49	5	8	0

	GP	GG	GF	GS	TGR
96-97	76.32	4.83	44	6	13.64
97-98	65.79	8.33	44	3	6.82
Averages	71.05	6.58	44.00	4.50	10.23

NILSSON, Roland

Coventry C. ❶❷ D
Fullname: Roland Nilsson
DOB: 27-11-63 Sweden

Gordon Strachan knew exactly what he was getting when he signed the very experienced Swedish defender Nilsson at the start of last season for a modest £200,000. Calm in possession and comfortable moving out of defence with the ball, his quality was one of many reasons why Coventry enjoyed a better season than has been their norm in the Premiership.

Played in 39 league and cup games last season – his first in England since leaving Sheffield Wednesday in 1994 – but may find his appearances reduced this year as he approaches his 35th birthday.

Form Factors

Season	Team	Tot	St	Sb	Y	R
92-93	Sheffield W.	32	32	0	0	0
93-94	Sheffield W.	38	38	0	1	0
97-98	Coventry C.	32	32	0	3	0
Total		102	102	0	4	0

	GP	GG	GF	GS	TGR
92-93	84.21	32.00	55	1	1.82
93-94	100.00	0.00	76	0	0.00
97-98	84.21	0.00	46	0	0.00
Averages	89.47	10.67	59.00	0.33	0.61

NOLAN, Ian

Sheffield W. ❶❷❸ FB

Fullname: Ian Robert Nolan
DOB: 09-07-70 Liverpool

Since signing for Sheffield Wednesday from Tranmere Rovers for £1.5m in August 1994, Nolan has been an almost permanent fixture in the Owls side and was ever present for their first 32 league and cup games of last season until a broken leg against Tottenham in February brought his season to a premature close.

Although a right-footed full-back he has spent much of his time at Hillsborough playing on the opposite flank but still manages to cut inside to get over good crosses.

Formerly with Northwich Victoria and then Marine, he made his debut in the Football League with Tranmere, whom he joined for just £10,000.

Form Factors

Season	Team	Tot	St	Sb	Y	R
95-96	Sheffield W.	29	29	0	1	0
96-97	Sheffield W.	38	38	0	1	0
97-98	Sheffield W.	27	27	0	1	0
Total		94	94	0	3	0

	GP	GG	GF	GS	TGR
95-96	76.32	0.00	48	0	0.00
96-97	100.00	38.00	50	1	2.00
97-98	71.05	0.00	52	0	0.00
Averages	82.46	12.67	50.00	0.33	0.67

O'KANE, John

Everton ❶❷ D

Fullname: John Andrew O'Kane
DOB: 15-11-74 Nottingham

Having not quite made the grade at Old Trafford, O'Kane switched across to Everton in a £400,000 move in January 1998 and launched his career in the Premiership by appearing in 12 of Everton's final 15 matches of last season.

A talented right-back he won a Second Division championship medal whilst on loan to Bury in 1996-97 and made his Premiership debut for Manchester United against Aston Villa in August 1995.

Form Factors

Season	Team	Tot	St	Sb	Y	R
95-96	Manchester U.	1	0	1	0	0
96-97	Manchester U.	1	1	0	0	0
97-98	Everton	12	12	0	5	0
Total		14	13	1	5	0

	GP	GG	GF	GS	TGR
95-96	2.63	0.00	73	0	0.00
96-97	2.63	0.00	76	0	0.00
97-98	31.58	0.00	41	0	0.00
Averages	12.28	0.00	63.33	0.00	0.00

OAKES, Michael

Aston Villa ① ② GK

Fullname: Michael Christian Oakes
DOB: 30-10-73 Northwich

A more than capable understudy to Mark Bosnich at Aston Villa but after making 20 appearances during 1996-97 was used just eight times in the Premiership last season and once in the UEFA Cup. Conceded 13 goals in his league appearances at an average of 1.62 compared to Villa's overall Premiership average for the season of 1.26. Having kept nine clean sheets in '96-97 he was unfortunate not to complete any shut-outs this time although only three goals were conceded in his last three games.

Has the potential to go far but needs regular first team football to gain experience.

Form Factors

Season	Team	Tot	St	Sb	Y	R
96-97	Aston Villa	20	18	2	0	0
97-98	Aston Villa	8	8	0	0	0
Total		28	26	2	0	0

	GA	GkA	GAp	CS	SO	R
96-97	34	17	0.85	9	3	2
97-98	48	13	1.63	0	0	0
Averages	41.0	15.0	1.24	4.5	1.5	1.0

OAKES, Scott

Sheffield W. ① M

Fullname: Scott John Oakes
DOB: 05-08-72 Leicester

Midfield player whose days at Hillsborough do look to be numbered having made just four Premiership appearances last season, all as substitute. Of his 19 league games the previous season 12 were again after named as substitute. Joined Sheffield Wednesday from Luton Town for £450,000 having started his career with Leicester City. At all three clubs he has played under the since-sacked Wednesday boss David Pleat.

A constructive midfield player who can play at full-back or wing-back and, particularly during his time at Kenilworth Road, has a proven goalscoring record.

Form Factors

Season	Team	Tot	St	Sb	Y	R
96-97	Sheffield W.	19	7	12	1	0
97-98	Sheffield W.	4	0	4	0	0
Total		23	7	16	1	0

	GP	GG	GF	GS	TGR
96-97	50.00	19.00	50	1	2.00
97-98	10.53	0.00	52	0	0.00
Averages	30.26	9.50	51.00	0.50	1.00

OAKLEY, Matthew

Southampton ❶❷❸ M

Fullname: Matthew Oakley
DOB: 17-08-77 Peterborough

A midfielder who can work from either flank to equal effect, Oakley has progressed at a rapid rate over the past few seasons from a trainee at the Dell to an established member of the Saints Premiership side. Going into the 1998-99 season he has already played 72 league games for the Saints at the age of 21 and with his pinpoint passing ability and long throws he will continue to make forward strides which could ultimately see him take the next step up from playing for England at Under-21 level.

Form Factors

Season	Team	Tot	St	Sb	Y	R
95-96	Southampton	10	5	5	0	0
96-97	Southampton	28	23	5	0	0
97-98	Southampton	33	32	1	3	0
Total		71	60	11	3	0

	GP	GG	GF	GS	TGR
95-96	26.32	0.00	34	0	0.00
96-97	73.68	9.33	50	3	6.00
97-98	86.84	33.00	50	1	2.00
Averages	62.28	14.11	44.67	1.33	2.67

Matthew Oakley

OGRIZOVIC, Steve

Coventry City ❶❷ GK

Fullname: Steven Ogrizovic
DOB: 12-09-57 Mansfield

An awesome sight for any advancing striker and an awesome playing record combine to give Steve Ogrizovic almost legendary status within the game. The giant keeper will be 41 early in the 1998-99 season but shows no sign of abdicating from his throne at Highfield Road. Last season saw him set a club record of appearances for Coventry City which included his 500th league game for the Sky Blues and over 600 league appearances in total during stints with City, Chesterfield, Liverpool and Shrewsbury Town.

During his 21 year career he has been ever present on six occasions but last season, despite having reclaimed pole position by the end of the campaign, he made 24 Premiership appearances which is his lowest in the league since the 1981-82 season.

Ogrizovic's acrobatics down the years have gone a long towards aiding Coventry's countless successful escape acts while the highlight of his career was the Sky Blues' 1987 FA Cup triumph.

Form Factors

Season	Team	Tot	St	Sb	Y	R
95-96	Coventry C.	25	25	0	0	0
96-97	Coventry C.	38	38	0	1	0
97-98	Coventry C.	24	24	0	0	0
Total		87	87	0	1	0

	GA	GkA	GAp	CS	SO	R
95-96	60	33	1.32	8	4	0
96-97	54	54	1.42	2	2	0
97-98	44	32	1.33	7	2	3
Averages	52.67	39.67	1.37	5.67	2.67	1.0

OMOYINMI, Manny
West Ham U.   ❶❷❸ S

Fullname: Emmanuel Omoyinmi
DOB: 28-12-77 London

Has worked his way through from the youth set-up at West Ham to make his first team league debut against Leeds United in March 1997. Made further progress last season with his first start for the Hammers and four more Premiership appearances from the substitutes' bench and also had a spell on loan at Dundee United. An exciting winger with good speed, excellent close skills and an eye for goal as proved by his two goals when coming on during a 3-3 draw at Crystal Palace towards the end of the season. Worth watching.

Form Factors

Season	Team	Tot	St	Sb	Y	R
96-97	West Ham U.	1	0	1	0	0
97-98	West Ham U.	5	1	4	0	0
Total		6	1	5	0	0

	GP	GG	GF	GS	TGR
96-97	2.63	0.00	39	0	0.00
97-98	13.16	2.50	56	2	3.57
Averages	7.89	1.25	47.50	1.00	1.79

ORMEROD, Anthony
Middlesbrough   ❶❷ M

Fullname: Anthony Ormerod
DOB: 31-03-79 Brotton, Middlesbrough

Was undoubtedly one of the success stories of last season. Going into the campaign aged just 18 he was not expected to challenge for a first team place much before the final weeks but instead got in early to score on his debut and add two more later in the season.

Finished the campaign with 17 league and four cup matches to his credit which should all provide useful experience for the big challenge that lies ahead in the Premiership.

OSTENSTAD, Egil
Southampton   ❶❷❸ S

Fullname: Egil Ostenstad
DOB: 02-01-72 Haugesund, Norway

Has proved a good acquisition at the Dell since signing for Southampton in October 1996 from Norwegian side Viking for whom he scored 25 times in 45 games during his final two seasons. With 20 Premiership goals in less than two full seasons in England he has been a complete success and would probably have scored more had he not been injured for two months last season.

Certainly the Southampton supporters are happy with him as he collected the Saints Player of the Year trophy at the end of the 1996-97 season. Very agile and quick which makes a handful for any defence, none more so than Manchester

United against whom he fully announced his arrival in this country with a hat-trick during a sensational 6-3 win for the Saints.

Went to France 98 with Norway and was used as a substitute during the 1-1 draw with Scotland.

Form Factors

Season	Team	Tot	St	Sb	Y	R
96-97	Southampton	30	29	1	3	0
97-98	Southampton	29	21	8	4	0
Total		59	50	9	7	0

	GP	GG	GF	GS	TGR
96-97	78.95	3.00	50	10	20.00
97-98	76.32	2.64	50	11	22.00
Averages	77.63	2.82	50.00	10.50	21.00

Egil Ostenstad

OSTER, John

Everton ❶❷❸ S

Fullname: John Oster
DOB: 08-12-78 Boston

When handed the opportunity to show his capabilities for Grimsby Town in January 1997, Oster grasped the chance with both hands and within six months he was on his way to Everton in exchange for £1.5m. Wasted no time in settling in at Goodison Park and featured in the starting line-up of 12 of Everton's first 15 games last season. After that meteoric start he had to settle for spending much of the rest of the season on the subs' bench but have no doubts, he will be back in a big way this season.

Form Factors

Season	Team	Tot	St	Sb	Y	R
97-98	Everton	31	16	15	2	0
Total		31	16	15	2	0

	GP	GG	GF	GS	TGR
97-98	81.58	31.00	41	1	2.44
Averages	81.58	31.00	41.00	1.00	2.44

OVERMARS, Marc

Arsenal ①②③④⑤ S

Fullname: Marc Overmars
DOB: 29-3-73 Emst, Holland

Marc Overmars

Arsenal's excellent £7m winger, whom they signed from Ajax in June 1997, had a fabulous first season at Highbury which culminated in him scoring the club's first goal in the FA Cup final victory over Newcastle and then playing a part in Holland's drive to the semi final of the World Cup.

Predominantly seen as a provider from either flank, Overmars also proved that he can get goals consistently with 16 successful strikes in 44 domestic matches last season. In keeping with most wingers he was frequently substituted as Arsène Wenger called him off early on 13 occasions in Premiership matches but unusually for Arsenal players in recent years he did not receive a single yellow card.

First broke into professional football with Dutch Division Two side Willem II before joining Ajax six years ago.

Form Factors

Season	Team	Tot	St	Sb	Y	R
97-98	Arsenal	32	32	0	0	0
Total		32	32	0	0	0

	GP	GG	GF	GS	TGR
97-98	84.21	2.67	68	12	17.65
Averages	84.21	2.67	68.00	12.00	17.65

OWEN, Michael

Liverpool ①②③④⑤ S

Fullname: Michael Owen
DOB: 14-12-79 Chester

France 98 – what price Michael Owen now? Every World Cup throws up one new star and this time round it was our turn to bring a goalscoring sensation to the biggest stage of the lot. Owen, just 18, was belatedly called upon by Glenn Hoddle but responded with two goals, the second of which – against Argentina – will surely be his launching-pad to super stardom.

He may not be particularly tall but his stature is gigantic. Despite his shortage of inches Owen is good in the air but his great asset is his speed which so nearly brought Argentina to their knees. His finishing is simply deadly. He made just two Premiership appearances for Liverpool during 1996-97, scoring once, but a year later his impact was awesome with 18 goals in 34 games; his Coca Cola Cup record was four games and four goals. He was also rightly dismissed against Manchester United but has hopefully learnt his lesson.

If your funds allow, then Owen must be in your team.

Form Factors

Season	Team	Tot	St	Sb	Y	R
96-97	Liverpool	2	1	1	0	0
97-98	Liverpool	36	34	2	4	1
Total		38	35	3	4	1

	GP	GG	GF	GS	TGR
96-97	5.26	2.00	62	1	1.61
97-98	94.74	2.00	68	18	26.47
Averages	50.00	2.00	65.00	9.50	14.04

Michael Owen

PALLISTER, Gary

Middlesbrough   CB

Fullname: Gary Andrew Pallister
DOB: 30-06-65 Ramsgate

After an absence of nine years Pallister returned to Middlesbrough in the summer of 1998 to mark the complete end of Manchester United's magnificent central pairing of himself and Steve Bruce, the latter having left Old Trafford two years earlier.

Pallister was the proverbial rock at the heart of Alex Ferguson's defence. Rarely beaten in the tackle, even less in the air and deceptively quick, he defied the ongoing changes to the Laws of the Game by conceding precious few free kicks in dangerous positions. But for injury, would have played more times for his country, 22, than he actually did.

His vast experience could make all the difference to Middlesbrough surviving for more than the two years they did the last time they visited the Premiership.

Form Factors

Season	Team	Tot	St	Sb	Y	R
95-96	Manchester U.	21	21	0	3	0
96-97	Manchester U.	27	27	0	4	0
97-98	Manchester U.	33	33	0	4	1
Total		81	81	0	11	1

	GP	GG	GF	GS	TGR
95-96	55.26	21.00	73	1	1.37
96-97	71.05	9.00	76	3	3.95
97-98	86.84	0.00	73	0	0.00
Averages	71.05	10.00	74.00	1.33	1.77

PALMER, Carlton

Southampton   ❶❷❸ M

Fullname: Carlton Lloyd Palmer
DOB: 05-12-65 Rowley Regis

Gangly midfielder who is nonetheless totally committed and quickly secured a permanent place in the starting line-up at Southampton following a £1m transfer from Leeds United in September 1997. Palmer has had his detractors down the years but 18 England caps and 10 years in the top flight are statistics that speak for themselves. Competitive in midfield and eager to support the attack, he is also a fine defender with good heading ability and tenacity in the tackle.

Started his career with West Bromwich Albion, and after almost four years at the Hawthorns spent over five seasons with Sheffield Wednesday before moving across Yorkshire to join Leeds.

Form Factors

Season	Team	Tot	St	Sb	Y	R
95-96	Leeds U.	35	35	0	8	0
96-97	Leeds U.	28	26	2	10	1
97-98	Southampton	26	26	0	6	1
Total		89	87	2	24	2

	GP	GG	GF	GS	TGR
95-96	92.11	17.50	40	2	5.00
96-97	73.68	0.00	28	0	0.00
97-98	68.42	8.67	50	3	6.00
Averages	78.07	8.72	39.33	1.67	3.67

PARKER, Garry
Leicester City ❶❷ M
Fullname: Garry Stuart Parker
DOB: 07-09-65 Oxford

Seems to have been around the scene for a long time and one has to go back to the 1982-83 season for his Luton Town debut. After just over three years at Kenilworth Road he moved for a similar period to Hull City before settling down in the midlands. His first central port of call was Nottingham Forest, where he was twice successful in the Coca Cola Cup, followed by Aston Villa from whom he joined Leicester City for £300,000 in February 1995.

An excellent play-maker who can be deadly from set pieces but with each passing season his number of appearances includes a greater number as substitute.

Form Factors

Season	Team	Tot	St	Sb	Y	R
94-95	Leicester C.	14	14	0	0	0
96-97	Leicester C.	31	22	9	0	0
97-98	Leicester C.	22	15	7	1	0
Total		67	51	16	1	0

	GP	GG	GF	GS	TGR
94-95	36.84	7.00	45	2	4.44
96-97	81.58	15.50	46	2	4.35
97-98	57.89	7.33	51	3	5.88
Averages	58.77	9.94	47.33	2.33	4.89

PARKER, Scott
Charlton A. ❶❷ M
Fullname: Scott Parker
DOB: 13-10-80

Has yet to appear in the starting line-up for Charlton Athletic but is tipped to break into the first team very soon. Came off the bench for three games last season making his debut at the age of 16. Said to be a very talented midfielder, he graduated through the FA National School of Excellence at Lilleshall.

PARLOUR, Ray
Arsenal ❶❷❸❹ M
Fullname: Raymond Parlour
DOB: 07-03-73 Romford

Parlour caught the eye when he first broke into the Arsenal first team under George Graham in 1992 but it is only since the arrival of Arsène Wenger's foreign legion that he has matured into one of the top midfielders in the country. Such was his consistency last season it was almost taken for granted that he would be going to France 98 but very surprisingly Glenn Hoddle decided to omit him from the squad.

Seen as a hardworking, ball-winning midfielder Parlour has added a better touch, greater awareness and more constructive passing to his game in recent years and he also benefited from the Gunners' very potent attacking force by getting in positions to return his best figures of five goals in 34 Premiership matches. His two goals at Ewood Park in Arsenal's 4-1 defeat of Blackburn was his first ever double in a game.

Form Factors

Season	Team	Tot	St	Sb	Y	R
95-96	Arsenal	22	20	2	7	0
96-97	Arsenal	30	17	13	6	0
97-98	Arsenal	34	34	0	6	0
Total		86	71	15	19	0

	GP	GG	GF	GS	TGR
95-96	57.89	0.00	49	0	0.00
96-97	78.95	15.00	62	2	3.23
97-98	89.47	6.80	68	5	7.35
Averages	75.44	7.27	59.67	2.33	3.53

PASCOLO, Marco

Nottingham F. ❶❷❸ GK

Fullname: Marco Pascolo
DOB: Switzerland

Swiss goalkeeper whose six appearances for Nottingham Forest last season cost the club a mere £125,000 per game (wages not inclusive). Pascolo was signed from Neuchatal Xamax for £750,000 but during the warm-up for Forest's first home match of the season he injured himself and once fit could not dislodge veteran 'keeper Dave Beasant.

PEACOCK, Darren

Blackburn R. ❶❷❸ CB

Fullname: Darren Peacock
DOB: 03-02-68 Bristol

A player who has shown tremendous determination to reach the very top of his profession and has a chance to further his Premiership career following a free transfer to Blackburn in the summer of 1998. During more than three years with Newcastle, Peacock belied his perhaps ungainly appearance with a calm use of the ball and excellent timing when going in for a tackle. Reliability is one of the main characteristics of his game.

Goes into the 98-99 season just four games short of 350 league appearances, Started his career with Newport County and also played for Hereford United and QPR before moving to Tyneside. Blackburn may care to note that two of Peacock's clubs are no longer in the Football League.

Form Factors

Season	Team	Tot	St	Sb	Y	R
95-96	Newcastle U.	34	33	1	3	0
96-97	Newcastle U.	35	35	0	2	0
97-98	Newcastle U.	20	19	1	0	4
Total		89	87	2	5	4

	GP	GG	GF	GS	TGR
95-96	89.47	0.00	66	0	0.00
96-97	92.11	35.00	73	1	1.37
97-98	52.63	0.00	35	0	0.00
Averages	78.07	11.67	58.00	0.33	0.46

PEARCE, Ian
West Ham U. ❶❷❸ CB
Fullname: Ian Anthony Pearce
DOB: 07-05-74 Bury St Edmunds

A West Ham supporter in his younger days, Pearce signed for the Hammers from Blackburn for £2.3m in September 1997 and by playing in 29 of their Premiership games he had more run-outs than in any of his seven seasons with Chelsea or Blackburn. His progress at Blackburn was thwarted by foot and leg injuries but he has the potential to be a major influence on the Hammers' fortunes for years to come.

A defender who can play in attack but his tally of three goals from 95 league games will not worry too many defences unduly. Good on the ball, Pearce, at 6'4", is understandably dominant in the air and shows a willingness to get forward whenever possible.

Form Factors

Season	Team	Tot	St	Sb	Y	R
96-97	Blackburn R.	12	7	5	0	1
97-98	Blackburn R.	5	1	4	1	0
97-98	West Ham U.	30	30	0	0	1
Total		47	38	9	1	2

	GP	GG	GF	GS	TGR
96-97	31.58	0.00	42	0	0.00
97-98	13.16	0.00	57	0	0.00
97-98	78.95	30.00	56	1	1.79
Averages	41.23	10.00	51.67	0.33	0.60

PEARCE, Stuart
Newcastle U. ❶❷ FB
Fullname: Stuart Pearce
DOB: 24-04-62 Hammersmith

Going into the 1998-99 season at the age of 35, former England captain Pearce is going to face increasing challenges to his left back position at St. James's Park. But if he remains fit, and selected, he will still be an influence on Newcastle's fortunes as the club looks to improve upon its lowly Premiership position of last season and use the FA Cup run as a platform to better times.

Pearce has achieved just about everything in the game having played in England's penalty heartache defeats of '90 and '96 during his 76 international appearances. In 12 years with Nottingham Forest he played in 401 league games for the club, also made 51 league appearances for Coventry who signed him from non-league Wealdstone in October 1983.

Form Factors

Season	Team	Tot	St	Sb	Y	R
95-96	N. Forest	31	31	0	3	0
96-97	N. Forest	33	33	0	8	0
97-98	Newcastle U.	25	25	0	4	0
Total		89	89	0	15	0

	GP	GG	GF	GS	TGR
95-96	81.58	10.33	50	3	6.00
96-97	86.84	6.60	31	5	16.13
97-98	65.79	0.00	35	0	0.00
Averages	78.07	5.64	38.67	2.67	7.38

PEDERSEN, Per

Blackburn Rovers ❶ S

Fullname: Per Pedersen
DOB: 30-03-69 Aalberg, Norway

A £2.4m signing from Odense in February 1997, Danish international striker Pedersen has made little impact at Ewood Park thus far with just 11 Premiership appearances under his belt, all of which came during the 1996-97 season. Last season his first team outings were restricted to just two games in the Coca Cola Cup.

Was expected to make greater in-roads under Roy Hodgson's leadership but his opportunities do look somewhat limited.

Form Factors

Season	Team	Tot	St	Sb	Y	R
96-97	Blackburn R.	11	6	5	0	0
Totals		11	6	5	0	0

	GP	GG	GF	GS	TGR
96-97	28.95	0	42	0	0.00
Averages	28.95	0	42	0	0.00

PEDERSEN, Tore

Blackburn R. ❶ D

Fullname: Tore Pedersen
DOB: 29-09-69 Fredrikstad

Signed for Blackburn Rovers in September 1997 from German side St. Pauli for £500,000 but Rovers fans saw little for the club's investment with Pedersen making a mere eight league and cup appearances. The defender arrived at Ewood Park with a good pedigree having played in excess of 40 games for his native Norway.

Form Factors

Season	Team	Tot	St	Sb	Y	R
97-98	Blackburn R.	5	3	2	0	0
Total		5	3	2	0	0

	GP	GG	GF	GS	TGR
97-98	13.16	0.00	57	0	0.00
Averages	13.16	0.00	57.00	0.00	0.00

PEMBRIDGE, Mark

Sheffield W. ❶❷❸ M

Fullname: Mark Anthony Pembridge
DOB: 29-11-70 Merthyr Tydfil

Was signed by former Sheffield Wednesday boss David Pleat who knew

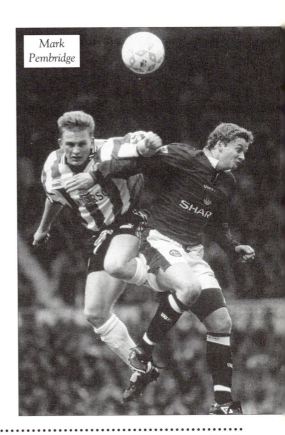

Mark Pembridge

the player well from a spell together at Luton Town. In between times Pembridge played for Derby County from where he joined Wednesday for £900,000 in July 1995. Has appeared in a high percentage of the Owls' Premiership matches since moving to Hillsborough and has missed just 10 games over the past two seasons although he was substituted in 15 of his 31 games last season.

Competitive Welsh international who plays on the left side of midfield and can be relied upon to knock in a goodly number of goals each season as his career total of 45 league goals testifies.

Form Factors

Season	Team	Tot	St	Sb	Y	R
95-96	Sheffield W.	25	24	1	0	9
96-97	Sheffield W.	34	33	1	7	0
97-98	Sheffield W.	34	31	3	4	0
Total		93	88	5	11	9

	GP	GG	GF	GS	TGR
95-96	65.79	12.50	48	2	4.17
96-97	89.47	5.67	50	6	12.00
97-98	89.47	8.50	52	4	7.69
Averages	81.58	8.89	50.00	4.00	7.95

PEREZ, Sebastien

Blackburn Rovers ❶❷ M

Fullname: Sebastien Perez
DOB: 24-11-73, Bastia, France

A versatile midfield player whose hard tackling style means he is also at home in defence. Started his career at St Etienne before moving to play for Bastia. Perez didn't make the final cut into the French World Cup squad. Roy Hodgson signed the player on a five-year deal which should provide Perez with enough time to prove his worth.

PERRY, Chris

Wimbledon ❶❷❸ CB

Fullname: Christopher John Perry
DOB: 26-04-73 Carshalton, Surrey

Has been the bedrock of the Wimbledon defence over the past three seasons during which time he has steered clear of injury and missed just three games. Possibly the shortest central defender in the top flight, he is nonetheless excellent when going for headers and is very swift in the tackle. Also has the ability to read situations quickly.

Scored one goal in the Premier League last season to double his career total and had the misfortune to score at Derby in the match which was abandoned due to floodlight failure.

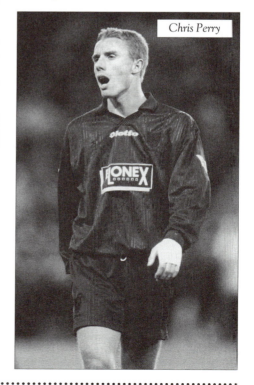

Chris Perry

Form Factors

Season	Team	Tot	St	Sb	Y	R
95-96	Wimbledon	37	36	1	8	0
96-97	Wimbledon	37	37	0	0	0
97-98	Wimbledon	35	35	0	7	0
Total		109	108	1	15	0

	GP	GG	GF	GS	TGR
95-96	97.37	0.00	55	0	0.00
96-97	97.37	37.00	49	1	2.04
97-98	92.11	35.00	34	1	2.94
Averages	95.61	24.00	46.00	0.67	1.66

PETIT, Emmanuel
Arsenal ❶❷❸❹ M

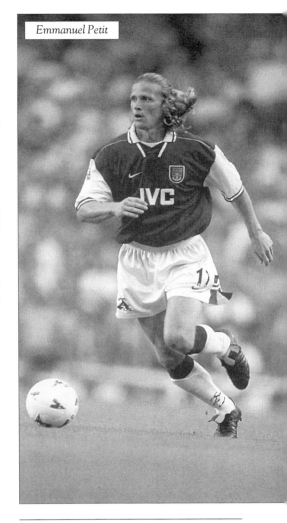

Emmanuel Petit

Fullname: Emmanuel Petit
DOB: 22-09-70 Dieppe, France

That a great deal of Arsenal's dominance of the Premiership last season was down to the £5m signing of brilliant French midfielder Petit only added to the frustration of neighbours Tottenham as the player had talks with them just hours before pledging his future to Highbury.

In Petit, Arsène Wenger again demonstrated his knowledge of the game as he brought another overseas player of whom little was known in this country – although they worked together at Monaco – but is now acknowledged as a hugely influential player on the pitch and a deep thinker off it. A good ball-winner who fills in just ahead of the defence, links well with the attack and proved himself on the world's biggest stage during the 1998 World Cup Final not only by the quality of his performances but also with his excellent goal in the final minute of the Final itself to clinch a place in history as France beat Brazil 3-0.

Form Factors

Season	Team	Tot	St	Sb	Y	R
97-98	Arsenal	32	32	0	4	1
Total		32	32	0	4	1

	GP	GG	GF	GS	TGR
97-98	84.21	16.00	68	2	2.94
Averages	84.21	16.00	68.00	2.00	2.94

PETRESCU, Dan
Chelsea ❶❷❸❹ FB
Fullname: Dan Vasile Petrescu
DOB: 22-12-67 Bucharest, Romania

Like his teammate in the Romanian national side, Viorel Moldovan, Petrescu showed a distinct lack of gratitude to those who have employed him for the past four years as he shrugged aside his Chelsea teammate Graeme Le Saux to score his country's last minute World Cup winner against England in France 98.

The goal was also somewhat out of character for the excellent right-sided wing-back who has found the back of the net just 13 times in 126 Premiership matches for Sheffield Wednesday and Chelsea.

He has settled well at Stamford Bridge with his £2.3m move in November 1995 ending a far from happy time at Hillsborough. Such is his importance to Chelsea now that only two other players made more Premiership appearances for the Blues last season than Petrescu.

Form Factors

Season	Team	Tot	St	Sb	Y	R
95-96	Chelsea	24	22	2	3	0
96-97	Chelsea	34	34	0	4	0
97-98	Chelsea	31	31	0	3	0
Total		89	87	2	10	0

	GP	GG	GF	GS	TGR
95-96	63.16	12.00	46	2	4.35
96-97	89.47	11.33	58	3	5.17
97-98	81.58	6.20	71	5	7.04
Averages	78.07	9.84	58.33	3.33	5.52

PETTERSON, Andy
Charlton A. ❶❷ GK
Fullname: Andrew Keith Petterson
DOB: 26-09-69 Fremantle, Australia

Has endured a stop-start career during six years with Luton Town and four years with Charlton Athletic. During his time with both clubs the Australian goalkeeper has done a fair amount of sight-seeing with loan periods at Swindon Town, Ipswich Town, Bradford City, Plymouth Argyle and Colchester United.

Petterson made a shaky start to his career at the Valley before establishing himself sufficiently to win the 1996-97 Player of the Year award. He began the Addicks' promotion season as first choice, was displaced, returned again but ultimately lost out to Sasa Ilic and goes into the new season back down the pecking order.

PISTONE, Alessandro
Newcastle U. ❶❷ D
Fullname:
DOB: 27-07-75 Milan, Italy

The 1997-98 season was his first in the Premiership following a £4.3m transfer from Internazionale in July 1997. Played at Wembley with the Geordies in the FA Cup final but had a dismal afternoon with a poor personal performance.

Predominantly a left-back he can fill other positions and is seen by some as a possible contender for a call up to the full Italian squad, having previously won caps at Under-21.

Form Factors

Season	Team	Tot	St	Sb	Y	R
97-98	Newcastle U.	28	28	0	6	0
Total		28	28	0	6	0

	GP	GG	GF	GS	TGR
97-98	73.68	0.00	35	0	0.00
Averages	73.68	0.00	35.00	0.00	0.00

POOM, Mart
Derby County ❶❷❸ GK

Fullname: Mart Poom
DOB: 03-02-72 Tallinn, Estonia

Since making his Derby County debut in a memorable 3-2 win over Manchester United at Old Trafford, Estonian goalkeeper Poom has firmly established himself as the Rams' number one. Missed just two Premiership matches last season, conceded 47 goals in his 36 games at an average of 1.30 per game – a marked improvement on the 58 league goals let in by the Rams the previous season.

Cost Derby a £500,000 transfer fee from FC Flora Tallinn but was one of the guilty Estonian players not at Tallinn when they were supposed to be facing Scotland in a World Cup qualifying match.

Mart Poom

Form Factors

Season	Team	Tot	St	Sb	Y	R
96-97	Derby Co.	4	4	0	0	0
97-98	Derby Co.	36	36	0	2	0
Total		40	40	0	2	0

	GA	GkA	GAp	CS	SO	R
96-97	58	7	1.75	0	0	
97-98	49	47	1.31	13	3	0
Averages	53.5	27.0	1.53	6.5	1.5	0

POTTS, Steve
West Ham U. ❶❷❸ CB

Fullname: Steven John Potts
DOB: 07-05-67 Hartford, USA

Longest-serving player currently on West Ham's books, Potts made his debut on 1 January 1985 and has since played 355 league games for the Hammers, 23 of which were last season – his testimonial year. Very useful player to have in any squad due to his versatility, he is happiest at right back but has also been used effectively in the middle of the defence and the midfield.

Despite being born in the States he won England Youth caps earlier in his career. If you decide to have him your squad don't look for his name on the scoresheet – his one and only goal in the league was against Hull City in October 1990.

Form Factors

Season	Team	Tot	St	Sb	Y	R
95-96	West Ham U.	34	34	0	3	0
96-97	West Ham U.	20	17	3	2	0
97-98	West Ham U.	23	14	9	2	0
Total		77	65	12	7	0

	GP	GG	GF	GS	TGR
95-96	89.47	0.00	43	0	0.00
96-97	52.63	0.00	39	0	0.00
97-98	60.53	0.00	56	0	0.00
Averages	67.54	0.00	46.00	0.00	0.00

POWELL, Chris

Charlton A.   ❶ FB

Fullname: Christopher George Robin Powell
DOB: 08-09-69 Lambeth

Given the frequency with which the promoted clubs swiftly return to the Nationwide League, the signing of Powell by Charlton Athletic boss Alan Curbishley looks a shrewd move in an attempt to bring experience to a side not familiar with the Premiership. Sound with either foot Powell missed just five Premiership games during his two full seasons with Derby County and was booked only a reasonable seven times during that time. Last season he finally ended a five year wait since his last Premiership goal.

Is now back closer to his birthplace having started his career with Crystal Palace before going on loan to Aldershot and then almost six years at Southend United before joining Derby where he won the Player of the Year award two seasons ago.

Form Factors

Season	Team	Tot	St	Sb	Y	R
96-97	Derby Co.	35	35	0	4	0
97-98	Derby Co.	36	34	2	3	0
Total		71	69	2	7	0

	GP	GG	GF	GS	TGR
96-97	92.11	0.00	45	0	0.00
97-98	94.74	36.00	52	1	1.92
Averages	93.42	18.00	48.50	0.50	0.96

POWELL, Darryl

Derby County   ❶❷❸ M

Fullname: Darryl Anthony Powell
DOB: 15-11-71 Lambeth

Has been used mainly in the centre of the Derby County midfield over the past two seasons but is very much an all-rounder with his passing ability and determination in the tackle making him ideal for any situation. In addition to midfield, he has served his various clubs in defence and attack and possesses one of the most cultured left feet in the Premiership.

Scored five times during his first season with Derby, the same total for each of his final two seasons with Portsmouth, but has scored just once, against Arsenal, in the past two years.

Cost Derby £750,000 when he decided to leave Pompey after seven years at Fratton Park.

Form Factors

Season	Team	Tot	St	Sb	Y	R
96-97	Derby Co.	33	27	6	7	0
97-98	Derby Co.	24	13	11	4	0
Total		57	40	17	11	0

	GP	GG	GF	GS	TGR
96-97	86.84	33.00	45	1	2.22
97-98	63.16	0.00	52	0	0.00
Averages	75.00	16.50	48.50	0.50	1.11

POYET, Gustavo
Chelsea   ❶❷❸ M

Fullname: Gustavo Poyet
DOB: 15-11-67 Montevideo, Uruguay

Despite the country of his origin, Poyet signed for Chelsea in the close season of 1997 from Spanish side Real Zaragoza where he had been for seven years. During that time he was in the Zaragoza side which defeated Chelsea in the semi final of the Cup Winners' Cup.

His first season at Stamford Bridge was not overly successful with the Uruguayan international midfielder only getting 14 Premiership run-outs during which time he scored four times. Given Chelsea's large and even growing international squad it is difficult to see Poyet being handed an improved number of chances this time round.

Form Factors

Season	Team	Tot	St	Sb	Y	R
97-98	Chelsea	14	11	3	2	0
Total		14	11	3	2	0

	GP	GG	GF	GS	TGR
97-98	36.84	3.50	71	4	5.63
Averages	36.84	3.50	71.00	4.00	5.63

PRESSMAN, Kevin
Sheffield W.   ❶❷❸❹ GK

Fullname: Kevin Paul Pressman
DOB: 06-11-67 Fareham

Missed just two games in the Premiership during 1997-98 and with eight clean sheets took his overall total in the top flight to 42 in 173 games. His goals conceded per game last season of 1.66 was well above his previous average of 1.40. Nonetheless he was called into one of Glenn Hoddle's England squads but didn't make the trip to France. In Sheffield Wednesday's two league games without Pressman the Owls conceded seven goals.

Kevin Pressman

Fantasy Football Handbook 1998/99 — **267**

The '97-98 campaign was the 10th anniversary of his Football League debut during which time he has had to overcome challenges from the likes of Chris Woods, Martin Hodge and Chris Turner. He also had a brief loan spell with Stoke City. Although he has never scored in open play, the left-footed Pressman has twice scored in penalty shoot-outs – surely a good enough reason for an England call-up.

Form Factors

Season	Team	Tot	St	Sb	Y	R
95-96	Sheffield W.	30	30	0	0	0
96-97	Sheffield W.	38	38	0	0	0
97-98	Sheffield W.	36	36	0	0	0
Total		104	104	0	0	0

	GA	GkA	GAp	CS	SO	R
95-96	61	48	1.60	6	1	0
96-97	51	50	1.32	10	2	2
97-98	67	60	1.67	7	2	1
Averages	59.67	52.67	1.53	7.67	1.67	1.0

PRIOR, Spencer
Leicester City ❶❷❸ CB

Fullname: Spencer Justin Prior
DOB: 22-04-71 Hockley

Has proved an excellent signing by manager Martin O'Neill who returned to one of his former clubs, Norwich City, to sign the dependable defender for £600,000 at the end of the 1995-96. Left Carrow Road on a high by collecting the Player of the Year trophy and produced his best form for the following season's Coca Cola Cup final matches with Middlesbrough. Finished last season in some discomfort after receiving three broken ribs during a 3-3 draw with Southampton.

Good on the ground and in the air but don't expect him to get you many goals as he has scored just once in 138 games for Leicester and Norwich but did bag three in 135 league games for Southend United.

Form Factors

Season	Team	Tot	St	Sb	Y	R
94-95	Norwich C.	17	12	5	2	0
96-97	Leicester C.	34	33	1	4	0
97-98	Leicester C.	30	28	2	2	0
Total		81	73	8	8	0

	GP	GG	GF	GS	TGR
94-95	44.74	0.00	37	0	0.00
96-97	89.47	0.00	46	0	0.00
97-98	78.95	0.00	51	0	0.00
Averages	71.05	0.00	44.67	0.00	0.00

RADEBE, Lucas
Leeds United ❶❷❸ CB

Fullname: Lucas Radebe
DOB: 12-04-69 Johannesburg, SA

Central defender who has been in superb form over the past couple of years with his consistency being recognised by his homeland when selecting him as captain for all three of South Africa's matches in France 98. Unfortunately was booked twice in those three games which makes poor reading when added to 10 yellow cards collected in the English domestic game last season.

Quick in the tackle and excellent at man-marking, Radebe is a class defender whose form over the past two years has coincided with Leeds' fine defensive record.

Joined Leeds from Kaiser Chiefs at a bargain price of £250,000 in August 1994 but had to overcome serious injuries before fully establishing himself at Elland Road.

Form Factors

Season	Team	Tot	St	Sb	Y	R
95-96	Leeds U.	13	10	3	2	0
96-97	Leeds U.	32	28	4	6	0
97-98	Leeds U.	27	26	1	10	1
Total		72	64	8	18	1

	GP	GG	GF	GS	TGR
95-96	34.21	0.00	40	0	0.00
96-97	84.21	0.00	28	0	0.00
97-98	71.05	0.00	57	0	0.00
Averages	63.16	0.00	41.67	0.00	0.00

REDFEARN, Neil
Charlton A. ❶❷❸ M

Fullname: Neil David Redfearn
DOB: 20-06-65 Dewsbury

Despite Barnsley's immediate relegation from the Premiership back to Division One last season, Neil Redfearn was one of the players of the season, particularly in fantasy football terms. It was no real surprise then when he was given the opportunity to stay in the top flight – Charlton Athletic splashing out £1 million for his services.

A captain who leads by example, he started his career as a junior at Nottingham Forest and having been released, did the rounds of a variety of clubs including Bolton, Lincoln, Doncaster, Crystal Palace, Watford and Oldham before signing for the Tykes in the summer of 1991. He should play his 700th senior game during the 1998-99 season.

Form Factors

Season	Team	Tot	St	Sb	Y	R
97-98	Barnsley	37	37	0	2	0
Total		37	37	0	2	0

	GP	GG	GF	GS	TGR
97-98	97.37	3.70	37	10	27.03
Averages	97.37	3.70	37.00	10.00	27.03

REDKNAPP, Jamie
Liverpool ❶❷❸❹ M

Fullname: Jamie Frank Redknapp
DOB: 25-06-73 Barton on Sea

Top quality midfield player who has been dogged by various injuries in

Jamie Redknapp

Fantasy Football Handbook 1998/99   **269**

recent years, the latest of which kept him out of France 98. Injury also restricted his appearances in Euro 96. When fully fit Redknapp should quickly re-establish himself not only with Liverpool but also with England, his precise passing and pinpoint accuracy from dead-ball situations marking him down as one of the most creative midfielders in the Premiership. Can be relied upon to score around four goals a season.

Moved to Liverpool in a £350,000 deal in January 1991 after just 13 league games for Bournemouth.

Form Factors

Season	Team	Tot	St	Sb	Y	R
95-96	Liverpool	23	19	4	1	0
96-97	Liverpool	23	18	5	0	0
97-98	Liverpool	20	20	0	3	0
Total		66	57	9	4	0

	GP	GG	GF	GS	TGR
95-96	60.53	7.67	70	3	4.29
96-97	60.53	7.67	62	3	4.84
97-98	52.63	6.67	68	3	4.41
Averages	57.89	7.33	66.67	3.00	4.51

RIBEIRO, Bruno
Leeds United ❶❷❸ M

Fullname: Bruno Ribeiro
DOB: 22-10-75 Setubal, Portugal

Enjoyed an excellent first ten months with Leeds United last season following a £500,000 transfer from Portuguese club Vitoria Setubal. Not the tallest of midfield players standing at only 5'7" he nonetheless hits the ball with great power with his left leg and has the ability to step up from being an Under-21 international with Portugal to the full side.

Scored three times in 29 Premiership games last season and don't be surprised to see him improve upon that tally this time round.

Form Factors

Season	Team	Tot	St	Sb	Y	R
97-98	Leeds U.	29	28	1	1	0
Total		29	28	1	1	0

	GP	GG	GF	GS	TGR
97-98	76.32	9.67	57	3	5.26
Averages	76.32	9.67	57.00	3.00	5.26

RIEDLE, Karl Heinz
Liverpool ❶❷❸ S

Fullname: Karl Heinz Riedle
DOB: 16-09-65 Weiler, Germany

Striker with a string of the game's highest honours locked away in his personal trophy cabinet. Won three Bundesliga championships, scored twice in the final of the European Cup in 1997 as Borussia Dortmund beat Juventus 3-1 in Munich, made two appearances for Germany in USA 94 and four appearances in the previous World Cup with West Germany but did not feature in the final.

His first season at Anfield, following a £1.75m transfer from Dortmund, did not quite match what has gone before as he started in just 18 Premiership games and was taken off in nine of those games. Unlikely that he will be more involved this season.

Form Factors

Season	Team	Tot	St	Sb	Y	R
97-98	Liverpool	25	18	7	1	0
Total		25	18	7	1	0

	GP	GG	GF	GS	TGR
97-98	65.79	4.17	68	6	8.82
Averages	65.79	4.17	68.00	6.00	8.82

RIPLEY, Stuart

Southampton ❶❷❸ M
Fullname: Stuart Edward Ripley
DOB: 20-11-67 Middlesbrough

One of the stars of Blackburn Rovers' 1995 championship winning side, Ripley ended his six year association with the Lancashire club with a move to Southampton in July 1998. The Saints have acquired a player who has been one of the best wide men in the top flight in recent years and won a couple of England call-ups in that time.

They will hope that he is over the injury problems which blighted his final couple of years at Ewood Park and will build on the three Premiership goals scored last season – his first since the 1993-94 season. Began his career with eight years at Middlesbrough.

Form Factors

Season	Team	Tot	St	Sb	Y	R
95-96	Blackburn R.	28	28	0	1	0
96-97	Blackburn R.	13	5	8	0	0
97-98	Blackburn R.	29	25	4	0	0
Total		70	58	12	1	0

	GP	GG	GF	GS	TGR
95-96	73.68	0.00	61	0	0.00
96-97	34.21	0.00	42	0	0.00
97-98	76.32	14.50	57	2	3.51
Averages	61.40	4.83	53.33	0.67	1.17

ROBERTS, Andy

Wimbledon ❶❷ M/D
Fullname: Andrew James Roberts
DOB: 20-03-74 Dartford

Became Wimbledon's second most expensive capture when switching from the Crystal Palace side of the Selhurst Park dressing room to join Wimbledon in a £1.6m deal in March 1998. Highly skilled midfielder who has also played plenty of times as sweeper and was a leading player in Palace's rise to the Premiership. Unflappable on the ball, he likes to get forward and usually chips in with a couple of goals each season. Scored once in his 12 games for Wimbledon towards the end of last season.

Form Factors

Season	Team	Tot	St	Sb	Y	R
97-98	C. Palace	25	25	0	5	0
97-98	Wimbledon	12	12	0	3	0
Total		37	37	0	8	0

	GP	GG	GF	GS	TGR
97-98	65.79	0.00	37	0	0.00
97-98	31.58	12.00	34	1	2.94
Averages	48.68	6.00	35.50	0.50	1.47

ROBERTS, Ben
Middlesbrough ❶❷ GK

Fullname: Benjamin James Roberts
DOB: 22-06-75 Bishop Auckland

Goalkeeper who has had to wait patiently at the Riverside for his chance to shine. Was given nine run-outs in the Nationwide League last season having made 10 first team appearances the previous year. His League experience came during a spell on loan to Hartlepool United and has subsequently been followed by loan spells with Wycombe Wanderers and Bradford City. Signed professional terms with Middlesbrough in March 1991 and has since represented England at Under-21.

ROBERTSON, David
Leeds United ❶❷❸ FB

Fullname: David Robertson
DOB: 17-10-68 Aberdeen

Although Robertson played 26 times for Leeds United in the Premiership last season, his first since transferring from Rangers for £500,000, it was not a season without its problems. Asked to play in a different position from the one he was used to, Robertson took time to find his form and once he had discovered his touch he picked up an injury, and given George Graham's summer signings he may indeed have a tough task in re-establishing himself at Elland Road.
 Was involved in a bizarre dispute with Scotland coach Craig Brown which culminated in the wing-back cum- full-back rejecting the opportunity of being involved in the Scotland France 98 squad.

Form Factors

Season	Team	Tot	St	Sb	Y	R
97-98	Leeds U.	26	24	2	0	0
Total		26	24	2	0	0

	GP	GG	GF	GS	TGR
97-98	68.42	0.00	57	0	0.00
Averages	68.42	0.00	57.00	0.00	0.00

ROBINSON, John
Charlton A. ❶❷ S

Fullname: John Robert Campbell Robinson
DOB: 29-08-71 Bulawayo, Zimbabwe

One of the few, in-fact probably only, Welsh international wingers to have been born in Zimbabwe, Robinson has become a firm favourite at Charlton Athletic after a start which was none too promising. Having taken time to find his best form he went on to win the 1995-96 Player of the Year award and over the past three seasons has missed only 14 of the Addicks 138 league games.
 A winger with sound crossing ability who favours his right foot, he can play on either flank as an out-and-out winger, or at wing-back and has also covered as full-back during an injury crisis.
 Has found the target 23 times in 187 league games for Charlton and six times in 62 games for his former club Brighton & Hove Albion.

ROGERS, Alan
Nottingham F. ❶❷❸D

Fullname: Alan Rogers
DOB: 03-01-77 Liverpool

Replacing Stuart Pearce is probably not the most welcoming challenge in the world but former Tranmere Rovers left-back Rogers rose to the task superbly at the City Ground last season following his £2m summer move from Prenton Park. A natural defender he also goes forward well and has proved himself capable of adding to Forest's attacking prowess with good crosses from the left flank.

Played 57 league games in two years at Tranmere and topped Forest's appearance chart last season with exactly 50 games under his belt.

ROWETT, Gary
Derby County ❶❷❸CB

Fullname: Gary Rowett
DOB: 06-03-74 Bromsgrove

Rowett's days in the Premiership looked set to be brief when he made little impression at Everton following a £200,000 move to Goodison Park from Cambridge United in May 1994. He left the Blues 14 months later, at an increased fee of £300,000, and has since blossomed into an outstanding defender who is equally adept playing down the right or as sweeper.

Played 35 times in the Derby side which won promotion in 1996 and has missed only three games during each of the Rams' two campaigns at the summit of British football. Has scored one league goal for the past two seasons which are his only goals since leaving Cambridge.

Form Factors

Season	Team	Tot	St	Sb	Y	R
94-95	Everton	2	2	0	0	0
96-97	Derby Co.	35	35	0	2	6
97-98	Derby Co.	34	32	2	3	0
Total		71	69	2	5	6

	GP	GG	GF	GS	TGR
94-95	5.26	0.00	44	0	0.00
96-97	92.11	17.50	45	2	4.44
97-98	89.47	34.00	52	1	1.92
Averages	62.28	17.17	47.00	1.00	2.12

RUDI, Petter
Sheffield W. ❶❷❸M

Fullname: Petter Rudi
DOB: 17-09-73 Norway

Norwegian international who made a big impression on Sheffield Wednesday supporters following his £800,000 move to Hillsborough from Molde in October 1997. Played 22 times in the Premiership last season, has yet to score but is quick and is seen more as a provider for others. Injury ruled him out for the whole of March but if he stays fit this season then he is almost certain to be a regular in the Owls' midfield.

Form Factors

Season	Team	Tot	St	Sb	Y	R
97-98	Sheffield W.	22	19	3	2	0
Total		22	19	3	2	0

	GP	GG	GF	GS	TGR
97-98	57.89	0.00	52	0	0.00
Averages	57.89	0.00	52.00	0.00	0.00

RUFUS, Richard
Charlton A. ❶❷❸ D
Fullname: Richard Raymond Rufus
DOB: 12-01-75 Lewisham

Local-born central defender who came into the side at 19 and was immediately a regular. Former Charlton youth player who has captained the England Under-21 side and on a few occasions carried out that role at club level. Has been very impressive in his four seasons with Charlton and over the next ten months or so faces the biggest challenge of his career to date.

Possesses everything needed to make a success of his time in the Premiership although he is sometimes criticised for wayward distribution. That aside, he is quick to recover lost ground, powerful in the air, a good reader of the play and impressive when tackling.

SAIB, Moussa
Tottenham H. ❶❷❸ M
Fullname: Moussa Saib
DOB: 05-03-69 Theniet-el-Had, Algeria

Technically gifted midfield player who made his debut for Tottenham in March after a £2.3 transfer from Valencia where he played just 14 games during a brief and unsuccessful spell. Was more impressive when scoring 24 times in 144 games for Auxerre the club he left to join Valencia. The rest of his background is equally impressive with success in the African Nations Cup, African League and Cup and the French League and Cup.

Although he made just three starts last season for Spurs, and was taken off in one of those games, he did make six other appearances from the bench, and he is tipped to be one of the star players at White Hart Lane this season. Has one Tottenham goal to his credit, which came during the 6-2 win at Wimbledon.

Form Factors

Season	Team	Tot	St	Sb	Y	R
97-98	Tottenham H.	8	2	6	0	0
Total		8	2	6	0	0

	GP	GG	GF	GS	TGR
97-98	21.05	8.00	44	1	2.27
Averages	21.05	8.00	44.00	1.00	2.27

SAVAGE, Robbie

Leicester City ❶❷❸ M

Fullname: Robert William Savage
DOB: 18-10-74 Wrexham

Robbie Savage

Once a member of one of Manchester United's successful youth sides, Savage made his breakthrough into the Football League with Crewe Alexandra. Scored 10 times in 77 league games for Crewe which persuaded Leicester City to snap him up for £400,000 in time for the 1997-98 season. Crewe transformed him from a forward into a midfield player to great effect. Scored just a couple of times last season and now that he has a season's Premier League experience behind him, one would look for him to use his 6'2" height to maximum advantage and improve upon that tally.

Form Factors

Season	Team	Tot	St	Sb	Y	R
97-98	Leicester C.	35	28	7	4	0
Total		35	28	7	4	0

	GP	GG	GF	GS	TGR
97-98	92.11	17.50	51	2	3.92
Averages	92.11	17.50	51.00	2.00	3.92

SCALES, John

Tottenham H. ❶❷ CB

Fullname: John Robert Scales
DOB: 04-07-66 Harrogate

Since joining Spurs in December 1996 from Liverpool for £2.6m, England defender Scales had suffered wretched ill-fortune culminating last season in a muscle virus which made him available for just a dozen games, taking his 18 month record with the club to a miserable 24 appearances.

His misfortune is, perhaps, in-keeping with Spurs' own fortunes as his undoubted skills in reading the game, quickness off the mark, good heading ability and fine close control would have gone some way towards easing the club's problems.

But even if now fit Scales faces further problems with the club's summer signings which include Italian defender Paolo Tramezzani.

Fantasy Football Handbook 1998/99

Form Factors

Season	Team	Tot	St	Sb	Y	R
96-97	Liverpool	3	3	0	0	0
96-97	Tottenham H.	12	10	2	0	0
97-98	Tottenham H.	10	9	1	0	1
Total		25	22	3	0	1

	GP	GG	GF	GS	TGR
96-97	7.89	0.00	62	0	0.00
96-97	31.58	0.00	44	0	0.00
97-98	26.32	0.00	44	0	0.00
Averages	21.93	0.00	50.00	0.00	0.00

SCHMEICHEL, Peter

Manchester U. ❶❷❸❹ GK

Fullname: Peter Boleslaw Schmeichel
DOB: 18-11-68 Gladsaxe, Denmark

Frequently touted as the best goalkeeper in the world and the statistics of his career in the Premiership go a long way towards supporting that claim. Kept 16 clean sheets in the league last season and completed the first five games of the season without conceding a single goal which equalled his previous best run. His total of 104 shut-outs is far and away a Premiership record and comes from just 219 games.

He has conceded a miserly 184 goals in those 219 games, giving him a remarkable average of 0.84 goals let in per game.

Schmeichel is almost unique in the way he dominates his penalty area, spreads himself when in eyeball contact with an oncoming striker, the way he launches attacks with long distance throw outs and the vociferous 'advice' he offers to his defence; his methods may be unorthodox but the results speak for themselves.

Played in all of Denmark's games in France 98 and will continue to dominate the domestic scene for many years to come.

Peter Schmeichel

Form Factors

Season	Team	Tot	St	Sb	Y	R
95-96	Manchester U.	36	36	0	1	0
96-97	Manchester U.	36	36	0	2	0
97-98	Manchester U.	32	32	0	0	0
Total		104	104	0	3	0

	GA	GkA	GAp	CS	SO	R
95-96	35	30	0.83	18	4	0
96-97	44	42	1.17	13	4	0
97-98	26	24	0.71	17	5	0
Averages	35.0	32.0	0.90	16.0	4.33	0

SCHNOOR, Stefan
Derby County ❶❷ D

Fullname: Stefan Schnoor
DOB: 18-4-71, Germany

A regular in the Hamburg side, Schnoor can play anywhere in defence or in a defensive midfield role. He was signed on a free transfer by Jim Smith courtesy of the Bosman ruling.

With Chris Powell having joined Charlton Athletic just days before Schnoor's signing, he could be in the manager's mind as a starting full-back.

SCHOLES, Paul
Manchester U. ❶❷❸❹ M/S

Fullname: Paul Scholes
DOB: 16-11-74 Salford

Seen as a striker in his younger days, Scholes has developed more into a midfield player who likes to push on. Had to be patient after first joining United but since claiming a place in the starting XI has gone from strength to strength. A hardworking, though not pacy, midfielder, he always makes himself available to whoever is in possession and is a tremendous team player. Only scored three times in the Premiership for Manchester United in 1996-97 but was back to his best in front of goal last season with nine league and cup goals to his credit.

Performed solidly rather than spectacularly in all of England's France 98 matches, scored an excellent goal against Tunisia, but also showed an unnecessary willingness to go down whenever in the penalty area. Still, it could earn your fantasy team points from possible penalties if you include one of his teammates in your side to take the spot-kicks.

Form Factors

Season	Team	Tot	St	Sb	Y	R
95-96	Manchester U.	26	16	10	2	0
96-97	Manchester U.	24	16	8	6	0
97-98	Manchester U.	31	28	3	7	0
Total		81	60	21	15	0

	GP	GG	GF	GS	TGR
95-96	68.42	2.60	73	10	13.70
96-97	63.16	8.00	76	3	3.95
97-98	81.58	3.88	73	8	10.96
Averages	71.05	4.83	74.00	7.00	9.53

SCHWARZER, Mark
Middlesbrough ❶❷❸ GK

Fullname: Mark Schwarzer
DOB: 06-10-72 Sydney

With Middlesbrough's promotion to the Premiership Schwarzer has become one of two Australian international goalkeepers currently plying their trade at the top level of English football. He arrived in this country from German Bundesliga side Kaiserslautern to join Bradford City for £350,000 in November 1996. Quite remarkably, just three months and 13 games later he was on his way to Middlesbrough in a deal worth £1.5m. Only managed seven appearances for Boro that season but last season he firmly established himself as number one at the Riverside with 42 appearances.

Started his career with Aussie side Marconi Sydney before trying his hand in Europe with Dynamo Dresden.

Mark Schwarzer

SCIMECA, Ricky

Aston Villa ❶❷ CB

Fullname: Riccardo Scimeca
DOB: 13-08-75 Leamington

An England Under-21 international, his parents are Italian. Scimeca has made steady progress with Aston Villa over the past three seasons with the 1997-98 campaign being his most successful to date. For the first time he appeared in more than half of Villa's Premiership games and enjoyed a run 10 successive starts which included games in the league, UEFA Cup and Coca Cola Cup.

Has shown himself to be a versatile player who can score goals from midfield although many feel that central defender is his best position. Definitely worth keeping an eye on.

Form Factors

Season	Team	Tot	St	Sb	Y	R
95-96	Aston Villa	17	7	10	1	0
96-97	Aston Villa	17	11	6	1	0
97-98	Aston Villa	21	16	5	0	0
Total		55	34	21	2	0

Season	GP	GG	GF	GS	TGR
95-96	44.74	0.00	52	0	0.00
96-97	44.74	0.00	47	0	0.00
97-98	55.26	0.00	49	0	0.00
Averages	48.25	0.00	49.33	0.00	0.00

Form Factors

Season	Team	Tot	St	Sb	Y	R
96-97	Middlesbrough	7	7	0	0	0
Total		7	7	0	0	0

Season	GA	GkA	GAp	CS	SO	R
96-97	60	7	1.00	2	1	1
Averages	60	7	1.00	2	1	1

SEAMAN, David

Arsenal ❶❷❸❹ GK

Fullname: David Andrew Seaman
DOB: 19-09-63 Rotherham

Without question England's Number One and despite his 35th birthday early in the new season is set to remain as Glenn Hoddle's first choice keeper for sometime to come. Last season saw Seaman win the championship and FA Cup for a second time during his eight years at Arsenal. Has also collected Cup Winners' Cup and League Cup winners medals with the Gunners and appeared in a losing Cup Winners' Cup final.

England's keeper during Euro 96 and this summer's World Cup, he dominates his penalty area with superb handling at crosses. Quick reflexes, good shot stopper, good long kicks and throws, the Yorkshireman has everything and during his eight years at Highbury has had the added bonus of playing behind one of the most stable and top quality defences in English football history.

Kept 13 clean sheets in 31 Premiership appearances last season, taking his Premiership total to 86 in exactly 200 games. Conceded less than a goal a game, taking his Premiership total with the Gunners to 165 at 0.82 per game.

Form Factors

Season	Team	Tot	St	Sb	Y	R
95-96	Arsenal	38	38	0	0	0
96-97	Arsenal	22	22	0	0	0
97-98	Arsenal	31	31	0	1	0
Total		91	91	0	1	0

	GA	GkA	GAp	CS	SO	R
95-96	32	32	0.84	16	2	4
96-97	32	15	0.68	10	5	0
97-98	33	29	1.07	13	4	0
Averages	32.3	25.3	0.86	13.0	3.67	1.33

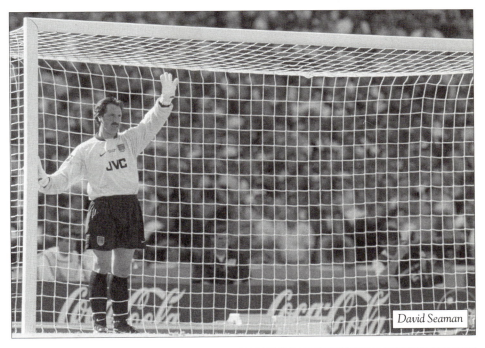
David Seaman

Fantasy Football Handbook 1998/99

SEDLOSKI, Goce
Sheffield W. ①② D
Fullname:
DOB: 10-04-74 Macedonia

A Macedonian international defender who joined Sheffield Wednesday from Hadjuk Split for an initial fee of £750,000 in February 1998. The then Wednesday manager Ron Atkinson had high hopes that Sedloski would prove to be a bargain capture but just three games into his Owls' career he picked up an injury which sidelined him for four games.

Form Factors

Season	Team	Tot	St	Sb	Y	R
97-98	Sheffield W.	4	3	1	0	0
Total		4	3	1	0	0

	GP	GG	GF	GS	TGR
97-98	10.53	0.00	52	0	0.00
Averages	10.53	0.00	52.00	0.00	0.00

SERRANT, Carl
Newcastle United ① F
Fullname: Carl Serrant
DOB: 12-09-75 Bradford

Serrant could prove to be amongst the best of Daglish's close season signings – despite being one of the cheapest at just £500,000. A talented left-back, who can also double up as a centre half or wing-back, the Bradford born player has already found his way into the England B team having been a regular in the Under-21 side while at Oldham.

Possessing terrific pace, he may find his opportunities at Newcastle limited initially but should he break into the side he might be difficult to dislodge.

SHARPE, Lee
Leeds United ①② M
Fullname: Lee Stuart Sharpe
DOB: 27-05-71 Halesowen

Former England international who had a glittering eight year career with Manchester United prior to becoming Leeds United's record signing in a £4.5m deal in July 1996. With his good close skills, excellent crosses and the knack of scoring a healthy quota of goals from wide positions, he looked to be on the path to continued success.

But since moving to Elland Road Sharpe has come through a disappointing first season only to miss the whole of the 1997-98 campaign after suffering a damaged cruciate ligament injury prior to the start of the season. Providing he makes a full recovery he has the ability to once again scale the heights, but having missed out on a year of George Graham's rebuilding at Leeds he may have already missed the boat.

Form Factors

Season	Team	Tot	St	Sb	Y	R
94-95	Manchester U.	28	26	2	7	0
95-96	Manchester U.	31	21	10	3	0
96-97	Leeds U.	26	26	0	1	0
Total		85	73	12	11	0

	GP	GG	GF	GS	TGR
94-95	73.68	9.33	77	3	3.90
95-96	81.58	7.75	73	4	5.48
96-97	68.42	5.20	28	5	17.86
Averages	74.56	7.43	59.33	4.00	9.08

Fantasy Football Handbook 1998/99

SHAW, Richard

Coventry City ①②CB
Fullname: Richard Edward Shaw
DOB: 11-09-68 Brentford

An unspectacular but reliable and consistent defender who is more than capable of filling in anywhere along the backline but is probably best either in the middle or doing a man-marking job. Joined Coventry City in November 1995, made 21 Premiership appearances for the Sky Blues that season and has missed just eight league games since.

Signed for Coventry after 10 years with Crystal Palace and all of his three goals came during his time at Selhurst Park. Will be remembered as the player against whom Eric Cantona got himself sent off before his infamous kung-fu kick.

Form Factors

Season	Team	Tot	St	Sb	Y	R
95-96	Coventry C.	21	21	0	2	1
96-97	Coventry C.	35	35	0	3	0
97-98	Coventry C.	33	33	0	2	0
Total		89	89	0	7	1

	GP	GG	GF	GS	TGR
95-96	55.26	0.00	42	0	0.00
96-97	92.11	0.00	38	0	0.00
97-98	86.84	0.00	46	0	0.00
Averages	78.07	0.00	42.00	0.00	0.00

SHEARER, Alan

Newcastle U. ①②③④⑤S
Fullname: Alan Shearer
DOB: 13-08-70 Newcastle

Injuries sustained during the 1996-97 season denied Shearer the opportunity of extending his already unique record of scoring over 30 Premiership goals in three successive seasons but it was nothing compared to the ankle injury which excluded the England captain from the 1997-98 season until January. Upon his return he scored just twice in the league but his five FA Cup goals carried the Geordies through to their first final in 24 years.

Alan Shearer

Newcastle paid a world record £15m to bring him back home from Blackburn in 1996 but, given today's prices, when he hangs up his boots his goals tally should comfortably justify that fee. He goes into the 1998-99 season 33 goals clear of Les Ferdinand as the highest scorer in the Premiership's six year history.

Top scorer in Euro 96 he scored twice in France 98 and may well have finished as top scorer there but for a certain penalty shoot-out. Shearer's assets are extensive; has an almost telepathic awareness of where the goal is, clever at holding the ball up with defenders at his back, amazingly strong in the air, and packs a blistering drive whether from set-pieces or open play.

Kicked off his career with a hat-trick on his debut for Southampton against Arsenal when he was a 17 year old apprentice and he hasn't looked back.

Form Factors

Season	Team	Tot	St	Sb	Y	R
95-96	Blackburn R.	35	35	0	4	0
96-97	Newcastle U.	31	31	0	5	0
97-98	Newcastle U.	17	15	2	2	0
Total		83	81	2	11	0

	GP	GG	GF	GS	TGR
95-96	92.11	1.13	61	31	50.82
96-97	81.58	1.24	73	25	34.25
97-98	44.74	8.50	35	2	5.71
Averages	72.81	3.62	56.33	19.33	30.26

SHERINGHAM, Teddy

Manchester U. ❶❷❸ S

Fullname: Edward Paul Sheringham
DOB: 02-04-66 Walthamstow

England striker who possesses one of the finest footballing brains around which enables him to read situations more quickly than most defenders. This skill alone more than compensates for Sheringham not being one of the most fleet of foot players around.

Last season, his first with Manchester United, was one in which Sheringham did not quite match the influence he had at Tottenham and with nine goals from 38 matches it was also not one of his most productive.

Sheringham went into France 98 under something of a cloud following a slating in the tabloids and quickly found himself falling behind Owen in the pecking order. Nonetheless with his excellent distribution and general awareness he still has the quality to play a major part in England's Euro 2000 bid and Manchester United will be looking for him to recapture the form which persuaded them to pay £3.5m for him in June 1997.

Form Factors

Season	Team	Tot	St	Sb	Y	R
95-96	Tottenham H.	38	38	0	2	0
96-97	Tottenham H.	29	29	0	6	0
97-98	Manchester U.	31	28	3	2	0
Total		98	95	3	10	0

	GP	GG	GF	GS	TGR
95-96	100.00	2.38	50	16	32.00
96-97	76.32	4.14	44	7	15.91
97-98	81.58	3.44	73	9	12.33
Averages	85.96	3.32	55.67	10.67	20.08

SHERWOOD, Tim

Blackburn R. ❶❷❸ M

Fullname: Timothy Alan Sherwood
DOB: 06-02-69 St Albans

Since signing for Blackburn Rovers for just £500,000 in December 1992, Sherwood has seldom been out of the Rovers line up and has matured into one most consistent midfielders in the Premiership. Rovers' captain, he had the honour of leading them to the championship in 1995. Hardworking, he is calm on the ball and not afraid to get stuck in and has missed just 24 of Rovers' 240 Premiership matches over the past six seasons. Scored five times in the Premiership last season which is slightly above his average and celebrated by winning the club's Player of the Year award.

An England Under-21 and B international who joined Rovers from Norwich City having begun his career with Watford.

Tim Sherwood

Form Factors

Season	Team	Tot	St	Sb	Y	R
95-96	Blackburn R.	33	33	0	8	0
96-97	Blackburn R.	37	37	0	7	1
97-98	Blackburn R.	31	29	2	5	0
Total		101	99	2	20	1

	GP	GG	GF	GS	TGR
95-96	86.84	11.00	61	3	4.92
96-97	97.37	12.33	42	3	7.14
97-98	81.58	6.20	57	5	8.77
Averages	88.60	9.84	53.33	3.67	6.94

SHORT, Craig

Everton ❶❷❸ CB

Fullname: Craig Jonathan Short
DOB: 25-06-68 Bridlington

Did well to put an injury-hit 1996-97 behind him to play a leading role in Everton's successful battle against relegation last season. A domineering central defender who missed seven Premiership games last season, of which Everton won just two. A strong and reliable player who can normally be called upon to add a couple or goals of his own but last season he failed to find the target for the first time in seven years.

Fantasy Football Handbook 1998/99   **283**

Craig Short

Former England Schoolboy who has played for Scarborough, Notts County and Derby County and been transferred for fees totalling over £5m.

Form Factors

Season	Team	Tot	St	Sb	Y	R
95-96	Everton	23	22	1	6	0
96-97	Everton	23	19	4	6	0
97-98	Everton	31	27	4	3	0
Total		77	68	9	15	0

	GP	GG	GF	GS	TGR
95-96	60.53	11.50	64	2	3.13
96-97	60.53	11.50	44	2	4.55
97-98	81.58	0.00	41	0	0.00
Averages	67.54	7.67	49.67	1.33	2.56

SINCLAIR, Frank

Chelsea   ❶❷❸ CB

Fullname: Frank Mohammed Sinclair
DOB: 03-12-71 Lambeth

A one club defender who started as a trainee at Stamford Bridge and has now made 169 league appearances for Chelsea with his 32 league and cup games last season being his most successful campaign for three years. Basically a central defender he scored once in the league and in two cup competitions last season, both of which were important strikes, against Middlesbrough at Wembley in the final of the Coca Cola Cup and in the last eight of the Cup Winners' Cup against Real Betis.

May have done enough last season to warrant an extended run in the side from the start of this season.

Form Factors

Season	Team	Tot	St	Sb	Y	R
95-96	Chelsea	13	12	1	5	1
96-97	Chelsea	20	17	3	5	0
97-98	Chelsea	22	20	2	3	1
Total		55	49	6	13	2

	GP	GG	GF	GS	TGR
95-96	34.21	13.00	46	1	2.17
96-97	52.63	20.00	58	1	1.72
97-98	57.89	22.00	71	1	1.41
Averages	48.25	18.33	58.33	1.00	1.77

SINCLAIR, Trevor

West Ham U. ❶❷❸❹ S

Fullname: Trevor Lloyd Sinclair
DOB: 02-03-73 Dulwich, London

Versatile striker who can play in wide or central positions up front as well as make useful contributions from midfield. Joined West Ham from Queens Park Rangers in January 1998 to finally make his bow in the Premiership after almost four years at Loftus Road and four seasons with Blackpool. Possesses great skill and will forever be remembered for his glorious overhead 20 yard volley for QPR against Barnsley in the FA Cup.

Form Factors

Season	Team	Tot	St	Sb	Y	R
94-95	QPR	33	32	1	4	1
95-96	QPR	37	37	0	4	0
97-98	West Ham U.	14	14	0	5	0
Total		84	83	1	13	1

	GP	GG	GF	GS	TGR
94-95	86.84	8.25	61	4	6.56
95-96	97.37	18.50	38	2	5.26
97-98	36.84	2.00	56	7	12.50
Averages	73.68	9.58	51.67	4.33	8.11

Trevor Sinclair

SINTON, Andy

Tottenham H. ❶❷ M

Fullname: Andrew Sinton
DOB: 19-03-66 Newcastle

It was something of a surprise when former Spurs boss Gerry Francis rescued Sinton from an unhappy spell at Sheffield Wednesday to take him south in exchange for £1.5m in January 1996. And certainly it seemed to take the former England player a long time to settle but during the 1997-98 season Sinton began reproducing some of his best form in the Spurs midfield.

On his day Sinton can cause problems for any defence with the quality of his crosses but as Christian Gross begins to rebuild Tottenham it could be that the former Cambridge United, Brentford and Queens Park Rangers wide-man, who finished the season on the injury list, has a battle on his hands to regain a place in the side.

Form Factors

Season	Team	Tot	St	Sb	Y	R
95-96	Tottenham H.	9	8	1	1	0
96-97	Tottenham H.	33	32	1	5	0
97-98	Tottenham H.	19	14	5	0	1
Total		61	54	7	6	1

	GP	GG	GF	GS	TGR
95-96	23.68	0.00	50	0	0.00
96-97	86.84	5.50	44	6	13.64
97-98	50.00	0.00	44	0	0.00
Averages	53.51	1.83	46.00	2.00	4.55

SOLIS, Mauricio

Derby County ❶ M

Fullname: Mauricio Mora Solis
DOB: 13-12-72 Costa Rica

Moved to Derby County from CS Herdiano as part of the deal which also brought Paulo Wanchope to these shores. Unfortunately for Solis he has to sit and watch his companion go from strength to strength while his career has stagnated not least because of Premiership rules governing the number of non-European players who can be fielded in any one game.

Is not short on skill but having played in just 10 league games since signing for Derby it looks unlikely that he will figure too much in Jim Smith's future plans.

Form Factors

Season	Team	Tot	St	Sb	Y	R
96-97	Derby Co.	2	0	2	0	0
97-98	Derby Co.	9	3	6	0	0
Total		11	3	8	0	0

	GP	GG	GF	GS	TGR
96-97	5.26	0.00	45	0	0.00
97-98	23.68	0.00	52	0	0.00
Averages	14.47	0.00	48.50	0.00	0.00

SOLSKJAER, Ole Gunnar

Manchester U. ❶❷❸ S

Fullname: Ole Gunnar Solskjaer
DOB: 26-02-73 Kristiansund, Norway

After a sensational first season with Manchester United, Solskjaer experienced, to a degree, the other side of the coin last season as his number of league appearances dropped by a third and his goals by two-thirds. Just for good measure he also received his first red card in English football but overall his disciplinary record is exceptionally good with his only other blemish being one yellow card a year earlier. There was, however, a silver lining to his cloud last season which came in the form of France 98 where the Norwegian made three appearances for his country.

After the summer recess expect Solskjaer to come back firing on all cylinders and given his ability to locate the target with both feet expect him to get closer to his tally of 17 league goals of two seasons ago rather than last season's disappointing six.

Fantasy Football Handbook 1998/99

Form Factors

Season	Team	Tot	St	Sb	Y	R
96-97	Manchester U.	33	25	8	1	0
97-98	Manchester U.	22	15	7	0	1
Total		55	40	15	1	1

	GP	GG	GF	GS	TGR
96-97	86.84	1.83	76	18	23.68
97-98	57.89	3.67	73	6	8.22
Averages	72.37	2.75	74.50	12.00	15.95

SOLTVEDT, Trond
Coventry C. ❶❷❸ M

Fullname: Trond Egil Soltvedt
DOB:

Midfield player who joined Coventry City prior to the start of last season for £500,000 and enjoyed a very successful first season at Highfield Road making 30 appearances in the Premiership. Used in a more defensive role than earlier in his career, he has good close control and is not lacking in experience having played in the Champions League with Rosenborg.

Form Factors

Season	Team	Tot	St	Sb	Y	R
97-98	Coventry C.	30	26	4	1	0
Total		30	26	4	1	0

	GP	GG	GF	GS	TGR
97-98	78.95	30.00	46	1	2.17
Averages	78.95	30.00	46.00	1.00	2.17

SOUTHGATE, Gareth
Aston Villa ❶❷❸❹❺ CB

Fullname: Gareth Southgate
DOB: 03-09-70 Watford

One of the best and certainly most consistent top quality defenders in the Premiership over recent seasons. Has won international recognition with England and was in outstanding form in Euro 96 only to have his achievements slightly tarnished in the penalty shoot-out defeat by Germany. Still an England regular, made two appearances in France 98, although not always in Glenn Hoddle's starting line-up.

First appeared in the Premiership with Crystal Palace, where he made 152 league appearances, before joining Aston Villa for £2.5m in July 1995. Was a midfield player at the time of his move and still uses many of the skills suited to that position nowadays. Seldom scores but more importantly for a defender is also rarely on the receiving end of a yellow card.

Form Factors

Season	Team	Tot	St	Sb	Y	R
95-96	Aston Villa	31	31	0	1	0
96-97	Aston Villa	28	28	0	1	0
97-98	Aston Villa	32	32	0	2	0
Total		91	91	0	4	0

	GP	GG	GF	GS	TGR
95-96	81.58	31.00	52	1	1.92
96-97	73.68	28.00	47	1	2.13
97-98	84.21	0.00	49	0	0.00
Averages	79.82	19.67	49.33	0.67	1.35

SPEED, Gary

Newcastle U. ❶❷❸❹ M

Fullname: Gary Andrew Speed
DOB: 08-09-69 Hawarden

Having joined Everton for £3.5m in June 1996, the Merseysiders conducted a good piece of business when selling Welsh international Speed to Newcastle less than two years later for £5.5m. During his brief spell at Goodison Park, the club he supported as a youngster, he was named as Player of the Year for 1996-97. His first Everton goal was, ironically, against Newcastle. Speed has spent most of his career with Leeds United where, apart from a couple of quiet seasons, he was a regular goalscorer. Although not one of the tallest players around, he is good in the air but his best position is attacking down the left from where he can get in telling crosses.

Form Factors

Season	Team	Tot	St	Sb	Y	R
96-97	Everton	37	37	0	8	0
97-98	Everton	21	21	0	4	0
97-98	Newcastle U.	13	13	0	0	1
Total		71	71	0	12	1

	GP	GG	GF	GS	TGR
96-97	97.37	4.11	44	9	20.45
97-98	55.26	3.00	41	7	17.07
97-98	34.21	13.00	35	1	2.86
Averages	62.28	6.70	40.00	5.67	13.46

SRNICEK, Pavel

Newcastle U. ❶❷ GK

Fullname: Pavel Srnicek
DOB: 10-03-68 Ostrava, Czechoslovakia

One of the very few overseas players to spend a good number of years with an English club, Srnicek found his chances at Newcastle United greatly reduced last season after putting in a transfer request. Was granted just one Premiership outing, a 1-1 draw with Blackburn Rovers. With just 38 appearances over the past three seasons it would appear that the former Czech international's days at St. James's Park are numbered despite Hislop's departure in the close season.

Has played 97 Premiership games for the Magpies since joining from Banik Ostrava and kept 33 clean sheets in that time.

Form Factors

Season	Team	Tot	St	Sb	Y	R
95-96	Newcastle U.	15	14	1	0	0
96-97	Newcastle U.	22	22	0	0	0
97-98	Newcastle U.	1	1	0	0	0
Total		38	37	1	0	0

	GA	GkA	GAp	CS	SO	R
95-96	37	18	1.20	5	2	0
96-97	40	19	0.86	7	4	0
97-98	44	1	1.00	0	0	0
Averages	40.3	12.67	1.02	4.0	2.0	0

STAM, Japp

Manchester U. ❶❷❸❹ CD

Fullname: Japp Stam
DOB: Holland

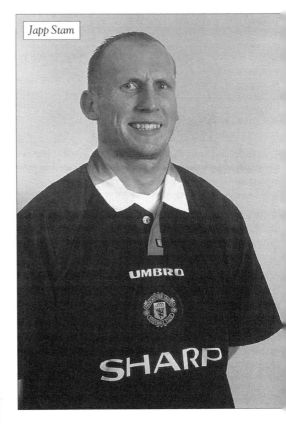
Japp Stam

Pretty much unknown to most followers in this country, Stam came to the fore during France 98 with performances which, on the whole, were competent for Holland rather than worthy of a £10.5m defender. That said, he was outstanding in the semi final even though he was nowhere to be seen for Brazil's goal. If Stam lives up to his billing, and with the excellent Schmeichel behind him he has perfect support, then he will be the ideal replacement for Gary Pallister.

Was in the Dutch squad for Euro 96 and a year later was named Player of the Year in Holland.

STAMP, Phil

Middlesbrough ❶ M

Fullname: Philip Lawrence Stamp
DOB: 12-12-75 Middlesbrough

Local-born midfielder whose only club has been Middlesbrough although in over four years as a professional he has yet to lay claim to a permanent place in the side. His personally most successful season was 1996-97 when he made 24 league appearances; it wasn't so good for the club though as they were relegated.

Has done well to force his way into the squad of the club he supported as a boy and with his non-stop total commitment performances he has the backing of the locals. But with just 10 Nationwide League games behind him from last season he does appear to have his work cut out to convince Bryan Robson that he can make it in the Premiership.

Form Factors

Season	Team	Tot	St	Sb	Y	R
95-96	Middlesbrough	12	11	1	0	0
96-97	Middlesbrough	23	15	8	1	0
Totals		35	26	9	1	0

	GP	GG	GF	GS	TGR
95-96	31.58	6	35	2	5.72
96-97	60.53	23	51	1	1.96
Averages	46.01	14.50	43	1.5	3.84

Fantasy Football Handbook 1998/99

STAUNTON, Steve

Liverpool ❶❷❸ FB
Fullname: Stephen Staunton
DOB: 19-01-69 Drogheda

Popular attack-minded defender who plays on the left side of the backline but loves to get forward whenever possible. Returned to his first club, Liverpool, in the summer on a free transfer having left the Reds in a £1m deal with Aston Villa back in August 1991. Spent seven years at Villa Park during which time he became a permanent member of the Eire side and played in all four of their USA 94 matches.

Made 27 Premiership appearances for Villa last season taking his career league games tally to 281 during which time he has scored 16 times although none came during his first spell at Anfield.

Form Factors

Season	Team	Tot	St	Sb	Y	R
95-96	Aston Villa	13	11	2	0	0
96-97	Aston Villa	30	30	0	5	1
97-98	Aston Villa	27	27	0	5	0
Total		70	68	2	10	1

	GP	GG	GF	GS	TGR
95-96	34.21	0.00	52	0	0.00
96-97	78.95	15.00	47	2	4.26
97-98	71.05	27.00	49	1	2.04
Averages	61.40	14.00	49.33	1.00	2.10

STEFANOVIC, Dejan

Sheffield W. ❶❷❸ CB
Fullname: Dejan Stefanovic
DOB: 20-10-74 Yugoslavia

Predominantly a central defender with a good left foot and close skills, Stefanovic found himself filling various positions last season to cover for injured teammates. He joined Sheffield Wednesday for £4.5m along with fellow Yugoslav Darko Kovacevic, the latter has since left Hillsborough and just yet it is debatable whether or not Wednesday have got value for money with Stefanovic. An international in his homeland he was frequently in trouble with match officials last season as eight yellow cards and a single red one were waved in his direction, leading to him missing a number of games through suspension.

Form Factors

Season	Team	Tot	St	Sb	Y	R
95-96	Sheffield W.	6	5	1	0	0
96-97	Sheffield W.	29	27	2	6	0
97-98	Sheffield W.	20	19	1	8	1
Total		55	51	4	14	1

	GP	GG	GF	GS	TGR
95-96	15.79	0.00	48	0	0.00
96-97	76.32	14.50	50	2	4.00
97-98	52.63	10.00	52	2	3.85
Averages	48.25	8.17	50.00	1.33	2.62

STIMAC, Igor

Derby County ❶❷❸ CD

Fullname: Igor Stimac
DOB: 09-06-67 Metkovic, Croatia

Croatian who capped a fine season with Derby County by helping his country to third place in the World Cup in France 98. A fine reader of the game, he tackles well, is more than comfortable on the ball and with his calming influence inspires those around him.

Joined Derby from Hadjuk Split almost three years ago and last season maintained his record of scoring one goal a season for the Rams. Managed to improve his poor disciplinary record but still collected six yellow cards taking his total in two seasons in the top flight to 15 which inevitably means suspensions and time out of the side.

Form Factors

Season	Team	Tot	St	Sb	Y	R
96-97	Derby Co.	21	21	0	9	0
97-98	Derby Co.	22	22	0	6	0
Total		43	43	0	15	0

	GP	GG	GF	GS	TGR
96-97	55.26	21.00	45	1	2.22
97-98	57.89	22.00	52	1	1.92
Averages	56.58	21.50	48.50	1.00	2.07

STONE, Steve

Nottingham F. ❶❷❸ M

Fullname: Steven Brian Stone
DOB: 20-08-71 Gateshead

Over the past two seasons there can be few players to have suffered the same amount of ill-fortune regarding injuries as Steve Stone. Just when he looked to be on the path to becoming an England regular

Steve Stone

Fantasy Football Handbook 1998/99

Stone went down with knee ligament problems which ended his 1996-97 season in September and early last season he underwent an operation for a hernia but still managed to play a part in 30 of Nottingham Forest's games on the way to promotion.

When fully fit he is the perfect midfield player, able to defend and attack when necessary, good in the tackle, creative and, up until his injury troubles, a regular goalscorer. With a good season in the Premiership behind him it is not inconceivable that he could force his way into Glenn Hoddle's European Championship plans.

Form Factors

Season	Team	Tot	St	Sb	Y	R
94-95	N. Forest	41	41	0	4	0
95-96	N. Forest	34	34	0	3	0
96-97	N. Forest	5	5	0	2	0
Total		80	80	0	9	0

	GP	GG	GF	GS	TGR
94-95	107.89	8.20	72	5	6.94
95-96	89.47	4.86	50	7	14.00
96-97	13.16	0.00	31	0	0.00
Averages	70.18	4.35	51.00	4.00	6.98

STRACHAN, Gavin

Coventry C. ❶❷ M

Fullname: Gavin Strachan
DOB: 23-12-78 Aberdeen

As the sun goes down on Gordon Strachan's glorious playing career up pops another Strachan, son Gavin, to keep the family name on Premiership teamsheets. Very much a taller version of his father, minus the famous red hair, Gavin also plays in midfield but by his own admission he relies on confidence and his head can go down if a couple of passes go astray.

Was twice in the starting line-up for Premiership games, came on as sub in seven other matches, but has yet to complete a full game and only gradual integration into the side can be expected this season.

Form Factors

Season	Team	Tot	St	Sb	Y	R
97-98	Coventry C.	9	2	7	0	0
Total		9	2	7	0	0

	GP	GG	GF	GS	TGR
97-98	23.68	0.00	46	0	0.00
Averages	23.68	0.00	46.00	0.00	0.00

STURRIDGE, Dean

Derby County ❶❷❸ S

Fullname: Dean Constantine Sturridge
DOB: 27-07-73 Birmingham

A very lively and exciting striker who made an instant impact at the highest level when he scored a brace in Derby County's first match in the Premiership, at home to Leeds United in August 1996, but has possibly just failed to live up to the high expectations that that start created for him.

Ended that season with a highly respectable 11 league goals but last season, from the same number of league appearances, 30, scored two goals less which, incidentally, contained another double at Leeds' expense.

Would not be a surprise to see him back amongst the goals this season with his excellent acceleration and nifty footwork always likely to cause defenders problems.

Form Factors

Season	Team	Tot	St	Sb	Y	R
96-97	Derby Co.	30	29	1	9	0
97-98	Derby Co.	30	24	6	8	0
Total		60	53	7	17	0

	GP	GG	GF	GS	TGR
96-97	78.95	2.73	45	11	24.44
97-98	78.95	3.33	52	9	17.31
Averages	78.95	3.03	48.50	10.00	20.88

SULLIVAN, Neil

Wimbledon ❶❷❸❹ GK

Fullname: Neil Sultan
DOB: 24-02-70 Sutton

Neil Sullivan

One time Wimbledon trainee who has taken giant leaps forward over the past couple of seasons, culminating in him winning his first cap for Scotland and being cover for Jim Leighton during France 98. Made slow progress with the Dons after first signing professional forms with just four league appearances in four years; also played one game on loan to Crystal Palace (presumably doesn't like travelling too far).

But over the past two seasons he has been absent for just two of the Dons' 76 Premiership games and has not missed any of the last 44 taking his career total of league games beyond the century mark. The 1997-98 season saw Sullivan keep 13 clean sheets – his best record to date – which included a run of six shut-outs in seven games. The run was marred by a 5-0 defeat at Arsenal and ended with a 6-2 thrashing by Tottenham, which stopped him from conceding his fewest goals in a season. An agile and athletic keeper he is now recognised as one of the leading custodians currently playing in the top flight.

Form Factors

Season	Team	Tot	St	Sb	Y	R
95-96	Wimbledon	16	16	0	0	0
96-97	Wimbledon	36	36	0	0	0
97-98	Wimbledon	38	38	0	0	0
Total		90	90	0	0	0

	GA	GkA	GAp	CS	SO	R
95-96	70	35	2.19	3	1	0
96-97	48	43	1.19	11	3	0
97-98	46	46	1.21	13	4	0
Averages	54.67	41.33	1.53	9.0	2.67	0

Fantasy Football Handbook 1998/99

SUTTON, Chris

Blackburn Rovers ①②③④⑤ S

Fullname: Christopher Roy Sutton
DOB: 10-03-73 Nottingham

Failed to score in Blackburn's opening game of last season but was soon assisting Rovers' free-scoring start to the season with a hat-trick in a 4-0 destruction of Aston Villa at Villa Park. Scored a second hat-trick in a 5-3 win over Leicester City in February and with his 18 Premiership goals — making him joint top scorer in the Premier League — many felt he should have been in France 98 with England but blotted his copybook in Glenn Hoddle's eyes when rejecting an invitation to play in the B team.

A one time defender who has suffered more than his fair share of injuries since joining Rovers from Norwich City for a then British record transfer fee of £5m in 1994, but when fully fit Sutton has everything going for him with his touch, distribution and sharpness in the penalty area likely to keep him amongst England's top strikers during 1998-99.

Has scored 79 times in 215 Football League and Premiership matches.

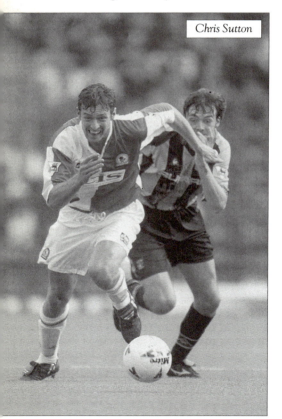

Chris Sutton

Form Factors

Season	Team	Tot	St	Sb	Y	R
95-96	Blackburn R.	13	9	4	3	0
96-97	Blackburn R.	25	24	1	4	0
97-98	Blackburn R.	35	35	0	10	1
Total		73	68	5	17	1

	GP	GG	GF	GS	TGR
95-96	34.21	0.00	61	0	0.00
96-97	65.79	2.27	42	11	26.19
97-98	92.11	1.94	57	18	31.58
Averages	64.04	1.41	53.33	9.67	19.26

TAYLOR, Ian

Aston Villa ①②③ M

Fullname: Ian Kenneth Taylor
DOB: 04-06-68 Birmingham

Has proved a tremendous acquisition in his four years at Villa Park following a £1m transfer from Sheffield Wednesday. Predominantly a midfielder of note, he has played at full-back and central defender although he seems well suited to wing-back with his high workrate enabling him to get up and down the field with ease.

Last season was his most successful in front of goal for four years with his six league goals being equal to Stan Collymore's tally. Taylor first broke into the Football League with Port Vale, having been picked up from non-league side Moor Green, and spent just one year with Sheffield Wednesday before his move to Villa Park.

Form Factors

Season	Team	Tot	St	Sb	Y	R
95-96	Aston Villa	25	24	1	5	0
96-97	Aston Villa	34	29	5	4	0
97-98	Aston Villa	32	30	2	6	0
Total		91	83	8	15	0

	GP	GG	GF	GS	TGR
95-96	65.79	8.33	52	3	5.77
96-97	89.47	17.00	47	2	4.26
97-98	84.21	5.33	49	6	12.24
Averages	79.82	10.22	49.33	3.67	7.42

Paul Telfer

TELFER, Paul

Coventry City ❶❷❸❹ M

Fullname: Paul Norman Telfer
DOB: 12-10-71 Edinburgh

A £1.5m signing from Luton Town at the end of the 1994-95 season Telfer has become an almost permanent fixture in the set-up at Coventry City. Is perfectly at home in the centre of midfield but many observers feel that his best position is right wing-back. Scored 16 goals during his last two seasons with Luton but has found goals much more difficult to come by in the Premiership although last season's tally of three, plus two in the FA Cup, suggests that he is again finding his goal touch.

Form Factors

Season	Team	Tot	St	Sb	Y	R
95-96	Coventry C.	31	31	0	4	0
96-97	Coventry C.	34	31	3	6	0
97-98	Coventry C.	33	33	0	9	0
Total		98	95	3	19	0

	GP	GG	GF	GS	TGR
95-96	81.58	31.00	42	1	2.38
96-97	89.47	0.00	38	0	0.00
97-98	86.84	11.00	46	3	6.52
Averages	85.96	14.00	42.00	1.33	2.97

TERRIER, David

Newcastle U. ❶ D

Fullname:
DOB: 04-08-73 Verdun, France

Joined Newcastle United in December 1997 after an unsuccessful spell with West Ham which was blighted by injury. Had been back in his native France just a week when Newcastle offered him the chance to try again on these shores. His original move to West Ham, from Metz, came shortly after a nomination as the best defender in his homeland

THATCHER, Ben

Wimbledon ❶❷ FB

Fullname: Benjamin David Thatcher
DOB: 30-11-75 Swindon

Wimbledon's record signing at £2m who, following an injury-disrupted first season at Selhurst Park, came more into his own last season and was pretty much a regular at left-back. Although not one of the tallest defenders around, Thatcher is proficient in the air, is a useful reader of the game and is excellent at knowing when to tackle. Likes to get forward to support the attack whenever possible but in the five years since making his debut for Millwall has scored just once.

Has represented England at Under-21 and played for an Endsleigh League rep side against the Italian counterparts.

Form Factors

Season	Team	Tot	St	Sb	Y	R
96-97	Wimbledon	9	9	0	2	0
97-98	Wimbledon	26	23	3	2	2
Total		35	32	3	4	2

	GP	GG	GF	GS	TGR
96-97	23.68	0.00	49	0	0.00
97-98	68.42	0.00	34	0	0.00
Averages	46.05	0.00	41.50	0.00	0.00

THOMAS, Geoff

Nottingham F. ❶❷ M

Fullname: Geoffrey Robert Thomas
DOB: 05-08-64 Manchester

Hard-working midfield player who made the last of his nine England appearances back in 1992 and since then has had to rebuild his career a couple of times following injury. Moved to Nottingham Forest at the start of last season after four years with Wolverhampton Wanderers and used his vast experience to good effect as he helped Forest back into the Premiership.

Was a regular goalscorer at Crystal Palace around the time of his England call-up but his quota of goals has dwindled in recent years, nonetheless his fine first touch, control and precise use of the ball make him a valuable member but at 34 he will doubtless have a tough battle on his hands to be a permanent fixture at the City Ground over the coming months.

Form Factors

Season	Team	Tot	St	Sb	Y	R
92-93	C. Palace	29	28	1	0	0
Total		29	28	1	0	0

	GP	GG	GF	GS	TGR
92-93	76.32	14.50	61	2	3.28
Averages	76.32	14.50	61.00	2.00	3.28

THOMAS, Tony

Everton ❶❷ D

Fullname: Anthony Thomas
DOB: 12-07-71 Liverpool

After nine years and 257 league games with Tranmere Rovers, Thomas departed Prenton Park to try his hand in the Premiership with neighbours Everton but spent most of the 1997-98 season on the sidelines as he was called upon for just seven league games.

A defender who can fill in at left or right-back he can also put over a decent cross but looks to have a tough battle to prove himself at Goodison Park.

Form Factors

Season	Team	Tot	St	Sb	Y	R
97-98	Everton	7	6	1	1	0
Total		7	6	1	1	0

	GP	GG	GF	GS	TGR
97-98	18.42	0.00	41	0	0.00
Averages	18.42	0.00	41.00	0.00	0.00

THOME, Emerson

Sheffield W. ❶❷❸ D

Fullname: Emerson Thome
DOB: Brazil

Brazilian-born defender signed for Sheffield Wednesday on a free transfer in March 1998 from Benfica by former Owls' boss Ron Atkinson. A defender who is flexible and may be used in other positions. Played six times for Wednesday towards the end of the season and is expected to make a big impact this term.

Form Factors

Season	Team	Tot	St	Sb	Y	R
97-98	Sheffield W.	6	6	0	1	0
Total		6	6	0	1	0

	GP	GG	GF	GS	TGR
97-98	15.79	0.00	52	0	0.00
Averages	15.79	0.00	52.00	0.00	0.00

THOMPSON, Alan

Aston Villa ❶❷❸ M

Fullname: Alan Thompson
DOB: 22-12-73 Newcastle

As Bolton Wanderers dropped back into the Nationwide League at the climax of the 1997-98 season, their midfield star Thompson opted to stay in the top flight with a move to Aston Villa. A goalscoring midfielder he should have little trouble in justifying Villa manager John Gregory's faith in him. An excellent signing who will help Villa build on the good start made under Gregory's leadership last season. An England Youth and Under-21 international.

Form Factors

Season	Team	Tot	St	Sb	Y	R
95-96	Bolton W.	26	23	3	8	0
97-98	Bolton W.	33	33	0	6	1
Total		59	56	3	14	1

	GP	GG	GF	GS	TGR
95-96	68.42	26.00	39	1	2.56
97-98	86.84	3.67	41	9	21.95
Averages	77.63	14.83	40.00	5.00	12.26

TILER, Carl

Everton ①②D

Fullname: Carl Tiler
DOB: 11-02-71 Sheffield

Joined Everton in November 1997 as part of a package which also took Mitch Ward to Goodison Park with Graham Stuart moving in the opposite direction to Sheffield United. Made 19 Premiership appearances for the Blues last season which is only four games short of his total league appearances for the previous four seasons.

At a massive 6'4" he is, needless to say, good in the air but is also comfortable when moving forward with the ball at his feet. But like Ward, he too has to prove himself to the new manager at Goodison Park.

Form Factors

Season	Team	Tot	St	Sb	Y	R
95-96	Aston Villa	1	1	0	0	0
96-97	Aston Villa	11	9	2	1	0
97-98	Everton	19	19	0	5	0
Total		31	29	2	6	0

	GP	GG	GF	GS	TGR
95-96	2.63	0.00	52	0	0.00
96-97	28.95	11.00	47	1	2.13
97-98	50.00	19.00	41	1	2.44
Averages	27.19	10.00	46.67	0.67	1.52

TODD, Lee

Southampton ①②FB

Fullname: Lee Todd
DOB: 07-03-72 Hartlepool

Very attack-minded defender who is equally comfortable playing at left wing-back. Joined Southampton in July 1997 as part of the deal which also took goalkeeper Paul Jones from Stockport County to the Dell for £1.5m. Made just 10 appearances in the Premiership last season and will surely make a more significant impact this season.

A former trainee with Hartlepool United he scored twice in 225 Football League games for Stockport prior to his move to the south coast.

Form Factors

Season	Team	Tot	St	Sb	Y	R
97-98	Southampton	10	9	1	1	0
Total		10	9	1	1	0

	GP	GG	GF	GS	TGR
97-98	26.32	0.00	50	0	0.00
Averages	26.32	0.00	50.00	0.00	0.00

TOWNSEND, Andy
Middlesbrough ❶❷❸ M

Fullname: Andrew David Townsend
DOB: 23-07-63 Maidstone

Maidstone-born holder of over 50 caps for the Republic of Ireland who was an inspired signing of Bryan Robson's as he sought experience to haul the Teeside club back into the Premiership. Townsend is tenacious in the tackle, hardworking and excellent at supplying telling passes to his strikers. For the third consecutive year the 35-year-old midfielder scored two league goals taking his career total to 35 in 433 league games.

Providing his legs can stand another season at the top level Townsend could come up against three of his former clubs currently in the Premiership; Southampton, Chelsea and Aston Villa, he has also played for Norwich City.

Form Factors

Season	Team	Tot	St	Sb	Y	R
95-96	Aston Villa	31	30	1	9	1
96-97	Aston Villa	34	34	0	8	0
97-98	Aston Villa	3	3	0	0	0
Total		68	67	1	17	1

	GP	GG	GF	GS	TGR
95-96	81.58	15.50	52	2	3.85
96-97	89.47	17.00	47	2	4.26
97-98	7.89	0.00	49	0	0.00
Averages	59.65	10.83	49.33	1.33	2.70

TRAMEZZANI, Paolo
Tottenham H. ❶❷❸ D

Fullname: Paolo Tramezzani
DOB: 20-07-70 Italy

Christian Gross's first summer signing at Tottenham was Italian defender Tramezzani who originally came to Spurs' attention when he played for Internazionale against his new club at White Hart Lane in the Fiorucci tournament in April 1993. Since then he has played for Cesena from whom the left-back joined Spurs during the World Cup.

ULLATHORNE, Robert
Leicester City ❶❷❸ FB

Fullname: Robert Ullathorne
DOB: 11-10-71 Wakefield

Leicester City supporters have yet to see the best of Ullathorne. Indeed, they have seen very little at all of their signing from Spanish club Osasuna who had the misfortune of breaking an ankle just 11 minutes into his debut against Wimbledon in the 1st Leg of the Foxes' Coca Cola Cup semi final. Was injured on his return to the side last December against the other Selhurst Park club, Crystal Palace, and managed one complete game on his next return in March before being dismissed at Bolton.

Put him in your team if you dare but it is time Ullathorne's fortunes took a twist for the better.

Form Factors

Season	Team	Tot	St	Sb	Y	R
94-95	Norwich C.	27	27	0	5	0
96-97	Leicester C.	0	0	0	0	0
97-98	Leicester C.	6	3	3	0	1
Total		33	30	3	5	1

	GP	GG	GF	GS	TGR
94-95	71.05	13.50	37	2	5.41
96-97	0.00	0.00	46	0	0.00
97-98	15.79	6.00	51	1	1.96
Averages	28.95	6.50	44.67	1.00	2.46

UNSWORTH, David

West Ham U. ❶❷❸ D

Fullname: David Gerald Unsworth
DOB: 16-10-73 Chorley

With Julian Dicks out injured it could be said that Unsworth provides the steel to the left side of the West Ham defence but that would do a great disservice to a consistently good defender who is sound in possession and potentially deadly from dead-ball situations. Adept in the air and technically proficient on the ground he scored 11 times in his six seasons with Everton prior to joining West Ham at the start of last season.

Form Factors

Season	Team	Tot	St	Sb	Y	R
95-96	Everton	31	28	3	3	1
96-97	Everton	34	32	2	5	1
97-98	West Ham U.	32	32	0	8	1
Total		97	92	5	16	3

	GP	GG	GF	GS	TGR
95-96	81.58	15.50	64	2	3.13
96-97	89.47	6.80	44	5	11.36
97-98	84.21	16.00	56	2	3.57
Averages	85.09	12.77	54.67	3.00	6.02

UPSON, Matthew

Arsenal ❶❷ CD

Fullname: Matthew James Upson
DOB: 18-04-79 Hartismere

Undoubtedly set to be a part of the next generation of top quality Arsenal defenders, teenager Upson joined the Gunners from Luton Town in April 1996 in a deal which could eventually cost the current champions £2m. As glorious as the 1997-98 season may have been for Arsenal, it got off to a dreadful start for the unfortunate young central defender as he was dismissed during a pre-season friendly against PSV Eindhoven due to a case of mistaken identity.

He overcame that setback to make his debut in the Premiership win over Crystal Palace in February and finished the campaign with eight league and cup appearances behind him. Will almost certainly improve upon that tally during the 1998-99 season and once that is achieved should step up a grade from being an England Youth international.

Form Factors

Season	Team	Tot	St	Sb	Y	R
97-98	Arsenal	5	5	0	0	0
Total		5	5	0	0	0

	GP	GG	GF	GS	TGR
97-98	13.16	0.00	68	0	0.00
Averages	13.16	0.00	68.00	0.00	0.00

VALERY, Patrick
Blackburn R.   ①② D
Fullname:
DOB: 03-07-69 Brignoles, France

The 1997-98 season was Frenchman Valery's first in the Premiership and he was quickly blooded into English football by starting in all nine of Blackburn Rovers opening league games. Made a total of 15 league appearances in the Rovers' defence last season, was sent off once, and was an unused substitute on a further five occasions. Could have his work cut out to improve upon that record this season.

Previously with Monaco and SC Bastia, from whom he joined Blackburn.

Form Factors
Season	Team	Tot	St	Sb	Y	R
97-98	Blackburn R.	15	14	1	2	1
Total		15	14	1	2	1

	GP	GG	GF	GS	TGR
97-98	39.47	0	57	0	0.00
Averages	39.47	0	57	0	0.00

VAN DER GOUW, Raimond
Manchester U.   ①② GK
Fullname: Raimond Van der Gouw
DOB: 24-03-63 Oldenzaal, Holland

Having made just two Premiership appearances during the 1996-97 season, last season was positively party time for Van der Gouw as the Dutch goalkeeper was afforded five games at the summit of the English game. Van der Gouw conceded just two goals and kept three clean sheets in his five games but fared less well in the cups with five goals put past him in single Champions League, FA and Coca Cola Cup ties.

With Schmeichel certain to rule the roost at Old Trafford for the foreseeable future his understudy will remain as just that and thereby earn you precious few fantasy points. His previous clubs are Dutch sides Go Ahead Eagles and Vitesse Arnhem from whom he joined United for £200,000 in 1996.

Form Factors
Season	Team	Tot	St	Sb	Y	R
96-97	Manchester U.	2	2	0	0	0
97-98	Manchester U.	5	4	1	0	0
Total		7	6	1	0	0

	GA	GkA	GAp	CS	SO	R
96-97	44	2	1.00	1	1	0
97-98	26	0	0.00	2	1	1
Averages	35.0	1.0	0.50	1.5	1.0	0.5

VAN HOOIJDONK, Pierre

Nottingham F. ①②③④ S

Fullname: Pierre van Hooijdonk
DOB: 29-11-69 Steenbergen, Holland

Striker who made light of the transition from Scottish to English football following a record £4.5m transfer from Celtic to Nottingham Forest. Came in towards the end of Forest's unsuccessful battle against relegation and could muster just one goal in eight games. But life in Division One was a roller-coaster ride as he rammed in 34 goals in 46 league and cup matches. It was form which earned him a place in the Dutch France 98 squad where he came on as a substitute against Brazil and almost won the game for his country.

An excellent header of the ball, quick on the deck, packs a powerful and accurate shot and deadly from set-pieces, van Hooijdonk has the quality to now make his mark at the top level of English football. His record in Holland was outstanding with 104 goals being scored in 168 league games.

Form Factors

Season	Team	Tot	St	Sb	Y	R
96-97	N. Forest	8	8	0	3	0
Total		8	8	0	3	0

	GP	GG	GF	GS	TGR
96-97	21.05	8.00	31	1	3.23
Averages	21.05	8.00	31.00	1.00	3.23

Pierre Van Hooijdonk

VEGA, Ramon

Tottenham H. ❶❷❸ CB

Fullname: Ramon Vega
DOB: 14-06-71 Olten, Switzerland

Swiss international defender who first caught the eye over here with his performances in England during Euro 96, was signed by Tottenham the following January from Cagliari for £3.75m. At 6'3" he is understandably good at dealing with aerial attacks and also likes to move forward at set-pieces with his three goals in 25 Premiership matches being slightly above his career average.

A very talented defender whose best position is sweeper but like most at White Hart Lane he was hindered by injury last season. Clear from injury and suspension – he was sent off a week after his debut and booked eight times last season – and with Sol Campbell playing just in front of him Tottenham have the basis for one of the best backlines in the Premiership

Form Factors

Season	Team	Tot	St	Sb	Y	R
96-97	Tottenham H.	8	8	0	2	0
97-98	Tottenham H.	25	22	3	4	1
Total		33	30	3	6	1

	GP	GG	GF	GS	TGR
96-97	21.05	8.00	44	1	2.27
97-98	65.79	8.33	44	3	6.82
Averages	43.42	8.17	44.00	2.00	4.55

VIALLI, Gianluca

Chelsea ❶❷❸ S

Fullname: Gianluca Vialli
DOB: 09-07-64 Cremona, Italy

A player who has experienced run-ins with those above him, Vialli was suddenly handed great responsibility in February 1998 when Chelsea dispensed with the services of Ruud Gullit and handed the task of managing the Blues to the Italian international striker who had no previous managerial experience. How well did he fare? Well, Chelsea have the Coca Cola Cup and the Cup Winners' Cup locked up at Stamford Bridge so one has to say 'the boy done great'.

As a player Vialli's days are probably drawing to an end, if only because of the demands made on him when managing the side. Certainly if left to concentrate on playing he probably could safely see out another season if his 13 goals in 25 league and cup appearances last season are anything to go by. As if to prove that you can't beat experience it was a marked improvement upon his first season at Chelsea but whether he wants to play and manage could depend on how well things are going on the pitch without him.

Form Factors

Season	Team	Tot	St	Sb	Y	R
96-97	Chelsea	28	23	5	5	0
97-98	Chelsea	21	14	7	4	0
Total		49	37	12	9	0

	GP	GG	GF	GS	TGR
96-97	73.68	3.11	58	9	15.52
97-98	55.26	1.91	71	11	15.49
Averages	64.47	2.51	64.50	10.00	15.51

VICKERS, Steve
Middlesbrough ❶❷❸ CD
Fullname: Stephen Vickers
DOB: 13-10-67 Bishop Auckland

Previously a Player of the Year winner at Middlesbrough, Vickers was in fine form last season as he master-minded Boro's return to the Premiership from the middle of their defence. Was one of ten players to appear in 30 or more Division One matches as Bryan Robson's side secured the second automatic promotion place on the final day of the season.

Joined Boro from Tranmere Rovers in December 1993 after playing 311 league games for the Prenton Park club which included two consecutive ever-present campaigns.

Form Factors

Season	Team	Tot	St	Sb	Y	R
95-96	Middlesbrough	32	32	0	1	0
96-97	Middlesbrough	29	26	3	4	0
Total		61	58	3	5	0

	GP	GG	GF	GS	TGR
95-96	84.21	32.00	35	1	2.86
96-97	76.32	0.00	51	0	0.00
Averages	80.26	16.00	43.00	0.50	1.43

VIEIRA, Patrick
Arsenal ❶❷❸❹❺ M
Fullname: Patrick Vieira
DOB: 23-06-76 Dakar, Senegal

From being a relatively unknown Frenchman in England when he arrived in this country, Vieira is now one of the most respected and sought after midfield players in Europe. His partnership with Petit in the Arsenal midfield has helped the massive improvement seen in Ray Parlour's game and that trio were just one of several vital clogs which gelled to help the Gunners to their second league and cup double last season.

His highly successful season had the perfect climax when he came on as substitute late in the World Cup Final victory and laid on the final goal for his Arsenal teammate Manu Petit. The tough tackling 22-year old will surely be a regular in the national side for many years to come.

The only problem for the former Milan player is his disciplinary troubles which will sideline him for several games each season; during the 1997-98 season due to suspension due to cautions and a sending off at Chelsea in the Coca-Cola Cup Semi Final.

Form Factors

Season	Team	Tot	St	Sb	Y	R
96-97	Arsenal	31	30	1	11	0
97-98	Arsenal	33	31	2	8	1
Total		64	61	3	19	1

	GP	GG	GF	GS	TGR
96-97	81.58	15.50	62	2	3.23
97-98	86.84	16.50	68	2	2.94
Averages	84.21	16.00	65.00	2.00	3.08

WALKER, Des

Sheffield W. ❶❷❸ CB
Fullname: Desmond Sinclair Walker
DOB: 26-11-65 Hackney

Since signing for Sheffield Wednesday from Sampdoria in 1993 following a disappointing year in Italy, Walker has continued to display the quality that marked him out as one of the best defenders in the country and earned him 59 England caps. Walker was one of just five players to start in every Premiership match last season and in five years at Hillsborough has missed just eight Premiership games out of a possible 156. Came to the fore during nine years with Nottingham Forest prior to his move to Italy.

Quick, calm, excellent reader of the game and although he will be 33 midway through the season Walker will continue to be an asset this season although goals is something he will not get your team – his one goal in professional football was scored seven seasons ago.

Form Factors

Season	Team	Tot	St	Sb	Y	R
95-96	Sheffield W.	36	36	0	2	0
96-97	Sheffield W.	36	36	0	1	1
97-98	Sheffield W.	38	38	0	0	0
Total		110	110	0	3	1

	GP	GG	GF	GS	TGR
95-96	94.74	0.00	48	0	0.00
96-97	94.74	0.00	50	0	0.00
97-98	100.00	0.00	52	0	0.00
Averages	96.49	0.00	50.00	0.00	0.00

WALKER, Ian

Tottenham H. ❶❷❸❹ GK
Fullname: Ian Michael Walker
DOB: 31-10-71 Watford

One of England's finest goalkeepers over the past four years, Walker has had a tough time over the past couple of seasons through injury to himself and due to Tottenham's other well-documented injuries which have seen the personnel in front of him frequently changed. The final knock-back came just before France 98 when he was dropped from Glenn Hoddle's 22 man squad. But he remains a top quality 'keeper who consistently pulls off outstanding saves with his excellent

Ian Walker

agility while his handling at crosses is sound.

Walker went into the season with a goals against record of 1.35 per game in Premiership matches but such was Spurs' form he conceded goals at 1.55 per game in '97-98. His tally of clean sheets was boosted by just seven with Tottenham failing to achieve a shut-out for two consecutive league games.

Despite a disappointing time last season Walker will be back and remains a good choice for your fantasy side.

Form Factors

Season	Team	Tot	St	Sb	Y	R
95-96	Tottenham H.	38	38	0	1	0
96-97	Tottenham H.	37	37	0	0	0
97-98	Tottenham H.	29	29	0	0	0
Total		104	104	0	1	0

	GA	GkA	GAp	CS	SO	R
95-96	38	38	1.00	11	5	0
96-97	51	49	1.32	13	2	2
97-98	56	46	1.59	7	1	6
Averages	48.33	44.33	1.30	10.33	2.67	2.67

WALLACE, Rod
Leeds United ❶❷❸ M

Fullname: Rodney Seymour Wallace
DOB: 02-10-69 Greenwich

The last surviving member of Leeds United's 1992 championship winning side, Wallace looked certain to depart from Elland Road during the close season having spent a year annoying manager George Graham by refusing to sign a one year deal.

Ironically a season which saw Wallace in the shop window ahead of a free transfer, with 10 Premiership goals he had his most productive time since scoring 17 times in 1993-94 – not that the majority of Leeds fans saw his goals as nine of them came in away matches.

An elusive player, it remains to be seen whether he can match the goalscoring exploits he enjoyed during four fruitful years with Southampton that persuaded Leeds to pay £1.6m for him.

Form Factors

Season	Team	Tot	St	Sb	Y	R
95-96	Leeds U.	24	12	12	1	0
95-96	Leeds U.	22	17	5	5	0
97-98	Leeds U.	31	29	2	1	0
Total		77	58	19	7	0

	GP	GG	GF	GS	TGR
95-96	63.16	24.00	40	1	2.50
95-96	57.89	7.33	40	3	7.50
97-98	81.58	3.10	57	10	17.54
Averages	67.54	11.48	45.67	4.67	9.18

WALLEMME, Jean-Guy
Coventry City ❶❷ D

Fullname: Jean-Guy Wallemme
DOB: 10-08-67, Maubeuge, France

Signed for a reported £700,000, Wallemme was a regular in the defence that helped Racing Lens to the French league title last season. Indeed he has been a near ever-present in the side since he made his debut in 1986. Now on the wrong side of 30, Wallemme will be looking to establish himself in the Sky Blues' starting line-up as soon as possible.

WALSH, Steve

Leicester City ❶❷❸ CB

Fullname: Steven Walsh
DOB: 03-11-64 Preston

Now at the veteran stage of his career Walsh has been an inspirational figure at Filbert Street over the past 12 seasons during which time he has amassed 335 league games for the Foxes, which probably represents just about the best £100,000 Leicester have ever spent on a player. Has always been relied upon to score a handful of goals in the league each season with his tally at Leicester standing at a very creditable 50, helped in no small part in '93-94 when he played in attack.

A tough, no nonsense central defender who has endured countless operations and red cards down the years that mount into double figures. Has a year left on his contract but will need to stay in peak fitness if he is to see off the challenge of a younger generation.

Form Factors

Season	Team	Tot	St	Sb	Y	R
94-95	Leicester C.	5	5	0	0	0
96-97	Leicester C.	22	22	0	3	1
97-98	Leicester C.	26	23	3	4	0
Total		53	50	3	7	1

	GP	GG	GF	GS	TGR
94-95	13.16	0.00	45	0	0.00
96-97	57.89	11.00	46	2	4.35
97-98	68.42	8.67	51	3	5.88
Averages	46.49	6.56	47.33	1.67	3.41

WANCHOPE, Paulo

Derby County ❶❷❸❹❺ S

Fullname: Paulo Cesar Wanchope
DOB: 31-01-76 Cost Rica

Paulo Wanchope

Made the nation sit up and take note as soon as he arrived in this country following a £600,000 transfer from CS Heridiano in March 1997. His debut was sensational with a mazy run being concluded by a cool finish to score in Derby County's 3-2 win at Manchester United. Has proved that it was no flash in the pan with 16 goals last season – 12 in the Premiership – making him the Rams' leading scorer.

He can appear cumbersome at times but he shields the ball effectively and at 22 his knack of getting goals should only be enhanced with experience.

Form Factors

Season	Team	Tot	St	Sb	Y	R
96-97	Derby Co.	5	2	3	0	0
97-98	Derby Co.	32	30	2	7	0
Total		37	32	5	7	0

	GP	GG	GF	GS	TGR
96-97	13.16	5.00	45	1	2.22
97-98	84.21	2.46	52	13	25.00
Averages	48.68	3.73	48.50	7.00	13.61

WARD, Mitch

Everton ⓘⓔ M

Fullname: Mitchum David Ward
DOB: 19-06-71 Sheffield

After eight seasons with Sheffield United, and a short spell on loan to Crewe Alexandra, Ward was given his chance in the Premiership last season by the then Everton boss Howard Kendall. The pair had previously worked together at Bramall Lane and Kendall was confident enough in the player's ability to try him at the highest level.

Unfortunately for the versatile Ward he did not collect a win bonus in any of his eight appearances and now has to prove himself all over again to new boss Walter Smith.

Form Factors

Season	Team	Tot	St	Sb	Y	R
92-93	Sheffield U.	26	22	4	3	0
93-94	Sheffield U.	22	20	2	0	0
97-98	Everton	8	8	0	0	0
Total		56	50	6	3	0

	GP	GG	GF	GS	TGR
92-93	68.42	0.00	54	0	0.00
93-94	57.89	22.00	42	1	2.38
97-98	21.05	0.00	41	0	0.00
Averages	49.12	7.33	45.67	0.33	0.79

WATSON, Dave

Everton ①②③ CB

Fullname: David Watson
DOB: 20-11-61 Liverpool

A pillar at the centre of the Everton defence since moving to Goodison Park from Norwich City in a bargain £900,000 deal way back in August 1986. Has since made 395 league appearances for the Blues, was a member of the '87 championship winning side and the '95 FA Cup winning team. Well into the veteran stage of his career but still never pulls out of a challenge whether on the ground or in the air.

Everton kept seven clean sheets in Watson's 26 Premiership games last season but at the opposite end of the pitch he was unable to contribute a goal himself for the first time since the 1984-85 season.

A former Liverpool youngster he played 12 times for his country and has already had one spell as player/manager with Everton.

Form Factors

Season	Team	Tot	St	Sb	Y	R
95-96	Everton	34	34	0	6	1
96-97	Everton	29	29	0	4	0
97-98	Everton	26	25	1	2	0
Total		89	88	1	12	1

	GP	GG	GF	GS	TGR
95-96	89.47	34.00	64	1	1.56
96-97	76.20	29.00	44	1	2.27
97-98	68.42	0.00	41	0	0.00
Averages	78.07	21.00	49.67	0.67	1.28

WATSON, Steve

Newcastle U. ①②③ FB

Fullname: Stephen Craig Watson
DOB: 01-04-74 North Shields

Since making his debut for Newcastle in November 1990, local born Watson has filled a variety of positions for the Magpies usually to good effect. The youngest player ever to turn out for Newcastle, he has caught the eye with some spectacular goals down the years although playing on the right-hand side of the defence is probably his best position. Won a dozen England Under-21 caps and was then promoted to the B side.

Scored one goal in 29 Premiership outings last season, and would have played more games but for a couple of post-new year injuries. Still only 24, he has already played more than 200 league games for his one club.

Form Factors

Season	Team	Tot	St	Sb	Y	R
95-96	Newcastle U.	23	15	8	0	0
96-97	Newcastle U.	36	33	3	3	0
97-98	Newcastle U.	29	27	2	3	0
Total		88	75	13	6	0

	GP	GG	GF	GS	TGR
95-96	60.53	7.67	66	3	4.55
96-97	94.74	36.00	73	1	1.37
97-98	76.32	29.00	35	1	2.86
Averages	77.19	24.22	58.00	1.67	2.92

WATTS, Julian
Leicester City ❶ CB

Fullname: Julian Watts
DOB: 17-03-71 Sheffield

After looking set to claim a regular place in the Leicester side following his 35 league and cup appearances during 1996-97, it was back to the drawing board for Watts last season as he was afforded just two run-outs in the Premiership, both as substitute, and was named as an unused sub on five occasions.

A tall central defender he joined Leicester in March 1996 for £210,000 from Sheffield Wednesday where he made 25 Premiership appearances in more than four seasons. Quick and comfortable with the ball at his feet he started his career with Rotherham United.

Form Factors

Season	Team	Tot	St	Sb	Y	R
95-96	Sheffield W.	11	9	2	3	0
96-97	Leicester C.	26	22	4	3	0
97-98	Leicester C.	2	0	2	0	0
Total		39	31	8	6	0

	GP	GG	GF	GS	TGR
95-96	28.95	11.00	48	1	2.08
96-97	68.42	26.00	46	1	2.17
97-98	5.26	0.00	51	0	0.00
Averages	34.21	12.33	48.33	0.67	1.42

WETHERALL, David
Leeds United ❶❷❸ CB

Fullname: David Wetherall
DOB: 14-03-71 Sheffield

Although just 27 years old, Wetherall is the longest-serving player currently with Leeds United having signed for the club from county neighbours Sheffield Wednesday in June 1991 for a mere £275,000. Did not make the first team at Hillsborough but with his 34 Premiership appearances last season he has played over 180 times in the league for Leeds.

Has done well to force his way back into the side over the past 18 months in the face of several big money signings. His strength in aerial combat and solidity when challenging for the ball will ensure that he continues to be at the heart of George Graham's defence.

Form Factors

Season	Team	Tot	St	Sb	Y	R
95-96	Leeds U.	34	34	0	5	0
96-97	Leeds U.	29	25	4	7	0
97-98	Leeds U.	34	33	1	6	0
Total		97	92	5	18	0

	GP	GG	GF	GS	TGR
95-96	89.47	8.50	40	4	10.00
96-97	76.32	0.00	28	0	0.00
97-98	89.47	11.33	57	3	5.26
Averages	85.09	6.61	41.67	2.33	5.09

WHELAN, Noel

Coventry City ❶❷❸ S
Fullname: Noel Whelan
DOB: 30-12-74 Leeds

Made a big impression when he joined Coventry City from Leeds United for £2m in December 1995. Within 11 games he had seven goals posted against his name but it was form which he has failed to sustain despite a prolonged run in the Sky Blues first team.

Scored six times in 35 Premiership games in 1996-97 and last season he again scored six times but from only 20 games. Part of the reason for his drop in goals has been the frequency with which Coventry have used him in midfield but other than for that brief spurt he has not been a prolific scorer throughout his career.

Uses his 6'2" frame well to shield the ball and win headers while on the deck he has decent close control and is capable of going past defenders with ease.

Noel Whelan

Form Factors

Season	Team	Tot	St	Sb	Y	R
95-96	Coventry C.	21	21	0	3	0
96-97	Coventry C.	35	34	1	9	0
97-98	Coventry C.	21	21	0	4	0
Total		77	76	1	16	0

	GP	GG	GF	GS	TGR
95-96	55.26	2.63	42	8	19.05
96-97	92.11	5.83	38	6	15.79
97-98	55.26	3.50	46	6	13.04
Averages	67.54	3.99	42.00	6.67	15.96

WHITTINGHAM, Guy

Sheffield W. ❶❷ M
Fullname: Guy Whittingham
DOB: 10-11-64 Evesham

An out-and-out striker and goalscorer during the early days of his career with Yeovil Town and Portsmouth, whom he joined after buying his way out of the army. He stepped into the big time with a £1.2m transfer to Aston Villa in August 1993. Scored just five times in 25 league games for Villa but perked up with eight goals in 13 games whilst on loan to Wolverhampton Wanderers. His success there persuaded Sheffield Wednesday to sign him for £700,000 in December 1994.

Began his time at Hillsborough with a flurry of goals but has since been converted into a right-sided midfielder. Found his chances more limited last season with 11 of his 28 Premiership appearances coming from the subs bench and may find his opportunities even more restricted this term as he approaches his 34th birthday.

Form Factors

Season	Team	Tot	St	Sb	Y	R
95-96	Sheffield W.	29	27	2	4	0
96-97	Sheffield W.	33	29	4	1	0
97-98	Sheffield W.	28	17	11	1	0
Total		90	73	17	6	0

	GP	GG	GF	GS	TGR
95-96	76.32	4.83	48	6	12.50
96-97	86.84	11.00	50	3	6.00
97-98	73.68	7.00	52	4	7.69
Averages	78.95	7.61	50.00	4.33	8.73

WIJNHARD, Clyde
Leeds United ❶❷❸ S

Fullname: Clyde Wijnhard
DOB: 09-11-73 Surinam

A new face in the Premiership this season the 24-year-old Dutchman signed for Leeds United from Willem II in May 1998. Has played for a number of Dutch clubs including Ajax and FC Gronigen. During his final two seasons in Holland he showed himself to be a high scoring striker with 28 goals in 46 games for RKC Waalwijk and Willem II.

WILCOX, Jason
Blackburn Rovers ❶❷❸ F

Fullname: Jason Malcolm Wilcox
DOB: 15-03-71 Farnworth

Blackburn Rovers may have seen a succession of multi-million pound players come and go in recent years but one of their proudest possessions has to be Jason Wilcox, the Bolton-born striker having come through the ranks at Ewood Park to win an England cap against Hungary in 1996.

His cap was ample reward for a gutsy return to the Premiership after suffering long term injuries and that Blackburn climbed the table again with a fully fit Wilcox in the side was more than coincidence.

Mainly a left-sided player he is happy to use either foot and supplies Sutton and co. with top quality crosses. Has great stamina and is willing to get back to help out in deeper positions. Three Premier League goals from 31 matches last season was just slightly below his average.

Form Factors

Season	Team	Tot	St	Sb	Y	R
95-96	Blackburn R.	10	10	0	0	0
96-97	Blackburn R.	28	26	2	3	0
97-98	Blackburn R.	31	24	7	4	2
Total		69	60	9	7	2

	GP	GG	GF	GS	TGR
95-96	26.32	3.33	61	3	4.92
96-97	73.68	14.00	42	2	4.76
97-98	81.58	10.33	57	3	5.26
Averages	60.53	9.22	53.33	2.67	4.98

WILLIAMS, Andy
Southampton ①②S
Fullname: Andrew Williams
DOB: 08-10-77 Bristol

Made his debut in the Premiership with Southampton early last season when still a teenager and went on to feature in 20 of his side's league games, 17 as substitute and he was named as an unused sub for seven more games. Young striker who didn't score last season but could force his way more into the side this term in light of Kevin Davies's move to Blackburn.

Form Factors

Season	Team	Tot	St	Sb	Y	R
97-98	Southampton	20	3	17	2	0
Total		20	3	17	2	0

	GP	GG	GF	GS	TGR
97-98	52.63	0.00	50	0	0.00
Averages	52.63	0.00	50.00	0.00	0.00

Andy Williams

WILLIAMS, Paul
Coventry City ①②CB
Fullname: Paul Darren Williams
DOB: 26-03-71 Burton

Moved across the midlands from Derby to Coventry City in June 1995 for just short of £1m. A gritty, tough-tackling player who usually operates from the centre of the defence but has also proved himself when playing in a defensive midfield position. Missed just six Premiership games during each of his first two seasons at Highfield Road but a mammoth ten bookings and two dismissals last season restricted him to just 21 league appearances and five cup ties.

Played for England Under-21s in his younger days and spent six years with Derby prior to joining the Sky Blues.

Form Factors

Season	Team	Tot	St	Sb	Y	R
95-96	Coventry C.	32	30	2	9	1
96-97	Coventry C.	32	29	3	7	0
97-98	Coventry C.	20	17	3	10	2
Total		84	76	8	26	3

	GP	GG	GF	GS	TGR
95-96	84.21	16.00	64	2	3.13
96-97	84.21	16.00	38	2	5.26
97-98	52.63	0.00	46	0	0.00
Averages	73.68	10.67	49.33	1.33	2.80

WILLIAMSON, Danny

Everton ①②M

Fullname: Daniel Alan Williamson
DOB: 05-12-73 Newham

Went straight into the Everton first team at the start of last season following a £3m deal with West Ham United which involved David Unsworth heading in the opposite direction. Williamson settled quickly at Goodison Park and had played in 15 matches by December when injury cut short his season. It was the second year in which he had to spend a great deal of time on the sidelines due to injury.

When fully fit Evertonians will see a high quality ball-playing midfielder who is also full of stamina but is seldom amongst the goals.

Form Factors

Season	Team	Tot	St	Sb	Y	R
95-96	West Ham U.	29	28	1	5	0
96-97	West Ham U.	15	13	2	0	0
97-98	Everton	15	15	0	1	0
Total		59	56	3	6	0

	GP	GG	GF	GS	TGR
95-96	76.32	7.25	43	4	9.30
96-97	39.47	0.00	39	0	0.00
97-98	39.47	0.00	41	0	0.00
Averages	51.75	2.42	41.00	1.33	3.10

WILSON, Clive

Tottenham H. ①FB

Fullname: Clive Euclid Aklana Wilson
DOB: 13-11-61 Rusholme, Manchester

A Football League career which began back on 28 December 1981 looked to finally be coming to an end last season when veteran defender Clive Wilson made just 16 Premiership appearances for Tottenham. But the full-back who can play down either side of the defence and still loves to go on forward forays was granted a new one-year deal which could well see him complete the 14 games required to chalk up his 550th game since making his debut for Manchester City.

Wilson maintained his good disciplinary record last season and if Spurs' injury problems should persist then he could well prove to be a very valuable squad member.

Form Factors

Season	Team	Tot	St	Sb	Y	R
95-96	Tottenham H.	28	28	0	1	0
96-97	Tottenham H.	26	23	3	0	0
97-98	Tottenham H.	16	16	0	1	0
Total		70	67	3	2	0

	GP	GG	GF	GS	TGR
95-96	73.68	0.00	50	0	0.00
96-97	68.42	26.00	44	1	2.27
97-98	42.11	0.00	44	0	0.00
Averages	61.40	8.67	46.00	0.33	0.76

WILSON, Stuart

Leicester City ❶❷ M

Fullname: Stuart Kevin Wilson
DOB: 16-09-77 Leicester

Former Leicester City trainee who made his first team debut during the 1996-97 season and scored his first goal on the final of the season during a 4-2 win over Blackburn Rovers. Made good progress last season with another 11 games for the Foxes in the Premiership although all were from the subs bench, even so he still scored two goals. Was an unused sub for 15 other matches.

Form Factors

Season	Team	Tot	St	Sb	Y	R
96-97	Leicester C.	2	0	2	0	0
97-98	Leicester C.	11	0	11	0	0
Total		13	0	13	0	0

	GP	GG	GF	GS	TGR
96-97	5.26	2.00	46	1	2.17
97-98	28.95	5.50	51	2	3.92
Averages	17.11	3.75	48.50	1.50	3.05

WINTERBURN, Nigel

Arsenal ❶❷❸❹ FB

Fullname: Nigel Winterburn
DOB: 11-12-63 Nuneaton

There will come a day when one of the veterans in the Arsenal back four needs replacing but Winterburn is determined to see that it will not be him who goes first and with another outstanding season was part of the bedrock defence which carried the Gunners to their latest league and cup double.

The former Wimbledon defender, he joined Arsenal in 1987, has missed just seven out of 118 league games over the past four seasons and missed just eight games in the season before his current run started. Not only an excellent defender but still gets forward well to support the attack and last season he scored a spectacular and important winning goal at Chelsea – it was his first for two seasons.

The only cloud on the horizon for Winterburn would appear to be his age but if he can stay injury free there is little reason why he should not continue his excellent form over the coming months.

Form Factors

Season	Team	Tot	St	Sb	Y	R
95-96	Arsenal	36	36	0	6	0
96-97	Arsenal	38	38	0	5	0
97-98	Arsenal	36	35	1	3	0
Total		110	109	1	14	0

	GP	GG	GF	GS	TGR
95-96	94.74	18.00	49	2	4.08
96-97	100.00	0.00	62	0	0.00
97-98	94.74	36.00	68	1	1.47
Averages	96.49	18.00	59.67	1.00	1.85

WISE, Dennis

Chelsea ❶❷❸❹ M

Fullname: Dennis Frank Wise
DOB: 15-12-66 Kensington

An exuberant character, the Chelsea captain and former England international is also highly talented and has been one of the few constant figures in the rebuilding of the Blues into the club it is today. Wise is a threat whenever he is on the ball with his defence-splitting passes and dangerous crosses creating plenty of chances for teammates to score. Is capable of playing down either flank and scoring goals although his tally has dropped from that of his early days at Stamford Bridge.

The one downside to putting him in your fantasy team is the 20 cautions handed to him over the past two seasons which has resulted, inevitably, in several suspensions.

Form Factors

Season	Team	Tot	St	Sb	Y	R
95-96	Chelsea	35	34	1	10	0
96-97	Chelsea	31	27	4	7	0
97-98	Chelsea	26	26	0	10	0
Total		92	87	5	27	0

	GP	GG	GF	GS	TGR
95-96	92.11	5.00	46	7	15.22
96-97	81.58	7.75	58	4	6.90
97-98	68.42	8.67	71	3	4.23
Averages	80.70	7.14	58.33	4.67	8.78

WOAN, Ian

Nottingham F. ❶❷❸ M

Fullname: Ian Simon Woan
DOB: 14-12-67 Heswall, Wirral

Was snapped by long-time Nottingham Forest boss Brian Clough for a paltry £20,000 from Runcorn in March 1990 and has since enjoyed and endured the good and bad times of Forest's yo-yo existence between the Football League and the Premiership. An elegant, stylish midfielder, Woan has scored a goodly number of goals down the years, many spectacular, although in the past two seasons his contribution has been just one in each campaign.

No stranger to life in the Premiership, he will have to demonstrate great determination to prove himself once again as half of his 20 Division One appearances last season were from the subs bench.

Ian Woan

Fantasy Football Handbook 1998/99

Form Factors

Season	Team	Tot	St	Sb	Y	R
94-95	N. Forest	37	35	2	5	0
95-96	N. Forest	33	33	0	5	0
96-97	N. Forest	32	29	3	7	0
Total		102	97	5	17	0

	GP	GG	GF	GS	TGR
94-95	97.37	7.40	72	5	6.94
95-96	86.84	4.13	50	8	16.00
96-97	84.21	32.00	31	1	3.23
Averages	89.47	14.51	51.00	4.67	8.72

WREH, Christopher
Arsenal ❶❷❸ S

Fullname: Christopher Wreh
DOB: 14-05-75 Monrovia, Liberia

At just £300,000 Wreh looks to have been a good piece of business for Arsenal boss Arsène Wenger although the Liberian is not yet the finished article. The former Monaco and Guincamp striker was used only sparingly at Highbury, being substituted in all seven of his starts; he was also used as a substitute in nine Pemiership matches. Scored three league goals including winners against Wimbledon and Bolton and also provided the goal in the FA Cup semi final against Wolverhampton Wanderers which took Arsenal to Wembley.

Now that he has a year's experience of playing in England he should be seen more from the start during the 1998-99 season.

Form Factors

Season	Team	Tot	St	Sb	Y	R
97-98	Arsenal	16	7	9	0	0
Total		16	7	9	0	0

	GP	GG	GF	GS	TGR
97-98	42.11	5.33	68	3	4.41
Averages	42.11	5.33	68.00	3.00	4.41

WRIGHT, Alan
Aston Villa ❶❷❸ FB

Fullname: Alan Geoffrey Wright
DOB: 28-09-71 Ashton-under-Lyne

Has been a revelation since his £1m move to Aston Villa from Blackburn Rovers in March 1995, having missed just one Premiership match over the past three

Alan Wright

seasons. Distinctive through his lack of inches but even more so for his all-action style down the left. Is the perfect player for the wing-back position with his ability to defend and keenness to attack and send over telling crosses. Very quick, clean striker of the ball but not a regular goalscorer as his tally of four in 293 league games testifies.

Form Factors

Season	Team	Tot	St	Sb	Y	R
95-96	Aston Villa	38	38	0	2	0
96-97	Aston Villa	38	38	0	2	0
97-98	Aston Villa	37	35	2	0	1
Total		113	111	2	4	1

	GP	GG	GF	GS	TGR
95-96	100.00	19.00	52	2	3.85
96-97	100.00	38.00	47	1	2.13
97-98	97.37	0.00	49	0	0.00
Averages	99.12	19.00	49.33	1.00	1.99

WRIGHT, Ian

West Ham ❶❷❸❹ S

Fullname: Ian Edward Wright
DOB: 03-11-63 Woolwich

Whatever supporters may feel about Ian Wright as a person there can be no denying his magnificent achievements since coming into the professional game at the relatively late age of 21. The 1997-98 season, his seventh at Highbury following a productive six years with Crystal Palace, saw him finally surpass Cliff Bastin's club record of 178 goals. Wright's total of 10 Premiership goals – which made him only the third player to break the century barrier in the Premier Leagues' history – was his lowest in his time at Arsenal but that they came from just 24 games is a record any other striker at the top level would be proud of. On the downside he continued to collect yellow cards at pace with seven more coming his way from limited appearances.

Even though Wright will be 35 in November it is far too early to write him off. He will, for certain, be amongst the goals for his new club West Ham in 1998-99.

Form Factors

Season	Team	Tot	St	Sb	Y	R
95-96	Arsenal	31	31	0	8	0
96-97	Arsenal	35	30	5	10	1
97-98	Arsenal	24	22	2	7	0
Total		90	83	7	25	1

	GP	GG	GF	GS	TGR
95-96	81.58	2.07	49	15	30.61
96-97	92.11	1.52	62	23	37.10
97-98	63.16	2.40	68	10	14.71
Averages	78.95	2.00	59.67	16.00	27.47

YORKE, Dwight

Aston Villa ①②③④⑤ S

Fullname: Dwight Yorke
DOB: 03-11-71 Canaan, Tobago, West Indies

Dwight Yorke

Born in Tobago, he is an international in his homeland and joined Aston Villa in a £120,000 deal from St. Clair's in 1991. Possessing an explosive turn of pace, good close skills and a ready smile on his face, Yorke is the most engaging of characters and vital to Aston Villa's fortunes. During three seasons of fluctuating fortunes for the club, Yorke has been Villa's top scorer, overshadowing the achievements (or lack of) of big money signings Milosevic and Collymore.

Still only 26-years-old Yorke should continue to score a sack full of goals and still create openings for others.

Form Factors

Season	Team	Tot	St	Sb	Y	R
95-96	Aston Villa	35	35	0	0	0
96-97	Aston Villa	37	37	0	2	0
97-98	Aston Villa	30	30	0	5	0
Total		102	102	0	7	0

	GP	GG	GF	GS	TGR
95-96	92.11	2.06	52	17	32.69
96-97	97.37	2.18	47	17	36.17
97-98	78.95	2.50	49	12	24.49
Averages	89.47	2.25	49.33	15.33	31.12

ZAGORAKIS, Theo

Leicester C. ①②③ M

Fullname: Theo Zagorakis
DOB:

Joined Leicester City in February of 1998 from Greek side PAOK Salonika for £750,000 and quickly worked his way into the starting line-up. Made 14 appearances before the season was out but was withdrawn in half of those games. Captain of his national side he holds the record for making the most consecutive appearances for Greece. Scored one goal for the Foxes last season; it was the one which spelled the end of Barnsley's top flight excursion.

Fantasy Football Handbook 1998/99 — 319

Form Factors

Season	Team	Tot	St	Sb	Y	R
97-98	Leicester C.	14	12	2	1	0
Total		14	12	2	1	0

	GP	GG	GF	GS	TGR
97-98	36.84	14.00	51	1	1.96
Averages	36.84	14.00	51.00	1.00	1.96

ZOLA, Gianfranco

Chelsea ①②③④ S

Fullname: Gianfranco Zola
DOB: 05-07-66 Oliena, Sardinia

One of the finest overseas players ever to grace these shores, Zola cemented his place in Chelsea folklore when coming on as substitute late in the day to score a spectacular winning goal in the 1998 Cup Winners' Cup final against VfB Stuttgart. It was his fourth goal in the CWC last season and 12th in all competitions.

A £4.5m signing from Parma in November 1996 the Italian international, who scored the goal which gave Italy a World Cup qualifying victory over England at Wembley, has made a huge impact since arriving in this country. He has maintained his career record of scoring a goal every three games since joining Chelsea with his brilliant left foot making him a constant threat from set-pieces.

Although individually gifted he works well with those around him making for a great team player and the combination of those factors resulted in Zola being voted the Football Writers' Player of the Year in 1997 despite not being in England for the first three months of the season.

Form Factors

Season	Team	Tot	St	Sb	Y	R
96-97	Chelsea	23	22	1	0	0
97-98	Chelsea	27	23	4	2	0
Total		50	45	5	2	0

	GP	GG	GF	GS	TGR
96-97	60.53	2.88	58	8	13.79
97-98	71.05	3.38	71	8	11.27
Averages	65.79	3.13	64.50	8.00	12.53

Appearance Files

Appearance Files

APPEARANCE FIGURES taken on their own can be very deceptive. Numbers most often quoted are those for the games played – but football these days, especially in the FA Premier League, is ever more a squad game. Thus very few players indeed actually get to compete in every minute of every season. Goalkeepers are about the only exception.

Equally a player might be seen to make 20 or so appearances but he might never have made the original starting line-up. Indeed his appearances might all have been in the last ten minutes of every game. For example, take Arsenal's David Platt during the 1997-98 season: he made 31 appearances, appearing therefore in all but seven of the Gunners' Premiership campaign. But well over half of these appearances – 20 in fact – came from the bench.

A player may also start many games but never actually complete them and this could also affect their ability to score points in your team. Eranio Baiano, for instance, played in 33 of Derby County's games during 1997-98 but was substituted in no less than 16 games!

The following pages contain a detailed analysis of every player who featured in first team league football last season for each of the 20 clubs playing in the 1997-98 Premiership season and provide the information behind the figures as related above. Use this, in conjunction with the information provided at the start of this handbook, to assist you in making your fantasy team selections.

Tot   Total number of appearances – this is St+Sb
St   Start – the number of times a player started the game.
Sb   Sub – the number of times the player came on as a substitute.
Snu   Sub Not Used – the number of times the player was on the bench but didn't get used.
Ps   Player Subbed – the number of times the player was substituted.
Gls   Number or league goals scored.
Y   Number of cautions. †
R   Number of dismissals. †
Lg   League – the league they played in last season, P = Premier, N = Nationwide League.

The teams indicated are the ones for whom the player performed last season.
† Not for Nationwide League teams.

Player	Team	Tot	St	Sb	Snu	Ps	Gls	Y	R	Lge
ABOU	West Ham	19	12	7	4	6	5	1	1	P
ADAMS	Arsenal	26	26	0	0	0	3	6	0	P
AGOGO	Sheffield W.	1	0	1	0	0	0	0	0	P
ALBERT	Newcastle	23	21	2	7	3	0	8	0	P
ALEXANDER	West Ham	0	0	0	1	0	0	0	0	P
ALEXANDERSON	Sheffield W.	6	5	1	1	2	0	0	0	P
ALLEN, B.	Charlton A.	12	7	5	9	2	2	0	0	N
ALLEN, G.	Everton	5	2	3	6	1	0	1	0	P
ALLEN	N.Forest	2	1	1	0	1	0	0	0	N
ALLEN, R.	Tottenham	4	1	3	2	1	0	0	0	P
ALVES	West Ham	4	0	4	4	0	0	0	0	P
ANDERSSON, A.	Blackburn	4	1	3	8	1	0	0	0	P
ANDERSSON, A.	Newcastle U.	12	10	2	2	5	2	0	0	P
ANDERTON	Tottenham H.	15	7	8	1	5	0	0	0	P
ANDREWS	Leicester C.	0	0	0	14	0	0	0	0	P
ANELKA	Arsenal	26	16	10	8	13	7	3	0	P
ARBER	Tottenham H.	0	0	0	2	0	0	0	0	P
ARDLEY	Wimbledon	34	31	3	0	6	2	1	0	P
ARMSTRONG, A.	Middlesbrough	11	7	4	0	2	7	0	0	N
ARMSTRONG, C.	N.Forest	17	4	13	17	1	0	0	0	N
ARMSTRONG, C.	Tottenham H.	19	13	6	2	5	5	2	0	P
ARPHEXAD	Leicester C.	5	5	0	23	0	0	0	0	P
ASANOVIC	Derby Co.	4	3	1	1	3	1	1	0	P
ASPRILLA	Newcastle U.	10	8	2	0	3	2	0	0	P
ATHERTON	Sheffield W.	27	27	0	0	2	3	7	0	P
AUSTIN	Tottenham H.	0	0	0	0	0	0	0	0	P
BAARDSEN	Tottenham H.	9	9	0	26	0	0	0	0	P
BABAYARO	Chelsea	8	8	0	1	1	0	0	0	P
BABB	Liverpool	19	18	1	8	1	0	5	0	P
BAIANO	Derby Co.	33	30	3	0	16	13	2	0	P
BAKER	Middlesbrough	3	2	1	0	2	0	0	0	N
BALL	Everton	25	21	4	6	2	1	2	0	P
BALMER	Charlton A.	16	13	3	4	1	0	0	0	N
BARMBY	Everton	30	26	4	1	7	2	7	0	P
BARNES, J.	Liverpool	0	0	0	1	0	0	0	0	P
BARNES, J.	Newcastle U.	26	22	4	8	8	6	0	0	P
BARNESS	Charlton A.	30	21	9	9	4	1	0	0	N
BARRETT, E.	Everton	13	12	1	4	5	0	3	0	P
BARRETT, E.	Sheffield W.	10	10	0	0	2	0	1	1	P
BARRY	Aston Villa	2	1	1	1	0	0	0	0	P
BART-WILLIAMS	N.Forest	33	30	3	0	2	4	0	0	N
BARTON	Newcastle U.	23	17	6	1	3	3	7	0	P
BASHAM	Southampton	9	0	9	1	0	0	0	0	P
BATTY	Newcastle U.	32	32	0	0	1	1	9	3	P

Fantasy Football Handbook 1998/99

Player	Team	Tot	St	Sb	Snu	Ps	Gls	Y	R	Lge
BEAGRIE	Everton	6	4	2	2	3	0	1	0	P
BEARDSLEY	Newcastle U.	0	0	0	1	0	0	0	0	P
BEASANT	N.Forest	39	39	0	0	0	0	0	0	N
BEATTIE	Blackburn R.	3	0	3	5	0	0	0	0	P
BECK	Middlesbrough	38	32	6	4	8	14	0	0	N
BECKHAM	Manchester U.	37	34	3	0	2	9	6	0	P
BEENEY	Leeds U.	1	1	0	35	0	0	0	0	P
BENALI	Southampton	33	32	1	1	2	1	2	2	P
BERESFORD, J.	Newcastle U.	18	17	1	0	3	2	3	0	P
BERESFORD, J.	Southampton	10	10	0	0	1	0	0	0	P
BERESFORD, M	Middlesbrough	3	3	0	0	0	0	0	0	N
BERG	Manchester U.	27	23	4	8	2	2	2	0	P
BERGER	Liverpool	22	6	16	9	2	3	0	0	P
BERGKAMP	Arsenal	28	28	0	0	2	16	6	0	P
BERKOVIC	West Ham U.	35	34	1	1	12	7	2	0	P
BERTHE	West Ham U.	0	0	0	5	0	0	0	0	P
BERTI	Tottenham H.	17	17	0	0	5	3	5	0	P
BILIC	Everton	24	22	2	3	1	0	4	3	P
BISHOP	West Ham U.	3	3	0	12	0	0	0	0	P
BJORNEBYE	Liverpool	25	24	1	3	4	0	4	0	P
BLACKMORE	Middlesbrough	2	1	1	2	1	0	0	0	N
BLACKWELL	Wimbledon	35	35	0	0	2	0	4	0	P
BLONDEAU	Sheffield W.	6	5	1	3	0	0	4	0	P
BOA MORTE	Arsenal	15	4	11	8	2	0	2	0	P
BOATENG	Coventry C.	14	14	0	0	4	1	4	1	P
BOHINEN, L.	Blackburn R.	16	6	10	7	2	1	0	0	P
BOHINEN, L.	Derby Co.	9	9	0	0	3	1	1	0	P
BOLAND	Coventry C.	19	8	11	10	2	0	4	0	P
BONALAIR	N.Forest	30	23	7	3	5	2	0	0	N
BOOTH	Sheffield W.	23	21	2	1	4	7	1	1	P
BORROWS	Coventry C.	1	1	0	1	0	0	0	0	P
BOSNICH	Aston Villa	30	30	0	0	0	0	1	0	P
BOULD	Arsenal	24	21	3	4	0	0	8	0	P
BOWEN, M.	Charlton A.	37	35	2	1	5	0	0	0	N
BOWEN	Southampton	3	1	2	0	2	0	0	0	P
BOWYER	Leeds U.	25	21	4	11	6	3	4	0	P
BRADY	Tottenham H.	9	0	9	0	0	0	0	0	P
BRANCA	Middlesbrough	11	11	0	1	3	9	0	0	N
BRANCH	Everton	6	1	5	1	1	0	0	0	P
BRAYSON	Newcastle U.	0	0	0	1	0	0	0	0	P
BREACKER	West Ham U.	19	18	1	1	5	0	3	0	P
BREEN	Coventry C.	30	30	0	2	2	1	1	1	P
BRIDGE-WILKINSON	Derby Co.	0	0	0	3	0	0	0	0	P

Player	Team	Tot	St	Sb	Snu	Ps	Gls	Y	R	Lge
BRIGHT	Charlton A.	17	14	3	1	3	7	0	0	N
BRISCOE	Sheffield W.	7	3	4	3	2	0	0	0	P
BROOMES	Blackburn R.	4	2	2	14	0	0	1	0	P
BROWN, S.	Charlton A.	35	27	8	2	6	2	0	0	N
BROWN	Manchester U.	2	1	1	0	0	0	0	0	P
BROWN	Tottenham H.	0	0	0	2	0	0	0	0	P
BURROWS	Coventry C.	32	32	0	0	0	0	8	0	P
BURTON	Derby Co.	29	12	17	3	8	3	0	0	P
BUTT	Manchester U.	33	31	2	1	6	2	7	0	P
BYFIELD	Aston Villa	7	1	6	6	1	0	1	0	P
CADAMARTERI	Everton	26	15	11	3	9	4	4	0	P
CALDERWOOD	Tottenham H.	26	21	5	10	5	4	3	0	P
CAMPBELL	Leicester C.	11	6	5	13	5	0	1	0	P
CAMPBELL, A.	Middlesbrough	8	4	4	7	2	0	0	0	N
CAMPBELL, K.	N.Forest	41	41	0	0	4	23	0	0	N
CAMPBELL, S.	Tottenham H.	34	34	0	0	2	0	5	0	P
CARBON	Derby Co.	4	3	1	2	2	0	1	0	P
CARBONE	Sheffield W.	33	28	5	0	7	9	8	1	P
CARLSTRAND	Leicester C.	0	0	0	1	0	0	0	0	P
CARR	Tottenham H.	38	37	1	0	3	0	2	0	P
CARRAGHER	Liverpool	20	17	3	10	2	0	2	0	P
CARSLEY	Derby Co.	34	34	0	0	1	0	11	0	P
CASPER	Manchester U.	0	0	0	3	0	0	0	0	P
CASTLEDINE	Wimbledon	6	3	3	4	1	0	1	0	P
CHAPPLE	Charlton A.	35	29	6	3	1	4	0	0	N
CHARLES	Aston Villa	18	14	4	11	3	1	1	0	P
CHARLTON	Southampton	3	2	1	1	2	0	0	0	P
CHARVET	Chelsea	11	7	4	1	0	2	3	0	P
CHETTLE	N.Forest	43	43	0	0	4	1	0	0	N
CLAPHAM	Tottenham H.	0	0	0	1	0	0	0	0	P
CLARIDGE	Leicester C.	17	10	7	3	8	0	0	0	P
CLARKE, S.	Chelsea	26	22	4	2	2	1	2	0	P
CLARKE, M.	Sheffield W.	3	2	1	32	0	0	0	0	P
CLARKE, A.	Wimbledon	14	1	13	13	0	0	0	0	P
CLEGG	Manchester U.	3	1	2	6	1	0	0	0	P
CLEMENCE	Tottenham H.	17	12	5	5	3	0	1	0	P
CLOUGH	Sheffield W.	1	1	0	3	1	0	0	0	P
COLE	Manchester U.	33	31	2	0	6	16	6	0	P
COLEMAN	Blackburn R.	0	0	0	0	0	0	0	0	P
COLGAN	Chelsea	0	0	0	1	0	0	0	0	P
COLLINS	Aston Villa	0	0	0	10	0	0	0	0	P
COLLINS, W.	Sheffield W.	19	8	11	1	4	5	2	0	P
COLLYMORE	Aston Villa	25	23	2	1	3	6	4	1	P
COOPER	N.Forest	32	32	0	0	1	5	0	0	N

Fantasy Football Handbook 1998/99 **325**

Player	Team	Tot	St	Sb	Snu	Ps	Gls	Y	R	Lge
CORT	Wimbledon	22	16	6	3	5	4	0	0	P
COTTEE	Leicester C.	19	7	12	6	4	4	0	0	P
COYNE	West Ham U.	0	0	0	7	0	0	0	0	P
CRAWFORD	Newcastle U.	0	0	0	4	0	0	0	0	P
CRICHTON	Aston Villa	0	0	0	3	0	0	0	0	P
CRITTENDEN	Chelsea	2	0	2	1	0	0	0	0	P
CROFT	Blackburn R.	23	19	4	5	5	1	0	0	P
CROWE	Arsenal	0	0	0	2	0	0	0	0	P
CRUYFF	Manchester U.	5	3	2	1	1	0	1	0	P
CULKIN	Manchester U.	0	0	0	2	0	0	0	0	P
CUNNINGHAM	Wimbledon	32	32	0	0	1	0	2	0	P
CURCIC	Aston Villa	7	3	4	6	3	0	0	0	P
CURTIS	Manchester U.	8	3	5	5	1	0	0	0	P
DABIZAS	Newcastle U.	11	10	1	0	0	1	2	0	P
DAHLIN	Blackburn R.	21	11	10	5	7	4	2	0	P
DAILLY	Derby Co.	30	30	0	1	0	1	7	0	P
DAVIDSON	Blackburn R.	1	1	0	3	1	0	0	0	P
DAVIES	Southampton	25	20	5	1	4	9	5	0	P
DAY	Arsenal	0	0	0	1	0	0	0	0	P
DE GOEY	Chelsea	28	28	0	0	0	0	0	0	P
DELAP	Derby Co.	13	10	3	1	3	0	2	0	P
DI CANIO	Sheffield W.	35	34	1	0	8	12	10	0	P
DI MATTEO	Chelsea	30	28	2	1	6	4	6	0	P
DIBBLE	Middlesbrough	2	2	0	1	0	0	0	0	N
DIXON	Arsenal	28	26	2	0	3	0	3	0	P
DODD	Southampton	36	36	0	0	2	1	2	0	P
DOMINGUEZ	Tottenham H.	18	8	10	3	2	2	4	0	P
DONALDSON	Sheffield W.	5	1	4	0	1	0	0	0	P
DOWIE	West Ham U.	12	7	5	6	1	0	2	0	P
DRAPER	Aston Villa	31	31	0	3	2	3	4	0	P
DRYDEN	Southampton	13	11	2	6	1	0	2	0	P
DUBERRY	Chelsea	23	23	0	0	0	0	2	0	P
DUBLIN	Coventry C.	36	36	0	0	0	18	4	1	P
DUCROS	Coventry C.	3	1	2	1	2	0	0	0	P
DUFF	Blackburn R.	26	17	9	4	5	4	0	0	P
DUNNE	Everton	3	2	1	4	0	0	0	0	P
EARLE	Wimbledon	22	20	2	2	2	3	0	0	P
EDINBURGH	Tottenham H.	17	14	3	0	5	0	4	1	P
EHIOGU	Aston Villa	37	37	0	1	2	2	7	1	P
EKOKU	Wimbledon	16	11	5	1	4	4	0	0	P
ELLIOTT, R.	Newcastle U.	0	0	0	3	0	0	0	0	P
ELLIOTT, S.	Derby Co.	3	3	0	5	2	0	0	0	P
ELLIOTT, M.	Leicester C.	37	37	0	0	0	7	6	0	P
EMBLEN	Charlton A.	4	0	4	1	0	0	0	0	N

Player	Team	Tot	St	Sb	Snu	Ps	Gls	Y	R	Lge
EMERSON	Middlesbrough	21	21	0	0	3	4	0	0	N
ERANIO	Derby Co.	23	23	0	0	6	5	9	2	P
EUELL	Wimbledon	19	14	5	2	10	4	1	0	P
EUSTACE	Coventry C.	0	0	0	1	0	0	0	0	P
EVANS	Southampton	10	6	4	0	2	0	0	0	P
FABIO	Middlesbrough	0	0	0	0	0	0	0	0	N
FARRELLY	Everton	26	18	8	5	6	1	3	0	P
FEAR	Wimbledon	8	5	3	2	0	2	2	0	P
FENN	Tottenham H.	4	0	4	2	1	0	0	0	P
FENTON	Leicester C.	23	9	14	14	7	3	1	0	P
FERDINAND, L.	Tottenham H.	21	19	2	0	7	5	2	0	P
FERDINAND, R.	West Ham U.	35	35	0	0	1	0	3	0	P
FERGUSON	Everton	29	28	1	0	1	11	6	1	P
FESTA	Middlesbrough	38	36	2	0	1	2	0	0	N
FETTIS, A.	Blackburn R.	8	7	1	20	0	0	0	0	P
FETTIS, A.	N.Forest	0	0	0	0	0	0	0	0	N
FILAN	Blackburn R.	7	7	0	3	1	0	0	0	P
FINN	West Ham U.	0	0	0	1	0	0	0	0	P
FLAHAVAN	Southampton	0	0	0	4	0	0	0	0	P
FLEMING	Middlesbrough	37	35	2	2	0	1	0	0	N
FLITCROFT	Blackburn R.	33	28	5	3	3	0	6	0	P
FLO	Chelsea	34	16	18	4	6	11	0	0	P
FLOWERS	Blackburn R.	25	24	1	3	1	0	0	1	P
FORREST	West Ham U.	13	13	0	21	0	0	0	0	P
FOWLER	Liverpool	20	19	1	0	4	9	1	1	P
FOX	Tottenham H.	32	32	0	3	9	3	3	0	P
FRANCIS	Wimbledon	2	0	2	5	0	0	0	0	P
FREESTONE	Middlesbrough	4	2	2	5	0	0	0	0	N
FRIEDEL	Liverpool	11	11	0	7	0	0	0	0	P
GAIN	Tottenham H.	0	0	0	1	0	0	0	0	P
GALLACHER	Blackburn R.	33	31	2	0	5	16	2	0	P
GARDE	Arsenal	10	6	4	3	1	0	3	0	P
GASCOIGNE	Middlesbrough	7	7	0	0	3	0	0	0	N
GAYLE	Wimbledon	30	21	9	6	13	2	1	0	P
GEMMILL	N.Forest	43	42	1	0	7	2	0	0	N
GERRARD	Everton	4	4	0	28	0	0	1	0	P
GHENT	Aston Villa	0	0	0	2	0	0	0	0	P
GIBBENS	Southampton	2	2	0	4	1	0	0	0	P
GIGGS	Manchester U.	29	28	1	1	4	8	1	0	P
GILLESPIE	Newcastle U.	29	25	4	2	8	4	2	0	P
GINOLA	Tottenham H.	34	34	0	0	7	6	7	0	P
GIVEN	Newcastle U.	24	24	0	11	0	0	1	0	P
GRANT	Everton	7	7	0	1	4	1	0	0	P
GRANVILLE	Chelsea	13	9	4	6	2	0	2	0	P

Fantasy Football Handbook 1998/99

Player	Team	Tot	St	Sb	Snu	Ps	Gls	Y	R	Lge
GRAY	Leeds U.	0	0	0	1	0	0	0	0	P
GRAYSON	Aston Villa	33	28	5	4	5	0	2	0	P
GREENING	Manchester U.	0	0	0	1	0	0	0	0	P
GRIFFIN	Newcastle U.	4	4	0	2	2	0	0	0	P
GRIMANDI	Arsenal	22	16	6	8	3	1	5	0	P
GROBELAAR	Sheffield W.	0	0	0	5	0	0	0	0	P
GRODAS	Tottenham H.	0	0	0	10	0	0	0	0	P
GUDNASON	Liverpool	0	0	0	3	0	0	0	0	P
GUINAN	N.Forest	2	1	1	11	1	0	0	0	N
GULLIT	Chelsea	6	0	6	1	0	0	0	0	P
GUPPY	Leicester C.	37	37	0	0	2	2	3	0	P
HAALAND	Leeds U.	32	26	6	1	2	7	6	1	P
HALL	Coventry C.	25	20	5	6	3	1	7	0	P
HALLE	Leeds U.	33	31	2	3	3	2	5	1	P
HAMILTON	Newcastle U.	12	7	5	9	4	0	0	0	P
HAMPSHIRE	Chelsea	0	0	0	0	0	0	0	0	P
HAREWOOD	N.Forest	1	1	0	0	0	0	0	0	N
HARKNESS	Liverpool	25	24	1	8	3	0	6	0	P
HARLEY	Chelsea	3	3	0	0	3	0	0	0	P
HARRISON	Middlesbrough	14	11	3	1	1	0	0	0	N
HARTE	Leeds U.	12	12	0	9	2	0	0	0	P
HARTSON	West Ham U.	32	32	0	0	1	15	4	2	P
HASSELBAINK	Leeds U.	33	30	3	3	7	16	5	0	P
HAWORTH	Coventry C.	10	4	6	8	2	0	1	0	P
HEALD	Wimbledon	0	0	0	38	0	0	0	0	P
HEANEY	Charlton A.	7	5	2	1	3	0	0	0	N
HEDMAN	Coventry C.	14	14	0	23	0	0	0	0	P
HENCHOZ	Blackburn R.	36	36	0	0	4	0	6	0	P
HENDRIE	Aston Villa	17	13	4	9	2	3	1	0	P
HENDRY	Blackburn R.	34	34	0	0	4	1	6	0	P
HESKEY	Leicester C.	35	35	0	0	2	10	5	1	P
HIDEN	Leeds U.	11	11	0	0	1	0	2	0	P
HIGGINGBOTTOM	Manchester U.	1	0	1	0	0	0	0	0	P
HIGNETT	Middlesbrough	33	27	6	2	7	7	0	0	N
HINCHCLIFFE, A.	Everton	17	15	2	0	1	0	3	1	P
HINCHCLIFFE, A.	Sheffield W.	15	15	0	0	0	1	0	0	P
HIRST, D.	Sheffield W.	6	3	3	0	0	0	0	0	P
HIRST, D.	Southampton	28	28	0	0	12	9	3	0	P
HISLOP	Newcastle U.	13	13	0	18	0	0	0	0	P
HITCHCOCK	Chelsea	0	0	0	36	0	0	0	0	P
HJELDE	N.Forest	28	23	5	4	3	1	0	0	N
HODGES	West Ham U.	2	0	2	11	0	0	0	0	P
HOLDSWORTH	Wimbledon	5	4	1	2	4	0	1	0	P
HOLMES	Charlton A.	16	10	6	1	2	1	0	0	N

Player	Team	Tot	St	Sb	Snu	Ps	Gls	Y	R	Lge
HOPKIN	Leeds U.	25	22	3	6	8	1	5	0	P
HOULT	Derby Co.	2	2	0	34	0	0	0	0	P
HOWE	N.Forest	0	0	0	0	0	0	0	0	N
HOWELLS	Tottenham H.	20	14	6	0	2	0	3	0	P
HOWEY	Newcastle U.	14	11	3	5	4	0	0	0	P
HOWIE	Coventry C.	0	0	0	2	0	0	0	0	P
HUCKERBY	Coventry C.	34	32	2	0	9	14	9	0	P
HUGHES, S.	Arsenal	17	7	10	10	2	2	0	0	P
HUGHES	Aston Villa	0	0	0	5	0	0	0	0	P
HUGHES, A.	Newcastle U.	4	4	0	11	1	0	0	0	P
HUGHES, D.	Southampton	13	6	7	5	1	0	1	0	P
HUGHES, M.	West Ham U.	5	2	3	2	0	0	1	0	P
HUGHES, M.	Chelsea	29	25	4	4	4	9	9	0	P
HUGHES, P.	Chelsea	9	5	4	4	2	0	1	0	P
HUGHES, C.	Wimbledon	17	13	4	8	5	1	1	0	P
HUGHES, M.	Wimbledon	29	29	0	1	2	4	7	0	P
HUMPHREYS	Sheffield W.	7	2	5	10	2	0	1	0	P
HUNT	Derby Co.	19	7	12	7	3	1	1	0	P
HUTCHISON	Everton	11	11	0	0	0	1	2	0	P
HYDE	Sheffield W.	21	14	7	4	10	1	7	0	P
ILIC	Charlton A.	15	15	0	1	0	0	0	0	N
IMPEY	West Ham U.	19	19	0	1	5	0	0	0	P
INCE	Liverpool	31	31	0	1	1	8	8	0	P
IRWIN	Manchester U.	25	23	2	1	4	2	4	0	P
IVERSEN	Tottenham H.	13	8	5	0	2	0	1	0	P
IZZET	Leicester C.	36	36	0	0	3	4	5	0	P
JACKSON	Leeds U.	1	0	1	8	0	0	4	0	P
JAMES	Liverpool	27	27	0	11	0	0	0	0	P
JEFFERS	Everton	1	0	1	3	0	0	0	0	P
JEVONS	Everton	0	0	0	4	0	0	0	0	P
JOACHIM	Aston Villa	26	16	10	7	3	8	0	0	P
JOHANSEN	Coventry C.	2	0	2	8	0	0	0	0	P
JOHANSEN, B.	Southampton	6	3	3	10	3	0	1	0	P
JOHNSEN	Manchester U.	22	18	4	1	7	2	2	0	P
JOHNSON, A.	N.Forest	32	23	9	5	6	4	0	0	N
JOHNSON, D.	N.Forest	6	5	1	0	3	0	0	0	N
JONES	Leeds U.	0	0	0	3	0	0	5	0	P
JONES, P.	Southampton	38	38	0	0	0	0	0	0	P
JONES, V.	Wimbledon	24	22	2	0	5	0	2	0	P
JONES, K.	Charlton A.	45	45	0	0	8	3	0	0	N
JONES, R.	Liverpool	21	20	1	3	6	0	1	0	P
JONES, S.	Charlton A.	24	18	6	1	7	7	0	0	N
JUPP	Wimbledon	3	3	0	5	1	0	1	0	P
KAAMARK	Leicester C.	35	35	0	1	4	0	2	0	P

Fantasy Football Handbook 1998/99

Player	Team	Tot	St	Sb	Snu	Ps	Gls	Y	R	Lge
KEANE	Manchester U.	9	9	0	0	0	2	3	0	P
KEIDEL	Newcastle U.	0	0	0	1	0	0	0	0	P
KEITH	West Ham U.	0	0	0	1	0	0	0	0	P
KELLER	Leicester C.	33	33	0	1	0	0	2	0	P
KELLY	Leeds U.	34	34	0	0	0	0	6	1	P
KENNA	Blackburn R.	37	37	0	0	0	0	0	0	P
KENNEDY, M.	Liverpool	1	0	1	1	0	0	0	0	P
KENNEDY, M.	Wimbledon	4	4	0	0	2	0	0	0	P
KEOWN	Arsenal	18	18	0	0	1	0	2	1	P
KERSLAKE	Charlton A.	0	0	0	1	0	0	0	0	N
KETSBAIA	Newcastle U.	31	16	15	4	4	3	3	0	P
KEWELL	Leeds U.	29	26	3	3	3	5	2	1	P
KHARINE	Chelsea	10	10	0	1	0	0	0	0	P
KIMBLE	Wimbledon	25	23	2	4	0	0	7	0	P
KINDER	Middlesbrough	34	33	1	3	3	2	0	0	N
KINSELLA	Charlton A.	53	47	6	0	3	5	0	0	N
KITSON	West Ham U.	13	12	1	1	7	4	1	0	P
KLINSMANN	Tottenham H.	15	15	0	0	2	9	1	0	P
KNIGHT	Derby Co.	0	0	0	3	0	0	0	0	P
KONCHESKY	Charlton A.	3	2	1	0	2	0	0	0	N
KOZLUK	Derby Co.	9	6	3	11	2	0	1	0	P
KVARME	Liverpool	23	22	1	8	3	0	2	0	P
LAMA	West Ham U.	12	12	0	6	0	0	1	0	P
LAMBOURDE	Chelsea	7	5	2	8	0	0	3	1	P
LAMPARD	West Ham U.	31	27	4	2	0	4	5	0	P
LAURENT	Leeds U.	0	0	0	3	0	0	0	0	P
LAURSEN	Derby Co.	27	26	1	0	5	1	5	0	P
LAZARIDIS	West Ham U.	28	27	1	0	3	2	2	0	P
LE SAUX	Chelsea	26	26	0	0	1	1	3	0	P
Le TISSIER	Southampton	26	25	1	2	15	11	6	0	P
LEABURN, C.	Charlton A.	14	13	1	0	2	3	0	0	N
LEABURN, C.	Wimbledon	16	15	1	0	3	4	0	0	P
LEBOEUF	Chelsea	32	32	0	0	4	5	8	1	P
LEE, D.	Chelsea	1	1	0	2	0	0	0	0	P
LEE, R.	Newcastle U.	28	26	2	0	3	4	3	0	P
LENNON	Leicester C.	37	37	0	0	1	2	6	0	P
LEONHARDSEN	Liverpool	28	27	1	0	7	6	2	0	P
LIDDLE	Middlesbrough	7	2	5	6	0	0	0	0	N
LIGHTBOURNE	Coventry C.	7	1	6	8	1	0	1	0	P
LILLEY	Leeds U.	12	0	12	13	0	1	1	0	P
LISBIE	Charlton A.	17	1	16	3	1	1	0	0	N
LOMAS	West Ham U.	33	33	0	0	0	2	6	1	P
LUKIC	Arsenal	0	0	0	14	0	0	0	0	P
LUNDEKVAM	Southampton	31	31	0	0	3	0	7	0	P

Player	Team	Tot	St	Sb	Snu	Ps	Gls	Y	R	Lge
LYTTLE	N.Forest	34	34	0	0	6	0	0	0	N
MABBUTT	Tottenham H.	11	8	3	11	2	0	1	0	P
MADAR	Everton	17	15	2	0	11	6	2	0	P
MADDISON, N.	Middlesbrough	16	10	6	1	3	4	0	0	N
MADDISON, N.	Southampton	6	5	1	3	2	1	0	0	P
MAGILTON, J.	Sheffield W.	20	13	7	7	4	1	1	0	P
MAGILTON, J.	Southampton	5	5	0	0	0	0	1	0	P
MAHORN	Tottenham H.	2	2	0	1	2	0	0	0	P
MANNINGER	Arsenal	7	7	0	24	0	0	0	0	P
MARSHALL	Arsenal	3	1	2	9	0	0	0	0	P
MARSHALL, I.	Leicester C.	24	22	2	0	10	7	2	0	P
MARTYN	Leeds U.	37	37	0	0	0	0	0	0	P
MATTEO	Liverpool	25	24	1	0	0	0	1	0	P
MATTHEWS	Leeds U.	3	0	3	5	0	0	0	0	P
MAY	Manchester U.	9	7	2	3	1	0	3	0	P
MAYBURY	Leeds U.	12	9	3	5	4	0	0	0	P
MAYRLEB	Sheffield W.	3	0	3	3	0	0	0	0	P
McALLISTER, G.	Coventry C.	14	14	0	0	2	0	1	0	P
McALLISTER, B.	Wimbledon	7	4	3	7	1	0	0	0	P
McATEER	Liverpool	21	15	6	3	2	2	3	0	P
McCANN	Everton	11	5	6	3	1	0	2	0	P
McCLAIR	Manchester U.	13	2	11	17	2	0	0	0	P
McGOWAN	Arsenal	1	0	1	0	0	0	0	0	P
McGREGOR	N.Forest	0	0	0	2	0	0	0	0	N
McKINLAY	Blackburn R.	30	26	4	3	6	0	7	0	P
McMAHON	Leicester C.	1	0	1	0	0	0	0	0	P
McMANAMAN	Liverpool	36	36	0	1	2	11	1	0	P
McPHAIL	Leeds U.	4	0	4	6	0	0	0	0	P
McVEIGH	Tottenham H.	0	0	0	0	0	0	0	0	P
MEAN	West Ham U.	3	0	3	11	0	0	0	0	P
MENDEZ	Arsenal	3	1	2	1	1	0	0	0	P
MENDONCA	Charlton A.	41	41	0	0	2	23	0	0	N
MERSON	Middlesbrough	45	45	0	0	4	12	0	0	N
MIKLOSKO	West Ham U.	13	13	0	0	0	0	0	0	P
MILLS	Charlton A.	10	10	0	0	1	1	0	0	N
MILOSEVIC	Aston Villa	23	19	4	8	7	7	5	0	P
MOLDOVAN	Coventry C.	10	5	5	6	3	1	0	0	P
MOLENAAR	Leeds U.	22	18	4	12	5	2	4	0	P
MONCUR	West Ham U.	20	17	3	1	5	1	7	0	P
MONKOU	Southampton	32	30	2	1	1	1	5	1	P
MOORE	Middlesbrough	4	3	1	1	0	0	0	0	N
MOORE, I.	N.Forest	9	2	7	4	0	1	0	0	N
MOORE	West Ham U.	1	0	1	2	0	0	0	0	P
MORENO	Middlesbrough	9	6	3	6	1	0	0	0	N

Fantasy Football Handbook 1998/99

Player	Team	Tot	St	Sb	Snu	Ps	Gls	Y	R	Lge
MORRIS	Chelsea	12	9	3	2	5	1	0	0	P
MORRISSON	Derby Co.	1	1	0	0	0	0	0	0	P
MORTIMER	Charlton A.	13	8	5	0	4	4	0	0	N
MOSS	Southampton	0	0	0	20	0	0	0	0	P
MULRYNE	Manchester U.	1	1	0	5	0	0	0	0	P
MUNTASSER	Arsenal	0	0	0	0	0	0	0	0	P
MURPHY	Liverpool	16	6	10	10	4	0	1	0	P
MURRAY	Aston Villa	0	0	0	2	0	0	0	0	P
MUSTOE	Middlesbrough	34	33	1	0	3	3	0	0	N
MYERS	Chelsea	12	11	1	5	1	0	0	0	P
MYRHE	Everton	22	22	0	1	0	0	1	0	P
NEILSON	Southampton	8	3	5	1	0	0	2	0	P
NELSON	Aston Villa	25	21	4	11	6	0	1	0	P
NEVILLE, G.	Manchester U.	34	34	0	2	5	0	2	0	P
NEVILLE, P.	Manchester U.	30	24	6	3	6	1	7	0	P
NEVLAND	Manchester U.	1	0	1	1	0	0	0	0	P
NEWSOME	Sheffield W.	25	25	0	0	2	2	2	0	P
NEWTON, S.	Charlton A.	42	34	8	2	9	5	0	0	N
NEWTON, E.	Chelsea	18	17	1	2	5	0	0	0	P
NICHOLLS	Charlton A.	6	1	5	1	0	0	0	0	N
NICHOLLS, M.	Chelsea	19	8	11	10	3	3	2	0	P
NICOL	Sheffield W.	7	4	3	6	2	0	1	0	P
NIELSEN	Tottenham H.	25	21	4	6	4	3	2	0	P
NIELSON	Liverpool	0	0	0	12	0	0	0	0	P
NILSSON	Coventry C.	32	32	0	1	0	0	3	0	P
NOLAN	Sheffield W.	27	27	0	0	2	0	1	0	P
NOTEMAN	Manchester U.	0	0	0	1	0	0	0	0	P
O'CONNOR	Everton	1	0	1	4	0	0	0	0	P
O'KANE	Everton	12	12	0	0	4	0	5	0	P
O'NEILL	Coventry C.	4	2	2	4	2	0	0	0	P
O'TOOLE	Everton	0	0	0	4	0	0	0	0	P
OAKES, M.	Aston Villa	8	8	0	29	0	0	0	0	P
OAKES	Leicester C.	0	0	0	1	0	0	0	0	P
OAKES, S.	Sheffield W.	4	0	4	10	0	0	0	0	P
OAKLEY	Southampton	33	32	1	0	10	1	3	0	P
OGRIZOVIC	Coventry C.	24	24	0	13	0	0	0	0	P
OMOYINMI	West Ham U.	5	1	4	2	0	2	0	0	P
ORMEROD	Middlesbrough	17	10	7	3	3	3	0	0	N
OSTENSTAD	Southampton	29	21	8	0	4	11	4	0	P
OSTER	Everton	31	16	15	5	5	1	2	0	P
OVERMARS	Arsenal	32	32	0	0	13	11	0	0	P
OWEN	Liverpool	36	34	2	1	4	18	4	1	P
PALLISTER	Manchester U.	33	33	0	0	5	0	4	1	P
PALMER	Southampton	26	26	0	0	0	3	6	1	P

Player	Team	Tot	St	Sb	Snu	Ps	Gls	Y	R	Lge
PARKER, S.	Charlton A.	3	0	3	1	0	0	0	0	N
PARKER, G.	Leicester C.	22	15	7	6	8	3	1	0	P
PARLOUR	Arsenal	34	34	0	0	15	5	6	0	P
PASCALO	N.Forest	6	6	0	9	0	0	0	0	N
PEACOCK	Newcastle U.	20	19	1	3	1	0	4	0	P
PEARCE, I.	Blackburn R.	5	1	4	1	0	0	1	0	P
PEARCE, I.	West Ham U.	30	30	0	1	1	1	1	0	P
PEARCE, S.	Newcastle U.	25	25	0	2	1	0	4	0	P
PEARSON	Middlesbrough	19	19	0	0	4	2	0	0	N
PEDERSEN, T.	Blackburn R.	5	3	2	12	0	0	0	0	P
PEDERSEN, P.	Blackburn R.	0	0	0	1	0	0	0	0	P
PEMBRIDGE	Sheffield W.	34	31	3	0	15	4	4	0	P
PERRY	Wimbledon	35	35	0	0	0	1	7	0	P
PETIT	Arsenal	32	32	0	0	5	2	4	1	P
PETRESCU	Chelsea	31	31	0	1	13	5	3	0	P
PETTERSON	Charlton A.	23	23	0	0	0	0	0	0	N
PHELAN	Everton	9	8	1	2	2	0	2	0	P
PHILLIPS	N.Forest	0	0	0	0	0	0	0	0	N
PILKINGTON	Manchester U.	2	2	0	6	0	0	0	0	P
PINAS	Newcastle U.	0	0	0	2	0	0	0	0	P
PISTONE	Newcastle U.	28	28	0	0	0	0	6	0	P
PLATT	Arsenal	31	11	20	1	3	3	4	0	P
POBORSKY	Manchester U.	10	3	7	6	3	2	1	0	P
POOM	Derby Co.	36	36	0	1	0	0	2	0	P
PORIC	Sheffield W.	3	0	3	2	0	0	0	0	P
POTTS	West Ham U.	23	14	9	12	2	0	2	0	P
POWELL, C.	Derby Co.	36	34	2	1	2	1	3	0	P
POWELL, D.	Derby Co.	24	13	11	1	4	0	4	0	P
POYET	Chelsea	14	11	3	0	1	4	2	0	P
PRENDERVILLE	Coventry C.	0	0	0	2	0	0	0	0	P
PRESSMAN	Sheffield W.	36	36	0	0	1	0	0	0	P
PRIOR	Leicester C.	30	28	2	2	5	0	2	0	P
QUINN	Sheffield W.	1	0	1	0	0	1	0	0	P
RACHEL	Aston Villa	0	0	0	3	0	0	0	0	P
RADEBE	Leeds U.	27	26	1	0	2	0	10	1	P
RANKIN	Arsenal	1	0	1	2	0	0	0	0	P
RAVANELLI	Middlesbrough	2	2	0	0	0	1	0	0	N
REDFEARN	Charlton A.	37	37	0	0	0	10	2	0	P
REDKNAPP	Liverpool	20	20	0	0	2	3	3	0	P
REEVES	Wimbledon	0	0	0	9	0	0	0	0	P
RIBEIRO	Leeds U.	29	28	1	0	6	3	1	0	P
RICARD	Middlesbrough	9	3	6	0	1	2	0	0	N
RICHARDSON, K.	Coventry C.	3	3	0	2	0	0	0	0	P
RICHARDSON, K.	Southampton	28	25	3	5	9	0	1	0	P

Fantasy Football Handbook 1998/99   **333**

Player	Team	Tot	St	Sb	Snu	Ps	Gls	Y	R	Lge
RIEDLE	Liverpool	25	18	7	5	9	6	1	0	P
RIEPER	West Ham U.	5	5	0	0	0	1	0	0	P
RIPLEY	Blackburn R.	29	25	4	2	14	2	0	0	P
RIZZO	Liverpool	0	0	0	4	0	0	0	0	P
ROBERTS	Liverpool	0	0	0	3	0	0	0	0	P
ROBERTS, B.	Middlesbrough	9	9	0	2	0	0	0	0	N
ROBERTS, A.	Wimbledon	12	12	0	0	0	1	3	0	P
ROBERTSON	Leeds U.	26	24	2	0	0	0	0	0	P
ROBINSON, J.	Charlton A.	38	37	1	0	8	8	0	0	N
ROBINSON	Leeds U.	0	0	0	4	0	0	0	0	P
ROBINSON	Southampton	1	0	1	3	0	0	0	0	P
ROGERS	N.Forest	45	45	0	0	7	1	0	0	N
ROSE	Arsenal	0	0	0	0	0	0	0	0	P
ROWETT	Derby Co.	35	32	3	3	2	1	3	0	P
ROWLAND	West Ham U.	7	6	1	11	0	0	0	0	P
RUDDOCK	Liverpool	3	2	1	2	1	0	0	0	P
RUDI	Sheffield W.	22	19	3	0	5	0	2	0	P
RUFUS	Charlton A.	43	43	0	0	7	0	0	0	N
RUSH	Newcastle U.	10	6	4	8	2	0	1	0	P
SAIB	Tottenham H.	9	3	6	0	1	1	0	0	P
SALAKO	Coventry C.	11	11	0	2	2	0	0	0	P
SALMON	Charlton A.	9	9	0	0	1	0	0	0	N
SANETTI	Sheffield W.	2	1	1	0	0	0	0	0	P
SAUNDERS	N.Forest	8	6	2	1	2	2	0	0	N
SAVAGE	Leicester C.	35	28	7	2	6	2	4	0	P
SCALES	Tottenham H.	10	9	1	9	1	0	1	0	P
SCHMEICHEL	Manchester U.	33	33	0	0	2	0	0	0	P
SCHOLES	Manchester U.	31	28	3	0	10	8	7	0	P
SCHWARZER	Middlesbrough	32	32	0	0	0	0	0	0	N
SCIMECA	Aston Villa	21	16	5	7	3	0	0	0	P
SEALEY	West Ham U.	0	0	0	10	0	0	0	0	P
SEAMAN	Arsenal	31	31	0	0	0	0	1	0	P
SEDLOSKI	Sheffield W.	4	3	1	0	1	0	0	0	P
SHAW	Coventry C.	33	33	0	2	1	0	2	0	P
SHEARER	Newcastle U.	17	15	2	0	0	2	2	0	P
SHEERIN	Chelsea	0	0	0	1	0	0	0	0	P
SHERINGHAM	Manchester U.	30	27	3	3	4	9	2	0	P
SHERWOOD	Blackburn R.	31	29	2	0	3	5	5	0	P
SHILTON	Coventry C.	2	2	0	5	1	0	0	0	P
SHORT	Everton	31	27	4	1	6	0	3	0	P
SIMPSON	Derby Co.	1	1	0	4	1	0	0	0	P
SINCLAIR, T.	Chelsea	22	20	2	0	4	1	3	1	P
SINCLAIR, T.	West Ham U.	14	14	0	0	1	7	5	0	P
SINTON	Tottenham H.	19	14	5	2	6	0	1	0	P

Player	Team	Tot	St	Sb	Snu	Ps	Gls	Y	R	Lge
SLATER	Southampton	11	3	8	3	3	0	1	0	P
SMITH	Derby Co.	0	0	0	1	0	0	0	0	P
SMITH	N.Forest	0	0	0	0	0	1	0	0	N
SOLBAKKEN	Wimbledon	6	4	2	5	0	1	1	0	P
SOLIS	Derby Co.	9	3	6	6	3	0	0	0	P
SOLSKJAER	Manchester U.	22	15	7	4	4	6	0	1	P
SOLTVEDT	Coventry C.	30	26	4	8	10	1	1	0	P
SOUTHALL	Everton	12	12	0	5	0	0	0	0	P
SOUTHGATE	Aston Villa	32	32	0	0	1	0	2	0	P
SPEDDING	Southampton	7	4	3	2	3	0	0	0	P
SPEED, G.	Everton	21	21	0	0	0	7	4	0	P
SPEED, G.	Newcastle U.	13	13	0	0	0	1	1	0	P
SPENCER	Everton	6	3	3	0	0	0	1	0	P
SRNICEK	Newcastle U.	1	1	0	9	0	0	0	0	P
STAMP	Middlesbrough	10	8	2	8	2	0	0	0	N
STAUNTON	Aston Villa	27	27	0	1	5	1	5	0	P
STEFANOVIC	Sheffield W.	20	19	1	3	2	2	8	1	P
STIMAC	Derby Co.	22	22	0	0	2	1	6	0	P
STOCKDALE	Middlesbrough	1	1	0	0	0	0	0	0	N
STONE	N.Forest	30	28	2	1	5	2	0	0	N
STRACHAN, Ga.	Coventry C.	9	2	7	11	2	0	0	0	P
STUART	Charlton A.	1	0	1	1	0	0	0	0	N
STUART, G.	Everton	14	14	0	0	1	2	6	0	P
STURRIDGE	Derby Co.	30	24	6	0	7	9	8	0	P
SULLIVAN	Wimbledon	38	38	0	0	0	0	0	0	P
SUMMERBELL	Middlesbrough	6	4	2	2	3	0	0	0	N
SUTTON	Blackburn R.	35	35	0	0	1	18	10	1	P
TAYLOR, I.	Aston Villa	32	30	2	0	3	6	6	0	P
TAYLOR	Southampton	0	0	0	14	0	0	0	0	P
TELFER	Coventry C.	33	33	0	0	4	3	9	0	P
TERRIER, D.	Newcastle U.	0	0	0	1	0	0	0	0	P
TERRIER, D.	West Ham U.	1	0	1	2	0	0	0	0	P
THATCHER	Wimbledon	26	23	3	4	2	0	2	2	P
THOM	N.Forest	0	0	0	0	0	0	0	0	N
THOMAS, T.	Everton	7	6	1	6	3	0	1	0	P
THOMAS, M.	Liverpool	11	10	1	2	2	1	3	0	P
THOMAS	Middlesbrough	11	11	0	0	2	0	0	0	N
THOMAS, G.	N.Forest	19	13	6	3	2	3	0	0	N
THOME	Sheffield W.	6	6	0	2	1	0	1	0	P
THOMPSON	Liverpool	5	1	4	5	0	1	1	0	P
THOMSEN	Everton	8	2	6	1	1	1	0	0	P
THORNLEY	Manchester U.	5	0	5	5	0	0	0	0	P
TILER	Everton	19	19	0	0	1	1	5	0	P
TODD	Southampton	10	9	1	7	1	0	1	0	P

Player	Team	Tot	St	Sb	Snu	Ps	Gls	Y	R	Lge
TOMASSON	Newcastle U.	23	17	6	11	6	3	1	0	P
TOWNSEND, A.	Aston Villa	3	3	0	0	0	0	0	0	P
TOWNSEND, A.	Middlesbrough	38	36	2	0	5	2	0	0	N
TREVOR	Middlesbrough	0	0	0	0	0	0	0	0	N
TROLLOPE	Derby Co.	10	4	6	1	0	0	0	0	P
TWISS	Manchester U.	0	0	0	2	0	0	0	0	P
ULLATHORNE	Leicester C.	6	3	3	1	1	1	0	1	P
UNSWORTH	West Ham U.	32	32	0	0	1	2	8	1	P
UPSON	Arsenal	5	5	0	6	1	0	0	0	P
VALERY	Blackburn R.	15	14	1	5	5	0	2	1	P
VAN DER GOUW	Manchester U.	5	4	1	26	0	0	0	0	P
VAN DER LAAN	Derby Co.	10	7	3	6	5	0	2	0	P
VAN GOBBEL	Southampton	2	1	1	0	1	0	0	0	P
VAN HOOIJDONK	N.Forest	41	40	1	0	1	29	0	0	N
VASSELL	Aston Villa	0	0	0	2	0	0	0	0	P
VEGA	Tottenham H.	25	22	3	0	0	3	4	1	P
VERNAZZA	Arsenal	1	1	0	0	1	0	0	0	P
VIALLI	Chelsea	21	14	7	10	6	11	4	0	P
VICKERS	Middlesbrough	35	32	3	2	2	0	0	0	N
VIEIRA	Arsenal	33	31	2	0	4	2	8	1	P
WALKER	Aston Villa	1	0	1	2	0	0	0	0	P
WALKER, D.	Sheffield W.	38	38	0	0	1	0	0	0	P
WALKER, I.	Tottenham H.	28	28	0	0	0	0	0	0	P
WALLACE	Leeds U.	31	29	2	2	6	10	1	0	P
WALLWORK	Manchester U.	1	0	1	0	0	0	0	0	P
WALSH	Leicester C.	26	23	3	1	6	3	4	0	P
WANCHOPE	Derby Co.	32	30	2	0	6	13	7	0	P
WARD	Derby Co.	3	2	1	0	0	0	0	0	P
WARD, M.	Everton	8	8	0	0	2	0	0	0	P
WARNER	Liverpool	0	0	0	7	0	0	0	0	P
WARNER	N.Forest	0	0	0	0	0	0	0	0	N
WARNER	Southampton	1	0	1	2	0	0	0	0	P
WATSON, D.	Everton	26	25	1	2	2	0	2	0	P
WATSON, S.	Newcastle U.	29	27	2	2	0	1	3	0	P
WATT	Blackburn R.	0	0	0	2	0	0	0	0	P
WATTS	Leicester C.	2	0	2	5	0	0	0	0	P
WETHERALL	Leeds U.	34	33	1	2	0	3	6	0	P
WHELAN	Coventry C.	21	21	0	0	2	6	4	0	P
WHITLOW	Leicester C.	1	0	1	2	0	0	0	0	P
WHITTINGHAM	Sheffield W.	28	17	11	7	6	4	1	0	P
WHYTE	Middlesbrough	8	5	3	4	0	0	0	0	N
WILCOX	Blackburn R.	31	24	7	2	6	3	4	2	P
WILLAMS	Blackburn R.	0	0	0	8	0	0	0	0	P
WILLEMS	Derby Co.	10	3	7	4	1	0	0	0	P

Player	Team	Tot	St	Sb	Snu	Ps	Gls	Y	R	Lge
WILLIAMS	Liverpool	0	0	0	1	0	0	0	0	P
WILLIAMS, A.	Southampton	20	3	17	7	2	0	2	0	P
WILLIAMS, P.	Coventry C.	20	17	3	8	1	0	10	2	P
WILLIAMSON	Everton	15	15	0	0	5	0	1	0	P
WILLIS	Coventry C.	0	0	0	1	0	0	0	0	P
WILSON, S.	Leicester C.	11	0	11	15	0	2	0	0	P
WILSON, C.	Tottenham H.	16	16	0	1	7	0	1	0	P
WINTERBURN	Arsenal	36	35	1	0	2	1	3	0	P
WISE	Chelsea	26	26	0	0	2	3	10	0	P
WOAN	N.Forest	20	10	10	7	6	1	0	0	N
WREH	Arsenal	16	7	9	3	7	3	0	0	P
WRIGHT, I.	Arsenal	24	22	2	0	7	10	7	0	P
WRIGHT, A.	Aston Villa	37	35	2	1	3	0	1	0	P
WRIGHT, M.	Liverpool	6	6	0	2	0	0	0	0	P
YATES	Derby Co.	9	8	1	2	2	0	2	0	P
YORKE	Aston Villa	30	30	0	0	2	12	5	0	P
YOUDS	Charlton A.	9	9	0	0	0	0	0	0	N
ZAGORAKIS	Leicester C.	14	12	2	0	7	1	1	0	P
ZOLA	Chelsea	27	23	4	4	11	8	2	0	P

Players who played in 30+ Games

Player	Team	Tot	St	Sb	Snu	Ps	Gls	Y	R
JONES, P.	Southampton	38	38	0	0	0	0	0	0
SULLIVAN	Wimbledon	38	38	0	0	0	0	0	0
WALKER	Sheffield W.	38	38	0	0	1	0	0	0
CARR	Tottenham H.	38	37	1	0	3	0	2	0
EHIOGU	Aston Villa	37	37	0	1	2	2	7	1
ELLIOTT	Leicester C.	37	37	0	0	0	7	6	0
GUPPY	Leicester C.	37	37	0	0	2	2	3	0
KENNA	Blackburn R.	37	37	0	0	0	0	0	0
LENNON	Leicester C.	37	37	0	0	1	2	6	0
MARTYN	Leeds U.	37	37	0	0	0	0	0	0
REDFEARN	Charlton A.	37	37	0	0	0	10	2	0
WRIGHT, A.	Aston Villa	37	35	2	1	3	0	1	0
BECKHAM	Manchester U.	37	34	3	0	2	9	6	0
DODD	Southampton	36	36	0	0	2	1	2	0
DUBLIN	Coventry C.	36	36	0	0	0	18	4	1
HENCHOZ	Blackburn R.	36	36	0	0	4	0	6	0
IZZET	Leicester C.	36	36	0	0	3	4	5	0
McMANAMAN	Liverpool	36	36	0	1	2	11	1	0
POOM	Derby Co.	36	36	0	1	0	0	2	0

Fantasy Football Handbook 1998/99

Player	Team	Tot	St	Sb	Snu	Ps	Gls	Y	R
PRESSMAN	Sheffield W.	36	36	0	0	1	0	0	0
WINTERBURN	Arsenal	36	35	1	0	2	1	3	0
OWEN	Liverpool	36	34	2	1	4	18	4	1
POWELL, C.	Derby Co.	36	34	2	1	2	1	3	0
BLACKWELL	Wimbledon	35	35	0	0	2	0	4	0
FERDINAND, R.	West Ham U.	35	35	0	0	1	0	3	0
HESKEY	Leicester C.	35	35	0	0	2	10	5	1
KAAMARK	Leicester C.	35	35	0	1	4	0	2	0
PERRY	Wimbledon	35	35	0	0	0	1	7	0
SUTTON	Blackburn R.	35	35	0	0	1	18	10	1
BERKOVIC	West Ham U.	35	34	1	1	12	7	2	0
DI CANIO	Sheffield W.	35	34	1	0	8	12	10	0
ROWETT	Derby Co.	35	32	3	3	2	1	3	0
SAVAGE	Leicester C.	35	28	7	2	6	2	4	0
CAMPBELL, S.	Tottenham H.	34	34	0	0	2	0	5	0
CARSLEY	Derby Co.	34	34	0	0	1	0	11	0
GINOLA	Tottenham H.	34	34	0	0	7	6	7	0
HENDRY	Blackburn R.	34	34	0	0	4	1	6	0
KELLY	Leeds U.	34	34	0	0	0	0	6	1
NEVILLE, G.	Manchester U.	34	34	0	2	5	0	2	0
PARLOUR	Arsenal	34	34	0	0	15	5	6	0
WETHERALL	Leeds U.	34	33	1	2	0	3	6	0
HUCKERBY	Coventry C.	34	32	2	0	9	14	9	0
ARDLEY	Wimbledon	34	31	3	0	6	2	1	0
PEMBRIDGE	Sheffield W.	34	31	3	0	15	4	4	0
FLO	Chelsea	34	16	18	4	6	11	0	0
KELLER	Leicester C.	33	33	0	1	0	0	2	0
LOMAS	West Ham U.	33	33	0	0	0	2	6	1
PALLISTER	Manchester U.	33	33	0	0	5	0	4	1
SCHMEICHEL	Manchester U.	33	33	0	0	2	0	0	0
SHAW	Coventry C.	33	33	0	2	1	0	2	0
TELFER	Coventry C.	33	33	0	0	4	3	9	0
BENALI	Southampton	33	32	1	1	2	1	2	2
OAKLEY	Southampton	33	32	1	0	10	1	3	0
BUTT	Manchester U.	33	31	2	1	6	2	7	0
COLE	Manchester U.	33	31	2	0	6	16	6	0
GALLACHER	Blackburn R.	33	31	2	0	5	16	2	0
HALLE	Leeds U.	33	31	2	3	3	2	5	1
VIEIRA	Arsenal	33	31	2	0	4	2	8	1
BAIANO	Derby Co.	33	30	3	0	16	13	2	0
HASSELBAINK	Leeds U.	33	30	3	3	7	16	5	0
CARBONE	Sheffield W.	33	28	5	0	7	9	8	1
FLITCROFT	Blackburn R.	33	28	5	3	3	0	6	0
GRAYSON	Aston Villa	33	28	5	4	5	0	2	0

Player	Team	Tot	St	Sb	Snu	Ps	Gls	Y	R
BATTY	Newcastle U.	32	32	0	0	1	1	9	3
BURROWS	Coventry C.	32	32	0	0	0	0	8	0
CUNNINGHAM	Wimbledon	32	32	0	0	1	0	2	0
FOX	Tottenham H.	32	32	0	3	9	3	3	0
HARTSON	West Ham U.	32	32	0	0	1	15	4	2
LEBOEUF	Chelsea	32	32	0	0	4	5	8	1
NILSSON	Coventry C.	32	32	0	1	0	0	3	0
OVERMARS	Arsenal	32	32	0	0	13	11	0	0
PETIT	Arsenal	32	32	0	0	5	2	4	1
SOUTHGATE	Aston Villa	32	32	0	0	1	0	2	0
UNSWORTH	West Ham U.	32	32	0	0	1	2	8	1
MONKOU	Southampton	32	30	2	1	1	1	5	1
TAYLOR, I.	Aston Villa	32	30	2	0	3	6	6	0
WANCHOPE	Derby Co.	32	30	2	0	6	13	7	0
HAALAND	Leeds U.	32	26	6	1	2	7	6	1
DRAPER	Aston Villa	31	31	0	3	2	3	4	0
INCE	Liverpool	31	31	0	1	1	8	8	0
LUNDEKVAM	Southampton	31	31	0	0	3	0	7	0
PETRESCU	Chelsea	31	31	0	1	13	5	3	0
SEAMAN	Arsenal	31	31	0	0	0	0	1	0
SHERWOOD	Blackburn R.	31	29	2	0	3	5	5	0
WALLACE	Leeds U.	31	29	2	2	6	10	1	0
SCHOLES	Manchester U.	31	28	3	0	10	8	7	0
LAMPARD	West Ham U.	31	27	4	2	0	4	5	0
SHORT	Everton	31	27	4	1	6	0	3	0
WILCOX	Blackburn R.	31	24	7	2	6	3	4	2
KETSBAIA	Newcastle U.	31	16	15	4	4	3	3	0
OSTER	Everton	31	16	15	5	5	1	2	0
PLATT	Arsenal	31	11	20	1	3	3	4	0
BOSNICH	Aston Villa	30	30	0	0	0	0	1	0
BREEN	Coventry C.	30	30	0	2	2	1	1	1
DAILLY	Derby Co.	30	30	0	1	0	1	7	0
PEARCE, I.	West Ham U.	30	30	0	1	1	1	1	0
YORKE	Aston Villa	30	30	0	0	2	12	5	0
DI MATTEO	Chelsea	30	28	2	1	6	4	6	0
PRIOR	Leicester C.	30	28	2	2	5	0	2	0
SHERINGHAM	Manchester U.	30	27	3	3	4	9	2	0
BARMBY	Everton	30	26	4	1	7	2	7	0
McKINLAY	Blackburn R.	30	26	4	3	6	0	7	0
SOLTVEDT	Coventry C.	30	26	4	8	10	1	1	0
NEVILLE P.	Manchester U.	30	24	6	3	6	1	7	0
STURRIDGE	Derby Co.	30	24	6	0	7	9	8	0
GAYLE	Wimbledon	30	21	9	6	13	2	1	0

Fantasy Football Handbook 1998/99

Players Who Were Subbed the Most

Player	Team	Ps	Tot	St	Sb	Snu	Gls	Y	R
BAIANO	Derby Co.	16	33	30	3	0	13	2	0
PARLOUR	Arsenal	15	34	34	0	0	5	6	0
PEMBRIDGE	Sheffield W.	15	34	31	3	0	4	4	0
Le TISSIER	Southampton	15	26	25	1	2	11	6	0
RIPLEY	Blackburn R.	14	29	25	4	2	2	0	0
OVERMARS	Arsenal	13	32	32	0	0	11	0	0
PETRESCU	Chelsea	13	31	31	0	1	5	3	0
GAYLE	Wimbledon	13	30	21	9	6	2	1	0
ANELKA	Arsenal	13	26	16	10	8	7	3	0
BERKOVIC	West Ham U.	12	35	34	1	1	7	2	0
HIRST	Southampton	12	28	28	0	0	9	3	0
ZOLA	Chelsea	11	27	23	4	4	8	2	0
MADAR	Everton	11	17	15	2	0	6	2	0
OAKLEY	Southampton	10	33	32	1	0	1	3	0
SCHOLES	Manchester U.	10	31	28	3	0	8	7	0
SOLTVEDT	Coventry C.	10	30	26	4	8	1	1	0
MARSHALL	Leicester C.	10	24	22	2	0	7	2	0
HYDE	Sheffield W.	10	21	14	7	4	1	7	0
EUELL	Wimbledon	10	19	14	5	2	4	1	0
HUCKERBY	Coventry C.	9	34	32	2	0	14	9	0
FOX	Tottenham H.	9	32	32	0	3	3	3	0
RICHARDSON	Southampton	9	28	25	3	5	0	1	0
CADAMARTERI	Everton	9	26	15	11	3	4	4	0
RIEDLE	Liverpool	9	25	18	7	5	6	1	0
DI CANIO	Sheffield W.	8	35	34	1	0	12	10	0
BURTON	Derby Co.	8	29	12	17	3	3	0	0
GILLESPIE	Newcastle U.	8	29	25	4	2	4	2	0
BARNES	Newcastle U.	8	26	22	4	8	6	0	0
HOPKIN	Leeds U.	8	25	22	3	6	1	5	0
PARKER	Leicester C.	8	22	15	7	6	3	1	0
CLARIDGE	Leicester C.	8	17	10	7	3	0	0	0
GINOLA	Tottenham H.	7	34	34	0	0	6	7	0
CARBONE	Sheffield W.	7	33	28	5	0	9	8	1
HASSELBAINK	Leeds U.	7	33	30	3	3	16	5	0
BARMBY	Everton	7	30	26	4	1	2	7	0
STURRIDGE	Derby Co.	7	30	24	6	0	9	8	0
LEONHARDSEN	Liverpool	7	28	27	1	0	6	2	0
WRIGHT	Arsenal	7	24	22	2	0	10	7	0
FENTON	Leicester C.	7	23	9	14	14	3	1	0
MILOSEVIC	Aston Villa	7	23	19	4	8	7	5	0
JOHNSEN	Manchester U.	7	22	18	4	1	2	2	0
DAHLIN	Blackburn R.	7	21	11	10	5	4	2	0

Fantasy Football Handbook 1998/99

Player	Team	Ps	Tot	St	Sb	Snu	Gls	Y	R
FERDINAND, L.	Tottenham H.	7	21	19	2	0	5	2	0
WILSON	Tottenham H.	7	16	16	0	1	0	1	0
WREH	Arsenal	7	16	7	9	3	3	0	0
ZAGORAKIAS	Leicester C.	7	14	12	2	0	1	1	0
KITSON	West Ham U.	7	13	12	1	1	4	1	0
SAVAGE	Leicester C.	6	35	28	7	2	2	4	0
ARDLEY	Wimbledon	6	34	31	3	0	2	1	0
FLO	Chelsea	6	34	16	18	4	11	0	0
BUTT	Manchester U.	6	33	31	2	1	2	7	0
COLE	Manchester U.	6	33	31	2	0	16	6	0
WANCHOPE	Derby Co.	6	32	30	2	0	13	7	0
SHORT	Everton	6	31	27	4	1	0	3	0
WALLACE	Leeds U.	6	31	29	2	2	10	1	0
WILCOX	Blackburn R.	6	31	24	7	2	3	4	2
DI MATTEO	Chelsea	6	30	28	2	1	4	6	0
McKINLAY	Blackburn R.	6	30	26	4	3	0	7	0
NEVILLE, P.	Manchester U.	6	30	24	6	3	1	7	0
RIBEIRO	Leeds U.	6	29	28	1	0	3	1	0
WHITTINGHAM	Sheffield W.	6	28	17	11	7	4	1	0
FARRELLY	Everton	6	26	18	8	5	1	3	0
WALSH	Leicester C.	6	26	23	3	1	3	4	0
BOWYER	Leeds U.	6	25	21	4	11	3	4	0
NELSON	Aston Villa	6	25	21	4	11	0	1	0
ERANIO	Derby Co.	6	23	23	0	0	5	9	2
TOMASSON	Newcastle U.	6	23	17	6	11	3	1	0
JONES, R.	Liverpool	6	21	20	1	3	0	1	0
VIALLI	Chelsea	6	21	14	7	10	11	4	0
ABOU	West Ham U.	6	19	12	7	4	5	1	1
SINTON	Tottenham H.	6	19	14	5	2	0	1	0
NEVILLE, G.	Manchester U.	5	34	34	0	2	0	2	0
GALLACHER	Blackburn R.	5	33	31	2	0	16	2	0
GRAYSON	Aston Villa	5	33	28	5	4	0	2	0
PALLISTER	Manchester U.	5	33	33	0	0	0	4	1
PETIT	Arsenal	5	32	32	0	0	2	4	1
OSTER	Everton	5	31	16	15	5	1	2	0
PRIOR	Leicester C.	5	30	28	2	2	0	2	0
LAURSEN	Derby Co.	5	27	26	1	0	1	5	0
STAUNTON	Aston Villa	5	27	27	0	1	1	5	0
CALDERWOOD	Tottenham H.	5	26	21	5	10	4	3	0
DUFF	Blackburn R.	5	26	17	9	4	4	0	0
JONES, V.	Wimbledon	5	24	22	2	0	0	2	0
CROFT	Blackburn R.	5	23	19	4	5	1	0	0
CORT	Wimbledon	5	22	16	6	3	4	0	0
MOLENAAR	Leeds U.	5	22	18	4	12	2	4	0

Player	Team	Ps	Tot	St	Sb	Snu	Gls	Y	R
RUDI	Sheffield W.	5	22	19	3	0	0	2	0
MONCUR	West Ham U.	5	20	17	3	1	1	7	0
ARMSTRONG	Tottenham H.	5	19	13	6	2	5	2	0
BREACKER	West Ham U.	5	19	18	1	1	0	3	0
IMPEY	West Ham U.	5	19	19	0	1	0	0	0
NEWTON	Chelsea	5	18	17	1	2	0	0	0
BERTI	Tottenham H.	5	17	17	0	0	3	5	0
EDINBURGH	Tottenham H.	5	17	14	3	0	0	4	1
HUGHES, C.	Wimbledon	5	17	13	4	8	1	1	0
ANDERTON	Tottenham H.	5	15	7	8	1	0	0	0
VALERY	Blackburn R.	5	15	14	1	5	0	2	1
WILLIAMSON	Everton	5	15	15	0	0	0	1	0
BARRETT	Everton	5	13	12	1	4	0	3	0
ANDERSSON	Newcastle U.	5	12	10	2	2	2	0	0
MORRIS	Chelsea	5	12	9	3	2	1	0	0
CAMPBELL	Leicester C.	5	11	6	5	13	0	1	0
VAN DER LAAN	Derby Co.	5	10	7	3	6	0	2	0

Players Who Were the Most Used Subs

Player	Team	Sb	Tot	St	Snu	Ps	Gls	Y	R
PLATT	Arsenal	20	31	11	1	3	3	4	0
FLO	Chelsea	18	34	16	4	6	11	0	0
BURTON	Derby Co.	17	29	12	3	8	3	0	0
WILLIAMS, A.	Southampton	17	20	3	7	2	0	2	0
BERGER	Liverpool	16	22	6	9	2	3	0	0
KETSBAIA	Newcastle U.	15	31	16	4	4	3	3	0
OSTER	Everton	15	31	16	5	5	1	2	0
FENTON	Leicester C.	14	23	9	14	7	3	1	0
CLARKE	Wimbledon	13	14	1	13	0	0	0	0
COTTEE	Leicester C.	12	19	7	6	4	4	0	0
HUNT	Derby Co.	12	19	7	7	3	1	1	0
LILLEY	Leeds U.	12	12	0	13	0	1	1	0
WHITTINGHAM	Sheffield W.	11	28	17	7	6	4	1	0
CADAMARTERI	Everton	11	26	15	3	9	4	4	0
POWELL, D.	Derby Co.	11	24	13	1	4	0	4	0
BOLAND	Coventry C.	11	19	8	10	2	0	4	0
COLLINS	Sheffield W.	11	19	8	1	4	5	2	0
NICHOLLS	Chelsea	11	19	8	10	3	3	2	0
BOA MORTE	Arsenal	11	15	4	8	2	0	2	0
McCLAIR	Manchester U.	11	13	2	17	2	0	0	0
WILSON, S.	Leicester C.	11	11	0	15	0	2	0	0

Player	Team	Sb	Tot	St	Snu	Ps	Gls	Y	R
ANELKA	Arsenal	10	26	16	8	13	7	3	0
JOACHIM	Aston Villa	10	26	16	7	3	8	0	0
DAHLIN	Blackburn R.	10	21	11	5	7	4	2	0
DOMINGUEZ	Tottenham H.	10	18	8	3	2	2	4	0
HUGHES, S.	Arsenal	10	17	7	10	2	2	0	0
BOHINEN	Blackburn R.	10	16	6	7	2	1	0	0
MURPHY	Liverpool	10	16	6	10	4	0	1	0
GAYLE	Wimbledon	9	30	21	6	13	2	1	0
DUFF	Blackburn R.	9	26	17	4	5	4	0	0
POTTS	West Ham U.	9	23	14	12	2	0	2	0
WREH	Arsenal	9	16	7	3	7	3	0	0
BASHAM	Southampton	9	9	0	1	0	0	0	0
BRADY	Tottenham H.	9	9	0	0	0	0	0	0
OSTENSTAD	Southampton	8	29	21	0	4	11	4	0
FARRELLY	Everton	8	26	18	5	6	1	3	0
ANDERTON	Tottenham H.	8	15	7	1	5	0	0	0
SLATER	Southampton	8	11	3	3	3	0	1	0
SAVAGE	Leicester C.	7	35	28	2	6	2	4	0
WILCOX	Blackburn R.	7	31	24	2	6	3	4	2
RIEDLE	Liverpool	7	25	18	5	9	6	1	0
PARKER	Leicester C.	7	22	15	6	8	3	1	0
SOLSKJAER	Manchester U.	7	22	15	4	4	6	0	1
HYDE	Sheffield W.	7	21	14	4	10	1	7	0
VIALLI	Chelsea	7	21	14	10	6	11	4	0
MAGILTON	Sheffield W.	7	20	13	7	4	1	1	0
ABOU	West Ham U.	7	19	12	4	6	5	1	1
CLARIDGE	Leicester C.	7	17	10	3	8	0	0	0
HUGHES, D.	Southampton	7	13	6	5	1	0	1	0
POBORSKY	Manchester U.	7	10	3	6	3	2	1	0
WILLEMS	Derby Co.	7	10	3	4	1	0	0	0
STRACHAN, Ga.	Coventry C.	7	9	2	11	2	0	0	0
HAALAND	Leeds U.	6	32	26	1	2	7	6	1
NEVILLE, P.	Manchester U.	6	30	24	3	6	1	7	0
STURRIDGE	Derby Co.	6	30	24	0	7	9	8	0
BARTON	Newcastle U.	6	23	17	1	3	3	7	0
TOMASSON	Newcastle U.	6	23	17	11	6	3	1	0
CORT	Wimbledon	6	22	16	3	5	4	0	0
GRIMANDI	Arsenal	6	22	16	8	3	1	5	0
McATEER	Liverpool	6	21	15	3	2	2	3	0
HOWELLS	Tottenham H.	6	20	14	0	2	0	3	0
ARMSTRONG	Tottenham H.	6	19	13	2	5	5	2	0
McCANN	Everton	6	11	5	3	1	0	2	0
HAWORTH	Coventry C.	6	10	4	8	2	0	1	0
TROLLOPE	Derby Co.	6	10	4	1	0	0	0	0

Player	Team	Snu	Tot	St	Sb	Ps	Gls	Y	R
SAIB	Tottenham H.	6	9	3	0	1	1	0	0
SOLIS	Derby Co.	6	9	3	6	3	0	0	0
THOMSEN	Everton	6	8	2	1	1	1	0	0
BYFIELD	Aston Villa	6	7	1	6	1	0	1	0
LIGHTBOURNE	Coventry C.	6	7	1	8	1	0	1	0
GULLIT	Chelsea	6	6	0	1	0	0	0	0
CARBONE	Sheffield W.	5	33	28	0	7	9	8	1
FLITCROFT	Blackburn R.	5	33	28	3	3	0	6	0
GRAYSON	Aston Villa	5	33	28	4	5	0	2	0
CALDERWOOD	Tottenham H.	5	26	21	10	5	4	3	0
DAVIES	Southampton	5	25	20	1	4	9	5	0
HALL	Coventry C.	5	25	20	6	3	1	7	0
SCIMECA	Aston Villa	5	21	16	7	3	0	0	0
EUELL	Wimbledon	5	19	14	2	10	4	1	0
SINTON	Tottenham H.	5	19	14	2	6	0	1	0
CLEMENCE	Tottenham H.	5	17	12	5	3	0	1	0
EKOKU	Wimbledon	5	16	11	1	4	4	0	0
IVERSEN	Tottenham H.	5	13	8	0	2	0	1	0
DOWIE	West Ham U.	5	12	7	6	1	0	2	0
HAMILTON	Newcastle U.	5	12	7	9	4	0	0	0
CAMPBELL	Leicester C.	5	11	6	13	5	0	1	0
MOLDOVAN	Coventry C.	5	10	5	6	3	1	0	0
CURTIS	Manchester U.	5	8	3	5	1	0	0	0
NEILSON	Southampton	5	8	3	1	0	0	2	0
HUMPHREYS	Sheffield W.	5	7	2	10	2	0	1	0
BRANCH	Everton	5	6	1	1	1	0	0	0
THORNLEY	Manchester U.	5	5	0	5	0	0	0	0

Players Who Were the Most Unused Subs

Player	Team	Snu	Tot	St	Sb	Ps	Gls	Y	R
HEALD	Wimbledon	38	0	0	0	0	0	0	0
HITCHCOCK	Chelsea	36	0	0	0	0	0	0	0
BEENEY	Leeds U.	35	1	1	0	0	0	0	0
HOULT	Derby Co.	34	2	2	0	0	0	0	0
CLARKE	Sheffield W.	32	3	2	1	0	0	0	0
OAKES	Aston Villa	29	8	8	0	0	0	0	0
GERRARD	Everton	28	4	4	0	0	0	1	0
BAARDSEN	Tottenham H.	26	9	9	0	0	0	0	0
VAN DER GOUW	Manchester U.	26	5	4	1	0	0	0	0
MANNINGER	Arsenal	24	7	7	0	0	0	0	0
HEDMAN	Coventry C.	23	14	14	0	0	0	0	0

Player	Team	Snu	Tot	St	Sb	Ps	Gls	Y	R
ARPHEXAD	Leicester C.	23	5	5	0	0	0	0	0
FORREST	West Ham U.	21	13	13	0	0	0	0	0
FETTIS	Blackburn R.	20	8	7	1	0	0	0	0
MOSS	Southampton	20	0	0	0	0	0	0	0
HISLOP	Newcastle U.	18	13	13	0	0	0	0	0
McCLAIR	Manchester U.	17	13	2	11	2	0	0	0
WILSON	Leicester C.	15	11	0	11	0	2	0	0
FENTON	Leicester C.	14	23	9	14	7	3	1	0
BROOMES	Blackburn R.	14	4	2	2	0	0	1	0
ANDREWS	Leicester C.	14	0	0	0	0	0	0	0
LUKIC	Arsenal	14	0	0	0	0	0	0	0
TAYLOR	Southampton	14	0	0	0	0	0	0	0
OGRIZOVIC	Coventry C.	13	24	24	0	0	0	0	0
CLARKE	Wimbledon	13	14	1	13	0	0	0	0
LILLEY	Leeds U.	13	12	0	12	0	1	1	0
CAMPBELL	Leicester C.	13	11	6	5	5	0	1	0
POTTS	West Ham U.	12	23	14	9	2	0	2	0
MOLENAAR	Leeds U.	12	22	18	4	5	2	4	0
PEDERSEN, T	Blackburn R.	12	5	3	2	0	0	0	0
BISHOP	West Ham U.	12	3	3	0	0	0	0	0
NIELSON	Liverpool	12	0	0	0	0	0	0	0
JAMES	Liverpool	11	27	27	0	0	0	0	0
BOWYER	Leeds U.	11	25	21	4	6	3	4	0
NELSON	Aston Villa	11	25	21	4	6	0	1	0
GIVEN	Newcastle U.	11	24	24	0	0	0	1	0
TOMASSON	Newcastle U.	11	23	17	6	6	3	1	0
CHARLES	Aston Villa	11	18	14	4	3	1	1	0
MABBUTT	Tottenham H.	11	11	8	3	2	0	1	0
KOZIUK	Derby Co.	11	9	6	3	2	0	1	0
STRACHAN,Ga.	Coventry C.	11	9	2	7	2	0	0	0
ROWLAND	West Ham U.	11	7	6	1	0	0	0	0
HUGHES, A.	Newcastle U.	11	4	4	0	1	0	0	0
MEAN	West Ham U.	11	3	0	3	0	0	0	0
HODGES	West Ham U.	11	2	0	2	0	0	0	0
CALDERWOOD	Tottenham H.	10	26	21	5	5	4	3	0
VIALLI	Chelsea	10	21	14	7	6	11	4	0
CARRAGHER	Liverpool	10	20	17	3	2	0	2	0
BOLAND	Coventry C.	10	19	8	11	2	0	4	0
NICHOLLS	Chelsea	10	19	8	11	3	3	2	0
HUGHES, S.	Arsenal	10	17	7	10	2	2	0	0
MURPHY	Liverpool	10	16	6	10	4	0	1	0
HUMPHREYS	Sheffield W.	10	7	2	5	2	0	1	0
JOHANSEN	Southampton	10	6	3	3	3	0	1	0
OAKES	Sheffield W.	10	4	0	4	0	0	0	0

Fantasy Football Handbook 1998/99

Player	Team	Snu	Tot	St	Sb	Ps	Gls	Y	R
COLLINS	Aston Villa	10	0	0	0	0	0	0	0
GRODAS	Tottenham H.	10	0	0	0	0	0	0	0
SEALEY	West Ham U.	10	0	0	0	0	0	0	0

PROMOTED CLUBS

Players Who Played in 30+ Games

Player	Team	Tot	St	Sb	Ps	Snu	Gls
KINSELLA	Charlton A.	46	46	0	3	0	5
JONES, K.	Charlton A.	45	45	0	8	0	3
MERSON	Middlesbrough	45	45	0	4	0	12
ROGERS	N.Forest	45	45	0	7	0	1
CHETTLE	N.Forest	43	43	0	4	0	1
RUFUS	Charlton A.	43	43	0	7	0	0
GEMMILL	N.Forest	43	42	1	7	0	2
NEWTON, S.	Charlton A.	42	34	8	9	2	5
CAMPBELL, K.	N.Forest	41	41	0	4	0	23
MENDONCA	Charlton A.	41	41	0	2	0	23
HOOIJDONK	N.Forest	41	40	1	1	0	29
BEASANT	N.Forest	39	39	0	0	0	0
ROBINSON, J.	Charlton A.	38	37	1	8	0	8
FESTA	Middlesbrough	38	36	2	1	0	2
TOWNSEND	Middlesbrough	38	36	2	5	0	2
BECK	Middlesbrough	38	32	6	8	4	14
BOWEN	Charlton A.	37	35	2	5	1	0
FLEMING	Middlesbrough	37	35	2	0	2	1
VICKERS	Middlesbrough	35	32	3	2	2	0
CHAPPLE	Charlton A.	35	29	6	1	3	4
BROWN	Charlton A.	35	27	8	6	2	2
LYTTLE	N.Forest	34	34	0	6	0	0
KINDER	Middlesbrough	34	33	1	3	3	2
MUSTOE	Middlesbrough	34	33	1	3	0	3
BART-WILLIAMS	N.Forest	33	30	3	2	0	4
HIGNETT	Middlesbrough	33	27	6	7	2	7
COOPER	N.Forest	32	32	0	1	0	5
SCHWARZER	Middlesbrough	32	32	0	0	0	0
JOHNSON, A.	N.Forest	32	23	9	6	5	4
STONE	N.Forest	30	28	2	5	1	2
BONALAIR	N.Forest	30	23	7	5	3	2

Players Who Were Subbed the Most

Player	Team	Ps	Tot	St	Sb	Snu	Gls
NEWTON, S.	Charlton A.	9	42	34	8	2	5
JONES, K.	Charlton A.	8	45	45	0	0	3
BECK	Middlesbrough	8	38	32	6	4	14
ROBINSON, D.	Charlton A.	8	38	37	1	0	8
ROGERS	N.Forest	7	45	45	0	0	1
GEMMILL	N.Forest	7	43	42	1	0	2
RUFUS	Charlton A.	7	43	43	0	0	0
HIGNETT	Middlesbrough	7	33	27	6	2	7
JONES, S.	Charlton A.	7	24	18	6	1	7
BROWN	Charlton A.	6	35	27	8	2	2
LYTTLE	N.Forest	6	34	34	0	0	0
JOHNSON, A.	N.Forest	6	32	23	9	5	4
WOAN	N.Forest	6	20	10	10	7	1
TOWNSEND	Middlesbrough	5	38	36	2	0	2
BOWEN	Charlton A.	5	37	35	2	1	0
BONALAIR	N.Forest	5	30	23	7	3	2
STONE	N.Forest	5	30	28	2	1	2
MERSON	Middlesbrough	4	45	45	0	0	12
CHETTLE	N.Forest	4	43	43	0	0	1
CAMPBELL, K.	N.Forest	4	41	41	0	0	23
BARNESS	Charlton A.	4	30	21	9	9	1
PEARSON	Middlesbrough	4	19	19	0	0	2
MORTIMER	Charlton A.	4	13	8	5	0	4

Players Who Were the Most Used Subs

Player	Team	Sb	Tot	St	Ps	Snu	Gls
LISBIE	Charlton A.	16	17	1	1	3	1
ARMSTRONG	N.Forest	13	17	4	1	17	0
WOAN	N.Forest	10	20	10	6	7	1
JOHNSON, A.	N.Forest	9	32	23	6	5	4
BARNESS	Charlton A.	9	30	21	4	9	1
NEWTON, S.	Charlton A.	8	42	34	9	2	5
BROWN	Charlton A.	8	35	27	6	2	2
BONALAIR	N.Forest	7	30	23	5	3	2
ORMEROD	Middlesbrough	7	17	10	3	3	3
MOORE, I.	N.Forest	7	9	2	0	4	1
BECK	Middlesbrough	6	38	32	8	4	14
CHAPPLE	Charlton A.	6	35	29	1	3	4
HIGNETT	Middlesbrough	6	33	27	7	2	7

Player	Team	Sb	Tot	St	Ps	Snu	Gls
JONES, S.	Charlton A.	6	24	18	7	1	7
THOMAS	N.Forest	6	19	13	2	3	3
HOLMES	Charlton A.	6	16	10	2	1	1
MADDISON	Middlesbrough	6	16	10	3	1	4
RICARD	Middlesbrough	6	9	3	1	0	2
HJELDE	N.Forest	5	28	23	3	4	1
MORTIMER	Charlton A.	5	13	8	4	0	4
ALLEN	Charlton A.	5	12	7	2	9	2
LIDDLE	Middlesbrough	5	7	2	0	6	0
NICHOLLS	Charlton A.	5	6	1	0	1	0
ARMSTRONG	Middlesbrough	4	11	7	2	0	7
CAMPBELL	Middlesbrough	4	8	4	2	7	0
EMBLEN	Charlton A.	4	4	0	0	1	0
VICKERS	Middlesbrough	3	35	32	2	2	0
BART-WILLIAMS	N.Forest	3	33	30	2	0	4
BRIGHT	Charlton A.	3	17	14	3	1	7
BALMER	Charlton A.	3	16	13	1	4	0
HARRISON	Middlesbrough	3	14	11	1	1	0
MORENO	Middlesbrough	3	9	6	1	6	0
WHYTE	Middlesbrough	3	8	5	0	4	0
PARKER, S.	Charlton A.	3	3	0	0	1	0

Players Who Were the Most Unused Subs

Player	Team	Snu	Tot	St	Sb	Ps	Gls
ARMSTRONG, C.	N.Forest	17	17	4	13	1	0
GUINAN	N.Forest	11	2	1	1	1	0
BARNESS	Charlton A.	9	30	21	9	4	1
ALLEN	Charlton A.	9	12	7	5	2	2
PASCALO	N.Forest	9	6	6	0	0	0
STAMP	Middlesbrough	8	10	8	2	2	0
WOAN	N.Forest	7	20	10	10	6	1
CAMPBELL	Middlesbrough	7	8	4	4	2	0
MORENO	Middlesbrough	6	9	6	3	1	0
LIDDLE	Middlesbrough	6	7	2	5	0	0
JOHNSON, A.	N.Forest	5	32	23	9	6	4
FREESTONE	Middlesbrough	5	4	2	2	0	0
BECK	Middlesbrough	4	38	32	6	8	14
HJELDE	N.Forest	4	28	23	5	3	1
BALMER	Charlton A.	4	16	13	3	1	0
MOORE, I.	N.Forest	4	9	2	7	0	1
WHYTE	Middlesbrough	4	8	5	3	0	0

Player	Team	Snu	Tot	St	Sb	Ps	Gls
CHAPPLE	Charlton A.	3	35	29	6	1	4
KINDER	Middlesbrough	3	34	33	1	3	2
BONALAIR	N.Forest	3	30	23	7	5	2
THOMAS, G.	N.Forest	3	19	13	6	2	3
LISBIE	Charlton A.	3	17	1	16	1	1
ORMEROD	Middlesbrough	3	17	10	7	3	3
NEWTON, S.	Charlton A.	2	42	34	8	9	5
FLEMING	Middlesbrough	2	37	35	2	0	1
BROWN	Charlton A.	2	35	27	8	6	2
VICKERS	Middlesbrough	2	35	32	3	2	0
HIGNETT	Middlesbrough	2	33	27	6	7	7
ROBERTS	Middlesbrough	2	9	9	0	0	0
SUMMERBELL	Middlesbrough	2	6	4	2	3	0
BLACKMORE	Middlesbrough	2	2	1	1	1	0
McGREGOR	N.Forest	2	0	0	0	0	0

Team Notes

Team Notes

Team Notes